Race Rights Reparations

This book considers institutional racism as a problem that exists within modern societies. Its roots lie with the transatlantic slave trade and slavery and the solution involves ridding society of the problem. It is argued here that, first, there needs to be an acceptance of its existence, then developing the tools needed to deal with it and, finally, to implement those tools so that institutional racism can be permanently removed from society. The book has four themes: the first considers the nature of institutional racism, the second theme looks at instances of institutional racism through matters such as deaths in custody and skin lightening, the third considers the concept of reparations and the final area looks at the development of social movements as a way of pushing institutional racism up the political agenda. The development of a social movement is part of a social discourse which would, for example, push mentoring as a form of reparations. There is a need for more research on the manifestations of institutional racism and this book is part of that discourse. It is argued that the legacy of the slave trade and slavery is continuing and contemporary through the presence of institutional racism in society. This problem has not been addressed through legislation and policies devised to combat racial discrimination. Institutional racism needs to be understood as being located in the processes and procedures of societal institutions.

Fernne Brennan is Senior Lecturer in Law, head of the Slave Trade Reparations Project (STeR) @ www.essex.ac.uk/reparation, School of Law and Human Rights Centre, University of Essex, UK. She has written on and regularly speaks on the subject of race crime, institutional racism, and reparations.

Race Rights Reparations

Institutional Racism and the Law

Fernne Brennan

Routledge
Taylor & Francis Group
LONDON AND NEW YORK

First published 2017
by Routledge

2 Park Square, Milton Park, Abingdon, Oxfordshire OX14 4RN
52 Vanderbilt Avenue, New York, NY 10017

Routledge is an imprint of the Taylor & Francis Group, an informa business

First issued in paperback 2020

British Library Cataloguing-in-Publication Data
A catalogue record for this book is available from the British Library

Library of Congress Cataloging-in-Publication Data
Names: Brennan, Fernne, author.
Title: Race rights reparations : institutional racism and the law / Fernne Brennan.
Description: Abingdon, Oxon ; New York, NY : Routledge, 2017.
Identifiers: LCCN 2016058260 | ISBN 9781472452627 (hardback) |
ISBN 9781317072256 (adobe reader) | ISBN 9781317072249 (epub) |
ISBN 9781317072232 (mobipocket)
Subjects: LCSH: Blacks--Civil rights. | Race discrimination--Law and legislation. |
Slavery–Law and legislation. | Blacks--Reparations. | Reparations for historical injustices.
Classification: LCC K3242 .B74 2017 | DDC 342.08/73--dc23
LC record available at https://lccn.loc.gov/2016058260

ISBN: 978-1-4724-5262-7 (hbk)
ISBN: 978-0-367-59499-2 (pbk)

Typeset in Galliard
by Taylor & Francis Books

To Laurette and Fredrick Josiah, Tony, Ashley
and Jonathan Brennan

Contents

Acknowledgements

Thanks go out to Tony Brennan, Janet Dine, Andrew Le Seuer, Anthony Gifford, Sabine Michalowski, Lorna Woods, and Laurette and Frederick Josiah. Without their help this project would not have been completed.

Preface

This work is excellent on two levels. It is a fine work of scholarship, and it ends with a call to action by a committed academic campaigner who wants to change the situation which she has analysed. She makes the link between two phenomena occurring centuries apart: institutional racism in Britain today, and the transatlantic trade in Africans and their enslavement in the Caribbean, which officially ended in 1838.

Fernne Brennan's study of institutional racism – a phrase brought into prominence by Sir William McPherson, Chair of the Stephen Lawrence Inquiry – breaks new ground in some of its chapters. What is the contribution of the Internet to the growth of race hate? Is the internet itself institutionally racist? What is the responsibility of Internet Service Providers, the 'doorkeepers' who hold the keys to the internet? These questions are addressed with a penetrating critique of the Council of Europe's Additional Protocol to the Convention on Cybercrime, an initiative which seeks to control race hate on the internet, but in the author's view fails to do so.

In another fascinating chapter the author traces the effect on institutional racism of the neo-liberal market economy, with particular reference to trade relations between Europe and the Caribbean, including the abolition of preferential trade agreements and the new Economic Partnership Agreements (EPAs). She describes the EPAs as a legacy of slavery and colonialism, perpetuating discrimination at an international level.

Ms Brennan discusses the 'internalized hatred of self', as demonstrated by black people who bleach their skin to make themselves less black, as being a consequence of racial discrimination. She shows how the dehumanization of the chattel slavery system was the origin of this self-hate, and then brings us right up to date with her analysis of how big business profits from the bleaching chemicals, and how the media and the fashion houses have shaped the images of black women which are portrayed as the most desirable. 'Education is the key', she observes.

In two later chapters she draws the threads together by advocating the importance of an effective reparations settlement as the key to overcoming institutional racism. This is a theme which I have advocated ever since I settled in Jamaica in the early 1990s. There is not only a moral but a legal case that Britain, who committed the crime against humanity which chattel slavery was, which profited massively from the labour of the enslaved Africans, and which never paid a penny in compensation (but rather compensated the slave-owners for the loss of their 'property'), is obliged to make reparation. Ms Brennan explains the case for reparations, and addresses some of the legal and practical obstacles to an effective claim.

In an exciting chapter Ms Brennan calls for a social movement for positive reparations. She writes at a time when the issue is gaining ground, in the Caribbean at least. National Reparations Committees have been set up in most of the Caribbean countries.

A CARICOM Reparations Commission has drawn up a ten point plan for reparatory justice, which includes a full apology, remission of debt, and programmes to address the still-enduring consequences of slavery. But as she rightly points out, there is not enough co-ordination between British and Caribbean activists, and little of the popular mobilization which is required for an effective social movement to 'complete the goals of the civil rights movement.'

I applaud this book which will not only add to our store of knowledge about the causes and effects of racial injustice, but will stimulate many to be part of the movement to end this cancer which blights societies in Britain and around the world.

Anthony Gifford QC, English Barrister and Jamaican Attorney-at-Law

1 Introduction

According to the United Nations Educational, Scientific and Cultural Organisation (UNESCO), the transatlantic slave trade and chattel slavery was a unique event in world history. This is because it was maintained over four centuries, it victimised 'black African men, women and children',[1] it intellectualised chattel slavery by creating an anti-black ideology with 'its legal organisation' being the infamous 'code noir'[2] or the regulation 'between slaves and colonists'[3] and, this book argues, it created a racist ideology that has become institutionalised in the organisations and socio-economic and socio-legal relations of modern society. Moreover, institutional racism has created an intersection where race and gender are relevant to its maintenance. For example, in terms of black men it is deaths in custody. For black women there is skin bleaching and hair straightening.

The main theme of this book is that the transatlantic slave trade and chattel slavery spawned modern day institutional racism. It is argued here that neither the law nor public and private institutions have dealt with institutional racism and that only a fundamental policy change, based on reparations, can provide a solution.

This book is not the first kind to explore institutional racism. Carmichael and Hamilton in *Black Power, the Politics of Liberation in America* (Vintage Books, 1967) saw institutional racism as 'acts by the total white community against the black community', p. 4. In *Institutional Racism: A Primer on Theory and Strategies for Social Change* (Burnham Publishers Book, 2002), Better argues in Chapter 3 that institutional racism is embedded in institutions. Whilst Law *et al.* suggest that there is institutional racism in higher education in *Institutional Racism in Higher Education* (Trentham Books, 2004). Moreover, the Stephen Lawrence Inquiry stated that institutional racism is:

> The collective failure of an organisation to provide an appropriate and professional service to people because of their colour, culture or ethnic origin. It can be seen or detected in processes, attitudes and behaviour which amount to discrimination through unwitting prejudice, ignorance, thoughtlessness and racist stereotyping which disadvantage minority ethnic people.[4]

However, this book is one the first to link institutional racism as a modern legacy sourced in the transatlantic slave trade and to argue that innovative reparations are due for this legacy.

Institutional racism is prevalent throughout society and can even be found in more recent developments in technology. An example of this is the way Internet service providers (ISPs) provide a service on the Internet that has a detrimental impact on black cyber users who may become cyber victims of cyber racists. It is argued that cyber racists that rely on the free speech label are not advocating free speech but racist speech. The latter is a danger to societal cohesion and should be struck down on that basis since it is argued that stable race relations are more important than the freedom to practise cyber racism. ISPs fall back on the mantra of free speech that they say ties their hands in dealing with cyber racism. It is contended that international law should provide ISPs with the powers to strike down cyber racism. This should be done on the basis that the legislation that abolished the slave trade and chattel slavery did not deal with racist ideology in society when it could and should have done. Furthermore, that current race relations legislation in England and Wales does not deal with ISPs as having some legal responsibility for cyber racism. The argument advanced here is that making ISPs liable should be part of a package of reforms based on reparations for the legacy of the slave trade, that is, institutional racism, which would be aimed at organisations which continue to perpetuate it.

Trade has also come under the spotlight of institutional racism. It is argued that the current Economic Partnership Agreement (EPA) that is aimed at liberalising trade between the European Union (EU) and the Caribbean countries is detrimental to Caribbean economies because their economic markets are vulnerable. This vulnerability is a hangover from the transatlantic slave trade and colonialism, and the failure of the EU to recognise this is an example of institutional racism. The EU has unwittingly provided a service through the EPA that is racially discriminatory in that it assumes economies of equals when this is clearly not the case with the Caribbean. The EU and the Caribbean should have retained the preferential agreements package which was dismissed by the World Trade Organisation on the grounds of being anti-free trade and discriminatory. It is argued that in the light of the transatlantic slave trade, chattel slavery and colonialism the moral thing to do is to bring back preferential agreements. These would be administered by a selected body made up of people from the Caribbean countries and the EU over a 10–15year period with intermittent periodic reviews that would make recommendations and highlight changes to be made that would benefit the Caribbean.

The EU has been active on the race relations front with the adoption of Council Directive 2000/43/EC (Race Directive). The Race Directive is important because it deals with public services and racial/ethnic discrimination. The problem is it has inherent flaws in its terms and in particular it excludes third-country nationals. Since a number of black people will fall into that latter category it is argued that the EU is institutionally racist in excluding them from protection when it comes to services such as housing. It is contended that the Race Directive should be amended to deal with interpretational difficulties and to include third-country nationals in its remit.

Another area in need of reform is the Criminal Justice System. Black custodial deaths where social actors have been involved in the killings and not prosecuted raise serious concerns for any faith in the Criminal Justice System, first for the way black people – primarily men – are restrained by the police until they die, and second in the failure by the Crown Prosecution Service to prosecute the state actors, despite Coroner Court findings of unlawful killings. The issue of restraint-led deaths of black people in custody is of particular concern. There are a disproportionate number of deaths in custody of the BAME community in England and Wales. This is according to a report by the NGO INQUEST.[5] According to Blaqfair[6] since 1969 there have been over 1,000 black people who have died in police custody.[7]

The main investigation into BAME custodial deaths in England and Wales was the Butler Inquiry into Crown Prosecution Service Decision-Making in Relation to Deaths in Custody and Related Matters, led by His Honour Gerald Butler QC that reported in August 1999. The inquiry found that there was incompetence in the service and bias but there was no finding of institutional racism, in any event the latter was not part of the brief. It is suggested that controversial black custodial deaths and the failure to prosecute the perpetrators are manifestations of institutional racism. What is needed is radical reform, it is suggested that given the serious nature of this issue, that judges alone (who are taught about institutional racism) deal with these cases and to dispense with the CPS and the jury until there is established a prima facie case against the defendant. This process would be controlled by judges. This is the way to ensure that the Criminal Justice System makes its contribution to the removal of the legacy of the transatlantic slave trade and chattel slavery which is institutional racism.

Institutional racism is not solely the preserve of national and inter/supra-national governments. Advertisers and other commercial enterprises, including multinationals in the beauty business have come under scrutiny for their persistent portrayal of the norm of beauty as being white skin and straight hair. This causes anguish amongst some female members of the black community who are not represented in the imagery on television, in magazines and on the Internet. It came as no surprise to me when in 2015 a friend's daughter who is eight and is one of the few black children in her local school, asked her mother why she had kinky hair and black skin. Years ago I asked my mother the same thing! This was based on me being some kind of curiosity as was the case with my friend's child. The solution that some/many black women turn to is to whiten their skin and/or straighten their hair through the use of chemicals. The view taken here is that the sale of white bleaching/hair straightening products should be banned by law. Furthermore, it is argued that there should be a legal requirement that relevant businesses publish annual statements stating how they are dealing with the image of black people in the media. There may also be a role for the Anti-Slavery Commissioner under the Modern Slavery Act 2015 in overseeing this process if the Act were amended to deal with the portrayal of imagery in the media that did not include black people.

The issue of reparations is dealt with in the book to highlight the need to provide a comprehensive programme of reform across the sectors of housing, education, health, criminal justice and other areas where it is argued that black people suffer from institutional racism. Government funds and monies from those businesses who continue to profit from the aftermath of the compensation given to them for the loss of their emancipated slaves, such as the Church of England,[8] should be used to set up a reparations programme in the UK. This programme would deal with matters such as public apologies and commemoration plaques set up in those areas such as Liverpool and London that dealt in and profited from slavery. These plaques would acknowledge their role played in the transatlantic slave trade and apologise. The reparations agenda could feed into Black History month to raise public awareness of the role of the transatlantic slave trade, chattel slavery, colonialism and institutional racism in the educational sector, targeting in relevant and appropriate ways primary and secondary schools and universities. Similar programmes could be devised in other countries that dealt in and profited from the trade in transatlantic slavery. Reparations would be practically realised by the Caribbean Community's (CARICOM) ten-point plan. That is a 'Full formal apology, Repatriation, Indigenous Peoples Development Program, Cultural Institutions, Public Health Crises, Illiteracy Eradication, African Knowledge Program, Psychological Rehabilitation, Technology Transfer [and] Debt Cancellation.'[9] In Britain reparations would primarily be aimed at raising public awareness on the link between the slave trade, colonialism, Empire and the industrial revolution. Furthermore, awareness raising would include the relationship between the slave trade, chattel slavery and institutional racism, suffered by people of African descent. There would also be campaigns to decolonise public awareness, the educational curricula and museums.

The book also goes on to consider that there is not only a new social movement for reparations but a global one that spans international borders. It has become integral to the process that could be deployed in tackling institutional racism that is locked into organisations. Its geographical focus deals with the African legacy, the Caribbean legacy and the European legacy of the slave trade in terms of its legacy of institutional racism. The African legacy deals with the ripping of African people in the prime of their life from their homes and shipping them to work on the Caribbean plantations leaving a large hole in the African economy and social way of life and turning the Caribbean plantations into a principally mono-crop countries. The Caribbean legacy is derived not only from the existence of the plantations but also from a lack of corrective programmes post-emancipation to right the wrongs wrought by slavery. Instead the Caribbean has consistently been treated unequally in its relations with Western Europe. The European legacy focuses on the psyche of black people in that they suffer trauma that they are not aware of.

The main concepts of the book

The key concepts important for the book are chattel slavery, institutional racism, causation, justice and reparations. When we consider the term chattel slavery it is understood in law as a non-human being, as property. Property is something that is owned, bought and sold, inherited and bequeathed, given away as a present. A chattel slave has no human agency and can be treated as well or as badly as the owner wants. A chattel slave is property and is therefore the subject matter of contract. The essence of property is that it can be controlled and for four centuries this type of control endured. Resistance was put down with brutal force and sometimes with lethal consequences. Unlike Equiano[10] (a freed slave and freedom activist), few slaves were able to buy their freedom. Most worked like beasts of burden on the plantations or worked in the houses of slavers as domestic slaves. What was common amongst the property of the plantation and that of the household was that they were not paid – after all, property does not require payment.

The relationship between chattel slavery and institutional racism can be seen as follows. Chattel slavery was built upon a system of racism where white people were on top and black people were at the very bottom of society (or in the views of some, possibly at the top of the animal chain).[11] Institutional racism is also built on a hierarchy where black people are part of society racialised as being at the bottom of human life, the bottom of society. This is despite legislation in many countries aimed at outlawing racial discrimination and racial hostility. Just like the emancipatory legislation that freed slaves but did not do anything about the ideological notion of how they were seen as black people and treated by white society, so to the twentieth and twenty-first-century legislation has so far done nothing to deal with the institutional racism built up in organisations that comprehend and treat black people in unwittingly racist ways.

The relationship between chattel slavery and institutional racism will be explored in relation to controversial deaths in custody and the skin bleaching/hair straightening chapters. In deaths in custody, black people are often treated as animals in the way they are restrained by the police in tense situations. There does not seem to be a policy of 'talking the alleged defendant down', of calming the situation. Rather, the police seem to go on the offensive and in some cases the victim has died from the force used to restrain. The use of 'him' is intentional here because in almost all cases the deceased is a black man so the gender issue must be raised. It is argued here that there should be legislation to deal with the way in which black men are treated in tense situations where they are held in restraint.

In skin bleaching/hair straightening, some darker skinned black women try to whiten their skin and/or straighten their hair. This is a problem because they do not see that they are playing into the very hands that institutionally and unwittingly see black women as the 'other'; as something not quite natural. This trait has evolved from chattel slavery and has not been addressed to such an extent that it may be seen as an enduring injury as to why black women would want to 'disfigure' themselves. It is a trait that has become internalised and beauty is very much perceived as that normalised by the white world, by white women. However, this is a relationship that has been neglected in discussions of institutional racism. It will be argued that the companies and multinationals that control the beauty industry should be required by legislation not to discriminate in unwitting ways. This would be a way of moving forward on a reparations programme.

Institutional racism and causation are dealt with in Chapter 8 but it would be useful just to discuss them in a preliminary way here. Institutional racism is critical to the book because it tells us part of the story in terms of where we are with respect to race relations today yet it is ignored by policy makers and generally not addressed in legislation. The fact that the problem is ignored in an unwitting, un-deliberate way is critical to our understanding of how racist social relations in institutions have existed down the ages in a tapestry format that has its origin in the slave trade

The link between the slave trade, institutional racism and reparations is one of causation. It is not causation in the narrow traditional legal sense of the term as such understood as 'but for' and 'legal' or 'proximate' cause, or factual cause and responsibility. It is causation in the wider sense. As a tapestry of interconnectedness with threads that are not linear nor are they clearly visible. It consists of strings that hold the institutions that are institutionally racist together. Those strings are made up of strong and weak threads. The strong threads are the social actors that reinforce the tapestry whilst the weaker threads are victims of the tapestry, black people. A section in Chapter 8 is devoted to causation and all the thematic chapters imply or infer causation in this wider sense.

When we discuss institutional racism as the legacy of the slave trade, there are a number of examples of which one will suffice for our purposes: the volatile relationship situated around the policing of people of African descent in Britain. Statistics from Her Majesty's Inspectorate of Constabulary (HMIC) in a report entitled, *The Treatment and Welfare of Vulnerable Adults and Children in Custody in England and Wales* show that people of African descent are disproportionately held in police cells and strip-searched compared to their white counterparts. People of African descent say that they experience discrimination from the police, rudeness, disrespect and the over-use of force (HMIC, p. 21, March 2015). The over-use of force is particularly problematic because it tends to be based on the stereotype that black people are 'big, black and dangerous'. That stereotype is entrenched in the ideological canteen culture of policing. The canteen culture is the way the world of black people is interpreted by the police as an institution. 'Racial stereotyping is the application of a generalised mental picture to all members of a particular group' (Bowling and Phillips, *Racism, Crime and Justice*, 2002, p. 37) and this depiction tends to lead to the over-use of force in some instances. Whilst racism from individual police officers cannot be discounted this cannot account for the racist relationship between the police as an institution and people of African descent. Institutional racism in the police force is an institutionalised, not an individual, phenomenon. Chapter 8 will demonstrate this relationship as will other chapters.

The study will show that institutional racism is more hidden than overt racism and racial discrimination that constitute intentional or unintentional forms of racial harm, or covert racism and racial discrimination that causes indirect racial harms. Similarly, there has been little discussion of institutions and why they are particularly prone to institutional racism. This work will consider these issues. This book will show that this veiled form of racism explains why, despite over 200 years of slave emancipation, institutional racism continues to prevail in those societies involved in the slave trade and chattel slavery – the source of institutional racism. This source of racism has been recognised at the universal level as a cause of racism in modern times (United Nation's production of the Declaration and Programme of Action, the World Conference Against Racism, Racial Discrimination, Xenophobia and Related Intolerance, Durban South Africa, 2001). Institutional racism is both inter-state (between states and societies) and intra-state (within states and societies). Given this level of complexity 'we need a broader and inclusive vision of what' constitutes institutionalised racial harm (S. Hays, 'Stalled at the Alter?' in D. Clawson *et al., Public Sociology* (University of California Press, 2007), p. 88).

The concept of justice is central to the arguments of this book. It is said that 'law and justice are not the same: both are abstract, but law is precise and as real as a number whereas justice is an aspiration and impossible to define ... martyrs have usually fought on behalf of justice and against law' (in J. Sassoon, *Ancient Laws and Modern Problems,* Intellect Ltd, 2005, p. 196). This is a book that challenges the law, in particular where there are gaps in the law but at the same time also asks that justice be done to fill in those gaps. It is argued that the law should recognise the problem of institutional racism as unwitting, as ignorance and that this be written into appropriate legislation to end institutional racism.

Reparations are the other important concept in the book. Reparations are not principally about financial compensation. It is about recognising what can be done to deal with the damage that institutional racism has caused because of its development from the slave trade. This damage can be seen in education where for example some children do not know enough about the slave trade so have no understanding of why they are here in the UK – this ignorance applies to both black and white children. It is to do with white children not understanding why their black neighbour is in the classroom and black children not understanding why they are there either. Other examples in education include the low expectations of teachers with respect to black children and their exclusion from school. In each chapter the area of reparations necessary to deal with the harm is highlighted and Chapter 8 is devoted to the topic.

Overview of the chapters as a navigational aid

Chapter 2 consists of the development of a process designed to identify these threads of institutional racism and to unpick them. It starts with a discussion of racism itself and then moves onto discourse regarding the constituent elements of institutional racism. The result is that there is found an organisational failure to provide relevant services to the black community that are both professional and appropriate. Indeed, Narayan and Andrews wrote in an article entitled *Malcolm X, Smethwick and BME Politics* (*Viewpoint,* issue 19, 1 April 2015), that a fifth of England's black African and black Caribbean populations live in the country's most deprived neighbourhoods, and are still over represented in relation to unemployment, prison populations, housing overcrowding, deaths in state detention and poor social mobility. They argue that there is a tendency to blame this group for their plight and to put the focus on a failure to perform as expected because of problems within the family, communities and culture as opposed to seeing the trouble as caused by structural racism – another word for institutional racism.

Chapter 3 explores a fairly new phenomenon which has arisen with respect to institutional racism and that is the area of Cyber Race Hate. It is argued that the Internet is a complex institution that contains a culture of race hate as part of its very being. The problem is whether and how to regulate the institution of race hate on the Internet given that there is a fundamental principle in the Western world of freedom of expression – a highly cherished right. When it comes to regulation there is a balancing exercise seen between the right to freedom of expression and the right to protection from cyber race hate.

There have been recent legislative efforts to control cyber race hate despite the golden chalice of freedom of expression. However, these efforts have been thwarted at the level of the Council of Europe (CoE), which has concerned itself with freedom of expression as well as race hate regulation. This weighting up of the freedom of expression with that of race hate regulation has resulted in a dilemma: what is to be protected when it comes to race hate speech and freedom of speech? Freedom of speech has won the day which means that ethnic minority communities are not protected from on-line racist abuse. The major piece of legislation, *CETS, No. 189 The Additional Protocol to the Convention on Cybercrime Concerning the Criminalisation of acts of a Racist and Xenophobic Nature through Computer systems 2003*, is optional. Furthermore, for Council of Europe Member States this discourse on cyber race hate is done without any reference to the notion of institutional racism and the very special relationship that it has to the transatlantic slave trade, and the need to make reparations. It is argued that this is the wrong way to go about the business of regulation. Both the nature of institutions and the nature of institutional racism need to be understood in order to provide effective regulation, as a form of reparation. Internet service providers need to be put under scrutiny in this regard. Internet service providers should protect those who suffer from institutional racism that Internet service providers perpetuate. This is because over the decades, Internet service providers have come to represent part of the media that influences and has opened up the public space by allowing racism to float into the public arena through its institutional mechanisms.

Chapter 4 investigates the role of institutional racism at an international level by focusing on the socio-economic relations and legal relations that exist between states. Scholarship on the existence of institutional racism and it impact on black people has tended to investigate it in terms of a focus on the intra-state domain. This can be found in the works of Carmichael and Hamilton (USA) and Tuitt (Britain) as well as the *Macpherson Report* (UK). There is a dearth of literature, however, on the relationship between institutional racism and the international domain and it is argued that institutional racism exists in this sector as well. The global picture is extremely complex with a background involving states, international institutions, multilateral treaties and bilateral treaties. Chapter 4 takes as its focus the Caribbean and trading issues between it and the West, in particular the pressure on countries like Guyana to move from preferential trading agreements to Economic Partnership Agreements (EPAs) – the latter is seen as good for European business interests, and imperialistic yet unwittingly racist as far as the Caribbean is concerned because it serves the economic interests of the European Union and not the socio-economic interests of Caribbean countries. It is argued that EPAs are an example of the legacy of institutional racism, and calls for a return to preferential trading agreements, although not perfect, they are better than EPAs, and this change could be achieved and justified within the framework of reparations.

In Chapter 5 the discussion surrounds the Council Directive 2000/43/EC (Race Directive).

This is an EU-level measure that member states have a legal duty to implement. The Race Directive is a legal tool set up to tackle race and ethnic discrimination in the market place, realising that free movement of persons cannot work if racial barriers are in the way. The question that concerns this chapter is whether the Race Directive incorporates the concept of institutional racism. Can the notion be *read* into the provisions?

The material scope of the Race Directive covers matters such as employment, vocational training, working conditions, membership of workers or professional organisations, social protection, healthcare, social advantages, education and access to and the supply of goods and services available to the public, including public housing. According to this directive the underlying problem is that racism and racial discrimination exist in these areas. Racism must be tackled in order to achieve the aims of the EU Treaty. These objectives include such matters as the attainment of a high level of employment, social protection, a better quality of life, and economic and social cohesion and inclusion. It is contended that the relevant institutions such as employment, healthcare and education cannot really be tackled in those countries where this phenomenon exists, unless the foundational elements of institutional racism are recognised, drawn out and outlawed. Unless the 'canteen culture'[12] of these organisations is tackled the principle of equal treatment that the EU wants to see will remain under threat.

Chapter 6 is a study into the deaths in custody of black people. These controversial deaths are said to arise from either the use of lethal force or the failure of a duty of care. The actors involved in these deaths are either state actors or private actors carrying out state functions. One death in custody through lethal force is one too many whether the deceased is black or white, however, INQUEST, an NGO that measures deaths in custody, shows that there is a disproportionate number of deaths in police custody where the victim is a member of the black and ethnic minority community and where the police use lethal force.[13] This chapter aims to situate these controversial black deaths in custody as an instance of institutional racism.

It will be argued that racial stereotyping of black people as aggressive and violent is part of the construction of the relationship between the police and the black community. This mythical stereotyping determines to some extent how state actors perceive black people and the concomitant treatment of them as necessitating that police 'go in hard' with tools of lethal force that are capable of killing some of the victims.

There is public concern about these controversial deaths in custody and, in this context, several documents will be consulted such as the Independent Inquiry into the death of David Bennett, the Sainsbury's Report on Mental Health and black People and the report from Black Mental Health UK as well as the Butler Report. The underlying question is to consider to what extent the role of institutional racism has been investigated as playing a role in the framework of these reports. Moreover, there will be some attention paid to the Crown Prosecution Service in terms of the use of the Code for Crown Prosecutors and the Independent Police Complaints Commission with respect to institutional racism and black deaths in custody.

Chapter 7 considers the issues of skin bleaching and hair straightening. The central concern is that some black people are bleaching their skin and/or straightening their hair to look white. This practice is reinforced by organisations involved in the beauty business that advertise white skin as being the norm in society. There is also the gendered nature of this practice since it seems to affect mostly black women. There is a whole beauty industry built up around the development and protection of white skin. Even those advertising agencies that portray a range of skin colours tend not use darker skinned models, yet this does not make business sense since darker skinned people wear makeup and use beauty products too.

The chapter will be dedicated to asking why this problem exists and the impact it has on some black people as one of internalised hatred of self. It will be argued that this self-hate in terms of skin bleaching stems from the time of chattel slavery when skin colour was either associated with black and the 'oppressed' or white and the 'liberated'. Indeed, the United Nation's produced a Declaration and Programme of Action in 2002 following the World Conference Against Racism, Racial Discrimination, Xenophobia and Related Intolerance, Durban South Africa, 2001(WCAR). The declaration states on page 16, paragraph 13 that the transatlantic slave trade is among the major sources and manifestations of racism, racial discrimination ... and that Africans and people of African descent ... continue to be victims of their consequences. It will further be argued that the beauty industry's framework is one that is institutionally racist and that has a direct consequence on those who wish to emulate the images that the beauty industry pursues, to their detriment.

Chapter 8 considers the issue of reparations. The chapter looks at what they are and whether they are appropriate as recompense for a legacy of the slave trade – institutional racism. Although the transatlantic slave trade has been seen by UNESCO as a one of the most horrific episodes in recorded human history there has been no recognition of it in terms of reparations. It is argued that institutional racism has been and continues to be the main reason behind this failure to make reparations. There is a culture, with respect to reparations, that thrives on the denial of the legacy and its source.

Causation is taken up in Chapter 8 on reparations where the necessary element in a sufficient set (NESS) theory developed by Hart and Honoré, *Causation in Law* (OUP, 1985) is used. In agreement with these theorists it is contended that causation in terms of the relationship between the transatlantic slave trade, chattel slavery, colonialism and institutional racism does not have to be seen as a uniform sequence but rather as a complex set of conditions that has produced institutional racism.

Their theory goes on to assert that 'there may be several independent causes of an event' (Hart and Honore, p. 19). This book parts company with that notion on the basis that the relationship between the transatlantic slave trade, chattel slavery, colonialism and institutional racism is interdependent and is strung along by racism itself. Racism being the imposition of harm and suffering reflected in the property status accorded black people justified on the basis of skin colour and language such as 'heathens', 'brutes' and 'dangerous' (H. Beckles, *Britain's Black Debt* (University of West Indies Press, 2013, p. 61), a racism that is today inculcated into the fabric of societal organisations.

Reparation is recognised as a form of 'payment' for the atrocities handed out by a particular regime. The Holocaust has been one of the most public examples of this. Another is the success of the Mau Mau survivors in terms of the right to sue for compensation from the UK government. In contrast, several reasons are stated for the refusal to grant reparations to victims of the transatlantic slave trade. The main one is that there are no survivors from the transatlantic slave trade and chattel slavery both in terms of claimants and defendants. However, it is argued that the claimants as survivors are those people of African descent who still suffer from the racism meted out by institutional racism and the defendants are principally the states involved. States have an intergenerational human rights responsibility to deal with the issue of reparations for those who suffer from institutional racism in modern times – those in Africa, the Caribbean and the diaspora. The chapter considers political campaigns for reparations as well as litigation strategies.

There are other issues such as the appropriate jurisdiction. Should the case be started in national courts or in the International Court of Justice? What would be the cause of action? Would it be a crime against humanity? Or would it be restitution in the sense of creating institutions that would house objects taken from Africa and provide educational tours or both. It has been argued that litigation is an educational tool.[14] It would fuel the public discourse on the transatlantic slave trade and chattel slavery and the reason why reparations is seen as an important tool to deal with the legacy, that is, institutional racism.

Guidelines were given at the international level as to what reparations should be by Van Boven[15] and Bassiouni,[16] subsequently adopted by the United Nations General Assembly in 2005. According to these guidelines, the scope of reparations include restitution which restore[s] the victim to the original situation before the gross violations of humanitarian law occurred. Although restoration to the original position would in fact be impossible as far as the actual victims are concerned, restoration of things such as artefacts would be possible, compensation for damage that is economically assessable, rehabilitation which consists of medical and psychological care, as well as legal and social services, satisfaction including public apology and guarantees of non-repetition. It is argued that some of these kinds of reparations should be given to those who suffer from the fall out of the transatlantic slave trade which is institutional racism.

Chapter 9 brings a new dimension to the debate surrounding reparations and institutional racism: the quest for reparations, and the use of reparations as a means of addressing the problem. Unlike the social movement that developed in the aftermath of the Jewish Holocaust, with the kernel being the concentration camps, highlighted by the story of Anne Frank, it has been argued by Howard-Hassmann in *Reparations to Africa* (University of Pennsylvania Press, 2008) that the cry for reparations for the wrongs of the transatlantic slave trade and chattel slavery is weakened by the fact, as she sees it, of no social movement.

It has been argued that the blue print of a social movement is one '*where a collection of* formal organisations, informal networks, and unaffiliated individuals engaged in a more *or less coherent struggle for change*' (Howard-Hassmann in *Reparations to Africa*, University of Pennsylvania Press, 2008) Moreover, Tarrow cited in Staggenborg in *Social Movements* (OUP, 2011), argues that the definition of social movements is 'as collective challenges, based on common purposes and social solidarities, in sustained interaction with elites, opponents, and authorities.' However, it is questioned whether given the nature of the transatlantic slave trade, chattel slavery and institutional racism there should be a movement that follows the blue print. Is it possible that there is not just a social movement but there is a global movement on reparations. In Jamaica there are attempts to build a social movement around the question of reparations. Similarly, the CARICOM has made a call for reparations engaging English lawyers and Caribbean academics. What makes these movements unique is that they are creatures of government rather than just organisations that have sprung from civil society. The elements of this global movement on reparations will be considered. There will also be the consideration of a charter to bring Caribbean government backed reparations movements together with those reparation movements that exist in civil society.

This book calls for reparations for the damage that continues as a result of institutional racism and traces this back to the transatlantic slave trade and chattel slavery. This damage can be seen in the education system, the policing of people of African descent, the delivery of services such as health and housing and through actions such as skin bleaching.

The book is a painful journey because after 400 years of chattel slavery one would not expect institutional racism to exist. We would expect that with abolition of that shameful episode in history that we would not be haunted by it in modern times. It is a sad fact that the past is very much still with us and as these chapters show, continuing to damage all of us. This book asks why and calls for a meaningful response and resolution.

Notes

1 'Transatlantic Slave Trade', UNESCO, Culture. Available at: www.unesco.org (accessed 2 December 2015).
2 Ibid.
3 Q. Taylor, 'Louisiana's Code Noir' (1724). Available at: www.faculty.washington.edu (accessed 2 December 2015). The 'code noir' was based on the code introduced into French Caribbean colonies in 1685 by the edict of Louis XIV. The code dealt with the policing of slaves.
4 W. Macpherson, *The Stephen Lawrence Inquiry* (London: Home Office, 1999), para. 6.34.
5 INQUEST, 'BAME Deaths in Police Custody, England and Wales, 2006–2015'. Available at: www.inquest.org.uk/statistics/bame-deaths-in-police-custody (accessed 12 March 2016). Another controversial area in the Criminal Justice System is racialised Stop and Search. A black person is six times more likely to be stopped and searched in England and Wales than a white person. See Equality & Human Rights Commission, 'Stop and Think'. Available at: www.equalityhumanrights.com/about-us/our-work/key-projects/past-projects/race-britain/stop-and-think (accessed 12 March 2016).
6 See Blaqfair, 'British Deaths in Custody: UN Must Investigate', 28 October 2016. Available at: www.blaqfair.com/blaqfair/dthcustody/unpet.htm (accessed 28 October 2016).
7 S. Hattenstone, 'Why?' *The Guardian*, 30 March 2001.
8 S. Bates, 'Church Apologises for Benefiting from Slave Trade', *The Guardian*, 9 February 2006. Available at: www.theguardian.com/uk/2006/feb/09/religion.world (accessed 12 March 2016). 'On 8 February 2006 the General Synod of the Church of England resolved to apologise for its role and complicity in the transatlantic slave trade.' See Reverend Tim Woods. Available at: www.rethinkingmission.org.uk/pdfs/Timwoods.pdf (accessed 12 March 2016). Also see *The Link* 2(1) Easter 2007. Available at: www.churchofengland.org/media/36359/easter07.pdf (accessed 12 March 2016).
9 D. Muhammad, 'CARICOM's 10 Point Program for Reparations for Slavery for African People', *The Final Call*, 9 May 2014. Available at: www.finalcall.com/artman/publish/World_News_3/article_101422.shtml (accessed 12 March 2016). Also see CARICOM Secretariat, Chairman of CARICOM Reparations Commission addresses British House of Commons, 25 July 2014. Available at: www.caricom.org/jsp/pressreleases/press_releases_2014/pres188_14.jsp (accessed 12 March 2016).
10 Olaudah Equiano, *The Interesting Narrative of the Life of Olaudah Equiano, or Gustavus, the African. Written by Himself* (London, 1789). A summary of Equiano's life can be found at: www.docsouth.unc.edu/neh/equiano1/summary.html (accessed 12 March 2016).
11 See the British Association for the Advancement of Science. In 1841 a speaker stated 'that the African variety of man bore anatomically "a nearer resemblance to the higher Quadrumana [i.e. apes] than to the highest varieties of his own species."' From P. Fryer, *Staying Power: The History of Black People in Britain* (London: Pluto Press, 1985) p. 176.
12 According to the *Oxford English Dictionary*, canteen culture means a set of conservative and discriminatory attitudes said to exist within the police force of the UK. Parallels are drawn in other institutions such as education, employment organisations and healthcare.
13 See www.inquest.org.uk/issues/bame-deaths (accessed 14 March 2016).
14 D. Shelton, 'Litigation and Political Action to Address Historic Injustices in the United States: Problems and Prospects', in F. Brennan and J. Packer (eds), *Colonialism, Slavery, Reparations and Trade: Remedying the Past?* (Abingdon: Routledge, 2012).
15 T. Van Boven, 'Basic Principles and Guidelines on the Right to a Remedy and Reparation for Victims of Gross Violations of International Human Rights Law and Serious Violations of International Humanitarian Law', New York, 16 December 2005. Available at: www.legal.un.org/avl/ha/ga_60-147/ga_60-147.html (accessed 14 March 2016).
16 See K. McCracken, 'Commentary on the Basic Principles and Guidelines on the Right to a Remedy and Reparation for Victims of Gross Violations of International Human Rights Law and Serious Violations of International Humanitarian Law'. Available at: www.cairn.inforevue-international (accessed 15 December 2016).

2 The nature of institutional racism

Introduction

Britain was the slave trafficker par excellence by the end of the eighteenth century though most Western European nations participated in the slave trade and the dehumanisation of millions of Africans. Britain ruled over her chattel slaves in the West Indies and parts of South America. Chattel slavery was the process by which African men, women and children were treated like animals and this was backed up by law and violence, and inhuman and degrading treatment. The labour from British slaves working for no money on the plantations was turned into profit for slaveholders. These profits in some way went to furnish the industrial revolution and enriched the state, church and many organisations that exist today such as Barclays bank.[1] When the British slave trade was abolished in 1807 by the Abolition of the Slave Trade Act and chattel slavery was de-legalised by the Slavery Abolition Act 1833, racism remained. The ex-slaves did not receive any compensation for their labour but the slave owners received £20 million for the loss of their labour force that is approximately £16 billion in modern currency. Racism manifested itself in overt and covert forms in Britain and her overseas West Indian colonies but also became institutionalised in organisations and race relations in the twentieth and twenty-first centuries. It was the case of Stephen Lawrence that brought institutional racism into the spotlight in the UK. Lawrence had been killed by a bunch of racist thugs when he was on his way home from college in London. This 19 year-old suffered from a lethal stab wound. Some of the perpetrators were eventually convicted. The investigation of the treatment of the way in which the police handled the case came under public scrutiny and resulted in a public inquiry that culminated in a report entitled the Stephen Lawrence Inquiry. It was this inquiry that stated that organisations in society such as education and housing[2] were institutionally racist, including the police.

The nature of some forms of institutional racism is much deeper and more hidden than other forms of racial harm such as overt and covert forms of racial discrimination and racism. Institutional racism occurs where institutions adopt policies that are overtly racist, such as Apartheid South Africa, or are 'inherently racist (adopting policies that result in the exclusion of blacks from services)',[3] or where black people receive an inadequate service. This chapter will consider racism and its source[4] in the slave trade and the whole notion of chattel slavery, and how this developed into institutional racism. Institutions will be examined generally along with the idea of the 'canteen' culture that can exist and survive within institutions. It will conclude that institutional racism is inherent within institutions and that is why it is difficult to detect, but by identifying it in public and private spaces we can make law and policy designed to eradicate it.

So where does institutional racism sit in the area of racism? There are three stages leading to institutional racism. The first is overt racism where, as in *Tower Boots*, individuals or groups or states[5] are the perpetrators of racial harm. Then there is covert racism where a group of people are victimised in that they are treated in the same way as others but the rule applied has a detrimental impact on that group as opposed to the others. And finally there is the institutionalisation of racism which is a form of racism that is embedded in practice and in the culture of organisations. This can be overt or covert or even more hidden than other forms of racism. A source of institutional racism comes from the chattelisation of Africans during the slave trade as well as an 'embedded colonial mentality [that] has continued to deny [black people] equal status in the legal order'[6] as well as in everyday life. But first we should consider what racism is.

Racism

Racism refers to a situation whereby there is an attempt 'to fix human social groups in terms of natural properties of belonging within particular political and geographical contexts. The assertion that racialised subjects do not belong within [particular] societies is then associated with social and cultural characteristics designated to them within the logic of particular racisms'.[7] A widespread definition of racism is 'the belief that certain groups are innately, biologically, socially, morally superior to other groups, based upon what is attributed to be their racial composition'.[8] The consequence of this is that the 'inferior' group suffers a form of racial harm that decreases their chance of living a 'normal' life and can cause them alarm and distress and even lead to death.[9] Racism can exist in overt, covert and institutional forms.

Overt racism

Examples of overt racism include the case of *Jones v Tower Boot*,[10] where the victim suffered racial abuse from his work colleagues. He was burned with hot screwdrivers and metal bolts were thrown at his head, moreover, on several occasions he was racially verbally abused. His case was successfully upheld. In another case[11] two black waitresses were subject to racist abuse that took place at a dinner engagement hosted by the racist comedian, Bernard Manning. The abuse took place at a policemen's ball, a certain structured environment that served to reinforce racism. This manifested itself in the language used which constituted a shared pattern of behaviour and particular way of thinking about race that had special significance with words used such as 'wog' 'nigger' and 'Sambo'. One guest was so comfortable in this environment that the question asked of Miss Rhule, one of the complainants, was 'what a black woman's vagina tasted like'.[12] In this way racism is connected with gender.

In the case of *Alexander v Home Office*[13] the racism took place in a prison where the most desirable work was in the kitchen. The prisoner complained that he was passed over for such jobs because he was black. The prison unsuccessfully[14] argued that the black prisoner

> displayed the usual traits associated with people of his ethnic background being arrogant, suspicious of staff, anti-authority, devious and possessing a very large chip on his shoulder ... common in most coloured inmates.[15]

This form of racism is quite overt and relatively easy to detect.

Covert racism

A more subtle form of racism is covert racism. This 'often appears hidden by norms of association, affiliation, group membership and/or identity'.[16] Thus in the U.S. 'hanging the Confederate flag "isn't meant to be racist, it's about tradition," say some Southern advocates. But the "tradition" while perhaps not wholly subsumed by is inherently saturated with slavery and Jim Crow'.[17] Similarly showing the Union Jack may not be meant to be racist but it is inherently tied to Britain's slavery and colonial past, as Gilroy says, 'There Ain't No Black in the Union Jack'.[18]

Coates argues that covert racism is a 'boundary keeping mechanism'[19] that serves to reinforce group separation. Stokely and Carmichael argue that covert racism is institutional racism[20] and is more subtle than overt racism because covert racism operates at an institutional level. It is the source of institutional norms and is difficult to detect but its consequences are quite severe because the policies and procedures of institutions serve, unintentionally, to victimise black people in public spaces.[21]

Institutional racism

It is argued that institutional racism is even deeper than covert racism as it is the 'bread and butter' of institutional norms meaning that it sits at the very soul of public and private institutions. It is part of the tapestry of institutions so much so that it is not noticed, unlike covert racism which would be seen, albeit with difficulty, as an indirect part of racism. Institutional racism has been identified by Macpherson in the *Stephen Lawrence Inquiry as*

> The collective failure of an organisation to provide an appropriate and professional service to people because of their colour, culture or ethnic origin. It can be seen or detected in processes, attitudes and behaviour which amount to discrimination through unwitting prejudice, ignorance, thoughtlessness and racist stereotyping which disadvantage minority ethnic people.[22]

Institutional racism 'pervades the very assumptions that shape our'[23] public institutions. It is argued here that it has its roots in the history of the transatlantic slave trade. It has survived colonialism and exists in modern times and has been identified as a phenomenon that is deeply hidden in the culture of institutions meant to serve all people but from which black people receive an inferior service. Gillborn argues that this is so in the education system[24] and, according to Gilroy,[25] at the very centre of British politics.[26] Institutional racism is in short the legacy of the slave trade and its emergence and survival is now to which we will turn.

Institutional racism: Sourced in the slave trade

We know from the discussion in Williams[27] that racism did not cause (but became a consequence of) the transatlantic slave trade. Rather, the slave trade was driven by greed and the quest for power, the push towards economic development and selfishness.[28] Rodney argues that there was an international trade from at least the latter part of the fifteenth century where 'Africa helped to develop Western Europe in the same proportion as Western Europe helped to under-develop Africa'.[29] Africa became Western Europe's satellite[30] community and existed as a victim of the triangular trade system. As an example of this, Rodney contends that although there was an international law[31] governing the seas, it was in effect European law.

Most Africans were merely victims – 'transportable merchandise'.[32] The Caribbean became known as the 'sugar islands' because much trade in sugar came from its plantations where the economies changed ownership following battles between various Western countries including Britain, Holland and France.[33]

The triangular slave trade was a complex phenomenon.[34] Sugar became one of the main industries because it complemented tea and coffee in Britain, but

> the slave-sugar complex … linked field slaves and slave boilers to colonial carters and dock workers, seamen, captains and ship's bursars to freight forwarders, insurance agents and customs agents, harbour officials, longshoremen and carters to refiners, grocers, confectioners; people who took sugar in their tea and spread jam on their bread to refiners, packagers and bakers; and shipbuilders and shipyard workers to brokers and commercial agents known as factors,[35]

not to mention the law and the courts.

This complex system included those who benefited from the trade and those who spoke out about the horrors of the crossing and the treatment of the slaves in order to change public opinion that the slave trade in Africans was a wicked matter. For instance, poet James Thomson (the author of 'Rule Britannia') in his *Seasons* (1726) wrote about a shark that was following a ship carrying slaves:

> *lured by the scent, of steaming crowds, of rank* disease and death. Behold! he rushing, cuts the briny flood, swift as the gale can bear the ship along; And from the partners of that cruel trade, Which spoils unhappy Guinea of her *sons, Demands his share of prey – demands themselves!*[36]

Wilberforce,[37] Clarkson[38] and Equiano (a freed slave)[39] and various organisations such as the Quakers[40] condemned the slave trade and were active in movements against slavers. Thomas[41] argues that a large amount of evidence was gathered from 320 ships that enabled Wilberforce from 1791 to bring several bills before Parliament to seek to abolish the slave trade[42] but they were unsuccessful.

Approximately 13 million Africans were lost to the transatlantic slave trade according to the Voyages database.[43] Sherwood[44] argues that a lot more died. If one takes account of the kidnapping, the march to the coast, prison overcrowding, disease and depression then the amount of people that Africa lost was nearer to 20 million.[45] There was vested interest in keeping the trade alive as many organisations were able to profit from it such as banking, heavy industry and insurance. At the time, this trading in and treatment of slaves was seen as morally justified. Several Acts such as 'An Act for the better ordering and governing of Negroes' was passed in 1661 in Barbados.[46] There was also the Code Noir (black code)[47] which came into being in 1685. What these pieces of legislation had in common was the policing of slaves by tyranny and providing for '"negroes" to be described as "heathenish", "brutish" and "a dangerous kind of people whose naturally wicked instincts should at all times be suppressed"'.[48]

It took an Act of Parliament to formally abolish the trade in slaves through the Slave Trade Abolition Act that came into force on the 25 March 1807.[49] It is argued 'formally' because as Sherwood points out, there was a lot of activity to circumvent 'the Act by Britons',[50] and little was done about it even when slave trading became punishable by death. Implementation was the major problem. Furthermore, the 1807 Act did not itself abolish slavery – only slave trading. This meant that the status of slaves as inferior beings, as property, still had to be tackled before the whole miserable business could be brought to an end.

Institutional racism: Sourced in chattel slavery

'The black must be discharged',[51] were the words Sommersett needed to free him from his master's wish to send him to the West Indies from England by force. A writ of Habeas Corpus[52] was issued to free Sommersett from this plight. However, millions of Africans faced the daily drudge and bad treatment and reduction to racialised chattel in order to generate profit for the metropolis. Thomas argues that Great Britain was the country that plunged most deeply into slavery.[53] Any guilt made easier through the notion of Africans as an inferior race which helped the slavers to justify racist treatment of slaves. But where did this idea of inferior race come from? Several sources were responsible for the construction of people of African descent as inferior beings of which a few can be mentioned here. In England in 1772 Samuel Estwick[54] urged that a Bill should be passed to prohibit negroes from entering England and thus rescue the country from contamination and stain.[55] The most important issue relating to slaves was that they were treated as a matter of private property,[56] as chattel racism and race and colour being pivotal to the status of the 'heathen Negro' under English Common Law according to Blackstone.[57] For Hume the best that could be expected from a Negro is that 'like a parrot [he] speaks a few words plainly'[58] but the negroes were inferior to whites.[59]

In England in the seventeenth century there were a number of newspaper adverts that gave strong clues to how African's were viewed: when they ran away, they could be identified with collars around their necks imprinted with the name of their owners.[60] Virey[61] went to great lengths to argue how different and inferior negroes were to whites. Blacks were like a curiosity that occupied his mind, that negroes were black inside and outside their bodies. However, this type of colourism was not surprising. Blackness had been equated with death and evil by the English before black people were even seen by most people. It is not beyond the realms of imagination that the English should equate black people with something to be scorned. Racism then has to be understood as a 'philosophy' that was adopted to justify the use of black people as chattels during the slave trade and slavery.[62] Mary Prince witnessed the beating of a male slave so badly and so many times that his skin was broken to the flesh and maggots were inside that flesh.[63] Olaudah Equiano talks of the stench in the hold of the ship – no fresh air, the fear that Africans had that they would be eaten and the pens they were put into like sheep on the dock when it came for them to be sold.[64]

The African moved from being a free person, to a captive to a slave[65] and a victim of racism.[66] There was the conversion of a free people to that of chattels. Chattel slavery constitutes the *complete* control of a person for the benefit of another[67] over the duration of their lives. 'De nigger woman is de mule uh de world so fur as Ah can see'.[68] Black slaves became a commodity that could be bought and sold, left in a will and given as gifts. In short their status was that of property. An example of this is found in the narrative of Mary Prince.[69] Prince's work is the first printed autobiography regarding the life of a black slave woman.[70] Born in Bermuda and sold to a slaver, Prince was bought for the amusement of the slaver's daughter. The daughter, Miss Betsy, 'used to lead me by the hand and call me her little nigger'.[71] Another example of this conversion from human to animal was in the incident that surrounded the British slave ship *Zong*[72] where the captain of the ship had 132 live slaves thrown overboard,[73] 'to allow the ship owners to make a cargo insurance claim for the loss of the slaves'.[74] The presiding judge at the time was Lord Chief Justice Mansfield.

Although the throwing of the slaves overboard was clearly a murderous act because the common law was and continues to be that of the unlawful killing of a person in being under the Queen's peace with malice aforethought.[75] Lord Mansfield's concern was the fraudulent claim by the captain and the ship owners against the insurance company. The Solicitor General was John Lee. He questioned the idea that the slaves were human. They were likened to the position as if wood was thrown overboard, rather than a case of the murder of innocent human beings.[76] Lord Mansfield likened black slaves to horses[77] having been thrown overboard. Krikler[78] argues that Lord Mansfield was not prejudiced against black people, after all, he had a loving relationship with a black female,[79] who was his niece. His main job in the commercial courts was to keep order and this 'drove him to deny humanity to the slaves of the Zong'.[80] Is that not the whole point, In this way, slaves were denied humanity which meant that in the court's eyes at least the slaves were not human and therefore there was no murder. As chattels the essence of the slaves 'being' was reinforced by cases such as the Zong.[81] At the time anti-slavery activists took a dim view of Lord Mansfield's position.[82] Olaudah Equiano,[83] a former slave who bought his freedom,[84] reported the Zong case to Granville Sharp[85] who tried without success to bring the slavers to justice.[86]

Racism[87] eased the distinction made between white servants and black slaves, because racism was used to dehumanise black slaves. The meaning of this dehumanisation is, Williams[88] argues, that 'racial difference made it easier to justify and rationalise negro slavery, to exact the mechanical obedience of a plough-ox or a cart-horse ... complete moral and intellectual subjection ... the slave was (also) cheaper'[89] than the white servant. The use of black slaves on the plantations in the West Indies was made easier by the justification that they were animals that could be used and abused – treated as such when kidnapped, on the crossing from Africa to the West Indies and on the plantations.[90]

Eventually, throughout the British Empire, the Abolition of Slavery Act 1833 gave slaves their freedom albeit after a number of years.[91] What the Act did not do, however, was to tackle racism. For example slaves became apprentices under the legislation and, as apprentices, some of them were still being flogged by their former masters.[92] The institution of racialised brutality was still part of the socio-economic system.[93]

Institutional racism: Its watershed moment

The definition of institutional racism can be extracted from instruments and scholarly works that deal with racial discrimination. The International Convention on Racial Discrimination (CERD)[94] states that racial discrimination

> shall mean any distinction, exclusion, restriction or preference based on race, colour, descent, or national or ethnic origin which has the purpose or effect of nullifying or impairing the recognition, enjoyment or exercise, on an equal footing, of human rights and fundamental freedoms in the political, economic, social, cultural or any other field of public life.[95]

This statement regarding ***economic, social, cultural and any other form of public life*** brings us closer to the idea that racism exists in institutions. In one of his conclusions, Lord Scarman[96] defined institutional racism following an investigation into civil disorders in Brixton one of Scarman's conclusions was,

> If by [institutional racism] it is meant that a society which knowingly, as a matter of policy, discriminates against [b]lack people, I reject the allegation.[97]

By this he meant that there was no evidence in terms of his investigation that institutional racism existed. He further argued that,

> if, however, the suggestion being made is that practices may be adopted by public bodies as well as private individuals which are unwittingly discriminatory against [b]lack people, then this is an allegation which deserves serious consideration, and, where proved, swift remedy.[98]

The critical points in Scarman's definitions are the notions of 'public bodies' and 'practice'. Although Scarman did not go so far as to argue that there were practices in the public domain that led to institutional racism he acknowledged that such might exist, he just did not go far enough. Scarman preferred the idea that there were a few 'bad apples' (individual racism) in the police service[99] and that this was the cause of poor race relations between the black community and the police.

It took the lethal wounding of a young black man to provide the context within which institutional racism became a watershed moment in British race relations. The Stephen Lawrence Inquiry set up to investigate the situation that followed the killing, defined institutional racism as follows:

> The collective failure of an organisation to provide an appropriate and professional service to people because of their colour, culture, or ethnic origin. It can be seen or detected in processes, attitudes and behaviour which amount to discrimination through unwitting prejudice, ignorance, thoughtlessness and racist stereotyping which disadvantage minority ethnic people.[100]

This definition of institutional racism encapsulates the full picture of what institutional racism is theoretically as well as practically. It is organisations that fail black people rather than individuals or groups (which is the notion that Scarman argues for). The problem we have with institutional racism is that it is the most stubborn form of racism. It is difficult to detect and hard to eradicate and people are generally blind to its existence. Its impact as a racial harm has been articulated in song, thus Jimmy Cliff sings

> You stole my history/Destroyed my culture/Cut out my tongue/So I can't communicate/Then you mediate/And separate/Hide my whole way of life/So myself I should hate.[101]

'You' is taken to mean society as a whole, and in that sense it is institutions that are represented as a central figure, in the analysis of what it is that perpetuates institutional racism. As Hall[102] remarks, 'Well-formed prejudices and institutional attitudes are deeply based and emotionally held in place; the culture of organisation is notoriously difficult to shift'.[103]

The concept of institutional racism is contested by some scholars such as Green.[104] He argues that the *Macpherson Report* was more a way in which a group could gain government recognition for its 'victim' status and that it is individuals not institutions that the focus on racism should be located.[105] Dennis[106] and others, also argue that the *Macpherson Report*'s evidence was too ready to draw assumptions and attribute blame to institutions.[107] However, Macpherson[108] argues that 'insidious forms of racism'[109] are not being faced up to in the public sector, and there is still an attitude in some quarters that institutions are not racist.[110] What is an institution and what is culture? These are the concepts we turn to next.

Institutions

What are institutions? This concept has troubled scholars for years because there is no common agreement as to what they are.[111] The custom of using institutions in the social sciences goes back to at least 1725.[112] Despite the lack of agreement and the desire by some scholars to work with the concept without challenging it,[113] it is argued that there is a need to explore the meaning of an institution in order to develop it at the empirical and theoretical level,[114] particularly when discussing institutional racism and the law.[115] The British monarchy, money and language are all institutions. As Hodgson contends, the monarchy does not 'cease to exist when the members of the royal family are all asleep and no royal ceremony is taking place'.[116] Similarly institutional racism does not disappear because institutions are obliged to monitor their staff ethnically and provide 'race' awareness training.[117] Institutions may be defined as 'a social arrangement through which collective action is taken to maintain and perpetuate the society and its culture'.[118] The notion of institutions in neo-classical economic theory at least has been questioned by Ankarloo and Parlemo.[119] However other scholars like Tolbert and Zucker[120] have highlighted that there is a wealth of work on institutional theory. Institutions may be defined as 'systems of established and prevalent social rules that structure social interactions',[121] thus law, the police and trade agreements are all institutions. Moreover, Rawls[122] states

> by an institution I shall understand a public system of rules which defines offices and positions with their rights and duties, powers and immunities and the like. These rules specify certain forms of action as permissible, others as forbidden; and they provide for certain penalties and defences, and so on, when violations occur.[123]

Rawls argues that 'an institution may be thought of in two ways … as an abstract object, that is, as a possible form of conduct expressed by a system of rules; and second, as the realisation in the thought and conduct of certain persons at a certain time and place of the actions specified by these rules'.[124]

Furthermore Weber[125] and Pogge[126] have commented on institutions. For Weber, an institution is 'a technical category which designates the ways in which various types of services are continuously combined with each other and with non-human means of production'.[127] From Pogge's point of view institutions are understood 'as a social system's practices or 'rules of the game' which govern interactions among individual and collective agents as well as their access to material resources. Such social institutions define and 'regulate property, the division of labour … political and economic competition … and also govern how collective projects are adopted and executed, how conflicts are settled, and how social institutions themselves are created, revised, interpreted and enforced'.[128] Hodgson[129] argues that institutions are not reducible to the individuals that occupy those institutions and interact with its practices. Thus institutions are independent of individuals although they depend for their operation on the thoughts and activities of the latter[130] as social actors.

In the definition of institutions, the critical elements are: rules, human interaction with those rules, and practice. We are born into a society structured by rules and our conduct is ordered by them, to some extent we are not conscious of the ways in which institutions mould our behaviour. 'Some rules are followed without any subjective formulation in thought of the rule'.[131] These rules are manifest in the 'social practices involving both expressive and practical aims and outcomes'.[132] One form of racism is institutional because it emerges 'out of the normal functioning of the institution rather than being … parasitic to it'.[133] Racism is institutional because it materialises out of practice which requires a reinforcement of rules within an institution by social actors. An example comes from law. As Hodgson says, 'we may define *institutions* as systems of established and prevalent social rules that structure social interactions ... language ... [and] table manners, are thus all institutions'.[134]

An example comes from Bolivia. Lipski[135] tells us there are Afro-Bolivians that directly descend from the Africans who were taken from Africa by the Spanish to work the Bolivian mines in the sixteenth century.[136] Afro-Bolivians are still discriminated against in many areas of social and domestic life as well as in the economic field.[137] The 350,000 Afro-Bolivians are some of the economically poorest groups in the world and this can be traced back to their relation with the transatlantic slave trade.[138] Cocoa growing is what many Afro-Bolivians do now, as opposed to working in the silver mines which they have done from the sixteenth century. Morales,[139] who is an Afro-Bolivian, comments that, 'we might not be slaves any more but we Afros are very poor, which is similar to slavery ... if we don't take good care of our small plantations, we have nothing, nothing at all. And we are always hated and discriminated against'.[140] The treatment of the Afro-Bolivians in this way has developed into an institutional practice which has evolved as the norm in Bolivian society that has structured social relations so that, for the most part, racism affects the usual way of doing things.

According to Douglas[141] institutional racism has been taking place since at least the latter part of the nineteenth century. This is contrary to the more general scholarly view that institutional racism is a twentieth- or twenty-first century phenomena. To some scholars in the context of South Africa it is seen as a post-apartheid development.[142] Romm writes in terms of 'old' and 'new' racisms. The 'old racism' draws on the 'use of apartheid-style racial labelling that denigrates others, marks them as inferior, and affronts their dignity, thus overtly still drawing on notions of white superiority'.[143] Where 'new racism' in post 1990's South Africa bore witness to a situation where 'people refuse to admit the continued need for social policies designed to address past as well as continuing discrimination against those suffering the effects of apartheid following the move to a post-apartheid society'.[144]

In the US institutional racism is said to play itself out in the post-civil rights era. This takes the form of the use of power relations in a way that maintains the inferiority of black people and the superiority of white people.[145] According to Feagin[146] this subtle form of racism was identified by Douglas in his writings and speeches in the 1880s. Institutional racism displayed itself so that

> in nearly every department of American life [black Americans] are confronted by this insidious influence. It fills the air. It meets them at the work-shop and factory, when they apply for work. It meets them at the church, at the hotel, at the ballot-box, and worst of all, it meets them in the jury box ... [the black American] has ceased to be a *slave of an individual*, but has in some sense become *the slave of society*.[147]

In Britain institutional racism has been identified as a phenomenon of public institutions by the Stephen Lawrence Inquiry.[148] It is to do with power and 'the way in which power is distributed throughout an organisation [which] has a major impact on the organisation's propensity to discriminate against individuals'.[149] It is also about privilege which is defined as 'the systematic conferral of benefit and advantage'.[150] Those benefits and advantages accrue to white people even if they are not aware of it, whilst black people are conscious of it[151] but can do nothing about it. Black people are conscious that there is this 'invisible knapsack of provisions that one counts on each day but [which] are largely invisible and unacknowledged'.[152] Moreover, it is difficult to get hold of this knapsack of provisions because they accrue to the dominant culture and the dominant groups within organisations and this is the very place where institutional racism resides. Institutional racism is part of the 'canteen' culture of public organisations[153] and this is where we turn to next.

Canteen culture

Canteen culture means a set of conservative and discriminatory attitudes said to exist within the police force.[154] It is contended that other public and private institutions also harbour a canteen culture that can be racially discriminatory in nature.[155] The canteen culture is a way of shaping institutional policies and practices that can have a negative impact on people. Culture can mean different things depending on the context in which it is located. Executive and scientific cultures relate to stakeholder responsibility and innovation respectively,[156] but none of this defines what culture is and how it works. In the context of institutional racism, culture is particularly relevant because it forms the net through which institutional racism is reinforced. According to Schein[157] 'culture is both a 'here and now' dynamic phenomenon and a coercive background structure that influences us in multiple ways'.[158] Furthermore, our culture is provided and reinforced by language that gives meaning to our day to day lives. So too culture is 'the foundation of the social order that we live in and of the rules we abide by'.[159] And culture is particularly important because it is one of the ways dominant groups maintain and reinforce their superiority over minorities.[160] An example is demonstrated in the way the police do targeted stops and searches of black people on the racist assumption that the person is up to no good. For instance, 'in Dorset (England) a black person was 17 times more likely to be stopped and searched … than other ethnic groups'.[161]

In Britain the issue of institutional culture has arisen recently in a number of cases.[162] Two of these cases surround policing and prosecutorial decision-making by the Crown Prosecution Service (CPS). With regard to policing, the *Macpherson Report*[163] stated that the 'canteen' culture in the police was a breeding ground for institutional racism.[164] Unthinking, unintentional and unwitting institutional racism is a layer of racial harm that often goes undetected. There are unthinking racial stereotypes that influence policing. This stereotyping is embedded in the culture[165] of policing. In terms of prosecutorial decision-making where there is a lethal black death at the hands of state and non-state actors acting on behalf of the state, there is a culture of not bringing a prosecution. The culture of institutions is critical in developing an understanding of institutional racism because it enables us to see how this phenomenon is embedded.

Put together institutions and racism and you find the canteen culture of institutional racism. Lea[166] has referred to this notion of institutional racism as one that shows there is a pattern of behaviour that is not reducible to the conduct of individuals – an example of behaviour that can be located in the patterns of institutional practices.[167] Like a number of institutions such as the police, education and mental health,[168] they harbour a culture of racism so harmful that there is no regard taken to the relations between white and black people in an institutional setting.[169] There is, as Better[170] argues, 'cultural blindness and cultural deafness'.[171] This is the refusal to accept that there is racism inside the very institutions of society that support the social system.[172] This refusal is marked by the belief that racism is the playground of a few individuals who do not want to see equality afforded to all and that once those individuals are 'outed' racism will somehow wither away.[173] Whilst such individuals exist they cannot account for the racial harm caused by institutionalised racism, the racial harm that is created by an opaque glass ceiling applied against black people in every realm of public life, in particular, 'employment, housing and education'.[174] This form of racism is unwitting, unconscious and part of the everyday way of doing business in institutions reinforced by social actors. For this reason, institutional racism has to be pointed out as was done in the Macpherson Inquiry. That is why there should be legislation directly aimed at identifying and eradicating it and policy directed at sifting it out of institutions.

Institutional racism: A framework

In order to research the idea of institutional racism we need to establish a conceptual framework. The first thing to realise is that the form of institutional racism raised in this chapter is not deliberate or something that we are consciously aware of. That means that it has to be pointed out to people where in an organisational framework institutional racism resides. In public housing for example it might be disproportionate allocation to overcrowded conditions and the long-term effects that such allocation has on children in terms of health and education.[175] In 1985 Fryer[176] raised this as an issue and the same problem of disproportionate overcrowding for black people was still being raised by Shelter in 2005.[177] Next we have to accept that institutional racism consists of cultural deafness and cultural blindness. All institutions have a culture and some have cultures that are more dominant than others. It is the dominant culture that in its movement and its reinforcement by social actors leaves no room for other cultures to be heard and seen. Moreover, there is the canteen culture that keeps the machinery of institutions turning with its reinforcement of racism. This machinery informs what social actors do, how they think and how they work together through the maintenance of policies and practices that are racist. Furthermore, there is the phenomenon of privilege which plays a major role in employment particularly in recruitment and retention. Institutions tend to recruit like as like and provide the factors that ensure similar people are recruited and retained as one moves up the echelons. This also helps to maintain the opaque glass ceiling. Institutional racism consists of racial stereotyping and that tends to be reinforced in institutional settings. There is also the 'them' and 'us' dichotomy with the assumption that somehow black people are 'different' and that difference constitutes inferiority harking back to enslavement times when black people were made to believe they were inferior and treated that way by most white people. There is the refusal to acknowledge that there is a need for social policies made to take into account continuing institutional racism against those people who are subject to racial discrimination and racism. There is no desire to shake up the status quo because it might be too uncomfortable in terms of challenging the dominant social order.

However, we are in the twenty-first century and it is time that law was enacted to deal with institutional racism in the UK and the European Union. This law would obligate public and private institutions to ensure that their organisations were not practising institutional racism. With this new law would come the monitoring of organisations by the Equality and Human Rights Commission (ECHR) under what would be termed the 'institutional racism duty'. This duty would apply to both the public and private sectors. The organisations (consisting of ten or more employees) would be trained by the EHRC regarding institutional racism and taught to carry out a self-audit of their policies and practices to ascertain where institutional racism was live. They would be required to remove it and state in their annual reports what they had done to eradicate it.

This system of training, self-auditing, monitoring with the penalty of being shut down for non-compliance would operate like the Care Quality Commission which inspects social care providers and has the power to recommend that they are shut down if they do not comply with their statutory obligations. The institutional racism duty would work in much the same way with teams of inspectors that monitor organisations by visiting them, interviewing users and monitoring paperwork. Of course there is bound to be resistance on the part of providers and the government might not want to recommend legislation to deal with institutional racism, but all the government would have to do is to amend the Equality Act 2010 and expand the powers of the Equality and Human Rights Commission in order to achieve this

The World Conference against Racism (WCAR)

At the international level the problem of racism and racial discrimination has been raised through the declaration and programme of action which was hosted by the United Nations (UN) in Durban, South Africa in 2001. The Declaration stated that:

> slavery and the slave trade, including the transatlantic slave trade, were appalling tragedies in the history of humanity not only because of their abhorrent barbarism but also in terms of their magnitude, organised nature and especially their negation of the essence of the victims ... and are among the major sources and manifestations of racism [and] racial discrimination ... and that *Africans and people of African descent ... continue to be victims of their consequences.*[178]

In paragraph 14 of the Declarations of the (WCAR) the UN also outlined that colonialism has led to racism and racial discrimination and the African people and descendants continue to be victims of these consequences.

What is striking in these paragraphs is that the UN refers to Africans and people of African descent who still suffer the consequences of slavery. It has been argued that in the twenty-first century black people suffer overt and covert racism and institutional racism. This latter form is sourced in the theft from African people who had their own culture, languages, religions, agricultural systems, books, education, architectural designs, hunting, fishing, pottery, blacksmithing, weaving, dyeing and so on[179] None of this tends to be taught in schools where the place of black people in society begins with slavery and the role of black women remains relatively silent. This failure to teach children the history of African societies before slavery and the destruction of them by the slave trade and chattel slavery constitutes a failure to provide a professional service based on race and yet it is something that could so easily be rectified.

Conclusion

This chapter has argued that the nature of institutional racism is a hidden form of racism. It is different from overt racism which is highly visible and covert racism which tends to be less overt. Institutional racism operates in institutional settings rather than as a racial harm perpetrated by individuals or groups. Given the argument that it is hidden it is of course far harder to detect – although not impossible in the Macpherson sense – and much more difficult to eradicate. Institutional racism is compounded by the years of racism against black people stemming from the transatlantic slave trade and chattel slavery. Some of the adverse effects of slavery which has culminated over 400 years was eventually eradicated through the abolition of the slave trade and slavery but no work was done on racism at the time of abolition. Racism has been left to fester undetected until the 1960s in Britain where legislation was used to deal with racism but institutional racism remained untouched. This is still the case now despite duty bearing legislation that has evolved to target institutions, who are to have 'due regard'[180] to eliminate unlawful racial discrimination under the Equality Act 2010. With the concept of institutional racism is used throughout the book to highlight the problems that institutional racism throws up with suggestions for how matters should be changed.

Notes

1 See Quakers in the World, 'Origins of Barclays Bank'. Available at: www.quakersintheworld.org/quakers-in-action/327 (accessed 11 March 2016).
2 Paragraphs 46.27 and 46.4 of the Stephen Lawrence Inquiry.
3 V.R. Randall, 'What is Institutional Racism? Available at: www.academic.udayton.edu (accessed 24 May 2016).
4 It has been argued that racism was not caused by the transatlantic slave trade but developed from it, E. Williams, *Capitalism and Slavery* (Chapel Hill: The University of North Carolina Press, 1994), p. 7.
5 Such as Apartheid South Africa or Jim Crow America or the Colonial Caribbean.
6 Williams, *Capitalism and Slavery*, p. 25.
7 L. Back and J. Solomos (eds), *Theories of Race and Racism: A Reader* (Abingdon: Routledge, 2000), p. 23.
8 M. Kleg, *Hate, Prejudice and Racism* (Albany: State University of New York Press, 1993), p. 21.
9 An infamous case in the US is that of James Byrd, a black man who, having accepted a lift from a group of white men, was tied to the back of their truck and dragged for three miles. His head was severed from his body and bits of Byrd's remains were found in 75 places. The perpetrators were found guilty. Two received capital punishment whilst the third received life imprisonment. See The Associated Press, *Race and Ethnicity on MSN.com*, 2008. Available at: www.msnbc.msn.com/id/25008925/ns/us_news-life/t/years-later-dragging-death-changes-town/ (accessed 27 June 2014).
10 *Jones v Tower Boot Co* [1997] IRLR 168; [1997] 2 All ER 406; CA.
11 *Burton Rhule v De Vere Hotels* [1996] IRLR 596.
12 Ibid., racism is interconnected with gender as this case demonstrates.
13 [1988] 2 ALL ER 118.
14 The court decided that the decision of the prison authorities constituted discrimination.
15 *Alexander v Home Office* [1988] 2 ALL ER 118, p. 120h.
16 R.D. Coates, 'Covert Racism in an Age of Colour Blindness', *This Week in Sociology*. Available at: www.thisweekinsociology.com/2011/10/covert-racism-in-age-of-color-blindness.html (28 June 2014).
17 Ibid., Jim Crow referred to laws in the Southern USA that reinforced racial segregation.
18 P. Gilroy, *There Ain't No Black in the Union Jack* (Chicago: University of Chicago Press, 1991). Although modernity has captured the union jack through the notion of 'Big Society' such as the Olympic Games.
19 R.D. Coates, 'Covert Racism in an Age of Colour Blindness', *This Week in Sociology*. Available at: www.thisweekinsociology.com/2011/10/covert-racism-in-age-of-color-blindness.html (accessed 28 June 2014).
20 S. Carmichael and C.V. Hamilton, *Black Power the Politics of Liberation in America* (New York: Vintage Books, 1967), p. 4.
21 W. Macpherson, *The Stephen Lawrence Inquiry* (London: Home Office, 1999), para. 6.34.
22 12 Ibid.
23 D. Gillborn, *Education and Institutional Racism* (London: Institute of Education, 2002), p. 1.
24 Ibid., p. 2.
25 P. Gilroy, 'The End of Antiracism', in J. Donald and A. Rattansi (eds), *'Race', Culture and Difference* (London: Sage, 1992).

26 Ibid., p. 51.
27 Williams, *Capitalism and Slavery*, p. 7.
28 J. Walvin, *The Trader, The Owner, The Slave* (London: Vintage Books, 2007), p. 110.
29 W. Rodney, *How Europe Underdeveloped Africa* (London: Bogle-L'Ouverture Publications, 1978), p. 85.
30 A country that is subservient to or controlled by a greater power, *The Concise Oxford Dictionary* (1964).
31 It has been argued that slavery and the slave trade were considered lawful; see R.C. Redman and P. Finkelman, 'Legal Aspects of Slavery', in D. Shelton, *Encyclopedia of Genocide and Crimes against Humanity* (New York: Thomson, Gale, 2005). Available at: www.enotes.com/slavery-legal-aspects-reference/slavery-legal-aspects (accessed 5 September 2014).
32 Rodney, *How Europe Underdeveloped Africa*, p. 86.
33 E. Abbott, *Sugar: A Bitter Sweet History* (London: Duckworth Publishers, 2010), pp. 36–37.
34 'The Understanding Slavery Initiative – Trade and Commerce'. Available at: www.understandingslavery.com/.
35 Abbott, *Sugar: A Bitter Sweet History*, p. 148.
36 J. Thomson, 'Summer, Complete Works' (in H. Thomas, *The Slave Trade: The History of the Atlantic Slave Trade 1440–1870* (London: Papermac, 1998), p. 453.
37 William Wilberforce was a keen abolitionist regarding both the slave trade and slavery. He put many bills before the Houses of Parliament to abolish these practices. See BBC History. Available at: www.bbc.co.uk/history/historic_figures/wilberforce_william.shtml (accessed 15 September 2014).
38 Throughout the British Empire and Britain Thomas Clarkson was a major protagonist against both the slave trade and slavery. See BBC History. Available at: www.bbc.co.uk/history/historic_figures/clarkson_thomas.shtml (accessed 15 September 2014).
39 O. Equiano, *The Interesting Narrative of the Life of Olaudah Equiano or Gustavus Vassa. The African. Written by Himself*, vol. 1, edited by Paul Edwards (Oxford: Heinemann, 1969), first published 1789. In this book Equiano tells of the horrors he and other slaves endured due to kidnap and the conditions on the ship that took him from Africa to the West Indies.
40 Several Quakers condemned their own members for being involved in slavery from the seventeenth century, and were critical in the road to abolition of the slave trade and slavery. See *Quaker Protest against Slavery in the 17th Century*. Available at: www.quaker.org.uk/quaker-protests-against-slavery-17th-century (accessed 17 September 2014).
41 H. Thomas, *The Slave Trade: The History of the Atlantic Slave Trade 1440–1870* (London: Papermac, 1998).
42 Ibid., p. 523.
43 'Voyages, the Trans Atlantic Slave Trade Database 1501 to 1866'. Available at: www.slavevoyages.org/tast/assessment/estimates.faces (accessed 17 September 2014).
44 M. Sherwood, 'The Trade in Enslaved Africans and Slavery after 1807', in F. Brennan and J. Packer (eds), *Colonialism, Slavery, Reparations and Trade: Remedying the Past?* (Abingdon: Routledge, 2012), pp. 23–24.
45 J. Crawford, 'The Single Greatest Crime in History'. Available at: www.mobilization2-21.com (accessed 24 May 2016).
46 H. Beckles, *Britain's Black Debt* (Jamaica: University of West Indies Press, 2013).
47 'Liberty, Equality, Fraternity, Exploring the French Revolution'. Available at: https://chnm.gmu.edu (accessed 8 December 2015).
48 Beckles, *Britain's Black Debt*, p. 61.
49 *Parliament and the British Slave Trade 1600–1833*, available at: http://www.parliament.uk/about/living-heritage/transformingsociety/tradeindustry/slavetrade/overview/parliament-abolishes-the-slave-trade/ (accessed 17 September 2014). The British slave trade was abolished in all her colonies between 1787 and 1833. J. Oldfield, '*British Anti-Slavery*', February 2011. Available at: www.bbc.co.uk/history/british/empire_seapower/antislavery_01.shtml (accessed 6 January 2015).
50 M. Sherwood, 'The Trade in Enslaved Africans and Slavery after 1807', in F. Brennan and J. Packer (eds), *Colonialism, Slavery, Reparations and Trade: Remedying the Past* (Abingdon: Routledge, 2012), p. 24.
51 Lord Mansfield, *The Sommersett Case*, Howell's State Trials, vol. 20, cols 1–6, 79–82 (1771–1772). Available at: www.nationalarchives.gov.uk/pathways/blackhistory/rights/transcripts/somerset_case.htm (accessed 17 September 2014).

52 A writ of Habeas Corpus is a 'Latin term meaning you have the body'. This writ gave every prisoner the right to challenge the terms of his or her incarceration. See about.com, Civil Liberties. Available at: http://civilliberty.about.com/od/lawenforcementterrorism/g/habeas_corpus.htm (accessed 18 September 2014).
53 Thomas, *The Slave Trade*, p. 235, quoting from William Pitt the Younger, in the House of Commons, April 1792.
54 Estwick was an agent for the island of Barbados in London; see F. Shyllon, *Black People in Britain 1555–1833* (London: Oxford University Press, 1977), p. 4.
55 Shyllon, *Black People in Britain 1555–1833*, p. 4. Stain meaning a type of contamination.
56 R. Blackburn, *The Making of New World Slavery from the Baroque to the Modern 1492–1800* (London: Verso, 1998), p. 324.
57 Shyllon, *Black People in Britain 1555–1833*, p. 4.
58 D. Hume, 'Negroes … Naturally Inferior to the Whites' (b. Edinburgh, 26 April 1711; d. Edinburgh, 25 August 1776) in E.C. Eze, *Race and the Enlightenment: A Reader* (Oxford: Blackwell Publishers, 1997), p. 33.
59 Ibid., p. 32.
60 Shyllon, *Black People in Britain 1555–1833*, p. 10.
61 J.J. Virey, 'Natural History of the Negroes Particularly', in H.F. Augstein (ed.), *Race: The Origins of an Idea 1760–1850* (London: Thoemmes Press, 1996), chapter 14.
62 Port Cities Bristol, 'Racist Ideas'. Available at: http://discoveringbristol.org.uk/slavery/after-slavery/wider-world/black-white-in-britain/racist-ideas/ (accessed 19 September 2014).
63 S. Salih, *The History of Mary Prince: A West Indian Slave* (London: Penguin, 2004), p. 21.
64 Equiano, *The Interesting Narrative of the Life of Olaudah Equiano or Gustavus Vassa*, vol. 1, pp. 30–31.
65 Rodney, *How Europe Underdeveloped Africa*, p. 103.
66 In the US there is concern from the descendants of enslaved Africans and slavers surrounding 'the racial nature of slavery of the slave system and the persistence of institutional racism that emerged from it'. See H. McDonald Beckles, *Slave Voyages, the Transatlantic Trade in Enslaved Africans* (Paris: United Nations Education, Scientific and Cultural Organisation Slave Trade Education Project (UNESCO, 2001).
67 The Free Dictionary. Available at: http://legal-dictionary.thefreedictionary.com/Chattel+slavery (accessed 8 August 2014).
68 M. Prince, *Mary Prince: The History of Mary Prince* (London: Penguin, 2004) (1831), p. vii.
69 Ibid.
70 Salih, *The History of Mary Prince*, p. vii.
71 Prince, *Mary Prince*, p. 7.
72 *Gregson v Gilbert* (1783) 3 Dougl 232, 99 English Report 629. The ship owners were Gregson and the insurers were Gilbert. Available at: http://web.utk.edu/~gerard/romanticpolitics/zongcase.html (accessed 9 August 2014).
73 Understanding Slavery Initiative (USI), *The Zong Case Study*. Available at: www.understandingslavery.com/index.php?option=com_content&view=article&id=373&Itemid=248 (accessed 9 August 2014).
74 The National Archives. Available at: http://yourarchives.nationalarchives.gov.uk/index.php?title=Zong_Massacre_%28case_of_Grayson_v_Gilbert_1783&29.
75 The Crown Prosecution Service, Homicide: Murder and Manslaughter. Available at: www.cps.gov.uk/legal/h_to_k/homicide_murder_and_manslaughter/#definition (accessed 9 August 2014).
76 Understanding Slavery Initiative (USI), *The Zong Case Study*. Available at: www.understandingslavery.com/index.php?option=com_content&view=article&id=373&Itemid=248 (accessed 9 August 2012).
77 S. Usherwood, 'The Black Must be Discharged: The Abolitionists' Debt to Lord Mansfield', *History Today* 31(3): 1981.
78 J. Krikler, 'The Zong and the Lord Chief', *History Workshop Journal* 64(1) (2007): 29–47.
79 The black female 'was the illegitimate daughter of Lord Mansfield's nephew', Slavery and Justice Exhibition at Kenwood House, *English Heritage*. Available at: www.english-heritage.org.uk/discover/people-and-places/the-slave-trade-and-abolition/slavery-and-justice-exhibition-at-kenwood-house/ (accessed 9 August 2014).
80 Krikler, 'The Zong and the Lord Chief' *History Workshop Journal*, 29–47. Available at: http://hwj.oxfordjournals.org/content/64/1/29.short?rss=1 (accessed 9 August 2014).

81 Slavers aboard ships would throw slaves overboard rather than get caught with them by the British navy following the abolition of the slave trade in 1807. The Abolition Project, 'Suppressing the trade'. Available at: http://abolition.e2bn.org/slavery_155.html (accessed 10 August 2014).
82 P. Edwards (ed.), *Equiano's Travels* (Oxford: Heinemann Educational, 1969) (1789).
83 The Equiano Society, *Olaudah Equiano*, itzcaribbean.com. Available at: www.itzcaribbean.com/olaudah_equiano.php (accessed 9 August 2014).
84 Edwards, *Equiano's Travels*, pp. 96–97.
85 Was an anti-slavery activist who reported the case and gained recruiters to his cause for the abolition of the slave trade. Available at: www.twmuseums.org.uk/slavery/_files/learning-zone/Activity8b.pdf (accessed 9 August 2014).
86 The Abolition Project, 'Granville Sharp (1735–1813): The Civil Servant'. Available at: http://abolition.e2bn.org/people_22.html (accessed 10 August 2012).
87 Racism is defined as 'the belief that certain groups are innately, biologically, socially, morally superior to other groups, based upon what is attributed to be their racial composition'. The consequence of this is that the 'inferior' group suffers a form of racial harm that decreases their chance of living a 'normal' life and can cause them alarm and distress and even lead to the death of the victim. Kleg, *Hate, Prejudice and Racism*, p. 21.
88 Williams, *Capitalism and Slavery*.
89 Ibid., p. 19.
90 Edwards, *Equiano's Travels*.
91 The National Archives, 'Emancipation'. Available at: www.nationalarchives.gov.uk/pathways/blackhistory/rights/emancipation.htm (accessed 13 August 2014).
92 'Birmingham's Emancipation Movement', CO 137/222 (12 September 1836). Available at: www.nationalarchives.gov.uk/pathways/blackhistory/rights/emancipation.htm (accessed 13 August 2014).
93 Although Emmer argues that the situation, economically at least, was more complex than this and that slaves used their new found freedom to bargain with plantation owners for the use of their labour. P.C. Emmer, 'The Big Disappointment: The Economic Consequences of the Abolition of Slavery in the Caribbean, 1833–1888', *History in Focus* 12 (Spring 2007).
94 UN General Assembly, *International Convention on the Elimination of all Forms of Racial Discrimination*, 21 December 1965, United Nations, Treaty Series, vol. 660, p. 195. Available at: www.unhcr.org/refworld/docid/3ae6b3940.html (accessed 18 August 2014).
95 Article 1 of the International Convention on the Elimination of all Forms of Racial Discrimination.
96 L. Scarman, *The Scarman Report* (London: Home Office, 1981).
97 92 Ibid., para. 2.22, p. 11.
98 93 Ibid., para. 6.28.
99 B. Bowling and C. Phillips, *Racism, Crime and Justice* (Harlow: Pearson Education, 2002), p. 17.
100 Macpherson, *The Stephen Lawrence Inquiry*, para. 6.34.
101 Jimmy Cliff, 'The Price of Peace'. See B. Sundhu, *Reparations for Colonialism and the Trans-Atlantic Slave Trade*. Available at: www.billsundhu.ca (accessed 6 July 2014).
102 S. Hall, G. Lewis and E. McLaughlin, *The Report on Racial Stereotyping* (prepared for Deighton Guedalla, solicitors for Duwayne Brooks, June 1998) (Milton Keynes: Open University, 1998).
103 Ibid., p. 6.
104 D.G. Green (ed.), *Institutional Racism and the Police: Fact or Fiction?* (London: Institute for the Study of Civil Society, 2000).
105 Ibid., p. 40.
106 N. Dennis, G. Erdos and A. Al-Shahi, *Racist Murder and Pressure Group Politics* (London: Institute for the Study of Civil Society, 2000).
107 Ibid., p. x.
108 B. McPherson, 'Institutional Racism: The Hidden Problem'. *Public Service.co.uk* 10 April 2012. Available at: www.publicservice.co.uk/feature_story.asp?id=19561 (accessed 14 August 2014).
109 Ibid.
110 Ibid.
111 S. Miller, 'Social Institutions', in *The Stanford Encyclopedia of Philosophy*, Fall 2012 Edition, ed. E.N. Zalta. Available at: http://plato.stanford.edu/cgi-bin/encyclopedia/archinfo.cgi?entry=social-institutions (accessed 21 August 2014).

112 G. Hodgson, 'What are Institutions?', *Journal of Economic Issues* 40(1) (2006). Available at: www.geoffrey-hodgson.info/user/image/whatareinstitutions.pdf (accessed 12 July 2014).
113 J.A. Goguen and R.M. Burstall, 'Introducing Institutions', Proc. of Logics of Programming Workshop, Pittsburgh. *Springer Lecture Notes in Computer Science* 164 (1983): 221–256.
114 Hodgson, 'What are Institutions?'.
115 M. La Torre, *Law as an Institution* (London: Springer Dordrecht Heidelberg, 2010).
116 G. Hodgson, 'What are Institutions?', p. 2.
117 Training was one of the suggested methods for tackling racism laid down in the Stephen Lawrence Inquiry, recommendation 48–54.
118 S. Better, *Institutional Racism: A Primer on Theory and Strategies for Social Change* (Lanham: Rowman & Littlefield, 2008), p. 38.
119 D. Ankarloo and G. Parlemo, 'Anti-Williamson: A Marxian Critique of New Institutional Economics' *Cambridge Journal of Economics* 28(3) (2004).
120 P.S. Tolbert and L.G. Zucker, 'The Institutionalization of Institutional Theory', in S.R. Clegg and C. Hardy, *Studying Organization: Theory and Method, Part 1* (London: Sage, 1999).
121 Hodgson, 'What are Institutions?', p. 2.
122 J. Rawls, *A Theory of Justice* (Oxford: Oxford University Press, 1990).
123 Ibid., p. 55.
124 Ibid.
125 M. Weber, *The Theory of Social and Economic Organisation* (New York: The Free Press, 1964).
126 T. Pogge, *World Poverty and Human Rights* (Cambridge: Polity Press, 2002).
127 Weber, *The Theory of Social and Economic Organisation*, p. 221.
128 Pogge, *World Poverty and Human Rights*, p. 31.
129 Hodgson, 'What are Institutions?', p. 2.
130 Ibid.
131 Ibid., p. 4.
132 R. Harre, *Social Being* (Oxford: Blackwell, 1979), p. 98.
133 J. Lea, 'The Macpherson Report and the Concept of Institutional Racism', *Howard Journal of Criminal Justice* 39(3) (2000): 219–323, at p. 231.
134 Hodgson, 'What are Institutions?', p. 2.
135 J.M. Lipski, 'Afro-Bolivian Spanish and Helvecia Portugese: Semi-creole Portugese', Papia 16, 2206, pp. 96–116. The Pennsylvania State University, USA. Available at: www.personal.psu.edu/jml34/papia.pdf (accessed 14 February 2014).
136 Ibid., pp. 96–97.
137 *World Directory of Minorities and Indigenous Peoples.* Available at: www.minorityrights.org/2406/bolivia/afrobolivians.html (accessed 14 February 2014).
138 King Julio is one of the many poverty-stricken Afro-Bolivians. But a few years ago he discovered that he was a direct descendant of Bonifaz, a tribal king from central Africa. The original Bonifaz was brought to Bolivia as a slave in the sixteenth century to work in the silver mines of Potosi. A. Schipani, 'Hidden Kingdom of the Afro-Bolivians', BBC News, 17 April 2009. Available at: http://news.bbc.co.uk/1/hi/world/americas/7958783.stm (accessed 15 February 2014).
139 See A. Schipani, 'Hidden Kingdom of the Afro-Bolivians', BBC News, 17 April 2009. Available at: http://news.bbc.co.uk/1/hi/world/americas/7958783.stm (accessed 15 February 2014).
140 Ibid. Although the author of this article suggests that there is a shift in bad feeling towards the Afro-Bolivians in recent times.
141 J.R. Feagin, *Racist America: Roots, Current Realitie, and Future Reparations*, 2nd edition (Abingdon: Routledge, 2010), p. 9.
142 N. Romm, *New Racism: Revisiting Researcher Accountabilities* (South Africa: Springer, 2010).
143 Ibid., p. 1.
144 Ibid., p. 2.
145 Ibid., p. 3.
146 Feagin, *Racist America.*
147 Ibid., p. 9.
148 Macpherson, *The Stephen Lawrence Inquiry*, p. 28, para. 6.50.
149 B. Kandola, *The Value of Difference: Eliminating Bias in Organisations* (Oxford: Pearn Kandola Publishing, 2009).
150 Ibid., p. 83.

151 Ibid.
152 Ibid.
153 According to Bowling and Phillips, Scarman's point regarding discriminatory practices by public bodies as well as individuals constituted a 'bad apples' thesis. This represents a 'reflection of society' which means that if people are prejudiced in society that prejudice will be played out in the police service who are recruited from wider society. Bowling and Phillips, *Racism, Crime and Justice.*
154 Available at: www.oxforddictionaries.com (accessed 24 May 2016).
155 DeepDyve, 'Challenging the Canteen Culture in Medicine'. Available at: www.deepdyve.com/lp/wiley/challenging-the-canteen-culture (accessed 24 May 2016).
156 E.H. Schein, *Organizational Culture and Leadership*, 4th edition (San Francisco: John Wiley & Sons, 2010), p. x.
157 Ibid.
158 Ibid., p. 3.
159 Ibid.
160 A. Gramsci, *Selections from Prison Notebooks of Antonio Gramsci*, ed. Q. Hoare and G.N. Smith (London: Lawrence & Wishart, 1971), p. 57.
161 N. Morris, 'Black People still far more likely to be stopped and searched than other Ethnic Groups', *The Independent* 6 August 2015.
162 Denning argues that in terms of corporate institutions such as the World Bank, 'an organization's culture comprises an interlocking set of goals, roles, processes, values, communications practices, attitudes and assumptions, S. Denning, 'How do you Change an Organizational Culture?' *Forbes*, 2011. Available at: www.forbes.com/sites/stevedenning/2011/07/23/how-do-you-change-an-organizational-culture/ (accessed 25 July 2014).
163 Macpherson, *The Stephen Lawrence Inquiry.*
164 Ibid., para. 6.17.
165 Ibid.
166 J. Lea, 'The Macpherson Report and the Concept of Institutional Racism', *Howard Journal of Criminal Justice* 39(3) (2000): 219–323.
167 Ibid., p. 221.
168 F. Keating, D. Robertson, A. McCulloch and E. Francis, *Breaking the Circles of Fear: A Review of the Relationship between Mental Health Services and African and Caribbean Communities* (London: The Sainsbury Centre for Mental Health, 2002). Available at: www.centreformentalhealth.org.uk/pdfs/breaking_the_circles_of_fear.pdf (accessed 24 August 2014).
169 Panorama, 'Young Offenders at Risk'. Available at: http://news.bbc.co.uk/1/hi/programmes/panorama/archive/1211953.stm (accessed 30 August 2014).
170 Better, *Institutional Racism*, p. 24.
171 Ibid.
172 M. Rowe, *Policing, Race and Racism* (Cullompton: Willan Publishing, 2004).
173 Better, *Institutional Racism*, p. 24.
174 Fryer, *Staying Power*, p. 387.
175 Ibid., p. 389.
176 Ibid.
177 L. Reynolds and N. Robinson, *Full House? How Overcrowded Housing Affects Families* (London: Shelter, 2005).
178 U.N. *World Conference Against Racism, Racial Discrimination, Xenophobia and Related Intolerance Declaration and Programme of Action* (New York: United Nations, 2002), para. 13, p. 16.
179 K.C. Holmes, *Black Inventors Crafting over 200 Years of Success* (New York: Global Black Inventor Research Projects, 2008), p. 34.
180 The general and specific duty on public institutions came into effect in 2011.

Bibliography

Abbott, E., *Sugar: A Bitter Sweet History* (London: Duckworth, 2010).

Ankarloo, D. and G. Parlemo, 'Anti-Williamson: A Marxian Critique of New Institutional Economics', *Cambridge Journal of Economics* 28(3) (2004): 413–429.

Back, L. and J. Solomos (eds), *Theories of Race and Racism: A Reader* (London: Routledge, 2000).

Better, S., *Institutional Racism: A Primer on Theory and Strategies for Social Change* (Lanham: Rowman & Littlefield, 2008).

Blackburn, R., *The Making of New World Slavery* (New York: Verso, 1998).

Bourne, J., *The Life and Times of Institutional Racism* (London: Sage Publications, Institute of Race Relations, 2001).

Bowling, B. and C. Phillips, *Racism, Crime and Justice* (Harlow: Pearson Education, 2002).

Carmichael, S. and C.V. Hamilton, *Black Power the Politics of Liberation in America* (New York: Vintage Books, 1967).

Connolly, M., *Townshend Smith on Discrimination Law: Text, Cases and Materials*, 2nd edition (London: Cavendish Publishing, 2004).

Dennis, N., G. Erdos and A. Al-Shahi, *Racist Murder and Pressure Group Politics* (London: Institute for the Study of Civil Society, 2000).

Dick, P. and D. Jankowicz, 'A Social Constructionist Account of Police Culture and its Influence on the Representation and Progression of Female Officers: A Repertory Grid Analysis in a UK Police Force', *Policing: An International Journal of Police Strategies & Management* 24(2) (2001): 181–199.

Edwards, P. (ed.), *Equiano's Travels* (Oxford: Heinemann Educational, 1969 [1789]).

Feagin, J.R. *Racist America: Roots, Current Realities, and Future Reparations*, 2nd edition (Abingdon: Routledge, 2010).

Fredman, S., *Discrimination and Human Rights: The Case of Racism* (Oxford: Oxford University Press, 2001).

Fryer, P., *Staying Power: The History of Black People in Britain* (London: Pluto Press, 1985).

Gillborn, D., *Education and Institutional Racism* (London: Institute of Education, 2002).

Gilroy, P., 'The End of Antiracism', in J. Donald and A. Rattansi (eds), *'Race', Culture and Difference* (London: Sage, 1992).

Gilroy, P., *There Ain't No Black in the Union Jack* (Chicago: University of Chicago Press, 1991).

Gramsci, A., *Selections from Prison Notebooks of Antonio Gramsci*, edited by Q. Hoare and G.N. Smith (London: Lawrence & Wishart, 1971).

Green, D.G. (ed.), *Institutional Racism and the Police: Fact or Fiction?* (London: Institute for the Study of Civil Society, 2000).

Harre, R., *Social Being* (Oxford: Blackwell, 1979).

Kandola, B., *The Value of Difference: Eliminating Bias in Organisations* (Oxford: Pearn Kandola Publishing, 2009).

Keating, F., D. Robertson, A. McCulloch and E. Francis, *Breaking the Circles of Fear: A Review of the Relationship between Mental Health Services and African and Caribbean Communities* (London: The Sainsbury Centre for Mental Health, 2002).

Kleg, M., *Hate, Prejudice and Racism* (Albany: State University of New York Press, 1993).

Krikler, J., 'The Zong and the Lord Chief', *History Workshop Journal* 64(1) (2007): 29–47.

La Torre, M., *Law as an Institution* (London: Springer Dordrecht Heidelberg, 2010).

Lea, J., 'The Macpherson Report and the Concept of Institutional Racism', *Howard Journal of Criminal Justice* 39(3) (2000): 219–233.

Macpherson, W., *The Stephen Lawrence Inquiry* (London: Home Office, 1999).

McDonald Beckles, H., *Slave Voyages: The Transatlantic Trade in Enslaved Africans* (Paris: United Nations Education, Scientific and Cultural Organisation Slave Trade Education Project, 2001).

Pogge, T., *World Poverty and Human Rights* (Cambridge: Polity Press, 2002).

Prince, M., *Mary Prince: The History of Mary Prince* (London: Penguin, 2004) (1831).

Rawls, J., *A Theory of Justice* (Oxford: Oxford University Press, 1990).

Reddie, R.S. *Abolition! The Struggle to Abolish Slavery in the British Colonies* (Oxford: Lion Hudson, 2007).

Reynolds, L. and N. Robinson, *Full House? How Overcrowded Housing Affects Families* (London: Shelter, 2005).

Rodney, W., *How Europe Underdeveloped Africa* (London: Bogle-L'ouverture Publications, 1972).

Romm, N., *New Racism: Revisiting Researcher Accountabilities* (Durban: Springer, 2010).

Rowe, M., *Policing, Race and Racism* (Cullompton: Willan Publishing, 2004).
Scarman, L., (1981) *The Scarman Report* (London: Home Office).
Schein, E.H., *Organizational Culture and Leadership*, 4th edition (San Francisco: John Wiley and Sons, 2010).
Strand, S., 'The Limits of Social Class in Explaining Ethnic Gaps in Educational Attainment', *British Educational Research Journal* 37(2) (2011): 197–229.
Tolbert, P.S. and L.G. Zucker, 'The Institutionalization of Institutional Theory', in S.R. Clegg and C. Hardy, '*Studying Organization: Theory and Method, Part 1* (London: Sage, 1999).
Townshend-Smith, R.J., *Discrimination Law: Text, Cases and Materials* (London: Cavendish Publishing, 1998).
Usherwood, S., 'The Black Must be Discharged: The Abolitionists' Debt to Lord Mansfield', *History Today* 31(3) (1981). Available at: www.historytoday.com/stephen-usherwood/black (accessed 15 December 2016).
Wasserstorm, R., 'Racism, Sexism and Preferential Treatment: An Approach to the Topics', *UCLA L Rev* 24(581) (1997).
Weber, M., *The Theory of Social and Economic Organisation* (New York: The Free Press, 1964).
Williams, E., *Capitalism and Slavery* (Chapel Hill: The University of North Carolina Press, 1994) (1944).
Williams, P.J., *Seeing a Colour-Blind Future: The Paradox of Race* (London: Virago Press, 1997).

3 Institutional racism and cyber race hate

Introduction

The World Conference against Racism, Xenophobia and related intolerance, stated that Africans and those of African descent suffer from the consequences of the transatlantic slave trade and chattel slavery. One of those consequences is the spread of black hate via the Internet. An example is the website 'White Aryan Resistance'.[1] That website has a 'nigger gallery' with cartoons depicting black people in racial stereotypical positions and with racist messages. This website shows up as number 10 on the Google hit list under the search term 'nigger'.[2] Some will say that the website is a manifestation of free speech and freedom of expression and that is the mark of a democratic society. This chapter argues that racists hide behind the cloak of free speech to peddle cyber race hate. As such they should not be able to lay claim to free speech and should be banned. Internet and web service providers (ISPs) that do little to curb the use of their facilities to promulgate black hate speech can be said to be institutionally racist in that they fail to provide a service to black people by inadvertently allowing racism to be facilitated on line. This means that some black users who are subject to racism online, often from anonymous sources, can suffer from depression and anxiety.[3] It is argued that ISPs have a duty of care to protect black people (and other minority ethnic groups) from being subject to racism online. One way of protecting black people from racist online comment is to prevent anonymity of racist material.

Chapter 2 provided a framework for defining institutional racism. It consists of the unwitting and the unconscious culture of organisations that creates a barrier reinforcing the 'them' and 'us' dichotomy as far as Africans and Afro-Caribbean's in the Diaspora are concerned. It is argued here that the Internet is an institution that contains a culture of racism as part of its very being. When it comes to regulating this racist culture the international discourse surrounding legislation against race hate on the Internet tends to concern itself with a balancing exercise.[4] That is striking the balance between freedom of expression and the 'pursuit of racial, religious and communal justice and harmony'.[5] However, it would appear that legislative efforts on the part of the Council of Europe (CoE)[6] to criminalise race hate in cyberspace (cyber race hate) have been thwarted through the compromise they have made on concerns about freedom of expression[7] and resistance to state interference in the same. It is argued that such a compromise comes at the expense of effective legislative protection for racial and ethnic minority groups from cyber race hate. The regulation of cyber race hate in the context of freedom of expression poses a moral dilemma. To what extent should states regulate hate speech in the light of the fact that we regard freedom of speech as fundamental in a liberal democracy? This discourse on regulating cyber race hate is done without reference to institutional racism as part of the culture of the Internet. The focus tends to be on moderating individuals and groups of the far right wing variety rather than dealing with the culture they inhabit. This chapter argues that there is a culture of racism in the Internet that cannot be narrowed down to the machinations of individuals, rather cyber race hate must be understood as a culture within which institutional service providers operate and that requires a different way of dealing with the problem of cyber race hate.

Background

Racism on the Internet and has been termed 'cyber racism'.[8] This has come to mean 'racism which occurs in the cyber world ... this includes racism which occurs on the internet such as racist websites, images, blogs, videos and online comments ... emails or on social networking sites'.[9] The Internet is a place that can be used for the display of racist language and images. 'Twitter Explodes with Racism After Hockey Game' read a number of sport outlets following the winning goal of Joel Ward (black person) in a hockey game 'when the Washington Capitals beat the Boston Bruins'.[10] People use racism on the Internet for a number of reasons. such as when like-minded people becoming more extreme when they talk to each other online, to the desire to get noticed through racism. There is a misconceived belief that the law cannot act on your racist beliefs promulgated online through to the view that the Internet allows freedom of speech and freedom of expression of which racism is one form of expression. Moreover, there is the idea that the anonymity of the Internet means that you cannot get caught spreading racism online. Putting racist materials online 'some people self-disclose or act out more frequently ... than they would in person',[11] this is called 'online disinhibition' where people are not inhibited from going further than they would in real space in the self-assured knowledge that they will not get caught. Some do not get caught but it is not true to believe that by downloading or uploading racist materials online the law will not intervene. The international nature of racism on the Internet can be seen from case law in Moscow, the US and the UK.

In Moscow, for instance there was the case of a 21-year-old who was convicted for setting up a racist group on a social network[12] and there was also an employee in the US who was traced through the racist emails sent to an African American woman.[13] In the UK a man was convicted for uploading racist video clips calling for a 'racist holy war' on YouTube.[14] Indeed, there is precedent from the UK that uploading unlawful materials from outside the UK is an offence. This was decided in the case of *R v Perrin*.[15] This means that accessing unlawful information outside the jurisdiction of the UK will not serve to protect the individual or group. However, it should be noted that *Perrin* was a case brought contrary to section 2(1) of the Obscene Publications Act 1959, rather than a case brought on cyber racism law.

Under UK law racist materials 'posted on any site anywhere in the world by a person in the UK ... falls under the "Obscene Publications Act 1959 and 1964" and therefore the person posting it is liable to arrest and prosecution'.[16] Moreover, under the Communications Act 2003 racist comments are a breach of UK law wherever the site is hosted.[17] There are relatively few cases on cyber racism compared to the number of race hate sites on the Internet. It has been reported that in terms of white supremacy online in the US there are between 762 (Southern Poverty Law Centre, SPLC) and 2,500,[18] whilst in the UK it is estimated that there are 'ten thousand such sites'.[19] Even so given the amount of general information online why should there be such concern over what amounts to words and images of a racist nature online? It has been argued that such materials are dangerous because of their global reach, and for the harm that their influence might cause in real life.

For example, the 'UK Nail Bomber', David Copeland, who was charged with bomb attacks on ethnic minorities and gay people, was found to have accessed 'internet files concerning white supremacist Eric Rudolph'.[20]

There is also the threat that cyber racism poses to the notion of racism on the international level. Article 1 of the *International Convention on the Elimination of All Forms of Racial Discrimination*, this states that

> 'racial discrimination' shall mean any distinction, exclusion restriction or preference based on colour, descent, or national or ethnic origin which has the purpose or effect of nullifying or impairing the recognition, enjoyment or exercise, on an equal footing, of human rights and fundamental freedoms in the political, economic, social, cultural or any other field of public life.[21]

It is argued that cyber racism impacts on this universal declaration in that it nullifies the enjoyment of social freedoms for those who are victims of cyber racism. In this chapter the focus is on Africans and Afro-Caribbean's around the world who are cyber victims and may very well feel the effects of this racism in real space.

The racial-historical context of cyber racism

Cyber racism needs to be understood in its racial-historical context of race hate. Race hate may be defined as bias conduct whose impact reaches beyond the individual victim to members of the individual victim's group or presumed group.[22] The effect is that by attacking individuals the group suffers racial harm that serves to marginalise it and destabilise its position in society, so that it is trapped in the role of the inferior 'other'. In real space 'the most commonly motivating factor in hate crime was race'[23] The perpetrators tend to be society's misfits who join white supremacist groups, those who do not belong to supremacist groups but dabble in racism or those who sympathise with racism. For these people this cyber race 'hate [is] itself … normal, rational and conventional. It is part of the culture-the way of life-of the society in which it exists, appealing typically to the most conventional and traditional of its members.'[24]

For black people this race hate has stemmed from the times of the transatlantic slave trade when they were treated as commodities. There was a transfer in the vocabulary from the talk of black people as human (servants for example) to the talk of them as things to be bought and sold in the market place like any other commodity in the seventeenth century,[25] that solidified their position as the substandard 'other'. Walvin[26] tells us that one can perceive the way in which black people were understood in the eighteenth century by reading the general magazines that were popular at the time. In one magazine black people were typified as Negroes who were, 'peculiarly sexual, musical, stupid, indolent, untrustworthy and violent'.[27]

This kind of racial stereotype continued in England until at least the nineteenth century. In the twentieth century black people met with blatant racial discrimination as they moved around Britain looking for work and housing because white people did not want to work with them[28] or live near them. Even during World War I when soldiers were required the mixing of black troops with white was fiercely resisted, 'even in war blacks were consigned to their age-old role of being the beast of burden for their white masters'.[29] Those who were injured during the war found a mixed reaction in the hospitals where some white soldiers protected them whilst others attacked them.[30] Black people also suffered their homes being attacked and their clubs being desecrated by whites. There was little if any protection afforded by the police. Whites victimised black people in the 1940s. This racism was particularly so with seamen where whites refused to work with them. There was blatant racial discrimination in economic and violent racism in social terms.[31] In the 1950s black West Indians were welcomed by the government to do the work that white people did not want to do such as drive tube trains, collect bus fares and empty the bed pans of hospital patients[32] but there was still widespread racial prejudice. Fryer tells us that:

> More than two-thirds of Britain's white population ... held a low opinion of black people or disapproved of them. They saw them as heathens who practiced head-hunting, cannibalism, infanticide, polygamy and 'black magic'. They saw them as uncivilised backward people, inherently inferior to Europeans, living in mud huts "in the bush", wearing few clothes, eating strange foods and suffering from unpleasant diseases. They saw them as ignorant and illiterate, speaking strange languages, and lacking proper education.[33]

Some white folk were prejudiced in a mild sort of way but others were 'deeply prejudiced'[34] and would not mix with black people in any way at work or at home and just wanted them to 'go home'.[35] This is the racial backdrop from which racism in society has been articulated online.

Cyber racism and the law

We see racism morphing onto the Internet where it has been allowed to spread as hate speech and online harassment. Over 605 million users of the Internet have among them 'racist, violent and extremist groups[who] have been quick to learn how to take advantage of this medium through systematic and rational use. They use and exploit the internet relatively effectively'.[36] From 1995 one website incited racial hatred but by 2002 there were 3,300.[37] There is a growing use of the Internet to harass and intimidate individuals in the UK[38] and perpetrators can hide behind the anonymity that the Internet gives them.[39] Given this backdrop, unsurprisingly, there have been reports[40] looking at exactly what problems the Internet causes in terms of racism. A cross-country study conducted by the Broadcasting Standards Commission, identified racism as a problem.[41] Two of the main problems are online harassment and stalking. Online harassment has been defined as the sending of threatening, obscene or abusive emails that are unwanted[42] or the sending of thousands of racist emails or sending computer viruses.[43] Whilst, stalking online refers to 'persistent and frequent unwanted contact from another individual which is highly undesirable [causing] discomfort and annoyance ... severe distress and mental trauma'.[44] In short, 'racism persists online in ways that are both new and unique to the internet'.[45]

Ellison and Akdeniz suggest that there are ways of regulating some of these problems. For instance, by using the Telecommunications Act 1984 section 43, one can catch messages that are grossly offensive, indecent, obscene or menacing in nature. The difficulty is the 'Act will not apply ... in cases where the data is transmitted by using a local area network unless part of the transmission is routed through a public telecommunications system'.[46] An alternative route is to use other speech crimes such as the Protection from Harassment Act 1997. This Act deals with stalking and is wide raging. Stalking involves causing fear of violence or serious alarm or distress under section 4A. There is also the Crime and Disorder Act 1998 that deals with stalking under section 32(1). Furthermore, there is the Protection of Freedoms Act 2012, section 111 that inserted two new offences of stalking into the Protection from Harassment Act 1977, so for instance stalking examples include where there is a course of unwanted conduct and the victim is 'contacted by any means,'[47] 'publishing any statement or other material … relating to a person'[48] and more importantly for our purposes 'monitoring the use by a person of the internet, email or any other form of electronic communication'.[49]

There are also the Public Order Act 1986 offences that can be used to deal with broadcasting racist materials, the improper use of public electronic communications network under section 127 of the Communications Act 2003, according to the British Crown Prosecution Service the provision can be used for cyber-stalking and cyber-bullying.[50] Moreover, Section 1 of the Malicious Communications Act 1988 is available to deal with electronic communications and this would also deal with the issue where there is an 'intent to cause distress or anxiety to the recipient'.[51] By far the most useful instrument for police to usurp in catching people who use the Internet to propagate racist material is the Police and Criminal Evidence Act 1984.[52] There must be '"reasonable grounds for believing' that a 'serious arrestable offence' has been committed'.[53] These instruments are necessary in the fight against racism on the Internet and are adequate when it comes to dealing with national perpetrators but when those perpetrators are abroad they are out of the jurisdiction and so beyond the reach of national law.

Although the Internet does not recognise geographical borders, states do. An attempt to deal with this problem has come through UNESCO and the Office of the United Nations of the High Commission for Human Rights (OHCHR). The OHCHR has made combating racism on the Internet one of its top priorities, and has sought to elevate the profile of this problem through various awareness raising campaigns.[54] Under the auspices of the UN umbrella several conferences have been held looking at the issue of racism and the Internet, the World Conference against Racism that produced the Durban Declaration and Programme of Action (2001) being one of them. An intergovernmental working group was set up to consider the Durban Declaration and Programme of Action in terms of the implementation and they came back with the following conclusions: 'promote the use of the internet to create educational and awareness raising networks against racism; adopt legislative and administrative measures to establish as criminal offences the distribution or making available to the public, through computer systems, of racist and xenophobic material which incites hatred or violence'.[55]

An initiative from the Council of Europe has been the Additional Protocol to the Convention on Cybercrime,[56] also known as the Additional Protocol, its job is to encourage Member States to create and implement legislative measures to handle race hate on the Internet. Generally, the European Court of Human Rights (ECtHR) has come down on the side of freedom of expression as expressed in Article 10 (1) of the European Convention of Human Rights curtailing the state's ability to control this freedom and that is as it should be except when it comes to cyber racism, including homophobic and misogynistic material that might be directed at black people. In the *Handyside*[57] case the Court said that 'information and ideas that offend, shock or disturb the State are in principle protected by Article 10,'[58] but it is argued that cyber racism that shocks or offends is too damaging to societal race relations to be left unchecked, to be 'protected' by Article 10 (1). Moreover in *Wingrove*[59] the ECtHR held that 'No restriction on freedom of expression, whether in the context of religious beliefs or in any other, can be compatible with Article 10 unless it satisfies … the test of necessity as required'[60] by Article 10(2) which gives states a limited right to control freedom of expression. What is meant by the test of necessity is that there must be 'a pressing social need,'[61] it must be proportional to the legitimate aim and it must be relevant and sufficient.[62] It is argued that the suppression of cyber racism is necessary as satisfying a pressing social need to protect human rights and promote racial equality. The ECtHR is alive to this considering the *Feret*[63] case where the Court held that:

> it may be considered necessary in certain democratic societies to sanction or even prevent all forms of expression which spread, incite promote or justify hatred based on intolerance ... provided that any formalities, conditions, restrictions, or penalties imposed are proportionate to the legitimate aim pursued ...[64]

Since the Durban conference on Racism and Xenophobia, the Council of Europe, the European Court of Human Rights and some states such as the UK and Australia are concerned about the use of the Internet to spread of racism on the Internet, what escapes the narrative is the role of institutional racism as an important facet in the consideration of how states and organisations operate with respect to this phenomenon.

Institutional racism and cyber racism

Racism No Way, an Australian non-governmental organisation, defines institutional racism as 'forms of racism which are structured into political and social institutions. It occurs when organisations, institutions or governments discriminate, either deliberately or indirectly, against certain groups of people to limit their rights'.[65] It has been argued by Macpherson[66] that institutional racism is unwitting and unconscious rather than a form of racism that is deliberate. Institutional racism forms a culture to which we are for the most part both deaf and blind. It is maintained by social actors where there is reliance for its existence on them keeping the culture alive. It is argued that institutional racism is part of the culture of Internet service providers (ISPs) because they fail to provide an Internet service that is cyber racist free. The Internet is a place where the culture of cyber racism has flourished in the form of infrastructures that form the backdrop through which racist social actors operate. For instance, its infrastructure has been used to bring 'together European and American [and other] extremist groups, the latter having previously been somewhat isolated'.[67] In favour of the argument that the Internet is a neutral place and it is its *use* by cyber racists that is the problem with cyber racism on line, Sorensen[68] contends that the Internet is merely there for us to use and cannot be blamed for the fact that it is used by extremist groups to promulgate their propaganda. This contention is supported by the fact that the elimination of racist hate substance on the Internet is quite difficult. 'The boundless, global nature of the internet makes it practically impossible to eradicate all objectionable material or to impede access to that material by anyone with a computer and a modem,'[69] but this chapter argues that without the Internet we would not have the problem of cyber racism so somebody with respect to the Internet has to be responsible for removing cyber racist materials, such as the state together with Internet service providers.

Esteban[70] tells us that the Internet is multifaceted and it is this that, not only makes it different from other media, but requires understanding. The Internet has been defined as 'the use of electronics and electromagnetic spectrum to store, modify, and exchange data via networked systems and associated physical infrastructures',[71] as an information highway that merely '... enables information spaces created by the technology of digital networked computer systems, most of which ultimately connect with the mother of all networks,'[72] the Internet can, it may be argued, be seen as akin to any other 'broadcasting' mechanism in the sense that it puts information into the public domain much as does a radio or television show or a book.

We are at liberty to switch the machinery through which this information comes on or off, we can filter the information as we choose and put in place regulation to control the harm that some of this information might cause, by preventing it, restricting access to it or grading the content. The Internet merges the functions that were associated with 'previously distinct media of telephony, TV, publishing and computing'.[73] There is an immediate difference in that one can access and engage in these distinct media in one place and evidence from the work of James and others[74] suggests this use reduces the time spent on other media such as TV, phone and books. Apparently coined by Gibson,[75] cyberspace was described as the 'projection of disembodied consciousness into the consensual hallucinations … matrix'.[76] It is this disembodied faceless form which creates communities that communicate with each other over thousands of miles. Like global backpackers the disembodied can hitch lifts into cyberspace by using the World Wide Web as a transporter.[77] As a social realm cyberspace needs to be understood not only as a place where information is obtained but where information is created[78] and transported without geographical boundary,[79] thus it is not a physical entity in the same way as traditional broadcasting mechanisms are, there are not the various levels in place by which one could hold those who publish content accountable, there are not the editorial mechanisms that attract responsibilities for control. An individual can engage with the world instantaneously from the privacy of their bedroom with anonymity, they can avoid jurisdictional controls by engaging in 'regulatory arbitrage'[80] to steer clear of national restrictions. We are faced with trying to imagine a space hard to define by reference to the property of physical boundaries, where borders may be articulated as domains with technical specifications, moreover, these 'boundaries in cyberspace are still linked to real effects in physically bounded real-space'.[81] Chon[82] suggests that cyber law has to

acknowledge, make coherent and demarcate 'these rezoned spaces' if we are to deal with its effects. Reno I[83] was the first American case to deal with the question of the nature of the Internet. As well as its evolving methods of communication and retrieval of information via word, sound picture and moving video images, the Internet has the capacity to connect individuals to other individuals and groups, and for individuals to enter chat rooms 'to engage in real time dialogue'.[84] For consumers the Internet is 'a vast library including millions of readily available and indexed publications and a sprawling mall offering goods and services'.[85]Moreover, it 'constitutes a vast platform from which to address and hear from a worldwide audience of millions of readers, viewers, researchers, and buyers. Any person or organisation with a computer connected to the internet can "publish" information'.[86]

ISPs provide the connection to this world and should be held morally accountable as well as legally responsible where the sprawling mall consists of cyber racist content. This means that ISPs do not adopt a policy of 'network neutrality' when it comes to the emission of cyber racism on the Net. It is argued that the role that ISPs might play amounts to a 'role as content controller and thus censor,'[87] but such a role is critical since it leads the way in constructing responsible use of what is a fantastic publication platform. My argument is that the understanding of the Internet must be its capacity as an infrastructure that provides the means by which users communicate with each other and cyber racists survive and grow. This growth is a threat to social stability for black people who already face racial discrimination in the social institutions such as education, health, housing and employment as well as racism in real space. Cyber racism just presents another problem area for black people. There is what Esteban alludes to as an 'electronic community of hate'[88] where groups are well structured and 'highly organised'.[89] They are able to use 'top-level domains where they can install their webpages'[90] and market it to the world particularly targeting disaffected young males.

Esteban talks about institutional racism as 'being supported by a most disconcerting form of modern racism and hatred spread through internet websites'.[91] It is critical to my argument that the Internet harbours cyber racism created by cyber racist. The Net is not institutionally racist it is ISPs that are so because it is they that fail to provide a service free of cyber racism. Arguably, the Net is not just a myriad of 'wires and cables strung loosely across the globe'[92] connecting computers together. The Internet is likened to a hive where cyber racism can lay its eggs that grow. The cyber racists are the social actors that use the Internet as the carrier of racist messages whether the individual or group are extremists or just dabblers of these racist messages and images.

The hive is the place where 'a cross-pollination of ideologies of hatred'[93] takes place. This hive is created by Internet service providers (ISPs) whether they be Facebook, Google, Myspace or the many others. It is argued that ISPS have a moral obligation in the name of racial equality and human rights, to disenable the racist part of the hive, that will consist of IP addresses, hubs, routers and the domain name system. In this age of modern technology this should not be hard to do but the question is whether it is in the providers interest to invest in the relevant technology. They may say that they provide a service for any user regardless of his or her intention. It is argued here that the provision of Internet services to cyber racists is institutionally racist because it fails to provide a service to black people who become cyber racist victims. It should not just be left up to the law enforcement agencies to catch cyber racists because they rely on a complaints driven system that cyber racist victims in the black community may not know about or have the confidence to use given the real space tensions between black users and the state. ISPs make profit from the Net and this should not be at the expense of black cyber racist victims. The individual states and ISPs should shoulder the responsibility of the financial burden that might ensue from dealing with cyber racists.

Internet service providers as an institution and as part of the legacy of the slave trade

It is argued that Internet service providers (ISPs) form an institution that has failed to provide a professional service to black people due to their failure to stop cyber racists from using the Internet to spread race hate ideology. Race hate ideology means that white supremacist groups believe that the white race is superior to all other races and characterise these other races in derogatory ways. White supremacists believe in racial separation and want to have separate societies that serve different groups. Some white supremacists allow 'outsiders' in so long as those outsiders accept the dominance of the white group.[94] Amongst others means, this race hate ideology is spread through the Internet, emails etc. Infrastructural arrangements that constitute the Internet are how cyber racists access the cyber world to create cyber racism. As has been previously established, institutional racism is the legacy of the transatlantic slave trade and this form of racism requires institutions to be accountable. It is held here that Internet service providers are part of an institution. As service providers, some 'host content'[95] they are companies that provide access to the Internet, usually for a fee.

Many ISPs [afford] additional services such as email accounts, web browsers, and space for you to create a website'.[96] These ISPs, 'individual companies, universities and governments … run tens of thousands of interconnected networks'..[97] ISPs supply the infrastructure together with thousands of technicians and other resources to provide access to the Internet and through these emails, for example, appear instantaneously. Internet service providers control the Internet space through which racism is promulgated such as 'facebook, YouTube, websites, email lists, online music and book stores such as Amazon, and iTunes, online games, social networking and chat rooms'.[98] These ISPs constitute 'a social arrangement through which collective action is taken to maintain and perpetuate the [internet]society and it's culture'[99] that society being the Internet itself and those who have been given access to it. The ISPs may be defined as 'systems of established and prevalent social rules that structure social interactions'.[100] So although the British National Party (a Far Right organisation) uses the Internet to spread its racist propaganda, such as people should go back to their homelands,[101] it is able to access the web through an ISP, the ISP is an institution that enables cyber racist information to appear on the web as a consequence of its relative 'hands off' policy.

As a more balanced argument about the role of Internet service providers it is probably fair to say that the exchange of data on the Internet occurs 'without the networks knowing the content of the data, or without any true idea of who in real life the sender of a given bit of data is'[102] according to Lessig.[103]Lessig argues that the Internet is so complex in terms of who is using it and what is being done with it that governments find it hard to regulate the kind of data being sent. Moreover, an important factor of the Internet is that it promotes or defends free speech, in a democratic society that is the right to speech no matter who it offends. But for those who cherish free speech and its appearance on the Internet regardless of its racist content (which some may argue is regrettable but the side effect of free speech), Lessig says that things are changing. 'The code of the internet implements a set of protocols called TCP/IP'.[104] For the code 'other architectures can be layered onto the basic TCP/IP protocols [that] can make behaviour on the Net fundamentally regulable'.[105] The potential to regulate the Net raises important issues concerning civil liberties. There is concern that these architectures will interfere with free speech on the Internet. I would argue that we must be concerned with free speech but that cyber racism is not free speech, it is racist speech that provides an opportunity to devalue part of humankind – a humankind that the law otherwise seeks to protect through human rights and racial equality laws. Cyber racism provides an opportunity for cyber racists to indulge in behaviours that would generally not be countenanced in real space or would be regulated in real space in some countries if it proved harmful to others. It is cyber racism that should be regulated by this new architecture not free speech in general. Technology should be developed (if it has not been already) to distinguish cyber racism from other forms of speech since it is cyber racism that serves to infiltrate and support the already racist factors that exist in real space such as the incitement to racial hatred.

It is society that stands to lose its multicultural cohesion if cyber racism is to remain unregulated given that this reinforces the racial dominance of white over black, a dominance that harks back to the transatlantic slave trade and slavery, Cyber racism needs to be regulated because it is dangerous and, as described by Black, is a form of 'translocal whiteness',[106] meaning a 'global white identity … [that]fosters a racist cyber culture that becomes much harder to fight head on'.[107] The involvement of the ISPs is essential in the desire to control online racist content.

Cultural deafness and cultural blindness

Institutional racism also consists of cultural deafness and cultural blindness. But the institution must have a culture for these conditions to develop. It is contended that there are several types of culture associated with the Internet one of these is the culture of ISPs the other is the culture of users of the Net itself. The ISPs culture consist of customs and practices that hold it apart from its users. These customs and practices consist of 'traditional and widely accepted way[s] of behaving or doing something ... '[108] particular to the Internet society of ISPs. The ISPs' culture can further be 'defined as an evolving set of collective beliefs, values and attitudes'.[109] This is part of a business culture that has 'its own unique dimension ... [and will]encompass [an] organisation's values, visions, working style beliefs and habits'.[110] The ISPs' culture is distinct from the culture of its users. Dutton and Blank[111] argue that there are five cultures of users of the Internet: e-Mersives who are comfortable with the Internet, Techno-pragmatists who see the Internet as instrumental to their everyday life, Cyber-savvy's who are ambivalent about the Internet, Cyber-moderates who appear to be both moderate and fearful about Internet use and Adigitals where the Internet appears to them to be 'out of their control'.[112] Within the user culture can be found cyber racism, a type of sub-culture that consists of a group within a larger group of users that follow racist beliefs that people such as black people should not be allowed to mix with whites and they also convey hatred of black people. It is argued that when it comes to regulating cyber racism on the Net the ISP culture is both deaf and blind to the harm caused by their persistence in playing a neutral role. It is true that they have been asked by the Council of Europe to 'promote greater respect for privacy, security and freedom of expression of users'[113] and 'ensure peoples enjoyment of a maximum of rights and services, subject to a minimum of restrictions, while at the same time seeking to ensure the level of security that users are entitled to expect,'[114] but this should not extend to a culture that unwittingly ignores cyber racism. Some ISPs have woken up to racism on line. Vodafone and Virgin have dealt with racism on Facebook either by refusing to share the same space with the right wing British National Party, a right wing party that has a policy that all non-white people should 'go home'[115] or, in the case of Richard Branson of Virgin, the use of Facebook to condemn a racist incident that occurred at a Virgin Active health club in South Africa.[116] There are also complaints led mechanisms used by YouTube, Facebook and Twitter where users can make an objection regarding cyber racism on the ISP's systems. But with the extent of cyber racism on line there is little evidence that a complaints led system is successful. It is debatable that the user victim will even have confidence that the ISPs will challenge cyber racism. Wertheim[117] argues that self-regulation by ISPs is one of the best ways to fight cyber racism. This argument holds that it is voluntary arrangements by the ISPs to deter cyber racists that are necessary to drive the cyber racist away from the use of the Internet as a forum to peddle dangerous racist ideas. It is counter-argued here that cyber racism is too important to be left with the underlying notion that really ISPs are just 'mere conduits and disclaim all responsibility for the way their services are used'.[118] Some ISPs do have a policy against what is sometimes called Net hate and they have successfully taken hate off of the Internet. The problem is the policy against cyber racism is not a general one in that not all ISPs and search engines adhere to it. More importantly the cyber racist information is already on the Net for all to see before it is taken off the site. Cohen-Almagor[119] suggests that the search engines could change the way searches are conducted by changing some of the words that come up[120] so that a search for 'race hate' could flag up websites on 'race equality' a search for 'white supremacy' could come back with the sites on 'racial harmony'.

Internet service providers need to accept that they are a culture that has provided the hive through which cyber racists peddle cyber racism. They also need to consider from a moral viewpoint that their black users suffer as user victims on line and in the real world when cyber racism is allowed to perpetuate racist myths 'about … racial and ethnic groups, that devalues and renders inferior those groups, that reflects and is perpetuated by deeply rooted historical, social, cultural and power inequalities in society'.[121]Internet service providers as gateways to the Internet have been questioned about their role in controlling racist content.[122] ISPs have been seen to be part of the chain which contributes to the distribution of illegal content on the Internet.[123] There would appear to be little recognition that they have a moral responsibility to block cyber racism. Partly this is down to the position that freedom of expression means they are limited in what they can block on the Net. The other aspect is that they are a business out to make profit and can seek comfort in their income generating activity that the Net covets free speech.

In America, for example, the constitution protects freedom of expression. 'The U.S. Constitution protects even the most offensive and controversial speech from government suppression, and permits regulation of speech only under certain limited and narrow circumstances. The US system is built on the idea that the free and open exchange of ideas encourages understanding, advances truth-seeking and allows for the rebuttal of falsehoods. The United States believes, and experience has shown, that the best way to counter offensive speech is not with regulation but with more speech'.[124] But the problem with Net access to free speech is the racist poison it can generate not only on the Internet but in real space. Certainly litigation in the American courts tends to protect free speech. In the *Reno*[125]ruling the court held that a content-based blanket restriction on speech is overly broad by prohibiting protected speech as well as unprotected speech and is unconstitutional. The quest here is not to counter all speech merely cyber racist speech. A case in the US that was not on cyber racism but nevertheless relates to this discussion here was the Nuremberg Files. This was a case where a website published the names and other private information about abortion providers. Nuremberg Files was legally challenged on the content of the website under the Freedom to Access Clinic Entrances Act 1994 that prohibits the use of force or threat to anyone seeking to provide 'reproductive health services'.[126] The appellants won after a long battle and the site was taken down, however anti-abortion extremists still use the Internet to harass, intimidate and threaten reproductive health service providers and this has had an impact in real space where up to nine abortion providers have been killed.[127]

There does seem to be a connection between the Internet and the spread of white extremism to intimidate and kill ethnic minorities and black people, for instance, the case of Keith Luke who killed two black people and 'raped and nearly killed a third on the morning after Barak Obama was inaugurated as president'.[128] Not having any contact with white extremist groups Luke said he had been reading 'white power' websites and used this as a basis for the racial harm caused. The trend is for cyber racists to use the Internet to spread racist ideas of the extreme variety such as the message on the British People's Party website that 'our only uniform is the colour of our skin'[129] (referring to white people) and to incite violence against ethnic minority groups. This is why it is important that ISPs control Internet access to such individuals and groups since they pose a dangerous threat to society. 'Threat' is the key word that ISPs should be alert to because it is this that makes for social instability in cyber space and in real space.

The US Supreme Court had the opportunity to consider the meaning of the word 'threat' in *Elonis v United States.*[130] Elonis argued that he was not guilty of posting threats on line when he came before the courts. He argued before the Court on the basis that the Federal law under which the government sought to control his Internet speech – that is the use of the term 'threat' was not contrary to 18 U.S.C. S875(c) of the Federal law that 'makes it a crime to transmit in interstate commerce any communication containing any threat … to injure the person of another'.[131] Elinos argued that his communication must have the *mens rea* of an intention to create a threat and this was not the case when he posted information on the Internet. According to the Supreme Court the statute in question was silent on the *mens rea* requirement and that negligence was not sufficient to find criminal liability under the statute. The Court stated, that is not to say that just because a statute does not 'specify any required mental state … that none exists … mere omission … of any intention of criminal intent should not read as dispensing with it'.[132] Furthermore, Elonis' conviction 'was premised solely on how his posts would be understood by a reasonable person … a familiar feature of civil liability in tort law, but is inconsistent with … criminal conduct'.[133] The defendant's conviction was not allowed to stand because it had to be proved that 'wrongdoing had to be conscious to be criminal'.[134] This ruling makes it difficult in the context of the US at least to hold Net users criminally liable where the Federal law does not convey what the appropriate men srea in a criminal statute should be. And in any event cyber racism on the Net in the US is generally construed as 'hyperbole'[135] which it should not be argues Cohen-Almagor. This is because cyber racism poses a real threat to law and order and the safety of black people as ethnic minorities.

Cyber racism hurts

Internet service providers probably stick to the old saying that 'sticks and stones may break my bones but words will never hurt me'[136] but this can be taken to refer to the erection of a barrier to insults which may cause psychological injury. Whether these 'injurious' words in fact cause hurt is a moot point.[137] Neu[138] argues that the answer to this (if there is *an* answer) is made complex by the intricacies of the meaning of words, to whom the words are said, who uses them and how the words are received. Thus the words 'welshing',[139] 'gyp',[140] 'hunk'[141] and 'niggardly'[142] may or may not be insulting words depending on time, geographical space, speaker, listener and context.

There is a school of thought[143] which adheres to the view that race hate words hurt. Matsuda[144] argues for us to understand these words as a form of assault or injury. Thus in *Virginia* v *Black*[145] the opinion of the US Supreme Court on race hate messages was 'while a burning cross does not inevitably convey a message of intimidation, often the cross burner intends that the recipients of the message fear for their lives. And when a cross burning is used to intimidate, few if any messages are more powerful'.[146] Similarly under English law an assault can be committed by words, thus in the British case of *Ireland and Burstow*[147] Lord Steyn was of the opinion that 'a man accosting a woman in a dark alley saying 'come with me or I will stab you,'[148] would constitute an example of assault by words. The essence of this type of assault is the apprehension of fear or injury that is generated by the words used towards the intended victim.[149] However there is a potential problem with treating race hurt words in cyber space in the same category as those conveyed through vocal means or cross burning. The sight of a cross burning on someone's front lawn is clearly frightening and meant to elicit fear in the mind of the individual. A crowd of white people estimated at between 1,500 and 4,000 shouting, 'let's get the blacks',[150] similarly terrifying. Such incidents, in the context of the US and UK respectively have a particularly despicable history,[151] rooted in hate, discrimination and exploitation. With the Internet the space between the perpetrator and potential victim is, however, separated by technology. The victim can choose not to use such sites and the perpetrator is never a 'real' threat.

It is argued that the questions of space, choice and real threat are important in our consideration of whether race hate words hurt when conveyed through cyberspace. It has been suggested that 'a person must actively search for information ... in order to be exposed to cyber-hate messages and images'.[152] However, evidence from the USA[153] suggests that hate speech takes place through a number of outlets on the Internet such as email and other sites e.g. football sites,[154] which are not necessarily accessed because the person is actively searching for such racist information. Moreover, the underlying message regarding actively searching for such information appears to be that the recipients 'deserve' the hurt generated from hurtful messages – so do not go there! Race hate words by their nature are designed to create victims.[155] These words damage community cohesion creating a 'them' and 'us' culture that destabilises multiculturalism and good race relations. Cyber racist words are 'like a constantly dripping tap'[156] meant to eat away at the very core of the soul of black people so that any confidence they have in social relations is destroyed. It is not just words that hurt but 'pictures, videos and music'[157] where the content has cyber racist words and images. The fact that cyber racist victims in the UK can report cyber racism to the web administrator, the hosting company and the police is some comfort that hopefully the offending material will be taken down and the cyber racist dealt with by the police. Nonetheless, 'much material that can be viewed in the UK is outside the jurisdiction of our courts',[158] and so whether the website administrator or host provider will remove the offensive material depends very much on the legal rules in force in that country or the voluntary arrangements of the ISP.

Orwick and Settles[159] suggest the culture of hate speech is prevalent on the Internet, it provides another 'venue for bullying behaviour'[160] and its propensity to injure its victims should not be underestimated. It is the content of the message and the context in which such messages are generated that needs to be focused on. Lawrence[161] argues for hate crimes[162] to be understood as more than a 'personal predilection of the perpetrator'.[163] Its dangerous nature lies in the social context within which such messages are portrayed, rooted in particular histories of discrimination and hatred against particular groups. Furthermore, the aim of the perpetrator[164] is to use the stereotyped characteristics of individual victims as a stepping stone to an attack on the general community to whom that victim belongs or is perceived to belong.[165] Akdeniz[166] suggests that the 'internet has thus become the medium of choice for propaganda, disseminating hatred, recruitment, training, fundraising, and for communications by racist ... organisations'.[167] The Net is an infrastructure that supports cyber racism as a culture. The Net consists of 'globally accessible tools, know-how and experience in order to support[cyber racism as a] local culture and to make it ... open to a wide international public'.[168] It has already been pointed out that there are at least five cultures of users of the Net (Dutton and Blank).[169] Cyber racists inhabit a racist culture that can cause great harm to social organisations and the black people contained therein. One example occurred in Louisiana US where Facebook was used as a means to threaten violence against black students at a local school. Many students left school early, some did not attend school and race relations became strained.[170]

The control of cyber racism raises huge human rights issues concerning freedom of expression and speech on the one hand, and on the other hand the desire to protect the human rights of ethnic minority groups. It is argued that free speech should be an absolute value but that cyber racism is not free speech but a culture that has piggy-backed onto the vehicle of the Net to find an outlet to vent racism. Certainly in some countries, such as France, freedom of expression is more restricted than it is in, say, the US[171] This was proved in the *Yahoo Inc*[172] case where in France it was held illegal[173] to put Nazi propaganda on its website. However, when the case was brought by Yahoo! in the US, the court decided that the French court's decision that Yahoo could not sell Nazi memorabilia on its website, was not enforceable under the US Constitution's First Amendment.[174] This tells us that in terms of cyber racism on line there needs to be common ground, a common international policy that will reach a consensus that cyber racist speech is not free speech, or at the very least that racist speech is so damaging in democratic societies that it presents a danger to democracy and its citizenry.

Cyber racism and international law

Imagine cyber racism as existing in a Net bubble. Outside of this bubble are various attackers. The attackers come in the form of cyber racist victims who use the complaints led system, some of the Internet service providers and the use of national laws. However, these three attackers have in-built limitations. Cyber racist victims may not know of the complaints led system, or if they do they may not have sufficient confidence in its efficacy. Not all ISPs are vigilant or quick enough to take down cyber racist content and in any event there is a conflict between them being a business in the pursuit of profit as well as the argument that they are bound by the ethics of free speech. National laws have their limitations in that there are jurisdictional boundaries as we saw in Yahoo! Inc. Another route of attack against this cyber racism bubble is international law. This international law comes in the form of the Additional Protocol to the Convention on Cybercrime, Concerning the Criminalisation of acts of Racist and Xenophobic Nature Committed through Computer Systems 2003 (Protocol).The Additional Protocol to the Convention on Cybercrime, Concerning the Criminalisation of acts of Racist and Xenophobic Nature Committed through Computer Systems 2003[175] (Protocol) is supplementary to the Cybercrime Convention[176] because of the 47 members 'some delegates expressed strong concern about including such a provision on freedom of expression grounds'[177] in the Cybercrime Convention itself. So from the outset the control of cyber racism has been met with human rights concerns over the freedom of expression as of higher importance than cyber racism on the Net. Nevertheless, we do have the Protocol and it is important to know how it is envisaged that it would provide an additional attack on the cyber racism bubble described above. This Protocol seeks to restrict access to cyberspace for those who wish to use it to commit racist and xenophobic crimes.[178] The Protocol with regard to racist and xenophobic crime is concerned with preventing a 'dark side'[179] to the Net taking hold. This is described as 'the emergence of new types of crime as well as the commission of traditional crimes by means of new technologies'.[180] This includes conduct of a racist or xenophobic nature 'committed through computer systems'.[181]

Member States of the Council of Europe who bring the Protocol into force are required to harmonise computer related offences in their national legal systems in order to attain a common minimum standard of relevant offences and to instil international cooperation. To date there are 24 members of the Council of Europe who have brought the Protocol into force and that does not include the UK[182] or the USA (the latter is not a member of the Council of Europe). The Protocol recognises the need for the harmonisation of the substantive law of Member States to provide a more effective tool in the fight against racism and xenophobia[183] because it is clear that in the world of global communication networks piecemeal and solitary national regulation can be thwarted where the perpetrator resides in a jurisdiction different from that in which the offence is committed. Kaplan et al[184] surmise that Internet hate crime offenders surf the Internet highway without fear of physical boundaries – they are non-existent; which means 'it is at least possible that a perpetrator of a threat or harassing speech need not be at the actual scene of the crime (or within 5,000 miles, for that matter) to prey on his or her victim'.[185]

The Protocol thus supplements the Convention by providing for a number of matters: a definition of racist and xenophobic material as the representation of

> ideas or theories *which advocates, promotes or incites hatred, discrimination or violence, against* any individual or group of individuals, based on race, colour, descent or national or ethnic origin, *as well a religion if used as a pretext for any of these factors,*[186]

the criminalisation of conduct that is intentional with respect to the distribution of or otherwise making available, racist or xenophobic material to the public through a computer system,[187] intentional threats to persons or groups on the basis of race, colour and so on, intentional insults in public with respect to the same where this is committed through a computer system,[188] and the intentional denial of genocide or crimes against humanity.[189]It can be argued that the approach of having states co-ordinate their legislative effort to provide a common approach to the prohibition of cyber race hate may be a better way of attacking cyber racist material. Such conduct, in the case of black people and the legacy of the slave trade – institutional racism – would acknowledge the growing pain that continues when cyber racism is allowed to appear on the Net and states cry 'freedom of speech' when asked to intervene to wipe cyber racism off of our Internet screens.

On reading the Protocol a number of issues become apparent. There are definitional problems in the way race hate crime is defined. The Protocol seeks to criminalise 'acts of a racist and xenophobic nature committed through the use of computer systems'.[190] This measure is admirable in its attempt to capture the type of offending behaviour that should be prohibited when using the Internet since such conduct serves to undermine social stability. The fabric with which the provision is concerned relates to written material, any image or other representation of ideas or theories which are of a racist or xenophobic nature.[191] The requirement is that these materials advocate, promote or incite hatred, discrimination or violence against any individual or group based on race, colour, descent or national or ethnic origin.[192] The type of conduct the Protocol seeks to criminalise is the use of the Internet to disseminate racist or xenophobic materials,[193] threats of a racist or xenophobic nature[194] and racist or xenophobic public insults.[195] Finally, Article 6 of the Protocol seeks to criminalise the denial, gross minimisation, approval or justification of genocide or crimes against humanity.

What is the common understanding of some of these words? Whose definition will be followed if at all? The words 'advocate', 'promote', or 'incite' hatred, discrimination or violence are words for which paragraph 14 of the Explanatory Report provides guidance on the meaning of these terms[196] which is fairly vague in the sense that 'a plea in favour of hatred',[197] 'encouragement or advancing of hatred'[198] and 'urging others to hate'[199] are meant to provide some sense of what it means to advocate, promote and incite respectively. Not only are these definitions unclear, Member States are not bound to refer to them in deciding criminal culpability since 'the text of this Explanatory Report does not constitute an instrument providing an authoritative interpretation of the Protocol'.[200] Nevertheless, it may be asking too much to expect these provisions to meet anything other than some general sense of the ingredients of bad behaviour and leave it to the good sense of prosecuting authorities to converse with and learn from each other in terms of their respective practices in different Member States.

Race and ethnicity

Should we take the same stance with respect to the groups the Protocol aims to protect those who may be cloaked in the cloth of racist or xenophobic hatred based on distinctions of race, colour, descent or national or ethnic origin? States are required to put in place measures that punish the intentional dissemination of racist or xenophobic materials or threats or public insults of a xenophobic nature. The term race is to be understood by reference to its national and international law and practice.[201] This is of great concern since it is not immediately obvious that all national systems subscribe to the theory that race is not a biological or genetic reality but a social construction. The International Convention on the Elimination of All Forms of Racial Discrimination (ICERD) makes it clear that there is no science in the drawing of racial distinctions in order to claim supremacy,[202] yet this is precisely what cyber racists do. In the case of white cyber racists and black people the former claim superiority over the latter. White racists have shifted their movements on to the Net in defence of already held views in real space that white people are a superior being. This use of the Internet to pursue a racist agenda threatens racial equality.[203] It also threatens the work already done to move away from ideas since the transatlantic slave trade that black people are inferior beings.

Solomos[204] argues that whilst race does not exist in an objective sense, a number of societies act as though this were a foregone conclusion.[205] Consequentially, some human beings are negatively constructed as the Other[206] which Fanon[207] equates with the 'experience of his being through others'[208] by the accentuation of difference based on association of somatic factors such as skin colour, clothing, language, diet and religion with racism, that is 'mental states of individuals or groups, of ideologies, of social practices of institutions'[209] that maintain 'relationships of domination and subordination',[210] that perpetuate hatred of the 'Other' in defence of 'Self'.[211] The fact the European Union has stated publicly that it 'rejects theories which attempt to determine the existence of separate human races'[212] affords little guarantee that national legal systems will follow suit, since an alternative was not provided for in this instrument. Some national legal systems have discussed the term race. In *Saint Francis College v Al-kharaji*[213] it was suggested that 'scientifically' based racial classifications were not a sensible way to define human beings. Furthermore in England and Wales in the case of *Mandla* v *Dowell Lee*[214] Lord Fraser said in the House of Lords, there would be practical difficulties of proof and 'the briefest glance at the evidence ... is enough to show that, within the human race, there are very few, if any, distinctions which are scientifically recognised as racial'.[215] It is important that the Protocol is amended to provide a clearer definition of race. This is so that when it comes to national implementation of the Protocol states are operating with definitions that are not construed on the back of pseudo science. In the case of the legacy of the slave trade – institutional racism – Member States would be in a better position to provide a professional service that does not discriminate against black people in refusing to see them as other than a category in a list of scientific definitions with black people at the bottom of the pile and white people on top, and not included as cyber victims in some states because they are not seen as a racial group.

The term ethnicity suffers from similar problems in so far as there is no definition in the Protocol and no generally agreed definition, moreover, there are those who consider themselves as an ethnic group who are not recognised as such.[216] Indeed for some countries such as Germany[217] and France[218] where there is a tradition of adherence to nationhood and notions of citizenship rather than ethnicity. The presence of ethnic or minority groups may be seen to constitute a threat to the idea of the liberal nation state, not conducive to the public good and a cause of social tensions due to the perceived failure to assimilate with the majority culture.[219] For instance whilst 'minorities tend to hold strong British identities … there are variations in identity acculturation across minority groups and by generation'.[220] There are those who express a desire to retain their cultural/ethnic identity but suffer from a castigation of the very things they hold dear, as Silverman[221] points out a 'simple piece of cloth on someone's head could send a whole country into a prolonged frenzy'.[222] As with race the failure to provide guidelines on the meaning of the term ethnic will not lend itself to a discourse that seeks to internationalise the fight against cyber race hate and the education of Internet users and regulators as to what constitutes acceptable and responsible behaviour in cyberspace. Moreover, black people, as one of the ethnic minority groups, are likely to find that their concerns over cyber racism are not taken into consideration by Member States that do not have an international working definition of ethnicity. Once again institutional racism is evident in the form of Member States not having to take account of the relentless discrimination suffered by black people, a discrimination that has its roots in the slave trade and has not to this day been dealt with by appropriate legislation that targets cyber racism.

Mens rea: The mental element

The fault element requirement for cyber race crime relies on a vague definition of intention which is subject to national variation.[223] The Protocol requires that the offences under the measures must be committed 'intentionally' albeit the meaning of intention is to be determined by the law of Member States.[224] Danner[225] has argued, however, that hate crimes (or bias crimes as she calls them) can be committed intentionally or recklessly by the perpetrator. This raises two related issues. One is whether these measures should have provided guidance on the meaning of intention the other is whether the focus on intentional conduct alone has gone far enough.

Under English Criminal law the concept of intention has raised difficult questions of interpretation and what are the boundaries to be drawn between the meaning of intentional and reckless conduct.[226] The concept of intention may be understood as a person's 'aim, objective or purpose'[227] but has also been defined as 'virtual certainty' in *Nedrick*.[228] The term recklessness has come to take on two meanings determined in the cases of *Cunningham*[229] and that of *Caldwell*.[230] *Cunningham* recklessness is said to arise when the perpetrator foresees the risk of a prohibited result and goes on to take that risk without necessarily intending that result, whilst a *Caldwell*[231] reckless defendant incurs criminal liability because she does an act which creates an obvious risk and gives no thought to the possibility of the risk of damage and has gone on to take it where a reasonable person would not have done.[232]

When we consider other jurisdictions a different story emerges. Under German law it has been argued that the concept of intentional criminal conduct includes not only knowledge and desire but also recklessness.[233] The obvious result of the application of national standards to the *mens rea* of cyber racism is that depending on the jurisdiction different legal rules will apply putting the claim for the provision of a minimal base point from which cyber racism is dealt with in international law in jeopardy. The Protocol aims to cover the *mens rea* of an offence with respect to cybercrime at the most basic or obvious level by providing that all Member States encompass as, a minimum, offences that are committed intentionally. This bare minimum requirement is no bar to raising the definition to include crimes committed with a state of mind less than intention. But since this approach by the Council of Europe (CoE) is to alleviate, 'the fight against such crimes on the national level and on the international level as well'[234] which makes sense if a country is to prosecute a person who commits a cyber racism offence abroad when they are domiciled or a foreigner in the prosecutorial country,[235] how is this minimum to be assured when countries can determine the content of the requirement with respect to an offenders' state of mind? Intention defined at the national level will surely re-manufacture the problem that the Protocol was designed to avoid – that the definition of such crimes by reference to national standards fails to provide a standard by which to prosecute cybercrime committed across territorial boundaries for which perpetrators have no respect. Schjolberg and Hubbard[236] argue that 'in order to establish standards in cyberspace, penal laws must be enacted with as much clarity and specificity as possible, and not rely on vague interpretations in existing legislation'.[237] This is particularly important for cyber racism where the channel through which cyber racist messages are spread and minorities targeted is the Net.[238]

A clearer definition of intention at the international level in the Protocol is necessary to deal with cyber racism, a definition that all Member States should observe. Such a definition would pave the way for the provision of a service that takes the cyber racism suffered by black people into account – a racism that comes from real space but has its origins in the transatlantic slave trade. In providing an international definition of intention for the protocol this would show that the C of E was providing an appropriate service to black people who suffer from the legacy of racism.

Freedom of expression

Fundamentally however the power of the Protocol is undermined by its own legislative 'get out clause' by virtue of Article 3(3). This provision accords a 'reservation possibility'[239] to states where 'due to established principles of its legal system concerning freedom of expression, it may reserve the right not to 'criminalise distributing or otherwise making available racist and xenophobic material to the public'[240] over the Internet. Since the central tenet upon which the Protocol stands is the protection of human rights, such as freedom of speech and expression and the protection of people from cyber racism this measure represents a tension between the two, that is to say the protection of free speech and the protection of people from cyber racist speech. It remains to be seen how Member States who adopt the Protocol will reconcile this conflict. It has already been argued here that cyber racist speech is not free speech and this is not only because it offends. Cyber racist speech not only offends and is hurtful to black people but it poses a real danger to stable race relations, it presents a threat to peaceful race relations and the existence of multiculturalism. Cyber racist speech does not deserve the protection of human rights since its purpose is to undermine racial equality. Cyber racism serves to maintain the racism that the transatlantic slave trade and chattel slavery produced via the Net. The acceptance of cyber racism as free speech undermines the other important argument that states fail to provide a professional service to black people if they do not deal with cyber racism. More importantly the notion that cyber racism is free speech serves to fundamentally undermine the C of E's own position that racism and xenophobia pose a threat to the rule of law, and so must be prohibited.[241]

The Council advocates that the instrument is not motivated by a desire to control national legal systems' freedom of expression principles,[242] whilst requiring states to adopt legislative and other measures to criminalise racist and xenophobic material disseminated through computer systems.[243] Moreover, the Explanatory Memorandum points to Article 10(2)[244] of the European Convention of Human Rights (ECHR) as a provision that gives states the right to regulate the freedom of expression where necessary to protect the rights of others not to be discriminated against.[245] The requirement to criminalise this conduct is undermined by Article 3(3) of the Protocol which provides the State can constrain itself where 'due to established principles in its national legal system concerning freedom of expression, it cannot provide for effective remedies'.[246] What are these 'established principles'? In *Handyside v United Kingdom*[247] the European Court of Human Rights (ECtHR) was of the opinion that freedom of expression constitutes one of the fundamental elements of a democratic society which includes the moral fibre to tolerate ideas that might 'offend, shock or disturb the State or any sector of the population'.[248] However, the ECtHR also took the view that where the State sought to regulate this freedom it must be 'proportionate to the legitimate aim pursued'. This is not the same thing as saying States do not have to criminalise the dissemination of racist materials on the Internet rather the ECtHR requires that States exercise their powers proportionately. The idea of not interfering with established principles must also surely take into account another established fundamental principle, globally agreed that 'steps [should] be taken to put an end to racism, racial discrimination, xenophobia and related intolerance to prevent their future occurrence'.[249] So the question is whether freedom of expression/speech with respect to dissemination of cyber racism on the Internet should take second place to cyber racism.

McGonagle[250] argues that currently the 'balancing of the rights' of free speech with that of 'regulating "hate speech" i.e. racist or otherwise identity-assailing expression'[251] has so far eluded the realms of international law. In part this appears due to the 'outer definitional demarcations of the right'[252] to free speech with the right to protection from racial discrimination with which cyber racism tussles. Both the UN Human Rights Committee (HRC) and the European Court of Human Rights (ECtHR) have been criticised regarding these issues. In the case law[253] insufficient detail has been provided to help identify the point at which free speech constitutes hate speech thereby making the latter an abrogation of international law principles regarding racism.[254] Similar criticism has been levied against the ECtHR in the cases where the International Convention on the Elimination of All Forms of Racial Discrimination (ICERD)[255] has been raised. Article 4 of ICERD provides that racial propaganda and racist organisations based on such misinformation should be condemned, moreover, the dissemination of racist materials should be criminalised, organisations that promote racism should be declared illegal and the promotion of racism by public authorities should be prohibited. In *Jersild v Denmark*[256] the ECtHR found a violation of Article 10 (freedom of expression) of the ECHR when the national court convicted a journalist of aiding and abetting the broadcast of racist views on television. Whilst the Court considered ICERD to be of great weight in the analysis of the issue and said that there was no conflict between ICERD and Article 10 holding that 'the potential impact of the medium concerned was an important factor,'[257] the Court would not, however, give guidance on what techniques of reporting should be adopted by journalists in such situations and said that this was not a matter for national courts either. McGonagle[258] suggests the Court's failure to deal with the relationship between freedom of expression and the regulation of cyber racist speech with regard to Articles 10 of the ECHR and Article 4 of ICERD is regrettable. It is also problematic for black people because this demonstrates that there is a failure to provide a professional service that deters racial discrimination in cyberspace where a provision such as Article 4 of ICERD is there to protect them.

Similar comments have been made of the *Glimmerveen*[259] and *Feldek*[260] cases.[261] The ECtHR treads carefully with respect to national state restrictions on the exercise of freedom of expression under Article 10(2) requiring that if, an applicant is dismissed from employment because of membership of extremist political parties, for instance, that the sanction must be proportionate to the legitimate aim to be achieved *Vogt*,[262] and necessary in a democratic society *Wille*.[263] In *Aslef v United Kingdom*[264] the European Court of Human Rights took the view that a Trade Union's expulsion of a member with views contrary to its principles (in this case, because he was a member of the British National Party, an extreme right wing organisation) was within its constitutional powers, moreover the UK's statutory limitations on the right to expel members constituted a violation of Article 11 of the ECHR related to freedom of association. The Article 10 (1) point raised by the UK government in the proceedings before the Court referred to the consequences that would attach to expulsion of members – that this would have a bearing on freedom of expression were trade unions entitled to expel members who held contrary views to that of the organisation. The Court took a 'common sense' approach in holding that 'where associations are formed by people, who, espousing particular values or ideals, intend to pursue common goals, it would run counter to the very effectiveness of the freedom at stake if they had no control over their membership'.[265]

Similarly in the successful prosecution of Norwood,[266] the applicant sought to exercise Article 10 as a protection for him to display racist propaganda in the window of his first floor flat. The Court held that such an invocation would breach Article 17 of the ECHR that provides for the ban on engaging in activity aimed at the destruction of any rights set out in the Convention. The application was deemed inadmissible. The ECtHR at least has given some direction on the conflict between free speech and racism and this is something that should be welcomed by nation states.

But few cases reach the courts and it becomes increasingly difficult for nation states to control mediums such as the Internet.[267] This is where ISPs could be called upon. They, ultimately, control access to the Net. They, of course, should consider the difference between free speech and racist speech when refusing to provide a service to or blocking the use of the Internet from cyber racists. Yahoo and the Anti-Defamation League (ADL) provide an example where ISPs can work together with NGOs to remove offending sites from the World Wide Web. ADL found hate sites being used on Yahoo in clear contravention of Yahoo's own policy and was able to get Yahoo to 'pull the plug on these haters, resulting in the company's removal of some of the most offensive clubs because they stood in violation of the site's terms of service agreement, which clearly prohibits hate speech'.[268] It would appear that some Internet service providers have as part of their policy that they will not tolerate the use of their services for hate speech, but that is not general, it is argued that it needs to be. An example of the contradiction between free speech and the regulation of hate speech is demonstrated through Earthlink. Whilst stating that they will not tolerate illegal activity on their site they allow hateful material to appear under the argument that the US First Amendment protects freedom of expression.[269] Fundamentally ISPs that do not condemn and remove hate speech are institutionally racist because they fail to provide a fair service to the victims of cyber racist speech. It is argued here that action needs to be taken to change this behaviour. There is a need for clear legislation, at international and national level that works together to target ISPs both with respect to their terms and conditions and their conscious and active engagement as providers of Internet services with regard to cyber racism on line.

Conclusion

The World Conference against Racism raised concern about the potential of the Internet to reinforce ideas of racial superiority.[270] This chapter maintains that any 'real' challenge to cyber race hate must begin with the principle that cyber racism constitutes a gross violation of human rights rather than the right to free speech. Nation states and ISPs should consider this perspective rather than one of freedom of expression or speech. International law in the form of the Additional Protocol requires amendment so that race, ethnicity and *mens rea* are more clearly defined. This is desired so that nation states provide a professional service to cyber racist victims such as black people who have borne the brunt of racism in real space and now experience it in cyber space.

Legislation could be fashioned with respect to ISPs to make them liable for cyber racism. This would demand of them as key stake holders that they use their powers to address the problem. This would include a change in their behaviour. Moreover, this type of leadership will be required if the most important stake holders – citizens – are to adjust their behaviour also. This chapter suggests that if we are to tackle the problem of race hate as it occurs in cyberspace we must all reconsider how we perceive race hate on the Internet and its effect on our fellow human beings, and refashion the tools we have developed to deal with it.

Cyberspace has become a virtual society which has real consequences for real space. It is argued that the defence of freedom of expression in this context does not hold because the harm to others and the consequences for societal cohesion far outweigh individual desires to express hatred of others. Freedom to surf the web and the right to communicate belong to all members of society and vulnerable minorities should not be restricted from doing so because of the barriers that come with the language of hate. We have a code by which we are governed which is fairly well developed with respect to the social contract. That includes the protection of minorities from the damage that can be caused through the expression of hate. Mills refers to the present social contract as a 'racial contract' in the sense that it is an 'obfuscation of the ugly realities of group power and domination'.[271] Whilst we fight to dismantle this we must pay attention to its duplication in attempts to regulate cyberspace. If the law merely replicates what happens in real space, it will fail. It is this chapter's contention that the law can shape and change behaviour in a way that does not repeat the mistakes that have been made in society thus far. Law is not simply a reflection of society it tends to react to problems rather than pre-empt issues. The current combination of laws are unclear and do not send the definite message that virtual race hate is unacceptable. We need to examine the contents of this social contract with respect to the commodification of cyber race hate, the vulnerable and the responsibility of gatekeepers to the Internet. Members and potential members of cyberspace need to have a real space dialogue where the rules with respect to race hate speech are fashioned, where we articulate how those rules are to be enforced and where we agree that the sanctions for breaking those rules will be that ISPs withdraw their service.

Notes

1 Available at: www.resist.com (accessed 14 July 2016).

2 Available at: http://niggermania.com/niggerjokes (accessed 14 July 2016) also using the search term nigger and white Aryan resistance and click on images.

3 NewsOne Staff, 'Racism is Still Alive and well in Online Comment Sections'. Available at: www.newsone.com (accessed 14 July 2016).

4 Hence the Committee of Experts on Crime in Cyberspace set up inside the Council of Europe to design up the Cyber-Crime Convention (Convention), decided that concerns expressed by delegates who advocated that freedom of expression would be hampered by content-related offences aimed at the distribution of racist propaganda militated against its inclusion in the Convention. See *Explanatory Report of the Additional Protocol to the Convention on Cybercrime*,

concerning the criminalisation of acts of a racist and xenophobic nature committed through computer systems, as adopted by the Committee of Ministers on 7 November 2002, para. 4. Available at: http://conventions.coe.int/Treaty/en/Reports/Html/189.htm (accessed 4 November 2014).

5 K. Boyle, 'Overview of a Dilemma: Censorship versus Racism', in S. Coliver (ed.), 'Striking a Balance: Hate Speech, Freedom of Expression and Non-discrimination' (Article 19, International Centre Against Censorship, Human Rights Centre, University of Essex, 1992), p. 1.

6 CETS, no. 189 'The Additional Protocol to the Convention on Cybercrime Concerning the Criminalisation of acts of a Racist and Xenophobic Nature through Computer systems 2003'. Available at: www.conventions.coe.int/treaty (accessed 5 November 2014).

7 Y. Akdeniz, *An Advocacy Handbook for the Non-governmental Organisations: The Council of Europe's Cyber-Crime Convention and the Additional Protocol on the Criminalisation of Acts of a Racist or Xenophobic Nature Committed through Computer Systems* (first published December 2003, updated May 2008, Cyber-Rights and Cyber Liberties, Leeds). On the USA's constitutional position see Y. Akdeniz, 'Stocktaking on Efforts to Combat Racism on the Internet', Commission on Human Rights Sixty-Second Session, Intergovernmental Working Group on the Effective Implementation of the Durban Declaration and Programme of Action, Fourth Session, Geneva', 16–27 January 2006, E/CN.4/2006/WG.21/BP.1, 9 January 2006, pp. 10–11.

8 Racismnoway, 'Anti-racism Education for Australian Schools, about Racism'. Available at: www.racismnoway.com.au (accessed 2 November 2015).

9 Ibid.

10 T. Manfred, 'Why is the Internet So Racist?' Available at: www.businessinsider.com (accessed 2 November 2015).

11 J. Suler, 'The Online Disinhibition Effect', *CyberPsychology & Behavior*, 7(3) (2004): 321.

12 J. Daniels, 'Cyber Racism and the Future of Free Speech', 16 November 2010. Available at: www.racismreview.com (accessed 2 November 2015).

13 Ibid.

14 Ibid.

15 [2002] EWCA Crim 747.

16 Standuptohate.blogspot.co.uk.

17 Ibid.

18 J. Daniels, *Cyber Racism: White Supremacy Online and the New Attack on Civil Liberties* (Lanham: Rowman & Littlefield, 2009), p. 5.

19 Ibid., Daniels argues that this figure is possibly inflated and there is no information on how this figure was arrived at.

20 Ibid., p. 7.

21 Article 1 of the International Convention on the Elimination of All Forms of Racial Discrimination, entry into force 4 January 1969.

22 F.M. Lawrence, 'Racial Violence on a 'Small Island': Bias Crime in a Multicultural Society', in P. Iganski (ed.), *The Hate Debate: Should Hate be Punished as a Crime?* (London: Profile Books, 2002), p. 38.

23 Home Office, Office for National Statistics and Ministry of Justice, 'An Overview of Hate Crime in England and Wales, December 2013', p. 6. Available at: www.gov.uk (accessed 2 November 2015).

24 J. Levin, 'Hatemongers, Dabblers, Sympathizers and Spectators: A Typology of Offenders', in P. Iganski (ed.), *The Hate Debate: Should Hate be Punished as a Crime?* (London: Profile Books, 2002), p. 79.

25 J. Walvin, *Black and White: The Negro and English Society 1555–1945* (London: Allen Lane, the Penguin Press, 1973), p. 39.

26 Ibid., ch. 10.

27 Ibid., p. 160.

28 Ibid., ch. 13.

29 Ibid., p. 205.

30 P. Fryer, *Staying Power: The History of Black People in Britain* (London: Pluto Press, 1985), pp. 296–297.

31 Ibid., pp. 368–369.

32 Ibid., p. 373.

33 Ibid., p. 374.
34 Ibid., p. 375.
35 Ibid.
36 B. Sorensen, 'Racism, the Media and the Internet', in United Nations, *Dimensions of Racism*, Anti-Discrimination Series, vol. 1. (New York and Geneva: 2005), p. 169.
37 Simon Wiesenthal Centre, *Digital Hate* (Los Angeles: SWC, 2002).
38 O. Bowcott and K. Roberts, 'Twitter Racism: How the Law is Taking on the "'Twacists"', *The Guardian*, March 2012. Available at: www.theguardian.com (accessed 15 July 2016).
39 The Leadership Conference on Civil and Human Rights, *The State of Hate: Exploiting the Internet to Promote Hatred* (2009).
40 Broadcasting Standards Commission, 'Regulating the Internet, No. 4, Briefing Update'. Available at: www.ofcom.org.uk/static/archive/bsc/pdfs/research/Update4RegulatingtheInternet.pdf (accessed 17 August 2014).
41 Ibid.
42 D. McGraw, 'Sexual Harassment in Cyberspace: The Problem of Unwelcome E-mail', *Rutgers Computer and Technology Law Journal* 492 (1995).
43 L. Ellison and Y. Akdeniz, 'Cyber-Stalking: The Regulation of Harassment on the Internet', *Criminal Law Review*, December special edition: Crime, Criminal Justice and the Internet, (1998): 29–48.
44 'Get Safe Online, Cyberstalking'. Available at: www.getsafeonline.org (accessed 14 July 2016).
45 J. Daniels, *Race and Racism in Internet Studies: A Review and Critique* (New York: Graduate Centre and Hunter College, 2013).
46 Ellison and Akdeniz, 'Cyber-Stalking', p. 6.
47 The Crown Prosecution Service, 'Stalking and Harassment'. Available at: http://cps.gov.uk (accessed 3 November 2015).
48 Ibid.
49 Ibid. There are defences to the offence of stalking and harassment where for example the course conduct is pursued to prevent or detect crime.
50 Crown Prosecution Service, *Communications Offences.* Available at: www.cps.gov.uk/legal/a_to_c/communications_offences/#an12 (accessed 18 August 2014).
51 Ibid.
52 Council of Europe, *Legal Instruments for Combating Racism on the Internet* (Strasbourg: Council of Europe, 2009).
53 Ibid., p. 63.
54 Ibid., p. 126.
55 Ibid., p. 127.
56 Additional Protocol to the Convention on Cybercrime, Concerning the Criminalisation of Acts of a Racist and Xenophobic Nature Committed through Computer Systems.
57 Handyside Judgment of 7 December 1976, Series A, no. 24, p. 23, para. 49.
58 Ibid.
59 Wingrove Judgment of 25 November 1996.
60 Ibid.
61 K. Lefever, *New Media and Sport: International Legal Aspects* (Leuven: Springer, 2012), p. 69.
62 Ibid.
63 *Feret v Belgium* no. 15615, 80, 16 July 2009.
64 The Council of Europe, 'Internet: Case Law of the European Court of Human Rights'. Available at: http://echr.coe.int (accessed 3 November 2015).
65 Racismnoway, 'Race, Racism and the Law', racism.org. Available at: www.racismnoway.com.au (accessed 2 November 2015).
66 *The Stephen Lawrence Inquiry*, 1999.
67 Sorensen, 'Racism, the Media and the Internet', p. 170.
68 Ibid.
69 Ibid.
70 M. Esteban, 'The Internet: A New Horizon for Racial Hatred', in S. Fredman (ed.), *Discrimination and Human Rights: The Case of Racism* (Oxford: Oxford University Press, 2001), p. 91.
71 Available at: http://searchsoa.techtarget.com/sDefinition/0,sid26_gci211883,00.html (accessed 4 November 2015).

72 M. Chon, *The Relation of Law to Cyberspace and Cyberspace to Law*. Available at: www.cyberspacelaw.org/chon/index.html (accessed 10 September 2015).
73 D. Atkin, L. Jefferies and K. Neuendork (1998). 'Understanding Internet Adoption as Telecommunication Behaviour', *Journal of Broadcasting and Electronic Media* 42(4) (1998): 470–490, at p. 475.
74 L. James, C. Wotring and E. Forest, 'An Exploratory Study of the Perceived Benefits of Electronic Bulletin Board Use and their Impact on other Communication Activities', *Journal of Broadcasting and Electronic Media*, 39 (1995): 30–50.
75 W. Gibson, *Neuromancer* (1984); see Chon, 'The Relation of Law to Cyberspace and Cyberspace to Law'.
76 Ibid.
77 http://w3.aces.uiuc.edu/AIM/scale/intro/whatiscyberspace.html (accessed 28 August 2014).
78 Chon 'The Relation of Law to Cyberspace and Cyberspace to Law'.
79 Ibid.
80 Ibid.
81 Ibid.
82 Ibid.
83 *Reno v ACLU* 521 U.S. 844 m (1997) U.S. Supreme Court.
84 Ibid.
85 Ibid.
86 Ibid.
87 Global Policy, 'Network Neutrality and Internet Service Provider Regulation: Are the Wise Monkeys of Cyberspace Becoming Stupid?'. Available at: www.globalpolicyjournal.com/ (accessed 26 August 2014).
88 Ibid., p. 77.
89 Ibid., p. 81.
90 Ibid., pp. 81–82.
91 Ibid., p. 82.
92 'What is the Internet made of?' *Smith Journal*. Available at: www.smithjournal.com.au/blogs/life/what-is-the-internet-made-of (accessed 4 November 2015).
93 Ibid., p. 83.
94 A.N. Milner, 'Hate Crimes in America', in C.A. Gallagher and C.D. Lippard (eds), *Race and Racism in the United States: An Encyclopedia of the American Mosaic* (Santa Barbara: Greenwood, 2014), p. 526.
95 JISC Legal Information, 'Hosting Liability Overview', 2007. Available at: www.jisclegal.ac.uk/legalareas/hostingliability/ispliabilityoverview.aspx#_Toc183596279 (accessed 21 August 2014).
96 Windows, *What is an Internet Service Provider (ISP)?* Available at: http://windows.microsoft.com/en-gb/windows/what-is-internet-service-provider#1TC=windows-7 (accessed 21 August 2014).
97 Internet Society, 'The Internet: How it Works'. Available at: www.internetsociety.org/internet/how-it-works (accessed 21 August 2014).
98 A. Jakubowicz, 'Free Speech, Democracy and New Media: Cyber Racism', in H. Sykes (ed.), *Free Speech Democracy and New Media* (Future Leaders, 2012). Available at: http://wwwandrewjakubowicz.com (accessed 4 November 2015).
99 S. Better, *Institutional Racism: A Primer on Theory and Strategies for Social Change* (Lanham: Rowman & Littlefield, 2008), p. 38.
100 G. Hodgson, 'What are Institutions?', *Journal of Economic Issues* 40(1) (2006): 2. Available at: www.geoffrey-hodgson.info/user/image/whatareinstitutions.pdf (accessed 12 July 2014).
101 British National Party, 'Foreign Affairs'. Available at: www.bnp.org.uk (accessed 10 November 2015).
102 L. Lessig, 'Code is Law: On Liberty in Cyberspace'. Available at: www.harvardmagazine.com (accessed 4 November 2015).
103 Ibid.
104 Ibid.
105 Ibid.
106 'California – The Not-so-Golden, Kind of Hateful State', 28 September 2014. Available at: www.raceandtechnology.wordpress.com (accessed 4 November 2015).
107 Ibid.

108 *Oxford Dictionary*. Available at: www.oxforddictionaries.com (accessed 6 November 2015).
109 Passport to Trade 2.0, *Business Culture*. Available at: http://businessculture.org/business-culture/ (accessed 22 August 2014).
110 Ibid.
111 W.H. Dutton and G. Blank, *Cultures of the Internet: The Internet in Britain* (Oxford: Oxford Internet Institute, 2013).
112 Ibid., p. 4.
113 Council of Europe, 'Human Rights Guidelines for Internet Service Providers and Online Game Providers'. Available at: http://hub.coe.int/human-rights-guidelines-for-internet-service-providers-and-online-games-providers (accessed 22 August 2014).
114 Ibid.
115 MashableUK, 'Facebook Loses Vodafone Advertising Due to Racist Profile'. Available at: www.mashable.com (accessed 6 November 2015).
116 S. Thomas, 'Richard Branson Weighs in on Virgin Active Racist Incident via Facebook'. Available at: www.memeburn.com (accessed 6 November 2015).
117 P. Wertheim, 'We Can Tame the Cyber Racism Beast'. Available at: www.smh.com.au (accessed 6 November 2015).
118 Ibid.
119 R. Cohen-Almagor, *Confronting the Internet's Dark Side: Moral and Social Responsibility on the Free Highway* (Washington, DC: Cambridge University Press, 2015), pp. 220–221.
120 Ibid., p. 127.
121 Racismnoway, 'About Racism'. Available at: http://www,racismnoway.com.au (accessed 6 November 2015).
122 Y. Timofeeva, 'Hate Speech Online. Restricted or Protected: Comparisons of Regulations in the United States and Germany', *Transnational Law and Policy* 12(2) (2003).
123 Y. Akdeniz, *Racism on the Internet* (Strasbourg: Council of Europe, 2009), p. 114.
124 United States of America Embassy IIP Digital. Available at: http://iipdigital.usembassy.gov/english/#axzz3BVCSgNE1 (accessed 25 August 2014).
125 *Reno v American Civil Liberties Union* 521 U.S 844, 117 S. Ct 2329, 138 L. Ed. 2d 874, 1997 U.S.
126 D. Cohen and K. Connon, 'Strikethrough (Fatality): The Origins in Online Stalking of Abortion Providers', 21 May 2015. Available at: www.slate.com (accessed 9 November 2015).
127 Ibid.
128 Cohen-Almagor, *Confronting the Internet's Dark Side*, pp. 210–211.
129 British People's Party. Available at: www.bpp.org.uk (accessed 10 November 2015).
130 *Elonis v U.S.*, Supreme Court of the United States no. 13–983, 1 June 2015.
131 Ibid.
132 Ibid.
133 Ibid.
134 Ibid.
135 Hyperbole is a natural exaggeration for the purpose of emphasis, *Dictionary.com*.
136 This is a phrase used in school playgrounds to establish that words do not hurt. According to Neu, this is a fallacy. For many people insults cause pain and injury, see J. Neu, *Sticks and Stones: The Philosophy of Insults* (Oxford: Oxford University Press, 2009).
137 Ibid.
138 Ibid.
139 To welch is to refuse payment but the word has come to mean a denigrating word for the Welsh, see: www.etymonline.com/index.php?search=welch&searchmode=none (accessed 3 November 2014).
140 The word 'gyp' means to cheat or swindle. 'Gyp' has its origins in the word gypsy, a word originated from Egyptian. Available at: www.etymonline.com/index.php?search=gyp&searchmode=none (accessed 3 November 2014).
141 The word 'hunk' means sexually appealing, see www.etymonline.com/index.php?search=hunk&searchmode=none but was used as hate speech against Hungarians according to Neu, *Sticks and Stones*, p. 23.
142 The word 'niggardly' appears to have its origins in the meaning for stingy or tight-fisted see www.etymonline.com/index.php?search=niggardly&searchmode=none (accessed 3 November 2014).

143 Critical Race Theory appears to have originated in the United States through the work of academic scholars like Derrick Bell, *Race, Racism and American Law*, 6th edition (New York: Aspen Publishers, 2008) whose work first appeared in the 1970s, here he took a critical look at issues of race and racism in the USA and the relationship between this and the law.
144 J. Mari Matsuda, R. Charles, Lawrence III, R. Delgado and K.W Crenshaw, *Words that Wound: Critical Race Theory, Assaultive Speech and the First Amendment* (Boulder: Westview Press, 1993).
145 *Virginia v Black* US Supreme Court 7 April 2003.
146 Justice O'Connor in *Virginia v Black* US Supreme Court 7 April 2003.
147 [1998] AC 147.
148 *R v Ireland and Burstow* [1998] AC 147, at 162.
149 A. Ashworth, *Principles of Criminal Law*, 3rd edition (Oxford: Oxford University Press, 1999) pp. 326–329.
150 Bowling writes that in Nottingham (UK) in 1958 a white crowd descended on the streets shouting this, whilst the people to whom these words were aimed stayed inside their houses. See B. Bowling, *Violent Racism: Victimization, Policing and Social Context* (Oxford: Oxford University Press, 1999), p. 30.
151 S. Bullard, *The Ku Klux Klan: A History of Racism and Violence* (Diane Publishing, 1996); K.M. Blee, 'Women and Organised Terrorism in the United States', *Studies in Conflict Terrorism* 28 (5) (2005): 421–433.
152 B. Orwick and D. Settles,*The Schools' Response to Online Bullying*, p. 1. Available at: www.kysafeschools.org/pdfs&docs/clearpdf/issuesbriefs/onlinebullying.pdf (accessed 19 November 2014).
153 Simon Wiesenthal Centre, *Digital Terrorism and Hate*, 2008. Available at: http://fswc.ca/digital_terrorism_hate.aspx (accessed 19 November 2014).
154 C. Balestri, 'Racism, Football and the Internet', European Union Monitoring Centre, Vienna, April 2002, which reports that whilst in 1995 there was one website inciting racial hatred by 1997 there were 600 sites and in 2002, 2,500 sites, p. 4.
155 L. Letts , 'Responses to Internet Hate Sites: Is Speech too Free in Cyberspace?' *Community Leadership and Policy* 6 (2001): 287–317.
156 M. Ricketson, 'Racism is more than Hurt Feelings. We've already had an Inquiry to Prove it', 10 June 2014, *The Guardian*.
157 'True Vision, Internet Hate Crime'. Available at: www.report-it.org (accessed 11 November 2015).
158 Ibid.
159 B. Orwick and D. Settles, *The Schools' Response to Online Bullying*. Available at: www.kysafeschools.org/pdfs&docs/clearpdf/issuesbriefs/onlinebullying.pdf (accessed 19 November 2014).
160 Ibid., p. 1.
161 F.M. Lawrence, *Punishing Hate: Bias Crimes under American Law* (Cambridge, MA: Harvard University Press, 1999).
162 Defined as a 'crime committed as an act of prejudice'. See Lawrence, *Punishing Hate*, p. 9.
163 Ibid., p. 11.
164 Research on the use of potential racial incitement on the Internet reveals that the host sites are mainly outside the UK, 'Internet Watch Foundation, Corporate Plan 2005–2007'. Available at: www.iwf.org.uk/corporate/page.128.275.htm#Trends_in_criminally_racist_content_allegations (accessed 4 November 2015.
165 Lawrence, *Punishing Hate*, p. 9.
166 Akdeniz, *Racism on the Internet.*
167 Ibid., p. 18.
168 S. Krekovic, 'New Media Culture: Internet as a Tool of Cultural Transformation in Central and Eastern Europe', *IWM Junior Visiting Fellows Conferences* 14(6) (2003).
169 W.H. Dutton and G. Blank, *Cultures of the Internet: The Internet in Britain* (Oxford: Oxford Internet Institute, 2013).
170 J. Daniels, 'Cyber Racism in High School', *Racism Review*, 21 September 2010.
171 E. Okoniewski, 'Yahoo!; Inc. V LICRA: The French Challenge to Freedom of Expression the Additional Protocol to the Convention on Cybercrime, Concerning the Criminalisation of Acts of Racist and Xenophobic Nature Committed through Computer Systems 2003 on the Internet', *American University International Law Review*, 18(1) (2002).

172 *League Against Racism and Anti-Semitism (LICRA), French Union of Jewish Students v Yahoo! Inc. (USA),Yahoo France*, Tribunal de Grande Instance de Paris (The County Court of Paris), Interim Court Order, 20 November, 2000.
173 French Penal Code R. 645–1.
174 See *Yahoo!, Inc.*, 169 F. Supp. 2d 1181 N.D. Cal. 2001, at 1194. In the French court it was decided that Yahoo take all necessary measures to render impossible any access via Yahoo.com to a Nazi auction site. Yahoo sought judgment in the US court that the French court's decision was not enforceable under the laws of the US and won.
175 Came into force 1 March 2006.
176 The Cybercrime Convention came into force on 1 July 2004 and entered into force in the UK on 1 September 2011.
177 Council of Europe, Explanatory Report to the Additional Protocol to the Convention on Cybercrime concerning acts of a Racist and Xenophobic Nature, ETS no. 189, 9/2/14.
178 Paragraph 3 of the Explanatory Report of the Additional Protocol to the Convention on Cybercrime, Concerning the Criminalisation of acts of Racist and Xenophobic Nature Committed through Computer Systems 2003 (ETS no. 189). Available at: www.conventions.coe.int/Treaty/en/Reports/Html/189.htm (accessed 5 August 2014).
179 Council of Europe, *Explanatory Report on the Convention on Cybercrime (ETS no. 185)*. 2 August 2008. Available at: http://conventions.coe.int/Treaty/en/Reports/Html/185.htm. (accessed 2 August 2014).
180 Ibid.
181 Council of Europe, *Additional Protocol to the Convention on Cybercrime, Concerning the Criminalisation of Acts of Racist and Xenophobic Nature Committed through Computer Systems 2003*, hereinafter Protocol. Available at: http://conventions.coe.int/Treaty/Commun/QueVoulezVous.asp?NT=189&CM=8&DF=&CL=ENG (accessed 2 August 2014).
182 Council of Europe Portal, Treaty Office, Chart of Signatures and Ratifications of Treaty 189, status at 13 November 2015. Available at: www.coe.int (accessed 13 November 2015).
183 Recital 7 of the Protocol.
184 J. Kaplan, M. Moss, M. Lieberman and S. Wessler, *Investigating Hate Crimes on the Internet* (Washington, DC: Partners Against Hate, 2003).
185 Ibid., pp. 12–13.
186 Article 2(1) of the Protocol.
187 Article 3(1) of the Protocol.
188 Articles 4 (1) and 5(1) of the Protocol.
189 Article 6 of the Protocol includes grossly minimising, approving or justifying such acts constituting genocide or crimes against humanity.
190 Article 1 of the Protocol.
191 Article 2(1) of the Protocol.
192 Ibid.
193 Ibid., Article 3.
194 Ibid., Article 4.
195 Ibid., Article 5.
196 Explanatory Report of the Additional Protocol to the Convention on Cybercrime, Concerning the Criminalisation of Acts of Racist and Xenophobic Nature Committed through Computer Systems 2003 (ETS no. 189). Available at: www.conventions.coe.int/Treaty/en/Reports/Html/189.htm (accessed 2 August 2015).
197 Ibid.
198 Ibid.
199 Ibid.
200 Ibid.
201 Ibid., Paragraph 18.
202 See the Recital to ICERD that states, Convinced that any doctrine of superiority based on racial differentiation is scientifically false, morally condemnable, socially unjust and dangerous, and that there is no justification for racial discrimination, in theory or in practice, anywhere.
203 Daniels, *Cyber Racism*.
204 J. Solomos, *Race and Racism in Britain* (London: Macmillan, 1993).
205 Ibid., pp. 8–9.

206 R.S. Wistrich (1997–98) *Nationalist Challenges in the New Europe.* 14 August 2008, The Stephen Roth Institute for the Study of Contemporary Antisemitism and Racism. Available at: www.tau.ac.il/Anti-Semitism/articles.htm (accessed 15 September 2015).
207 F. Fanon, 'The Fact of Blackness', in L. Back and J. Solomos (eds), *Theories of Race and Racism* (London: Routledge, 2000), pp. 257–266.
208 Ibid., p. 257.
209 D. Petrova, 'Racial Discrimination and the Rights of Minority Cultures', in S. Fredman (ed), *Discrimination and Human Rights: The Case of Racism* (Oxford: Oxford University Press, 2001), pp. 45–76.
210 Fredman, *Discrimination and Human Rights*, p. 10.
211 Ibid.
212 Recital 6 of the Council Directive 2000/43/EC, 29 June 2000 (Race Directive). However, unlike the Race Directive the Protocol goes further by including categories that go beyond merely racial and ethnic origin.
213 481 US 604 (Sup Ct 1987).
214 *Mandla v Dowell Lee* [1983] 2 A.C. 548, HL.
215 Ibid., p. 562.
216 *Crown Suppliers v Dawkins, ICR* 517 (1993), Rastafarians were not recognised by the English courts as an ethnic group because they were not perceived to have a sufficiently long history. In *Harris* v *NKL, Automotive* 3 October 2007, UKEAT/1034/07/DM, the appellate court found that Rastafarians could be protected from discrimination on the grounds of religion under the Employment Equality (Religion and Belief) Regulations 2003 on the basis that Rastafarianism constitutes a philosophical belief similar to a religious belief.
217 R. Koopmans , 'Challenging the Liberal Nation-State? Post-nationalism, Multiculturalism, and the Collective Claims Making of Migrants and Ethnic Minorities in Britain and Germany', *American Journal of Sociology* 105(3) (1999): 625–696.
218 M. Silverman, *Deconstructing the Nation: Immigration, Racism and Citizenship in Modern France* (London: Routledge, 1992).
219 Adask's Law, 'What We've Got Here is, "Failure to Assimilate"'. Available at: www.adask.wordpress.com (accessed 15 July 2016).
220 A. Nandi and L. Platt, 'British Identity Assimilation among the UK's Minority and Majority Ethnic Groups', *Institute for Social and Economic Research*, no. 2014-01, January 2014, p. 3.
221 Silverman, *Deconstructing the Nation.*
222 Ibid., p. 1.
223 *Explanatory Report of the Additional Protocol to the Convention on Cybercrime, Concerning the Criminalisation of Acts of a Racist and Xenophobic Nature Committed through Computer Systems, as Adopted by the Committee of Ministers on 7 November 2002*, para 32. Available at: http://conventions.coe.int/Treaty/en/Reports/Html/189.htm (accessed 4 November 2015).
224 Paragraph 39 of the *Explanatory Report on the Cybercrime Convention (ETS no. 185), Article 3 (1) of the Protocol and Article 25 of the Explanatory Report of the Additional Protocol to the Convention on Cybercrime, Concerning the Criminalisation of acts of Racist and Xenophobic Nature Committed through Computer Systems*, 2003 ETS no. 189.
225 A.M. Danner, 'Bias Crimes and Crimes against Humanity: Culpability in Context', Research Paper Number 02-08, Public Law and Legal Theory, Vanderbilt University Law School (2002).
226 A. Ashworth, *Principles of Criminal Law* (New York: Oxford University Press, 2006), p. 181.
227 Ibid., p. 175.
228 *R v Nedrick* [1986] AC 455, approved by the House of Lords in *R v Woollin* [1999] AC 82.
229 *R v Cunningham* [1982] AC 566, HL.
230 *R v Caldwell* [1981] 1 All ER 961. Caldwell is no longer the law.
231 Ibid.
232 A. Ashworth, *Principles of Criminal Law* (Oxford: Oxford University Press, 2006), p. 185. This version of recklessness has attracted wide criticism for its harshness on defendants because it is an objective test that takes little account of the frailty of the human condition, see *R v G* [2004] 1 AC 1034. This form of recklessness is out of favour now since R *v* G [2004].
233 G. Taylor, 'Concepts of intention in German Criminal Law', *Oxford Journal of Legal Studies*, 24 (1) (2004): 99–127.
234 Paragraph 33 of the Explanatory Report on the Cybercrime Convention (ETS no. 185).

235 Judge S. Schjolberg and A.M. Hubbard (10 June 2005) *Harmonizing National Legal Approaches on Cybercrime*, International Telecommunication Union, Document:CYB/04, 17 August 2008. Available at: www.itu.int/osg/spu/cybersecurity/docs/Background_Paper_Harmonizing_National_and_Legal_Approaches_on_Cybercrime.pdf.
236 Ibid.
237 Ibid., p. 5.
238 Senator Patrick Leahy, *Statement of Senator Patrick Leahy, Ranking Member, Senate Judiciary Committee, Hearing on 'Hate Crimes and the Internet'*, 14 September 1999. Available at: http://leahy.senate.gov/press/199909/990914.html (accessed 11 August 2014).
239 *Explanatory Report of the Additional Protocol to the Convention on Cybercrime, Concerning the Criminalisation of Acts of a Racist and Xenophobic Nature Committed through Computer Systems, as Adopted by the Committee of Ministers on 7 November 2002*, para. 32. http://conventions.coe.int/Treaty/en/Reports/Html/189.htm (accessed 5 November 2015).
240 Ibid., para. 27.
241 See the recital to the Protocol. Available at: http://conventions.coe.int/Treaty/en/Treaties/Html/189.htm (accessed 10 June 2015).
242 Ibid.
243 Article 3(1) of the Protocol.
244 The exercise of these freedoms, since it carries with it duties and responsibilities, may be subject to such formalities, conditions, restrictions or penalties as are prescribed by law and are necessary in a democratic society, in the interests of national security, territorial integrity or public safety, for the prevention of disorder or crime, for the protection of health or morals, for the protection of the reputation or the rights of others, for preventing the disclosure of information received in confidence, or for maintaining the authority and impartiality of the judiciary.
245 Paragraph 11 of the Explanatory Report of the Additional Protocol to the Convention on Cybercrime, Concerning the Criminalisation of acts of Racist and Xenophobic Nature Committed through Computer Systems 2003 (ETS no. 189).
246 Article 3(1) of the Protocol.
247 *Handyside v United Kingdom* (5493/72) [1976] ECHR 5 (7 December 1976), Series A, no. 24, the ECtHR found that the UK had violated the applicants right to freedom of expression under Article 10 of the ECHR when a prosecution was brought against him under the obscene publications provisions for the publication of a book entitled *The Little Red School Book* that advocated that the young should adopt a liberal attitude towards sex. Para. 49.
248 Ibid., Series A, no. 24, para. 49.
249 United Nations, *World Conference Against Racism, Racial Discrimination, Xenophobia and Related Intolerance, Declaration and Programme of Action*, foreword by Mary Robinson (New York: UN, 2002); also see the United Nations Declaration on the Elimination of all forms of Racial Discrimination of 20 November 1963 (General Assembly resolution 1904 (XVIII).
250 T. McGonagle (2001) *Freedom of Expression and Limits on Racist Speech: A Difficult Symbiosis.* 20 August 2008, 13 Interights Bulletin – A Review of the International Centre for the Legal Protection of Human Rights, pp. 135–136. Available at: www.ivir.nl/publications/mcgonagle/difficultsymbiosis.html (accessed 20 August 2014).
251 Ibid., p. 135.
252 Ibid.
253 *Faurisson v France* decision of 8 November 1996, Communication no. 550/1993, Ross *v Canada* decision of 18 October 2000, Communication no. 736/1997 and *J.R.T. and the W.G. Party v Canada* Decision of 6 April 1983, Communication no. 104/1981.
254 T. McGonagle, (2001). *Freedom of Expression and Limits on Racist Speech: A Difficult Symbiosis.* 20 August 2008, 13 Interights Bulletin – A Review of the International Centre for the Legal Protection of Human Rights, pp. 135–136. Available at: www.ivir.nl/publications/mcgonagle/difficultsymbiosis.html (accessed 4 November 2015).
255 21 December 1965 (Entry into force on 4 January 1969).
256 23 September 1994, Series A, no. 298.
257 See Summary 23 September 1994, Series A, no. 298. 22 August 2008. Available at: http://sim.law.uu.nl/SIM/CaseLaw/hof.nsf/1d4d0dd240bfee7ec12568490035df05/ac6f.5011c933625bc1256640004c2957?OpenDocument.
258 McGonagle, *Freedom of Expression and Limits on Racist Speech.*

259 *Glimmerveen & Hagenbeek v Netherlands* Appn. Nos. 8348/78 & 8406/78, ECommHR, Decision 11 October 1979, Decision and Reports 18, 187, a case where racist leaflets were distributed but the case was declared inadmissible under Article 17(the prohibition of abuse of rights).
260 *Feldek v Slovakia* Decision of 12 July 2001, where the national authorities restrictions on the activities of a journalist's reference to an official's fascist past was held to be a breach of Article 10 ECHR.
261 McGonagle, *Freedom of Expression and Limits on Racist Speech*, p. 135.
262 *Vogt* v *Germany* [1995] App. no. 17851/91, publication no. A323.
263 *Wille* v *Liechtenstein* [1999], 593 EHHR.
264 C1102/05, 27 February 2005.
265 *Aslef* v *UK*C1102/05, 27 February 2005, para. 39.
266 *Anthony Norwood v United Kingdom*, ECtHR, 16 November 2004, Application no. 23131/03.
267 Akdeniz, *Racism on the Internet*, pp. 21–22.
268 C. Wolf, *Racists, Bigots and the Law on the Internet* (Anti-Defamation League, 2000). Available at: http://archive.adl.org/Internet/print.html (accessed 28 August 2014).
269 P. Chronis, '"Smoking Holes" and the Age of Retail Cybersecurity', *Retailing Today*, 13 March 2015. The hack includes racist emails from company executives. Available at: www.retailingtoda y.com (accessed 15 July 2016).
270 World Conference against Racism, Durban 2001, para. 143.
271 C.W. Mills, *The Racial Contract* (New York: Cornell University Press, 1997) p. 3.

Bibliography

Akdeniz, Y., *Racism on the Internet* (Strasbourg: Council of Europe, 2009).

Ashworth, A., *Principles of Criminal Law*, 3rd edition (Oxford: Oxford University Press, 1999).

Ashworth, A., *Principles of Criminal Law* (New York: Oxford University Press, 2006).

Atkin, D., L. Jefferies and K. Neuendork, 'Understanding Internet Adoption as Telecommunication Behaviour', *Journal of Broadcasting and Electronic Media*, 42(1998): 475–490.

Better, S., *Institutional Racism: A Primer on Theory and Strategies for Social Change* (Lanham: Rowman & Littlefield, 2008).

Blee, K.M., 'Women and Organised Terrorism in the United States', *Studies in Conflict Terrorism* 28 (5) (2005): 421–433.

Bowling, B., *Violent Racism: Victimization, Policing and Social Context* (Oxford: Oxford University Press, 1999).

Boyle, K., 'Overview of a Dilemma: Censorship versus Racism', in S. Coliver (ed.), *Striking a Balance: Hate Speech, Freedom of Expression and Non-discrimination* (Article 19, International Centre Against Censorship, Human Rights Centre, University of Essex, 1992). Available at: www.article19.org.publications (accessed 15 December 2016).

Bullard, S., *The Ku Klux Klan: A History of Racism and Violence* (Diane Publishing, 1996).

Cutler, J., *Lynch-Law: An Investigation into the History of Lynching in the United States* (New York: Longmans Green, 1905).

Daniels, J., *Race and Racism in Internet Studies: A Review and Critique* (New York: Graduate Centre and Hunter College, 2013).

Daniels, J., 'Cyber Racism in High School', *Racism Review*, 21 September, 2010.

Danner, A.M., '*Bias Crimes and Crimes against Humanity: Culpability in Context*', Research Paper Number 2–8, Public Law and Legal Theory, Vanderbilt University Law School, 2002.

Devlin, Patrick, *The Enforcement of Morals* (Oxford: Oxford University Press, 1968).

Dubow, S., *Scientific Racism in Modern South Africa* (Cambridge: Cambridge University Press, 1995).

Dutton, W.H. and G. Blank, *Cultures of the Internet: The Internet in Britain* (Oxford: Oxford Internet Institute, 2013).

Ellison, L. and Y. Akdeniz, 'Cyber-Stalking: The Regulation of Harassment on the Internet', *Criminal Law Review*, December special edition (1998): 29–48.

Esteban, M., 'The Internet: A New Horizon for Racial Hatred', in S. Fredman (ed.), *Discrimination and Human Rights: The Case of Racism* (Oxford: Oxford University Press, 2001).
Fanon, F., 'The Fact of Blackness', in L. Back and J. Solomos (eds), *Theories of Race and Racism* (London: Routledge, 2000).
Fekete, L., 'The Emergence of Xeno-Racism', *Race and Class* 43(2001).
Foster, S., *Human Rights and Civil Liberties* (Harlow: Pearson Education, 2008).
Fredman, S. (ed.), *Discrimination and Human Rights: The Case of Racism* (Oxford: Oxford University Press, 2001).
Fryer, P., *Staying Power: The History of Black People in Britain* (London: Pluto Press, 1985).
Hall, N., *Hate Crime* (Cullompton: Willan Publishing, 2005).
Hochschild, A., *Bury the Chains: The British Struggle to Abolish Slavery* (Basingstoke: Macmillan, 2006).
James, M., C. Wotring and E. Forest, 'An Exploratory Study of the Perceived Benefits of Electronic Bulletin Board Use and their Impact on Other Communication Activities', *Journal of Broadcasting and Electronic Media*, 39(1995): 40–57.
Kaplan, J., M. Moss, M. Lieberman and S. Wessler, *Investigating Hate Crimes on the Internet* (Washington, DC: Partners Against Hate, 2003).
Koopmans, R., 'Challenging the Liberal Nation-State? Post-nationalism, Multiculturalism, and the Collective Claims Making of Migrants and Ethnic Minorities in Britain and Germany', *American Journal of Sociology* 105(1999): 652–696.
Lawrence, F.M., *Punishing Hate: Bias Crimes under American Law* (Cambridge, MA: Harvard University Press, 1999).
Lawrence, F.M., 'Racial Violence on a 'Small Island': Bias Crime in a Multicultural Society', in P. Iganski (ed.), *The Hate Debate: Should Hate be Punished as a Crime?* (London: Profile Books, 2002).
Lee, S., *Law and Morals* (Oxford: Oxford University Press, 1987).
Leets, L., 'Responses to Internet Hate Sites: Is Speech too Free in Cyberspace?' *Community Leadership and Policy* (2001): 287–317.
Levin, J., 'Hatemongers, Dabblers, Sympathizers and Spectators: A Typology of Offenders', in P. Iganski (ed.), *The Hate Debate: Should Hate be Punished as a Crime?* (London: Profile Books, 2002).
Macpherson, William, *The Stephen Lawrence Inquiry* (London: Home Office, 1999).
McGraw, D., 'Sexual Harassment in Cyberspace: The Problem of Unwelcome E-mail', *Rutgers Computer and Technology Law Journal* 21(491) (1995): 492.
Matsuda, M., C.LawrenceIII, R. Delgado, and K. Crenshaw, *Words that Wound: Critical Race Theory, Assaultive Speech and the First Amendment* (Boulder: Westview Press, 1993).
Mill, J.S., *On Liberty* (1859).
Mills, C.W., *The Racial Contract* (New York: Cornell University Press, 1997).
Nandi, A. and L. Platt, 'British Identity Assimilation among the UK's Minority and Majority Ethnic Groups', Institute for Social and Economic Research, No. 2014–01, January 2014. Available at: www.iser.essex.ac.uk/research/publications/working-papers/iser/2o14-01.pdf (accessed 15 December 2016).
Neu, J., *Sticks and Stones: The Philosophy of Insults* (Oxford: Oxford University Press, 2009).
Petrova, D., 'Racial Discrimination and the Rights of Minority Cultures', in S. Fredman (ed.), *Discrimination and Human Rights: The Case of Racism* (Oxford: Oxford University Press, 2001).
Silverman, M., (1992) *Deconstructing the Nation: Immigration, Racism and Citizenship in Modern France* (London: Routledge, 1992).
Simon Wiesenthal Centre, *Digital Hate* (Los Angeles: SWC, 2002).
Sorensen, B., 'Racism, the Media and the Internet', in United Nations, *Dimensions of Racism*, Anti-Discrimination Series, Vol. 1 (New York and Geneva: UN, 2005).
Strangelove, M., 'The Geography of Consciousness: Cyberspace and the Changing Landscape of the Self', *Wave* 4(1994). Available at: http://www.cybergeography-fr.org (accessed 16 February 2017).

Taylor, G., 'Concepts of intention in German Criminal Law', *Oxford Journal of Legal Studies* 24(1) (2004).

The Leadership Conference on Civil and Human Rights, *The State of Hate: Exploiting the Internet to Promote Hatred* (2009).

Walvin, J., *Black and White: The Negro and English Society 1555–1945* (London: Allen Lane, the Penguin Press, 1973).

Williams, E., *Capitalism and Slavery* (Chapel Hill and London: The University of North Carolina Press, 1994).

4 Institutional racism and markets

Introduction

This chapter argues that it is important to locate institutional racism at the international as well as the intra-state level. The international level focuses on what occurs between states, the European Union (EU) and the World Trade Organisation (WTO) whereas the intra-state concentrates on what happens within a state. Both are important in relation to this study. Scholarship tends to focus on institutional racism in terms of what happens within a state. So for instance the Macpherson report was a judicially led inquiry that focused on institutional racism in policing and suggested that public bodies as well as the police were institutionally racist in Britain.[1] Carmichael and Hamilton focused their work on institutional racism in America.[2] Furthermore, the Transitional Racial Justice Initiative[3] and work produced by Tuitt[4] consider the USA and Britain respectively. These works are to be celebrated for their contribution to what is a very contentious debate about institutional racism and its existence.[5] However, it is argued that institutional racism not only operates at an intra-state level but is also compounded by its existence between states or regions. The global picture is extremely complex with a background involving states, international institutions, multilateral treaties and bilateral treaties. My focus is on the Caribbean countries that trade with the EU and the role of the WTO.

Institutional racism is in operation in the trading relations between the Caribbean and the West generally and in its relationship with the WTO. For example, the Economic Partnership Agreements[6] (EPA) that purport to offer the eradication of poverty through trade partnership with developing countries such as the CARIFORUM[7] (CF) has been condemned by Brewster,[8] for example, as serving the interests of the EU and not the welfare of the Caribbean countries. Brewster argues that 'the EPA itself is replete with development rhetoric ... based on a template, provided by the European Commission, containing its own in-built ideological agenda'.[9] Moreover, Brewster points out that there is more than enough reciprocity between the richer EU and the poorer Caribbean states with '53per cent of imports from the EU',[10] that there should not be further concessions 'until some income or human development level relative to that of the EU is attained'.[11] It is also argued that the framework of institutional racism demonstrates that there is a failure to provide a service due to unwitting racism based on colour, of which the Caribbean countries are victims.

There is a pattern of behaviour that unwittingly leads to the West treating the Caribbean trading partners in a discriminatory way and it will be argued that this is the legacy of the slave trade – institutional racism. It will be concluded that preferential agreements need to be reinstated and given more time to work. There should be a special case for economies devastated by 400 years of chattel slavery. The Caribbean should be one of these cases where they are allowed to operate with respect to international trade on the basis of preferences in order to earn the foreign currency to build up their economy. This is so that they can eventually compete in the arena of goods and services on an equal footing because 'Western European nations participated in the traffic in enchained African bodies and reaped the benefits that the enslavement of these bodies conferred on investors'[12] in the Caribbean, therefore they should accept that this kind of intervention is required.

Background to institutional racism and markets

Upwards of 20 million Africans[13] had been turned into chattel slaves. The imposition of this status on African peoples profited Western states (that is those states involved in the lucrative trade in slaves) because they could work slaves to death without fear of consequences. The conduct towards the slaves constituted inhuman and degrading treatment[14] on millions of African human beings.[15] The terrible brutalities meted out to slaves is detailed in slave narratives such as the story of *Mary Prince*[16] where slaves were beaten to within an inch of their lives, killed and treated like animals by their owners.[17]

Thomas'[18] describes the market in slaves where 'the slaves were examined by us in like manner as our brother traders do beasts in Smithfield',[19] while the testaments divulged by the *Abolition Project*[20] show how abominably slaves were treated. This inhuman and degrading treatment continued through the imposition of imperialism and its manifestation in colonialism – the movement of people into a territory and settling them there under the conqueror's control,[21] and the 'policy or practice of acquiring full or partial political control'.[22] This control benefits the coloniser to the detriment of the colonised. The journey consisted of more than just the kidnapping and movement of people. Equiano[23] was a black slave who experienced the crossing. He said 'the closeness of the place and the heat of the climate, added to the number in the ship, which was so crowded that each had scarcely room to turn himself, almost suffocated us. This produced copious perspiration so that the air soon became unfit for respiration from a variety of loathsome smells, and brought on a sickness among the slaves, of which many died, thus falling victims to the improvident avarice … of their purchasers'.[24]

Eventually the British slave trade and slavery were abolished in 1807[25] and 1833[26] respectively. However, nothing was done to ensure equality for ex-slaves or rights to the lands they occupied This is the legacy we are left with and which is demonstrated through the relationship between the WTO, the EU and the Caribbean at the international level; and export processing zones within Caribbean countries at the intra-state level, with institutional racism embedded in the trading rules.

Institutional racism is defined as the culture of an organisation which is unwittingly racist due to ignorance about the way in which the decision-making impacts on the people of African descent. It can be seen or detected in organisational conduct that has a negative impact on people because of their race or ethnicity.[27]

Intra-state trade and institutional racism

The history of the Caribbean economies has seen the eras of slavery, colonialism driven by imperialism and the onslaught of globalisation under-develop the potential of these countries. This has had a knock-on effect on the black poor and has been responsible for the racial victimisation of the 'native' rather than the 'slave',[28] meaning that the latter status has been removed by legislation but for the former slaves their economic conditions remain relatively unchanged In *Race and Class Struggles in a Colonial State* Singh[29] tells us that schemes to set up agricultural production in the twentieth century run by black people in Trinidad were scorned by the governor who accepted the plantocracy's view that 'none of the men behind the scheme carried any weight in the agricultural world'.[30] Race was the primary organising norm used by Europeans in the colonial system. He argues that 'the presumption was that only the presence of a controlling class of European ancestry within the colony could be relied on to secure the major interests, economic and strategic, of the imperial power. This presumption was largely rationalised by the European power's proclamation of a civilising mission, a self-arrogated role of trusteeship over 'backward races' until such time in an indefinite future when such races would have been sufficiently civilised to assume the right to self-determination, thus relieving the White man of his self-assumed burden'.[31] Yet it was these very same 'backward races' that furnished the wheels of the industrial revolution and made very many Europeans very wealthy indeed. In England, Dine[32] points to the fortunes made in banking, heavy industry and the insurance industries.[33] Whilst Williams[34] shows that Quaker, Barclay and Baring families[35] were heavily involved in the slave trade and profited from it.

The West continues to perpetuate institutional racism in a time of global capital defined as 'the circulation of capital, commodities and money over a greater distance and at a greater velocity than before within a framework which is increasingly international as opposed to national,'[36] as 'the defining political, economic and social phenomenon of the new millennium,'[37] or as a non-democratic process that expects developing countries to comply with the 'benefits' of free trade whilst walking over their rights.[38] This occurs through the way in which these post-colonial economies are forced to engage with rules that are rigged against them and where it is contended that the imposition of double standards lock the black poor out of the benefits of trade, which are designed to, or in effect, substantially benefit the West.[39] These double standards amount to institutional racism because they form a service of racial exploitation in the guise of the framework of free trade.

A clear example of institutional racism operating in the economic sphere and one that shows the gendered dimension to institutional racism is the effect of trading rules on black women in Jamaica that relate to the export processing zones (EPZ) they work in. These zones are 'industrialised zones with incentives set up to attract foreign investors which import materials to undergo some degree of processing before being exported again'.[40] Women are attracted to this area of work by the dictates of the dollar. They work in factories, processing materials via assembly operations. They are poorly paid and discouraged to unionise. If they complain about the very poor working conditions or if they get sick they are sacked. In this respect they share similar experiences to the global poor. There is heavy reliance on women to work in this type of low skilled industry in order to generate foreign exchange but women are not protected from the harsh working conditions. Shrivastava[41] writes that the socio-economic pattern of industrialisation in Caribbean economies is a continuation from the establishment of the plantation system and slavery which was not sourced in racism but became racist, similarly according to Williams,[42] racism was a 'by-product' of the plantation system. This racism continues in the deployment of capital in the EPZs to exploit Caribbean women through the inequality of bargaining power and discrimination women face in terms of race and gender.

Recommendations to curtail the impact of EPZs on women have been made by the Women's Edge Coalition[43] who have produced a toolkit for the Jamaican government. This kit is called the Trade Review and it is designed for the government to use when negotiating with those who own and run these EPZs. The focus is on the gender dimension which causes harm to women who work in the EPZs. But there is an institutionally racial dimension also. This occurs because there is lack of care over the working conditions of women in these zones and they are not noticed unless they cause problems for the corporation. Similarly, women were not noticed in terms of their working conditions as slaves unless they caused trouble when forced to work as slaves. There is a racialisation of social relations in this economic sphere,[44] whereby there is a 'feminisation and racialisation of work as part of an expansion of part-time, temporary, non-unionised employment … '[45] Jamaican women, for instance, provide very cheap labour. The foreign manufacturer can take the opportunity that this situation provides to pay low wages.[46] Some 'sweatshops' have been unionised after mass pressure such as BJ&B hat factory.[47] This is not the norm. However due to lack of alternative employment women are forced to work in free trade zones. They are the poorest and least able to complain about their working conditions, suffer inequality of bargaining power and are 'left at the bottom of the market'[48] as racial and gendered minorities. This is an intersection[49] that black women face based on race as well as gender.[50] They are the most vulnerable in developing countries. For instance in '2000 Jamaican women accounted for 67 percent of all workers who were laid off'.[51] Furthermore, due to their vulnerability in the labour force when free trade zones move to another country this impacts on the lives of women and their employability. Thus when free trade zones moved from Jamaica to Mexico under the NAFTA,[52] Jamaica lost 16,000 jobs with a disproportionate impact on women who formed the majority of the work force in these zones,[53] in some cases 80 percent.[54] There is a failure to provide an economically viable service to these women that leaves them at the bottom of the labour market. It is argued here that conditions should be set in place such as the laid out in the Trade Review that would harness the working conditions in the EPZs to racial and gender equality.

International trade preferences and institutional racism

Sugar, rice and bananas are some of the commodities produced in the Caribbean and sold in the international market. However, the terms upon which these food stuffs are sold are detrimental to the Caribbean. These terms are both express and hidden, unconscious and unwitting in terms of institutional racism. Institutional racism can be traced back to at least the argument within the WTO[55] over the terms by which sugar and rice were sold from the Caribbean to the EU on preferential terms for example. The WTO, the successor to the General Agreement on Tariffs and Trade (GATT),[56] is the guardian of the free flow of trade between its members.[57] A subject that has cropped up as problematic is the 'erosion of preferences'[58] for developing countries. The WTO operates by consensus[59] meaning for Moore[60] the forging of a 'working consensus, of a diverse membership that runs the gamut from the poorest LDCs to economic superpowers … consensus by exhaustion'.[61] Kwa[62] argues that poor developing countries are subject to different strategies and different levels of economic activity that 'has been turned into one of the most powerful weapons used by the developed countries to divide and conquer'[63] there can be cliques around an issue that make it difficult for the Caribbean to maintain and argue for a particular position, particularly as Dine[64] argues, small developing countries do not have the power in terms of sanctions against super powers like the EU or the USA. These power blocks operate in an institutionally racist way in that they do not realise that their behaviour amounts to blocking the development of the Caribbean with respect to trade. It is particularly in the context of agriculture where differences can be found.[65]

The WTO incorporates dispute resolution machinery and this was used to deal with a dispute that successfully challenged preferential agreements between the EU and some

Caribbean countries. Preferential agreements that could be said to at least indirectly take into account the special relationship the Caribbean has with the West. This is in terms of the difficulties that the Caribbean inhabit due to the socio-economic problems inherited through the transatlantic slave trade and colonialism.

In the context of the WTO 'preference' generally refers to tariff preferences. The basic idea is that products from less developed countries that are to be imported into an industrialised nation would be subject to a tariff rate by the industrialised nation that would be less than the rate applied to products from a source other than a less developed country.[66] However, this principle goes against a more basic principle of the WTO which is that under the WTO agreements:

> countries cannot normally discriminate between their trading partners. Grant someone a special favour (such as a lower customs duty rate for one of their products) and you have to do the same for all other WTO members, this does not take into account the fact that the Caribbean, for instance, is not a 'developed' [region] with very little diversification and is not on an equal footing with Western states. This principle is known as most-favoured-nation (MFN) treatment ... It is so important that it is the first article of the General Agreement on Tariffs and Trade (GATT) which governs trade in goods ... Some exceptions are allowed. For example, countries can set up a free trade agreement that applies only to goods traded within the group – discriminating against goods from outside. Or they can give developing countries special access to their markets. Or a country can raise barriers against products that are considered to be traded unfairly from specific countries.[67]

In the context of sugar, Australia, Brazil and Thailand alleged that the EU's exports of sugar were subsidised in a way that conflicted with the rules of the WTO Agreement – a central tenet of the WTO is one of non-discrimination[68] in the treatment of goods from one country to another. Two grounds of challenge were made by the complainants. The first was that 'the export of so-called "C sugar" [benefited] from export subsidies with revenues from production under A and B quotas'.[69] With the second complaint the allegation was that there were 'export refunds on 1.6 million tonnes of sugar ... equivalent to preferential EU imports from ACP (African, Caribbean and Pacific)[70] countries and India'.[71] On the basis of these two points the complainants claimed that the EU went beyond subsidies allowed under the WTO Agreement. The EU countered that by refuting both claims. The EU made further arguments that its behaviour in relation to the 'exports of ACP/India sugar [were] in full conformity with EU's schedule of commitments and WTO provisions regarding agricultural export subsidies'.[72] In ruling against the EU (15 October 2004) on this issue the World Trade Organisation Panel decided that the EU had exported 'more sugar with export subsidies than it is permitted to do under the WTO Agreement'.[73]

The decision of the WTO panel[74] has been criticised as causing, amongst other things, concern in relation to the 'preferential access enjoyed by developing countries into the EU'.[75] The African, Caribbean and Pacific countries (ACP) have expressed concern that the ruling of the WTO will affect the preferential agreement that they have with the EU[76] very much needed if they are to get out of the institutionally racist trap they have found themselves in. Since it is difficult for these countries to compete in the world sugar market it has been suggested that these preferential arrangements give ACP countries a chance to trade on a more equal footing than would otherwise be the case and preferential agreements indirectly, at least, recognise the particular slave history of some of these countries. It is reported that under the agreement between the EU and the ACP countries concerning sugar, the EU would buy sugar from the ACP countries at more than three times the world price and then re-export it.[77] The ACP have expressed concern that the WTO ruling will not only endanger exports to the EU but also bring dire changes to the whole of the sugar industry for this region which has for some time had a relationship under the ACP/EU Sugar Protocol with the EU. There is some disagreement as to the extent of the impact of the ruling,[78] for instance Dean[79] argues that some studies show that there is no direct relationship between growth and preferential trade agreements. This ignores the time needed by the Caribbean countries to use preferences to their advantage.

However, it is clear that the new EU sugar regime will lock out many of the poor and their economies since it amounts to 'export dumping' that inhibits access for poor countries.[80] This 'export dumping' leads to a depression in the world market for sugar and consequently a reduction in foreign exchange.[81] The ACP have expressed fear that the challenge from Australia, Brazil and Thailand regarding the EU sugar regime will affect ACP states because of their vulnerability as single commodity producers.[82] For some countries in the Caribbean this lack of commodity diversification is one developed through the inheritance of plantation land, subsequently geared to the goods of value to the West.[83] Furthermore, the type of ruling from the WTO tends to conflict with agreements such as the Lomé Convention which provides that under the sugar protocol, the Community agrees to buy a fixed quantity annually of sugar from ACP producers at attractively high guaranteed prices aligned to the EU's own internal sugar price and establishes annual quotas for sugar producers, a preference which has been valuable to the economic development of certain ACP states – Mauritius, Fiji, Guyana and Barbados.[84] Thus a preferential system that was aimed at widening and protecting access for some of the most vulnerable economies in the world is itself under threat as a consequence of WTO rules that are based on liberal notions of equality, demanding market access on the grounds of free trade. There appears to be no awareness that institutional racism might be at work here within a culture that is apparently oblivious to the pain inflicted on countries that have been benefiting from preferences hitherto. The WTO rules conflict with the need for Caribbean countries to develop in a global economy. The rules are institutionally racist because they serve to lock the Caribbean into poverty by not providing a service that is free from racism. Developing countries trading in bananas have suffered a similar fate.[85] The WTO dispute panel ruled in favour of the US and its allies concerning preferential trade entry to Europe for Caribbean bananas. The history of this dispute (called the banana wars)[86] involved a decision by the EU in 1993 to improve the import banana market. This involved the granting of preferential treatment to the 'EU's overseas territories and former colonies'[87] and a correlative restriction on imports in bananas from a number of countries, including those in Latin America. This move by the EU enabled former African colonies, former colonies in the Caribbean and the Pacific to 'export bananas to the EU at lower costs and in higher quantities while'[88] other countries had elevated duties to pay and limitations placed on the number of bananas they could export to the European market. Furthermore, the EU obliged entities involved in the business of the export of bananas to the European market to acquire a licence. This system was more favourable to the African and Caribbean countries. Myers[89] argues that the Windward Islands 'which are the most vulnerable of the ACP banana exporting countries, have very little current or potential alternative sources of income apart from tourism'.[90] The banana trade is critical for the economies of these countries in terms of export earnings. Moreover, economic 'diversification is therefore only feasible alongside a core banana export'.[91]

The EU's regime was challenged by the US companies of Del Monte, Chiquita and Dole that were operating out of Latin America. Their argument was heard at the WTO dispute settlement panel. The allegation was that the EU's trade restrictions in bananas breached the GATT and a number of trade agreements that were the responsibility of the WTO. In addition they argued that there was an infringement of Article XIII of the WTO.[92] In its defence the EU argued that the regime it had set up was covered by the Lomé Convention of 1975. Of the four conventions the first Lomé Convention was signed in 1975. The aim of this Convention was to encourage trade relations with the Commonwealth upon Britain's accession to the European Community. In terms of the subject matter under discussion the relevant term of this agreement was 'the nonreciprocal preferences for most exports from ACP countries to the EEC'.[93] As an international aid and trade agreement dealing with relations between ACP and the EU this convention was 'aimed at supporting the "ACP states"'[94] efforts to achieve comprehensive, self-reliant and self-sustained development, through a mechanism of 'non-reciprocal preferences for most exports from ACP (African, Caribbean and Pacific) countries to the EEC'.[95] A further argument made by the EU was that the Uruguay Round Agreements also safeguarded the banana trade arrangements.[96] It is argued that such agreements between the EEC (now EU) and the Caribbean serve to make recompense for the racially contrived situation that they find themselves in through the global market. Despite the arguments mounted by the EU in defence of its preferential trade entry to Europe for Caribbean bananas, the WTO Appellate Panel found against the arrangement in 1997 on the basis that the import licence scheme breached the rules of non-discrimination in relation to the banana market participants in the non-ACP countries.[97] According to the panel, 'the tariff quotas enjoyed by ACP countries must be eliminated or provided to all'.[98] Such rules demonstrate institutional racism in that there is a failure to provide a service to Caribbean countries that have been ravaged by the slave trade, slavery and colonialism. This service would be one that considered the unequal status of Caribbean countries in the global economy due to their racialised economic history caused by the West.

The position today is that the 'banana wars', as they were known, have come to an end. Reporting in the Telegraph in 2012, WTO Director General Pascal Lamy stated, 'After so many twists and turns, these complicated and politically contentious disputes can finally be put to bed'.[99] But those in the Caribbean were not jumping up and down with joy states Crowther.[100] 'For small farmers and workers on banana plantations alike, the battle for a sustainable livelihood remains at a critical stage'.[101] Bananas are grown at the expense of cheap labour on large plantations with very poor working conditions and we in the West benefit from that in the sense that bananas are cheap for us.[102] The banana wars were never about better conditions for workers but a fight between the EU and multinationals. Once again the Caribbean suffers from the unwitting and unconscious racism that endured behind the arguments about equality of treatment, a racism that the Caribbean continues to suffer due to the impact of the rules that are not at all neutral – although they may look so – but are racially contrived by the powerful who do not see the racial aspect to the rules.

The banana ruling tends to reflect a traditional notion of equal treatment influenced by the Aristotelian perspective that equality is where a man is 'assumed to have no more than his share, if he is just (for he does not assign to himself more of what is good in itself unless such a share is proportional to his merits ... '[103] the imperative is thus based on the notion of equality of opportunity found in discrimination law, meaning that like should be treated alike. The idea of equality appears to be premised on the paradigm of 'equality of starting points' and not 'equality of outcomes'. Thus a situation can arise where if everyone is treated equally badly then that would satisfy the idea of equal treatment, as occurred in *Palmer v*

Thompson.[104] There is a principle of non-discrimination contained in the preamble to the WTO Agreement which reads: 'Being desirous of contributing to these objectives by entering into reciprocal and mutually advantageous arrangements directed to the substantial reduction of tariffs and other barriers to trade and to the elimination of discriminatory treatment in international trade relations'.[105] This principle, read in its narrow sense, would presuppose equality of treatment in terms of allowing all participants an equal chance to participate in the market for the trade in bananas. For mono-crop developing countries this is not the case because they start from a poor position, an unequal position and a position that has been entrenched by institutional racism. This has been the case of Guyana (Formerly British Guiana).

Guyana – A case study

The Guyanese economy is quite clearly affected by changes in its trade relations concerning sugar.[106] For instance, it is estimated that of its 750,000 population, 600,000 of them live in areas where the sugar industry employs people. About 20,000 of this number are employed in the industry and another 10,000 are employed in connecting areas. Thus it has been suggested that 'an average of four people depend on one employed person, (therefore) no less than 150,000 people rely on the sugar industry for their livelihood'.[107] It is through the slave trade and plantation system that has been 'inherited' by free labour that many find themselves locked in to this position of vulnerability. The relationship between the sugar trade, the Guyanese economy and its vulnerability can be traced back to the slave plantation systems developed by Western Europeans. The Dutch East India Company introduced the plantation system where products such as sugar were grown using West Africans as slaves when attempts to enslave the native Arawaks and Caribs generally failed.[108] Later the French and British took parts of Guiana for their own purposes with Britain taking three of the Dutch colonies which it renamed British Guiana.[109] The plantation system was developed to serve the needs of the markets of the plantation owners and their trade with the rest of the world. For instance by 1762, Demerara in Guyana had 93 plantations.[110] Evidence suggests that the social life of Western Europe in the eighteenth century had the clear aim of the development of the plantation system to make quick profits.[111] Many British people profited from the trade in slavery amongst who were John Gladstone (1764–1851), a large estate owner in British Guyana.[112]

According to Williams,[113] Gladstone was a slave owner in the West Indies who argued that the slave trade was necessary. He was able to obtain several large plantations in what was British Guiana (Guyana) which he used to grow sugar, and subsequently sold on the Liverpool Exchange.[114] The wealth generated from this trade activity helped to fuel trade with Russia, India and China.[115] Despite its appalling impact on the lives of those subject to the plantation system,[116] Gladstone and his family defended the system of slavery on the family estates in Guiana.[117] This system of exploitation was justified as essential to the progression of trade in areas such as sugar. As Williams put it, 'sugar meant labor – at times the labor has been slaves, at other times nominally free'.[118] Williams further observed that 'Ultimately, like other colonial territories, [Guyana] was essentially an area of exploitation, in which the European engaged in a narrow range of activities exclusively for the benefit of the master class'.[119] This system of exploitation of the land, the people used to work it and the racist ideology that unquestioningly exploited the skin of Black men, women and children, continued even after the emancipation of the African slaves in 1834 when slavery was abolished. However it was the skin of Indian indentured labour according to Williams that filled the hole created by the 'emancipation of the Negro and the inadequacy of the white worker'.[120]

'[D]eprived of his Negro'[121] the sugar plantation owners looked to the 'the Indian from the East. India replaced Africa; between 1833 and 1917'[122] importing 238,000 Indians into the region.[123] This was done to benefit the West. It was Indian indentured labour that is said to have been 'enticed by promises of land'[124] in Guyana to work the rice fields. Fried describes rice as the 'bloodline for Guyana'[125] because fluctuation in global price impacts on the 150,000 people who are directly or indirectly employed in the industry. When prices are good, the people and the economy benefit. The reverse is also true. Big and small farmers have been 'punished' for complying with rules in the world market for rice, whilst these rules which, it is argued, are based on a 'false presumption that markets can be free and equal',[126] allow 'wealthy nations to play fast and loose when it suits them'.[127]

In relation to the rice industry, Guyana sought to improve her position in the world market for rice by taking advantage in the 1990s of the EU's preferential trading agreement which was offered to ACP countries[128] under the Lomé I Convention. This entailed the use of 'non-reciprocal preferences for most exports from ACP countries to EEC'.[129] This understanding enabled Guyana to export 90 per cent of her rice duty-free. The profits made from rice exports enabled farmers and others to borrow money in order to invest in the infrastructural elements that would make them more productive. However, in the mid to late 1990s the EU put restrictions on the rice imports from Guyana. This restriction was imposed to meet with requirements imposed on the EU by WTO rules.[130] These rules had a negative impact on the preferential arrangements enjoyed by Guyanese rice exports. In 1996 the new quotas imposed reduced her rice exports to the EU from 90 per cent to 19 per cent of the total. Earnings also dropped[131] and with a ripple effect that was to impact on the lives of the Guyanese people. Not to be defeated, Guyana increased her rice exports to the CARICOM countries in the Caribbean.[132] Here Guyana was once again offered preferential treatment on her rice exports. The biggest importer of Guyanese rice was Jamaica, which absorbed 79,000 to 100,000 tonnes a year.[133] Guyana's market share rose in 1997 from 1 per cent to 44 per cent.[134] However, Guyana's competitor was the USA, traditionally the main supplier of this product. During this period the price for rice was deliberately driven downwards by rice brokers. Whilst the US Government was able to subsidise its participants in the production and export of rice to Jamaica, the same could not be said for Guyana. An already heavily indebted government had no leverage to support its rice farmers.

In terms of equal treatment, two related things should be noted at this juncture. One is that the rules of the WTO in relation to the use of preferential treatment by developing countries appear to be subject to the more general rule of equality of treatment between the membership. However, this notion of equality is limited and its application quite damaging in situations where it is quite clear that developing countries such as Guyana do not start off from an equal point. And further, this unequal starting point is one imposed through the historical relationship that created a plantation-mono-crop system in Guyana. The West has clearly had the advantage of using the slave trade and subsequent periods in ways that have allowed diversification and dominance in world trade markets.

Preferential trading rules are built on the understanding that historically, developing countries have poorer economies compared with the stronger economies of the West. This impoverished position is one that can be traced back to an international trading regime that 'has encouraged Guyana to develop a mono crop export sector oriented towards preferential markets in the industrialised countries'.[135] The recognition of this problem whilst apparently catered for within the idea of preferential treatment withers away when it comes to putting this idea into practice. Thus the relatively few gains made by the poorer countries are trumped by the way in which the richer countries are able to play the WTO rules (along with the shelter of state subsidies when market prices drop) to their advantage.[136] The link to institutional racism is clear in that the rules are applied in a way that ignores the racially contrived economic position of the Caribbean. Even when there is a solution in the form of preferences this is overcome by rich and powerful countries that have no concern for the economic poverty caused by relying on rules that have been contrived by the same powerful countries.

Like rice, the markets in sugar have been used to fuel the wealth of the industrialised nations. Also like rice, the interest in sugar and its profitability for the West has come at the expense of people and the lands they were forced onto or coerced into cultivating. No regard was paid to the slaves who were deliberately stolen from Africa to work the Guyanese plantations when attempts to enslave the local population of Caribs and Arawaks failed.[137] Nash points out that 'Sugar and tobacco production … developed hand-in hand with co-erced and degraded labor: grasping for wealth, profit-maximising English planters relentlessly sought overseas markets, ruthlessly exploited fellow humans, accumulated narrowly concentrated power, and resonated very little to liberal ideas and higher values'.[138] Despite the abolition of slavery in Guyana in 1834 and her eventual political independence in 1966 she remains a 'pawn' in the hands of the free trade market rules, like many similarly placed Caribbean countries. It is in this sense one sees institutional racism flourishing and this is why it is argued for the incorporation of a reparative framework in the operation of these trading rules. Evidence suggests that when economies like Guyana try to take advantage of preferential terms in trade agreements in relation to rice and sugar, there is a 'sting in the tail'. The complexities in the world trade arena which are buttressed by WTO rules tend to favour those economies where the resources of their governments are able to 'soften' the blow of the consequences of sticking to the rules. Thus the strict letter of WTO that required the EU to comply with non-discrimination requirements, that is 'mutually advantageous arrangements directed to the substantial reduction of tariffs and other barriers to trade and to the elimination of discriminatory treatment in international trade relations'[139] in relation to the rice and sugar markets, disadvantages Guyana. Her source for exports on preferential terms virtually dried up. Moreover, whilst the rice market was depressed by the brokers, her potential for export earnings also reduced significantly. At the same time the American agri-business was able to rely on government subsidies to assist them during this problematic era. In 1999 this was to the tune of US$446 million under the US Department of Agriculture's Production Flexibility Contract and further payments of US$470 million and loans of US$395 million.[140]

Clearly the market is not dealing with economies of equals. The Guyanese government had no reserves to provide a cushion for its farmers and related workers. It has not been in a position to acquire the reserves from export earnings that would enable it to do so. According to Bhagwab Lall (the Chairperson of Leguan district 3), 'Whether you be a big farmer or a small farmer, you are punished for being a rice farmer'.[141] Furthermore, despite her willingness to follow the trading rules of the WTO on its terms – with the promise of 'the need for positive efforts designed to ensure that developing countries, and especially the least developed among them, secure a share in the growth in international trade commensurate with the needs of their economic development',[142] this promise has not materialised. Like many Caribbean economies, she is still deprived of the income that would enable her to maintain a viable economy. The rules that give lip service to the recognition of the need for ex-colonies to have a fair share of the market – preferential agreements – have become just that. This is clearly an unacceptable position to be in, and one that needs to be given urgent attention because we are not only talking of a loss of profits but the way in which the present global economic order supported by the WTO Agreement contributes to the maintenance of huge debt in the developing countries and the 'persistence of poverty'.[143] Moreover, this is entrenched by institutionalised racist rules that keep developing countries poor.

Institutional discrimination

On the face of it the EU's system of favourable tariffs for ACP countries and the licensing requirements would seem unfair to other members of the WTO. However, some scholars in the field of discrimination law have argued that such liberal notions of equality equated with equality of opportunity are limited in terms of providing effective change in situations where there has been historical discrimination such as that between the 'developed' economies and the 'developing' ones. This is a factor explicitly recognised in the WTO Agreement that states recognising further that there is need for positive efforts designed to ensure that developing countries, and especially the least developed among them, secure a share in the growth in international trade commensurate with the needs of their economic development. Fredman argues that one of the problems with this notion of equality is that it does not have any substantive[144] underpinning. Such an underpinning should recognise that equality of treatment in its narrow liberal sense may in practice reinforce racial discrimination. Thus the impact of this statement is said to have caused 'enormous social and economic problems in the windward islands where bananas represent as much as 60 percent of their economies'.[145] Furthermore, the statement tends to ignore the important role of social institutions, such as the WTO, in playing a central, rather than a 'neutral' position in the distribution of justice.[146] Eroding preferential treatment on goods from the Caribbean such as sugar and bananas and rice play into the hands of institutional racism:

> The collective failure of an organisation to provide an appropriate and professional service to people because of their colour, culture or ethnic origin which can be seen or detected in processes; attitudes and behaviour which amount to discrimination through unwitting prejudice, ignorance, thoughtlessness and racist stereotyping which disadvantages minority ethnic people[147]

This racism is not deliberate in design or desire, nor a matter that can be tied to individual acts. Rather, there is a predominant institutional response that fails to address the root causes of racism against racial and ethnic minority groups even when there is the opportunity to do so through the device of preferential trading agreements. This blinkered attitude is more than the 'prejudiced or racist acts of people running institutions such as banks, corporations, government agencies, and so forth'.[148] It is a failure to make the link between the transatlantic slave trade, colonialism and the unfavourable treatment of post-colonial economies by Western regimes. Preferential trading rules are recognised by the WTO but often side-stepped when challenged in the arena of the desire to enforce the rules regarding non-discrimination. Those that challenge such preferences correctly predict that the WTO will take the minimalist option, which means determining disputes through the narrow legal paradigm of liberal equality. The impact of such a paradigm for developing countries is to devastate an economy and starve its people. The liberalisation of the commodity exchange rules that at first blush appear built on notions of 'free' trade serve to benefit strong Western economies, the EU and the USA, whilst the returns in terms of economic and social goods for developing economies in Africa and the West Indies come with onerous conditions attached that operate unfairly, unequally and serve to spiral the cycle of poverty experienced by the economies of these countries, caused by or compounded through the rules such as that of the WTO. It is contended that such rules need to be restructured to halt the potential destructive force of current globalisation in relation to the economies of these developing countries and to address the racist historical injustices of the past that continue to be perpetuated through these trading rules. As things stand for developing countries, the idea that there is a free market is nothing more than a myth.[149]

Institutional racism and economic partnership agreements

It has been argued that preferential agreements made very little difference to the local economies of the ACP.[150] The removal of preferential trading[151] agreements with the EU as a tool to help Caribbean economies survive in a competitive world has been replaced by EPAs. EPAs[152] are trade agreements between ACP[153] countries and the EU.[154] They purport to promote 'trade between the two groupings – and through trade development, sustainable growth and poverty reduction. The EPAs set out to help ACP countries integrate into the world economy and share in the opportunities offered by globalisation'.[155] The European Commission's remedy, for what it sees as the failure of the preferential trading agreements between the ACPs and the EU to get a firm foothold in the European market, is to create an instrument through the EPAs that 'will make it easier for people and businesses from the two regions to invest in and trade with each other and thus to help Caribbean countries grow their economies and create jobs'.[156] The EPAs came into existence between the Caribbean and the EU in 2008.[157] The European Commission argues that preferences have not been beneficial in terms of the development of developing countries over a 30-year period and that the EPA's will be beneficial to developing countries.[158]

To what extent have the Economic Partnership Agreements benefited the Caribbean countries? Despite the European Commission's assurance that the EPAs will create a 'virtuous circle of growth'[159] amongst other positives, Action Aid[160] argues that the EPAs are detrimental to the economies of the countries they are targeted at, namely '76 former colonies in Africa, the Caribbean and Pacific (ACP) countries'.[161] Specifically the problems are that 750 million people will be worse off because the EPAs are designed in favour of rich countries. Institutional racism is simply not a consideration. The ACP countries are not ready to open themselves to the rich countries even though in terms of free trade they should be. To force them to do so will mean crippling job losses, revenue deficit to governments, and public service cuts. Moreover, the ability of these governments to regulate corporations will be restricted as the notion of free markets take effect in practice. Furthermore, the hands of governments will be tied as their ability to design their own development strategies disappears.[162] There are shortcomings with the EPAs raised by Norman Girvan[163] who tells us that CARIFORUM[164] – a group of 14 Caribbean countries – signed the EPA, amongst a lot of controversy as to its benefits and problems for these countries. In EPA-Democratic Governance,[165] Girvan points out that the EPA is legally binding and difficult to change. Its scope is wide covering regional and national policy; it fastens the hands of government in several strands and is a grey area as far as the public is concerned. The EPA offers access for goods and services and the opening up of development support whilst the CARIFORUM countries provide the EPA with markets for goods and services and binding commitments.[166] However, there are a range of problems. There is duty-free and quota-free access to markets excluding sugar and rice.[167] There is insufficient explanation of the benefits under rules of origin and few 'SMEs will be able to afford to establish a market presence in Europe and expand exports of goods'.[168] In the area of services the EPA has facilitated free movement of individual persons but the EU states have considerable discretion and it is difficult to know how CARIFORUM states are to prepare service providers for the conditions of entry.[169] In terms of development support the problem that arises is that it is not quantified, specific or time-bound. There are no targeted funds for the development of infrastructure and the evolution of the private sector to ensure competitiveness in response to the imports from EU markets.[170]

Of the CARICOM[171] countries Jamaica is one of the worst affected in terms of 'making the biggest retreat from the European market'.[172] Some of the problems are to do with the type of packaging required by the EU. For instance, Sonya Dunstan, CEO of Taste of Caribbean Limited, argued that 'due to economies of scale, we will not be able to compete'.[173] 'The manufacturers are huge overseas and what one company can produce in a day is what local companies will take months to produce.'[174] Moreover there are inequalities of development and no taking into account the stage of development that Caribbean economies have compared with their United Kingdom, German and French counterparts.[175] This is not surprising since the West has had a head start with the surplus labour that was used in terms of the slave trade[176] and slavery[177] with its ability to develop its economies at the expense of the Caribbean through the triangular trade. As Williams tells us the great wealth secured from the plantations and the selling of slaves provided the money for investment in British industry, banking and insurance.[178] The legacy of the slave trade continues to fester in the contractual relations between the Caribbean and the Western European region as witnessed by the Economic Partnership Agreements. As Jackson and Wedderburn[179] argue, the Caribbean is very dependent on the USA and world markets in which they are quite vulnerable. It is argued that the principle problem is institutional racism where the West and the USA do not see why it is that the ACP countries cannot compete on an equal footing with them. They do not see the historical role of slavery as having anything to do with the economies of the Caribbean and Africa today. They do not recognise that there is a legacy of the slave trade that still exists and that is institutional racism. And so they see the ACP countries as 'equal' trade partners when they clearly are not.

Conclusion

The Caribbean does not suffer in economic trade matters just in terms of intra-state trade but also with respect to international trade. The preferential system that was meant to help them to build up their economies was taken away from them by the WTO rules and more powerful multinationals. This was clearly seen in the context of the Guyanese case study. Behind these trade wars lurks the problem of institutional racism which is evident in the failure to see the plight of developing countries such as those in the Caribbean. This was apparent in the 'banana wars' and the imposition of the EPAs. One of the major problems for Caribbean countries is their lack of economic diversification. As a hangover from slavery this makes them particularly vulnerable to the global market.[180] Race, argues Girvan[181] is a 'central factor in the political economy of exploitation'[182] as far as the Caribbean is concerned. 'There is a continuous reproduction of a structure of dependent underdevelopment which was at first created by European colonisation.'[183] Today the EPAs are still highly controversial and it remains to be seen how Caribbean countries will fair under this new regime. It would appear unlikely that they will succeed as a means of advancing the Caribbean into the twenty-first century, as there is 'inadequate, uncompetitive and undiversified productive capacity'.[184] Although in Barbados, it is one of the countries where the government is trying to get the manufacturing sector to embrace EPAs as a way to move forward economically,[185] nevertheless negotiations with African and Caribbean countries over the EPAs are still drawn out.[186] It is argued that a preferential economic trading system is required for the Caribbean region. This would be to address the problem with lack of diversification, the protection of their limited markets and the earmarking of their economies for development in a way that will reinforce growth. Otherwise all that happens is that the pretty negative status quo is repeated and reinforced behind which hides the political economy of racial exploitation. The WTO consists of 150 developing countries, that is two-thirds of its membership. The membership includes Caribbean countries. Many of the developing countries do not have the economic muscle that the developed countries have when it comes to rule making within the WTO. It is argued that the WTO agreements that have special provisions on developing countries should be amended so that preferential agreements for the Caribbean are part of that package. The GATT and the General Agreement on Trade in Services already contain some preferential treatment for developing countries. Moreover, developing countries have been given extra time to fulfil their commitments in many of the WTO agreements.[187] It is argued that in these agreements preferential treatment should be expanded to cover all the goods and services provided by developing countries and, in particular, those who have suffered from the transatlantic slave trade and chattel slavery. Furthermore, the time given to Caribbean countries to comply with WTO agreements should be measured by their state of development not numerical time. This would work by assessing the economic position of each Caribbean state and considering its impoverishment. There should be a risk assessment conducted that looks at the issue of the economic impact of EPAs. Other developing countries and the developed countries of the WTO would likely object on the grounds that attributing special status to the Caribbean countries is unfair. Developing countries not caught up in the transatlantic slave trade may argue that they also struggle in the global market. Developed countries are likely to argue that there are already preferences in WTO agreements and there should not be any more. To these arguments it is contended that Caribbean countries have had a particular economic and social history that has put them in the disadvantaged position that they are in, that is the transatlantic slave trade, chattel slavery and colonialism. Due to this history they are underdeveloped. It would therefore be appropriate to provide a service to them by giving them special treatment in terms of wider preferences for their goods and services. There is a committee called the Committee on Trade and Development (CTD) that could be given the task of looking at and making proposals for the amendment of WTO agreements so that Caribbean countries are identified for preferential treatment on all their goods and services. For the developed countries that call foul, that this is a breach of free trade, it could be pointed out to them that the Caribbean has been operating under an economic system that has played a discriminatory game with them. It is time to introduce some balance in the economic system in order to achieve justice. CTD already has a role in monitoring how WTO provisions work for developing countries. They could consider all WTO agreements that affect Caribbean countries and propose to amend those that relate to preferences. This is so that the Caribbean countries are able to seek reparations in terms of a change in the trading rules. The legacy of the transatlantic slave trade exists in the institutional racism of the power brokers in the WTO, in this case the developed countries many of whom played a role in the transatlantic slave trade and chattel slavery. The argument that preferences should be retained for Caribbean countries is a fundamentally moral and political one. However, the moral case has been made for the retention of preferences in trade and service agreements. The WTO with respect to the Caribbean should agree to this on the grounds that reparations for the slave trade legacy could be dealt with by way of preferential trade agreements.

Notes

1 Sir William Macpherson, *The Stephen Lawrence Inquiry* (London: Home Office, 1999), chapter 6, para 6.34.
2 S. Carmichael and C.V. Hamilton, *Black Power the Politics of Liberation in America* (New York: Vintage Books, 1967).
3 Transitional Racial Justice Initiative, 'The Persistence of White Privilege and Institutional Racism in US Policy. A Report on Government Compliance with the International Convention on the Elimination of All Forms of Racial Discrimination' (California, 2001); see www.arc.org/pdf/303pdf.pdf (accessed 3 July 2014).
4 P. Tuitt, *Race, Law, Resistance* (London: Glass House Press, 2004).
5 D.G. Green (ed.), *Institutional Racism and the Police: Fact or Fiction* (London: CIVITAS, 2000); see www.civitas.org.uk/pdf/cs06.pdf (accessed 7 March 2014).
6 'Economic Partnership Agreement between the CARIFORUM States, of the one part, and the European Community and its Member States, of the other part'. *Official Journal of the European Community*, L2819/1/4, 2008.
7 CARIFORUM consists of a range of countries in the Caribbean: 14 are members of the Caribbean Community (CariCom); see www.normangirvan.info/economic-partnership-agreement-epa/ (accessed 3 July 2014).
8 H.R. Brewster, 'The Anti-development Dimension of the European Community's Economic Partnership Agreement for the Caribbean'. See www.normangirvan.info/economic-partnership-agreement-epa/ (accessed 3 July 2014).
9 Ibid.
10 Ibid.
11 Ibid.
12 H. McDonald Beckles, *Britain's Black Debt* (Kingston: University of West Indies Press, 2013), p. 82.
13 F. Brennan and J. Packer (eds), *Colonialism, Slavery, Reparations and Trade: Remedying the Past?* (Abingdon: Routledge, 2012). According to statistics found by Marika Sherwood this number is made up of official figures from the website www.slavevoyages.org/tast/assessment.faces (accessed 1 December 2014) as well as those who died through enslavement, the march to the barracoons, those locked up in the cells waiting to be shipped out and those who died during capture, pp. 23–24.
14 It has been recommended that the UN Committee on the Elimination of Racial Discrimination (CERD) state that racial discrimination constitutes 'degrading treatment' within the meaning of Article 3 of the European Convention on Human Rights, see D. Petrova, 'Racial Discrimination and the Rights of Minority Cultures', in S. Fredman, *Discrimination and Human Rights: The Case of Racism* (Oxford: Oxford University Press, 2001).
15 H. Thomas, *The Slave Trade: The History of the Atlantic Slave Trade 1440–1870* (London: Papermac, 1997).
16 S. Salih (ed.), *The History of Mary Prince* (London: Penguin Books, 2000 [1831]).
17 Ibid., pp. 14–15.
18 Thomas, *The Slave Trade.*
19 Ibid., p. 393. Smithfield was a famous meat market in the middle of London that had been on the same site for over one thousand years www.smithfieldmarket.com/content/market/the-market-today (accessed 22 February 2014).
20 The Abolition Project with testament of Dr Thomas Trotter discussing the Middle Passage where slaves were moved from the cells in the barracoons to the ships and taken to the Americas.
21 L.H. Gann and P. Duignan (eds), *Colonialism in Africa 1870–1960* (Cambridge: Cambridge University Press, 1975). Difference Between.net, *Difference between Colonialism and Imperialism.* Available at: www.differencebetween.net/miscellaneous/difference-between-colonialism-and-imperialism/. Also see 'South African Study: Israel Practicing Apartheid and Colonialism'. Available at: https://electronicintifada.net (accessed 16 July 2016).

22 www.oxforddictionaries.com (accessed 16 July 2016).
23 P. Edwards (ed.), *Equiano's Travels* (Oxford: Heinemann Publishers, 1969 [1789]).
24 Ibid., pp. 28–29.
25 The Abolition of the Slave Trade Act 1807.
26 The Abolition of Slavery Act 1833 (came into effect in most of the British colonies in 1834). The Act did not free most people. They were to be apprentices for six years. This did not go down well with the slaves because it was seen as another way to retain slavery. Demonstrations saw this part of the Act rescinded in 1838. See The Abolition Project at http://abolition.e2bn.org/slavery_69.html (accessed 2 January 2014).
27 Adapted from the definition of institutional racism put forward by Sir W. Macpherson in the *Stephen Lawrence Inquiry*, chapter 6, para 6.34.
28 Working Group of Experts on People of African Descent, 2 Session, 3–7 February 2003, at 4, see S. Paneerselvam, intern, International Movement Against All Forms of Discrimination and Racism – UN Office.
29 K. Singh, *Race and Class Struggles in a Colonial State Trinidad 1917–1945* (Jamaica: University of the West Indies Press, 1994).
30 Ibid., pp. 77–78.
31 Ibid., p. 223.
32 J. Dine, *Companies, International Trade and Human Rights* (Cambridge: Cambridge University Press, 2005).
33 Ibid., p. 142.
34 E. Williams, *Capitalism and Slavery* (Chapel Hill: University of North Carolina Press, 1994).
35 Ibid., p. 43.
36 G. Bhattacharyya, J. Gabriel and S. Small, *Race and Power: Global Racism in the Twenty-First Century* (London: Routledge, 2003), p. 30.
37 Ibid., p. 15.
38 A. Kwa, *Power Politics in the WTO* (Bangkok: Focus on the Global South, 2002), p. 10.
39 See Oxfam, 'Rigged Rules and Double Standards: Trade, Globalisation, and the Fight against Poverty' at www.maketradefair.com (accessed 9 January 2014).
40 See ILO, 'Employment and Social Policy in Respect of Export Processing Zones', ILO, Committee on Employment and Social Policy, GB285/ESP/5, Geneva, November 2002.
41 M.K. Shrivastava, 'Review: Women and Trade Liberalisation: The Caribbean Experience' (Review, CAFRA, 2002, Gender and Trade Liberalisation in the Caribbean) at www.cafra.org/article391.html (accessed 10 June 2014).
42 Williams, *Capitalism and Slavery*, p. 29.
43 An NGO based in Jamaica.
44 Bhattacharyya, Gabriel and Small, *Race and Power*.
45 Ibid., p. 30.
46 L. Lamphere, *Situated Lives: Gender and Culture in Everyday Life* (Abingdon: Routledge, 1997).
47 D. Gonzalez, 'Latin Sweatshops Pressed by U.S. Campus Power', *New York Times*, 2003. Available at: www.commondreams.org/headlines03/0404-10.htm (accessed 6 March 2014).
48 S. Pradhan-Malla, in 'Racism and Gender', *Dimensions of Racism* (Paris: the Office of the United Nations High Commissioner for Human Rights and the United Nations Educational, Scientific and Cultural Organization, 2003).
49 J. Conaghan, 'Intersectionality and the Feminist Project in Law' in E. Grabham *et al., Intersectionality and Beyond* (Abingdon: Routledge-Cavendish, 2009).
50 Pradhan-Malla, p. 182.
51 Policy Briefing, http://womenthrive.org/sites/default/files/images/jamaicapolicyanalysis-1.pdf (accessed 6 March 2014).
52 North American Free Trade Agreement.
53 Global Envision, 'Exploring Market-Driven Solutions to Poverty, Jamaican Case Study Released'. See www.globalenvision.org/library/6/678 (accessed 6 March 2014).
54 Y-Dang Troeung, 'Disciplinary Power, Transnational Labour, and the Politics of Representation in Stephanie Black's Life and Debt, *Politics and Culture* 2007(2) published 10 August 2010. See www.politicsandculture.org/2010/08/10/y-dang-troeung-disciplinary-power-transnational-labour-and-the-politics-of-representation-in-stephanie-black%E2%80%99s-life-and-debt-2/ (accessed 6 March 2014).

55 The WTO consists of 157 members, some of whom are African and Caribbean countries; see www.wto.org/english/thewto_e/whatis_e/tif_e/org6_e.htm (accessed 31 December 2014).
56 GATT was the entity that had overall responsibility for the multilateral trading system.
57 There are 157 country members, including some Caribbean and African countries as well as the European Community.
58 'Understanding the WTO – Developing Countries'. Available at: www.wto.org/english/thewto_e/whatis_e/tif_e/dev4_e.htm (accessed 31 December 2014).
59 Ibid.
60 M. Moore, *A World without Walls: Freedom, Development, Free Trade and Global Governance* (Cambridge: Cambridge University Press, 2003).
61 Ibid., p. 110.
62 A. Kwa, *Power Politics in the WTO* (Bangkok: Focus on the Global South, 2002).
63 Ibid., p. 10.
64 J. Dine, *Companies, International Trade and Human Rights* (Cambridge: Cambridge University Press, 2005), p. 128.
65 'Understanding the WTO – Developing Countries'.
66 N.B. dos Santos, R. Farias and R. Cuhna, 'Generalised System of Preferences in General Agreements on Tariffs and Trade/World Trade Organisation: History and Current Issues', *Journal of World Trade* 39(4) (2005): 637–670, at p. 638. Available at: www.academia.edu/254533/Generalized_System_of_Preferences_in_General_Agreement_on_Tariffs_and_Trade_World_Trade_Organization_History_and_Current_Issues (accessed 4 January 2014).
67 'Understanding the WTO: Basic Principles'.
68 Ibid.
69 EUROPA, Press Release, 'Commission Appeals against WTO Sugar Ruling', Reference IP/04/1237, 15/10/2004, Brussels.
70 The Georgetown Agreement on the Organisation of the African, Caribbean and Pacific Group of States, 1975, the ACP.
71 EUROPA, Press Release, op. cit.
72 Ibid.
73 Ibid.
74 In April 2005 the WTO confirmed its initial decision that the EU sugar subsidies were illegal. It is reported that the decision is likely to cause problems for developing countries, although Oxfam maintains that the judgment should not cause a problem for countries with preferential access agreements; see *Financial Times*, 29 April 2005, p. 8.
75 EUROPA, Press Release, op. cit.
76 See BBCCaribbean.com, 16 October 2004.
77 Ibid.
78 D.A. Armstrong, 'The Potential Impact of Trade Policy Changes on Caribbean Sugar', (2004). Available at: http://etd.lsu.edu/docs/available/etd-1121103-010631/unrestricted/Armstrong_thesis.pdf (accessed 8 January 2014).
79 J.M. Dean, 'Do Preferential Agreements Promote Growth?' US International Trade Commission, Working Paper, July 2002.
80 WWF, European Policy Office, 4 August 2004.
81 Ibid.
82 ACP Sugar. Available at: www.acpsugar.org/ (accessed 8 January 2014).
83 Williams, *Capitalism and Slavery*.
84 This was part of the Treaty of European Union in 1993. The object of which was to advance economic, social and cultural developments in Africa, the Caribbean and the Pacific States; see http://europa.en.int/comm/development/body/cotonou/lome_history_en.htm (accessed 8 January 2014).
85 B. Ahmed, 'The Impact of Globalization on the Caribbean Sugar and Banana Industries', in S. Courtman (ed.), *The Society for Caribbean Studies Annual Studies Annual Conference Paper*, vol. 2, 2001. Available at: www.caricom.org/jsp/community/donor_conference_agriculture/preferences.pdf (accessed 8 January 2014).
86 BBC News, 'Banana War ends after 20 Years'. Available at: www.bbc.co.uk/news/business-20263308 (accessed 1 September 2014).
87 State of the Union Initiative, *Trade in Bananas*.
88 Ibid.

89 G. Myers, *Banana Wars: The Price of Freedom* (London: Zed Books, 2004).
90 Ibid., p. 143.
91 Ibid.
92 Relating to the non-application of Multilateral Trade Agreements between Particular Members, see Agreement Establishing the WTO, *Article XIII Non-Application of Multilateral Trade Agreements.*
93 The European Commission, Development,*The Lomé Convention*. 'Membership of the United Kingdom to the then EEC in 1973 led to the signing of the wider reaching Lomé I agreement between 46 ACP and the then 9 EEC member states (1975–80)'.
94 See the Georgetown Agreement on the Organisation of the African, Caribbean and Pacific Group of States, 1975, the ACP. By Article 1 of this agreement Members of the ACP are signatories to the Lomé Convention.
95 European Commission, Development, the Cotonou Agreement, The Lomé Convention.
96 State of the Union Initiative, *Trade in Bananas.*
97 State of the Union Initiative, *Trade in Bananas.* Also see WTO Ruling.
98 M. Dolan, Field Director, Public Citizen's Global Trade Watch.
99 'Banana War Ends after Twenty Years', *The Telegraph*, 9 November 2012; see www.telegraph.co.uk/finance/globalbusiness/9666147/Banana-war-ends-after-20-years.html (accessed 5 March 2014).
100 B. Crowther, *End of the Banana Wars?* 9 November 2012. Available at: http://fairtradeblog.tumblr.com/post/35345212089/end-of-the-banana-wars (accessed 1 September 2014).
101 Ibid.
102 Ibid.
103 See L.P. Pojman and R. Westmoreland (eds), *Equality, Selected Readings* (Oxford: Oxford University Press, 1997) p. 24; Aristotle, *The Nichomachean Ethics*, trans. W.D. Roass (Oxford: Oxford University Press,1925).
104 *Palmer v Thompson* (1971) 403 US 217, 91 S Ct 1940. The city ran a 'whites only' policy in its swimming pools. When required to desegregate the city closed the service down. The court decided that since '... identical treatment had been applied to both whites and blacks ... there was no breach of the equality guarantee'. See S. Fredman, *Discrimination Law*(Oxford: Oxford University Press, 2002) p. 8.
105 This is from one of the recitals of the Agreement Establishing the World Trade Organization, an overall agreement which forms parts of legal documents called the 'Final Act', signed in Marrakesh in 1994.
106 Rhoee suggested that the whole of the economy would be disrupted by a WTO decision against the EU's preferential agreement regarding sugar; see *Stabroek News*, 8 April 2004.
107 See *Stabroek News*, 8 April 2004: 'Sugar Protocol Challenge Case, Rhoee Makes Plea for Differential Treatment'.
108 See Guyana – A Look at the Past; see www.settlement.org/cp/english/guyana/alook.html (accessed April 2014).
109 Ibid.
110 See M. Ifill, 'Guyana under Siege, Legacies of the Early Colonial Era: The Plantation System and the Export Economy in British Guyana', 2001. Available at: www.guyanaunderseige.com (accessed 5 June 2014).
111 Williams, *Capitalism and Slavery*, chapter 3.
112 Merseyside Maritime Museum, 'European Profits'. Available at: www.liverpoolmuseums.org.uk/maritime/slavery/eprofits.asp (accessed June 2014).
113 Williams, *Capitalism and Slavery.*
114 Ibid., pp. 89–90.
115 Ibid., p. 89.
116 Williams writes that not all those who were brought into slavery remained so: 'the Bush Negroes of British Guiana were runaway slaves who had extracted treaties from the British Government and lived independently in their mountain fastness or jungle retreats'. See Williams, ibid., p. 202.
117 Ibid., p. 93.
118 Williams also points out that this labour was sometimes 'black, white or brown or yellow', ibid., p. 29.
119 See M. Ifill, 'Guyana under Siege, Legacies of the Early Colonial Era'.
120 Williams, *Capitalism and Slavery*, p. 28.

121 Ibid., pp. 28–29.
122 Ibid., pp. 28–29.
123 Ibid.
124 M. Fried, *Guyana's Rice Farmers and the Myth of the Free Market* (Ottawa: Oxfam, 2001).
125 Ibid.
126 Ibid.
127 Ibid.
128 The Caribbean Community and Common Market (CARICOM) states are concerned. This body was set up under statute by the Treaty Establishing the Caribbean Community in 1974. This consists of Antigua, Barbados, Belize, Dominica, Grenada, Guyana, Jamaica, Montserrat, St Kitts-Nevis-Anguilla, St Lucia, St Vincent, Trinidad and Tobago.
129 See http://europa.eu.int/comm/development/body/cotonou/lome_history_en.htm (accessed 14 December 2013).
130 Fried, *Guyana's Rice Farmers and the Myth of the Free Market.*
131 Ibid.
132 Ibid.
133 Ibid.
134 Ibid., p. 2.
135 Ibid., p. 4.
136 According to Fried, US farmers received millions in government aid and guarantees to help them during the 1999 crisis in the price for rice on the world market, whilst the Guyanese farmers received nothing from their impoverished government; see Fried, ibid., pp. 2–3.
137 See www.settlement.org/cp/english/guyana/alook.html (accessed 23 January 2014).
138 G. Nash 'Foreword', in R. Dunn *Sugar and Slaves: The Rise of the Planter Class in the English West Indies, 1624–1713* (Chapel Hill: University of North Carolina Press, 1972).
139 This sentence is from one of the recitals of the Agreement Establishing the World Trade Organization, an overall agreement which forms part of legal documents called the 'Final Act', signed in Marrakesh in 1994.
140 Fried, *Guyana's Rice Farmers and the Myth of the Free Market*, p. 2.
141 Ibid., p. 3.
142 WTO Agreement, preamble.
143 T. Pogge, *World Poverty and Human Rights* (Cambridge: Polity Press, 2002), pp. 115–116.
144 The idea of substantive equality is based on the work of Fredman, *Discrimination Law*, pp. 128–9.
145 J. Dow, 'A Clash of Global Forces', Women's Environment and Development Organisation, March 2000.
146 Fredman, *Discrimination Law*, refers to the substantive approach as one that rejects State neutrality, p. 129. I have transposed that idea to entities such as the WTO.
147 Macpherson, *The Stephen Lawrence Inquiry*, chapter 6, para 6.34.
148 L.G. Carr, *'Colour-Blind' Racism* (London: Sage, 1997) p. 167, footnote 3.
149 Fried, *Guyana's Rice Farmers and the Myth of the Free Market.*
150 D.A. Armstrong, 'The Potential Impact of Trade Policy Changes on Caribbean Sugar', (2004). Available at: http://etd.lsu.edu/docs/available/etd-1121103-010631/unrestricted/Armstrong_thesis.pdf (accessed 8 January 2014).
151 It has been argued that preferential trading agreements did not do the job they were expected to in order to lift the economies of developing countries out of poverty and increase their competitiveness. For developing countries there has been a 'race to the bottom', for rich countries they protect their exports, see European Commission, Trade, Economic Development, http://ec.europa.eu/trade/wider-agenda/development/economic-partnerships/. Also see Global Policy Forum, International Trade Agreements. Available at: www.globalpolicy.org/globalization/globalization-of-the-economy-2-1/trade-agreements-2-4.html (accessed 24 January 2013).
152 EPAs are also known as CARIFORUM-EU Economic Partnership Agreement. See European Commission, Trade, Caribbean at http://ec.europa.eu/trade/creating-opportunities/bilateral-relations/regions/caribbean/ (accessed 24 January 2013).
153 The African, Caribbean and Pacific countries. The ACP/EPA countries are grouped into seven regions – five in Africa, one in the Caribbean and one in the Pacific. Guyana, Jamaica and Trinidad and Tobago are some of the countries in the Caribbean region; see European

Commission, Trade, Caribbean. See http://ec.europa.eu/trade/creating-opportunities/bilateral-relations/regions/caribbean/ (accessed 24 January 2013).

154 See European Commission, Trade, Economic Development. Available at: http://ec.europa.eu/trade/wider-agenda/development/economic-partnerships/ (accessed 24 January 2013).

155 Ibid.

156 European Commission, Trade, Caribbean. Available at: http://ec.europa.eu/trade/creating-opportunities/bilateral-relations/regions/caribbean/ (accessed 24 January 2013).

157 http://ec.europa.eu/trade/wider-agenda/development/economic-partnerships/ (accessed 5 February 2014).

158 European Commission, The CARIFORUM- EC Economic Partnership Agreement. Available at: http://europa.eu (accessed 10 October 2016). It is argued that development should not be measured in time but rather in capacity.

159 http://ec.europa.eu/trade/wider-agenda/development/economic-partnerships/ (accessed 5 February 2014).

160 Action Aid, Economic Partnership Agreements. Available at: www.actionaid.org.uk/1412/epas.html (accessed 5 February 2014).

161 Ibid.

162 Ibid.

163 N. Girvan (a professorial research fellow at the University of the West Indies), Caribbean Political Economy, Economic Partnership Agreements. Available at: www.normangirvan.info/economic-partnership-agreement-epa/ (accessed 5 February 2014).

164 CARIFORUM stands for Caribbean forum.

165 N. Girvan, 'The EPA a Critical Evaluation'. Available at: www.normangirvan.info/the-epa-a-critical-evaluation-norman-girvan-powerpoint-presentation-270408/ (accessed 5 February 2014).

166 Ibid.

167 In the transitional period.

168 Girvan, 'The EPA a Critical Evaluation'.

169 Ibid.

170 Ibid.

171 CARICOM stands for Caribbean Community.

172 J. Richardson, 'No European Trojan Horse', *Jamaica Observer*, 14 December 2012.

173 'Small Manufacturers More Worried after European Tour', *Jamaican Gleaner*, 1 August 2012. Available at: http://jamaica-gleaner.com/gleaner/20120801/business/business6.html (accessed 8 February 2014).

174 Ibid.

175 Ibid.

176 Abolition of the Slave Trade Act 1807 abolished the British slave trade.

177 The Slave Emancipation Act 1833 abolished British slavery.

178 Williams, *Capitalism and Slavery* (Chapel Hill: The University of North Carolina Press, 1994), chapter 5.

179 J. Jackson and J. Wedderburn, 'Gender and the Economic Partnership Agreement: An Analysis of the Potential Gender Effects of the CARIFORUM-EU EPA', *Caribbean Development Report, Volume 2.* Available at: www.eclac.cl/publicaciones/xml/3/38253/LCARL.245part3.pdf (accessed 5 June 2014).

180 PriceWaterhouseCoopers, *Sustainability Impact Assessment of the EU-ACP Economic Partnership Agreements*, Final Report 30 January 2004. Available at: http://trade.ec.europa.eu/doclib/docs/2005/january/tradoc_121202.pdf (accessed 8 September 2014).

181 N. Girvan, *Aspects of the Political Economy of Race in the Caribbean and the Americas* (Jamaica: University of West Indies, Institute of Social and Economic Research, 1981).

182 Ibid., p. 1.

183 Ibid., p. 2.

184 H. Brewster, 'The Anti-Development Dimension of the EPA', Text of a paper presented at the Commonwealth Secretariat High Level Technical Meeting: EPAs: The Way Forward for the ACP, Cape Town, South Africa, 7–8 April, 2008. Available at: www.normangirvan.info/the-anti-development-dimension-of-the-european-communitys-economic-partnership-agreement-for-caribbean-havelock-brewster/ (accessed 8 September 2014).

185 T. Blackman, 'Make Use of Trade Agreement, says Barbados Minister',*Caribbean News Now*, 1 August 2014. Available at: www.caribbeannewsnow.com/topstory-Make-use-of-trade-agreements,-says-Barbados-minister-22235.html (accessed 8 September 2014).

186 A. Kwa, P. Lunenborg and W. Musonge, 'African, Caribbean and Pacific (ACP) Countries' Position on Economic Partnership Agreements (EPAs)', Directorate General for External Policies, Policy Department, European Parliament, April 2014. Available at: www.europarl.europa.eu/RegData/etudes/etudes/join/2014/433843/EXPO-DEVE_ET(2014)433843_EN.pdf (accessed 8 September 2014).

187 The World Trade Organisation, 'Understanding the WTO: Developing Countries'. Available at: www.wto.org (accessed 20 November 2015).

Bibliography

Ahmed, B., 'The Impact of Globalization on the Caribbean Sugar and Banana Industries', in S. Courtman (ed.), *The Society for Caribbean Studies Annual Studies Annual Conference Paper*, Vol. 2 (Nottingham: The University of Nottingham, 2001).

Bhattacharyya, G., J. Gabriel and S. Small, *Race and Power: Global Racism in the Twenty-First Century* (London: Routledge, 2003).

Brennan, F. and J. Packer (eds), *Colonialism, Slavery, Reparations and Trade: Remedying the Past?* (Abingdon: Routledge, 2012).

Carmichael, S. and C.V. Hamilton, *Black Power the Politics of Liberation in America* (New York: Vintage Books, 1967).

Carr, L.G., *'Colour-Blind' Racism* (London: Sage, 1997).

Dean, J.M., 'Do Preferential Agreements Promote Growth?', US International Trade Commission, Working Paper, July 2002.

Dine, J., *Companies, International Trade and Human Rights* (Cambridge: Cambridge University Press, 2005).

Dolan, M., Field Director, Public Citizen's Global Trade Watch. Available at: http://depts.washington.edu/wtohist/interviews/Dolan-pfaff%20Murphy.pdf (accessed 16 February 2017).

Dow, J., 'A Clash of Global Forces', Women's Environment and Development Organisation (March 2000). Available at: http://www.wedo.org (accessed 16 February 2017).

Edwards, P. (ed.), *Equiano's Travels* (Oxford: Heinemann, 1969 [1789]).

Fredman, S., *Discrimination Law* (Oxford: Oxford University Press, 2002).

Fried, M., *Guyana's Rice Farmers and the Myth of the Free Market* (Ottawa: Oxfam, 2001).

Girvan, N., *Aspects of the Political Economy of Race in the Caribbean and the Americas* (Jamaica: University of West Indies, 1981).

Green, D.G. (ed.), *Institutional Racism and the Police: Fact or Fiction* (London: CIVITAS, 2000).

Kwa, A., *Power Politics in the WTO* (Bangkok: Focus on the Global South, 2002).

Macpherson, William, *The Stephen Lawrence Inquiry* (London: Home Office, 1999).

McDonald Beckles, H., *Britain's Black Debt* (Kingston: University of West Indies Press, 2013).

Moore, M., *A World without Walls: Freedom, Development, Free Trade and Global Governance* (Cambridge: Cambridge University Press, 2003).

Myers, G., *Banana Wars the Price of Freedom* (London: Zed Books, 2004).

Nash, G., 'Foreword', in R. Dunn, *Sugar and Slaves: The Rise of the Planter Class in the English West Indies, 1624–1713* (Chapel Hill: University of North Carolina Press, 1972).

Petrova, D., 'Racial Discrimination and the Rights of Minority Cultures', in S. Fredman (ed.), *Discrimination and Human Rights: The Case of Racism* (Oxford: Oxford University Press, 2001).

Pogge, T., *World Poverty and Human Rights* (Cambridge: Polity Press, 2002).

Pojman, L.P. and R. Westmoreland (eds), *Equality: Selected Readings* (Oxford: Oxford University Press, 1997).

Richardson, J., 'No European Trojan Horse', *Jamaica Observer*, 14 December 2012.

Salih, S. (ed.), *The History of Mary Prince* (London: Penguin Books, 2000 [1831]).

Santos, B. dos N., R. Farias and R. Cuhna, 'Generalised System of Preferences in General Agreements on Tariffs and Trade/World Trade Organisation: History and Current Issues', *Journal of World Trade* 39(4) (2005): 637–670.

Singh, K., *Race and Class Struggles in a Colonial State Trinidad 1917–1945* (Jamaica: The University of the West Indies Press, 1994).

Thomas, H., *The Slave Trade: The History of the Atlantic Slave Trade 1440–1870* (London: Papermac, 1997).

Transitional Racial Justice Initiative, 'The Persistence of White Privilege and Institutional Racism in US Policy. A Report on Government Compliance with the International Convention on the Elimination of All Forms of Racial Discrimination' (California, 2001). Available at: www.raceforward.org>files>pdf (accessed 16 February 2017).

Tuitt, P., *Race, Law, Resistance* (London: Glass House Press, 2004).

Williams, E., *Capitalism and Slavery* (Chapel Hill: University of North Carolina Press, 1994).

5 The race directive – Recycling the legacy of institutional racism

Introduction

The thesis of this book is that institutional racism is rife in Europe. Major European countries such as France, Portugal, the Netherlands, Spain, German families[1] and Britain were heavily involved in the transatlantic slave trade and chattel slavery. It is argued that this history is the source of institutional racism. The European Union had an opportunity to deal with institutional racism (and therefore the consequences of the transatlantic slave trade and chattel slavery) with Council Directive 2000/43/EC (Race Directive). This was the first EU legislation dealing with race relations and service provision. However, what remains strange is that the Directive did not make explicit reference to and legislate for institutional racism, given that the European Commission was alive to its existence as a watershed moment in British race relations in 1999.[2] All 28 Member States have transposed the Race Directive into their domestic law and the European Union institutions have had the opportunity to deliberate on the Directive.[3] It is argued that due to weaknesses in this law there are difficult implementation and application considerations. This has an impact on Africans and Afro-Caribbeans who are descendants of the victims of the transatlantic slave trade and chattel slavery, in other words, those who are now victims of its legacy, institutional racism.

The problem also means that some of the Member States involved in the slave trade including Britain, France, Denmark and the Netherlands, Spain and Portugal are not made to be accountable for their responsibilities for institutional racism as a legacy of the slave trade and chattel slavery. It is argued here that the Race Directive could and should be amended so that it is able to deal with the anomalies and effects of institutional racism. Although it was not the purpose of the Race Directive to deal with past wrongs of transatlantic slavery, the fact that it is dealing with racial discrimination makes the link with the legacy of transatlantic slavery, that is the modern day form of racism – one of which is institutional racism. On 29 June 2000, the European Council of Ministers adopted Council Directive 2000/43/EC (Race Directive)[4] implementing the principle of equal treatment between persons irrespective of racial or ethnic origin.[5] The Race Directive may be understood as a mechanism for implementing international legal obligations.[6] The Directive lays down a common framework for combating racial or ethnic discrimination in the Member States of the European Union.[7] The object of this common framework is to enable Member States to deliver an anti-race discrimination regime by putting into effect the principle of 'equal treatment'[8] in their domestic laws, regulations and administrative provisions.[9] Individuals[10] who consider themselves wronged may rely on national provisions brought in to give effect to the Race Directive. In this way, the European Union's promise[11] to provide measures to combat racism in the EU can start to take shape. The existence of a Directive as an instrument to provide minimum protection for victims of racial discrimination is useful. The adoption of such a tool takes account of the divergent legal and cultural systems of different Member States when pursuing the principle of equal treatment. By its nature a Directive imposes obligations only on Member States[12] to achieve the end whilst leaving them choice as to form and method.[13] This choice of form and method enables account to be taken of the social and political differences of Member States.[14]

The older Member States had until 19 July 2003 to complete the processes necessary to ensure that the Directive would be complied with.[15] Whilst the newer Member States that joined in May 2004 had to implement the Race Directive immediately.[16] The Race Directive is one of the latest measures adopted by the Council of Ministers under powers aimed at combating racism in the EU. This Race Directive reflects the strategic thinking behind EU policy directed towards combating racist constraints on the free movement of persons within the European Community. The Race Directive represents a landmark in the evolution of EU policy on race discrimination, since it is the first time that a legal duty has been placed on Member States to provide a 'common minimum level of legal protection from discrimination in public and private sectors'[17] in the context of racism. Its objective is to provide a foundational, common framework for Member States to put into place anti-race discrimination measures by requiring the abolition of any laws, regulations or administrative provisions contrary to the principle of equal treatment[18] on the grounds of racial or ethnic origin. What the Directive does not do is to refer to the transatlantic slave trade and chattel slavery as having anything to do with race relations and the fact that black people suffer from its legacy in the form of institutional racism. The Race Directive can be seen as an equal opportunities measure that addresses two related problems – market and social integration. Market integration can be understood as requiring the dismantling of racially and ethnically determined barriers to the marketplace. The business case for removing these barriers concern questions about, 'effective service delivery, concerns with the public image of an organisation … and issues surrounding recruitment and retention'.[19] It is argued that the business case should also include the removal of racial barriers wrought by institutional racism. Social integration raises questions of equity that resonate beyond the market. The obligations imposed by the Race Directive concern both market and social integration. Successful implementation should mean that no person is prevented from pursuing economic and social opportunities on racial or ethnic grounds.

The scope of the Race Directive covers employment, vocational training, working conditions, membership of workers' or professional organisations, social protection, healthcare, social advantages, education and access to and the supply of goods and services available to the public, including public housing. The Directive requires that Member States remove racial and ethnic barriers in these areas in order to achieve the objectives of the EU Treaty such as a high level of employment, social protection, a better quality of life, and economic and social cohesion and inclusion. But it makes no reference to people of African descent who have suffered from the consequences of the slave trade and their exclusion in terms of a better quality of life.

During the Stephen Lawrence Inquiry[20] it was stated that institutions are an important medium through which racism has evolved. It is the 'canteen culture' of these organisations that has made institutional racism so difficult to eradicate. It is argued that this manifests itself in a number of ways including in the paucity of legislation to tackle it. In this respect, we may ask if the Race Directive is a missed opportunity to tackle the problem of institutional racism.

Historical background

Several Western European countries were involved in the transatlantic slave trade and chattel slavery. They created a racist ideology to support these exploitative systems and that racist ideology lives on unwittingly in institutional racism. European Union institutions such as the former European Monitoring Centre[21] state that racism is a multifaceted phenomenon.[22] According to the former Commission for Racial Equality (CRE)[23] in Britain, '"racism" is the belief that some "races" are superior to others – based on the false idea that different physical characteristics (such as skin colour or hair) or ethnic back ground (such as dress and culture) makes some people better than others'.[24] It takes many forms and may be expressed in a number of ways across the various Member States, but 'racism and xenophobia are universal. No country in the Union is immune.[25] It can be argued that this problem of perceived racial inferiority of black people is particularly acute in those Member States with a slave trading past.

Racism has an impact on equality: Fredman[26] contends that equality is a recent phenomenon that evolved with early capitalism in Britain in the sixteenth century and the development of the state with the shrinking of the role of the monarchy. Even then there were groups such as black people and other minority groups that were excluded from the benefits that accompanied this shift away from autocracy.[27] Well into the twentieth century black people and ethnic minorities continued to be discriminated against in employment, housing, 'social security and on the streets'.[28] Even after several pieces of legislation[29] deep seated racism continues in the twenty-first century, in particular institutional racism in the police force[30] and other organisations such as health, education and the criminal justice system.[31] Despite some changes, it is still the case that in Britain in unemployment,[32] educational retention,[33] inequality in health patterns,[34] incarceration in prison[35] and a reduced representation in political life have a detrimental impact on people of African descent more than a lot of other groups.[36]

EU-wide studies carried out by scholars such as Ford[37] show that hatred of foreigners has led to murderous killings of members of the Turkish, Roma and Iranian communities in Germany,[38] assassinations, and the physical and mental handicapping of North Africans and Romanians in France.[39] Similarities can be drawn in Britain, for example, with the racist killing of Stephen Lawrence.[40] There is general intimidation and harassment of foreigners and suggestion by some Eurobarometer opinion polls that approximately 25 per cent of European people are ambivalent towards minorities.[41]

Numerous campaigns from non-governmental entities show that many ordinary people believe that racism is unacceptable and do not subscribe to it. Nevertheless, the existence of an unacceptable level of tolerance of racism and the failure of Member States to adequately deal with it has prompted the European Union to legislate on a community-wide level for its eradication. It is important to point out that the public discourse on racism tends to focus on individual or group behaviour. One exception is the Stephen Lawrence Inquiry in Britain which highlighted racism in the form of institutional racial discrimination. The failure of the EU to respond to this forms the basis of discussion in this chapter. Generally speaking, the EU has had a relatively poor record in tackling racist/ethnic discrimination. Of particular relevance here, is the failure to deal with the racist forced migration of up to 15 million Africans[42] by some European countries leaving the resulting issues to be dealt with by individual Member States.[43] Several reports demonstrate the futility of this individualistic approach[44] because there was no comprehensive prohibition covering areas where racial/ethnic discrimination tended to occur in the civil, political, economic, social and cultural spheres.[45] Moreover, many of the legal instruments that exist at Member State level are rarely used.[46] Given the racism proceeding from the transatlantic slave trade, chattel slavery and their consequences, as well as the Holocaust that preceded the birth of the European Union, the legal response in this area seems highly inadequate. It has been argued that racism and intolerance have a detrimental effect on third-country nationals[47] and national ethnic minorities.[48] The failure to abolish racist barriers strikes at the very heart of the European idea in two fundamental respects. On a narrow internal market basis (the business case),[49] upwards of 13 million third-country nationals (that is people born outside the EU) are more or less discounted by EU law where questions of effectiveness of service delivery, markets and competition for the recruitment and retention of people is concerned. At the level of concerns over fairness and equity (the altruism model)[50] this necessitates that racial and ethnic groups are represented throughout EU countries, so that the creation of 'harmonious societies characterised by ethnic and cultural diversity … [as] a positive and enriching factor'[51] can be achieved.

In the light of these difficulties, the Khan Commission,[52] a body set up by the European Council and peopled by representatives of the Member States, recommended using EU law. This law would enshrine the principle that, 'all individuals, regardless of their colour, race, nationality, ethnic or national origin, or religion, should have the right of equal access to employment, equal pay and fair treatment'.[53] The Khan Commission emphasised that the right to equal treatment should apply whether or not a person was a Community citizen.[54] It is argued that within a human rights framework this is justified. Additionally, the 1996 European Parliament asked the Commission[55] to address the question of how the principle of equal treatment might be obtained beyond areas pertaining to the labour market.[56] This reflected an understanding that racist barriers might have a bearing on interstate (between Member States) and intrastate (within Member States) movement for 'racial' and 'ethnic' minorities. This understanding is important if the appropriate legislative tools are to be formulated in order to strike at the heart of racist practices and, where necessary, at the individuals who operate them.

Examples can be found in Austria and Germany where distinctions drawn between EU nationals and non-EU nationals (including third-country nationals who have permanent residence) are not seen as racially discriminatory. In Greece, public sector employment is not open to non-EU nationals and in Portugal a company with more than five employees can only employ foreign nationals as long as 90 per cent of the workforce remains Portuguese.[57] Yet the continuance of this demarcation does not make any sense unless it is understood as institutionalised racist barriers.

Although proposals to amend the EU Treaty had been advocated since the 1980s,[58] it was only in 1997 that the European Council meeting in Amsterdam accepted the principle that the EU should combat racism. Yet in this European policy it was not thought prudent to link slavery to racism and to institutional racism. Instead tackling racism was pursued by the implementation of Article 13.[59] This article empowers[60] the Council, acting unanimously on a proposal from the Commission,[61] to take appropriate action to combat discrimination on racial or ethnic grounds.[62] Article 13 is now Article 19 which reads

> Without prejudice to the other provisions of the Treaties and within the limits of the powers conferred by them upon the Union, the Council, acting unanimously in accordance with a special legislative procedure and after obtaining the consent of the European Parliament, may take appropriate action to combat discrimination based on sex, racial or ethnic origin, religion or belief, disability, age or sexual orientation.[63]

The addition of the words 'in accordance with a special legislative procedure' is unclear but it is hoped that this is not a way of slowing down the use of article 19 to combat discrimination based on racial or ethnic origin.

Article 19 is the main provision dealing with Union competence in tackling unlawful racial and ethnic discrimination and equal opportunities in employment and other fields. Its existence is motivated by the belief that equal opportunities in the labour market are, to some extent, contingent on equality of access to spheres that are necessary such as housing and health. Inequality in these spheres compound labour market discrimination.[64]

As well as having the power to develop measures to combat racism the EU monitoring of racism and xenophobia has become an important factor. The former European Monitoring Centre on Racism and Xenophobia (EUMC)[65] was set up with the express aim of providing the Community and its Member States with data at European level on racism, xenophobia and anti-Semitism, in order to help them in formulating policy in this area.[66]

> The mandate of the EUMC was to study the extent and development of the phenomena and manifestations of racism, xenophobia and anti-Semitism, analyse their causes, consequences and effects and examine examples of good practice. To these ends, it will collect record and analyse information communicated to it by research centres, Member States, Community institutions, non-governmental organisations and international organisations. It will also set up and coordinate a European Racism and Xenophobia Information Network (known as 'RAXEN').[67]

Amongst other achievements, the EUMC produced a report on housing and discrimination in 15 Member States. Here they found that in the area of housing the role of discrimination is not adequately researched or addressed.[68] However, the research found that whilst some Member States had addressed specific issues and had put measures in place to deal with discrimination, others had not done so and were actively hostile to the notion that migrants and minorities needed protection from discrimination in the housing field.[69] What was not clear in the report was the extent to which race or ethnic origin had to do with discrimination. that was problematic because Member States collection of such statistics were inadequate – 'many Member States lack an institutionalised framework for monitoring ethnic or national origin and measuring housing performance, and thus do not have the evidence base necessary for informed policy-making'.[70] In their annual report of 2006 the EUMC produced evidence that discrimination is experienced in housing, education and employment by migrants and ethnic minorities in the EU.[71] It is a missed opportunity that they did not link some of this to the consequence spawned by the transatlantic slave trade and chattel slavery in former slave trading states.

The EUMC[72] was succeeded by the Fundamental Rights Agency (FRA)[73] which also has the mandate to cover racism and xenophobia and related intolerance but these are to be perceived in the broader context of fundamental rights across the EU, rather than specifically racism, racial discrimination and related intolerance. So the FRA covers many other rights-related issues including disability, gender and minority rights but continues to provide information on racism and related intolerance for the EU policy makers. The FRA provided research on *Racism, Football and the Internet* and found that there were hundreds of sites dedicated to racism in football.[74] One in particular, the Pro Patria group, has an area on its website that contains downloadable songs that refer to monkey chants like 'there are no Italian niggers'[75] and 'the monkey imitation racist supporters make when a black player touches the ball'.[76] This kind of behaviour should be acted on by the Race Directive rather than left to voluntary arrangements. This conduct should also be dealt with by UEFA and national football organisations.[77]

The FRA forms the context within which the Race Directive now works.[78] It was not until 6 June 2000 that agreement was reached on a package of anti-discrimination measures put forward by the European Commission, which included the Race Directive.[79] The Race Directive was adopted by the Council of Ministers (Council)[80] on 29 June 2000. It is a European Union (EU) Community-wide instrument that came into effect[81] on 19 July 2003 in Member States,[82] and immediately in newer Member States. Given the concern over racism within Member States it is important to consider how effective the Race Directive is as an instrument both in terms of how it is to be interpreted and its implementation particularly with respect to people of African descent.

Key features

The object of the Race Directive is to lay down a common framework for combating racial or ethnic discrimination in Member States of the EU in order to enforce the application of the principle of equal treatment. Member States are under a duty to implement measures at the domestic level to ensure compliance and must report to the Commission on their work in this regard.[83] They must designate a body or bodies charged with the promotion of equal treatment on the grounds of racial or ethnic origin and imbued with the legal competence to provide assistance for victims. These bodies must also have competence to conduct surveys and publish independent reports.[84] Sanctions for non-compliance with the objective of the Race Directive must be developed that are *effective, proportionate and dissuasive*.[85] Provisions designed to deal with these matters must be notified to the Commission.[86] Whilst there are several areas aimed at the level of Member State obligation, our concern is with how the Race Directive help victims of racial discrimination.[87] There are a number of articles in the Directive that purport to lay down a level playing field for *those who consider themselves wronged by failure to apply the principle of equal treatment*[88] on the grounds of racial or ethnic discrimination. These include the right not to be discriminated against either directly or indirectly[89] and protection from harassment[90] and victimisation.[91] These rights apply in the private and public sectors[92] and cover a number of areas such as employment, training, and membership of organisations, social protection, security and healthcare.[93] Some important aspects involve the establishment of an independent body to provide individual assistance to victims,[94] a shift in the burden of proof to the respondent once a prima facie case of racial or ethnic discrimination has been made out[95] and a duty to disseminate information to inform people of the existence of these provisions.[96] A Directive is seen as the most feasible instrument to deal with a minimum level of protection from racial or ethnic discrimination in Member States.

A Directive[97] as an instrument to provide minimum protection to victims of racial discrimination is useful. It can take account of the divergent legal[98] and cultural systems of Member States when measuring compliance with the obligation to implement the principle of equal treatment because it is binding *as to the results to be achieved*, leaving the *form or method* of attaining the objective to Member States. A directive differs from other Union instruments such as regulations[99] and decisions[100] that are *binding in their entirety* and their implementation might require complete uniformity. Reliance on the latter might prove problematic when pursuing complex EU social policy such as the integration of people in the single market, in countries with divergent legal and historic systems. From a political point of view, a Directive is likely to be the most palatable instrument in seeking to achieve the consensus of 28 Member States. The Race Directive requires a minimum standard of compliance across all Member States.[101] It is aimed at the protection of victims of racial and ethnic discrimination by placing upon states a duty to provide national measures to give effect to this instrument. Where a Member State fails to implement a directive, individuals may rely on it directly. In other words, the individual does not have to wait for the state to implement the Race Directive before they can bring a discrimination claim. They can rely on the provisions of the Directive if they are sufficiently clear.[102] This opens the door to *horizontal direct effect*[103] as well as *vertical direct effect*[104] claims. An individual may also bring an action in damages against the state if there is a causal link between the state's failure to implement a Directive and the loss suffered.[105]

The idea behind the Race Directive is to prevent the use of characteristics such as racial or ethnic origin, as a ground for discrimination in the single European market. It could be argued then that the Directive is a potentially powerful instrument in challenging both intentional discrimination and prejudice and the social construction and ideological justification of racism[106] when manifested in the form of racial discrimination in the Union market place. This may be dealt with at an individual, group or institutional level. Thus the Directive appears to place an obligation on Member States to perform a 'policing' function in terms of controlling discrimination[107] and it can be seen as an agent of social change, in the sense that it also prohibits discrimination[108] against groups and so has the potential to deal with the results of past discriminatory practices and/or a 'concern for distributive justice'.[109] This ability to deal with past practices is why the Directive could have a role to play in dealing with institutional racism that is built on historical practices that are sourced in the transatlantic slave trade and chattel slavery.

Textual ambiguity

The problem with the Race Directive is that it presents textual ambiguity. This is particularly the case with the concepts of equal treatment, race, ethnicity, third-country nationals and institutional racism.

Equal treatment

Let us consider the concept of equal treatment as laid down in the Race Directive. Article 1 of the instrument states that: 'the purpose of this Directive is to lay down a framework for combating discrimination on the grounds of racial or ethnic origin, with a view to putting into effect in the Member States the principle of equal treatment'.[110] The use of a Directive as an instrument to provide minimum protection for potential victims of racial or ethnic discrimination is useful. The adoption of such a tool has the potential to take account of the divergent legal and cultural differences that reside within Member States when pursuing the principle of equal treatment. However the definition of equal treatment in the Directive is tied to discrimination and not to racial harm, particularly of the institutional kind, more generally. Equal treatment means that there shall be no direct or indirect discrimination based on racial or ethnic origin.[111] Direct discrimination means 'less favourable treatment', whilst indirect discrimination

> shall be taken to occur where an apparently neutral provision, criterion or practice would put persons of a racial or ethnic origin at a particular disadvantage compared with other persons, unless that provision, criterion or practice is objectively justified

by a legitimate aim and the means of achieving that aim are appropriate and necessary.[112]

The problem with the notion of equal treatment, however, is that it can mean different things in divergent jurisdictions As a form of equality its 'meaning shifts'[113] on closer examination although it may be argued that we have an intuitive grasp of what it means.[114] Conceptually the notion of equality can be said to mean several things.

In the UK jurisdiction there has been case law on the concept of equal treatment. Connolly[115] argues that the term involves less favourable treatment. In *De Souza v Automobile Association*[116] when a member of staff overheard her manager say that some typing should be given to 'the wog', the courts decided that this was not an incidence of being *treated* less favourably but one of being *considered* less favourably. It is not that racial insults would not amount to less favourable treatment, argues Connolly, but the threshold for the consideration of treatment needs to be higher. It is argued that this is precisely the arena where racism is manifest. This is where the ideological notions of racism persist based on the concept of inferiority and superiority. This concept is one that can be traced back to the transatlantic slave trade and chattel slavery.

Moreover, the term 'less favourable treatment' begs the question what is meant by 'less favourable' treatment. There have been cases on this issue, in *Chief Constable of West Yorkshire v Khan*[117] an employer's refusal to give a former employee a reference was seen as less favourable treatment on racial grounds. In *Macdonald v Advocate General for Scotland*[118] male and female homosexuals were treated badly by the Royal Air Force. However, since they were treated equally badly there was no less favourable treatment. This means that bad treatment, if it is equal, will not qualify as less favourable treatment.

In two cases this issue of what constitutes less favourable treatment has been demonstrated. In *Burton and Rhule v De Vere Hotels*[119] two black waitresses were harassed by a party of men who were being entertained by a comedian well known for racist and sexist jokes. The manager did nothing to protect the women and it was held in that case that the hotel was legally responsible for the harm caused to the women. However in *Pearce v Governing Body of Mayfield Secondary School*[120] a lesbian schoolteacher complained that the harassment she had been put through had not been dealt with by the school governors. In the House of Lords the court disapproved of *Burton Rhule*. The House of Lords[121] was of the opinion that employers should not be held liable for acts of a third party and there was no act of unlawful discrimination on the part of the employer. It is quite clear that bad treatment if experienced by all respondents does not amount to discrimination and therefore is not a failure of equal treatment. In terms of Africans and Afro-Caribbeans there needs to be a wider notion of equal treatment to take into account the very particular history of institutional racism that has impacted on their lives. This is a plea for positive discrimination in legislation to deal with the oppression suffered by this group rather than the narrow interpretation of the concept of equal treatment used, that holds that if white and black people are treated equally badly then there is lawful equal treatment. Such a construction fails to take into account their differing histories and the role institutional racism plays in the lives of black people.

'Race'

Regarding the question of 'race', the premise in the Directive is one that rejects theories of separate human races.[122] No doubt this is put in place to counter any suspicion that nineteenth-century scientific racism and its re-emergence in mainstream politics and Far Right discourse is accepted by the EU. Such racism is based on hatred of the 'Other'[123] and a belief in the superiority of one racial group over another, drawing on somatic features such as skin colour, skull size and hair texture-linked to mental characteristics.[124] However, the use of language such as 'racial origin', 'related to racial origin' and 'linked to racial origin', in Article 1 and 2 is ambiguous. In transposing the Directive who is the Member State to target? Should they put in place provisions to protect 'racial' groups or prohibit perceptions that there are separate 'racial' groups? It may be argued that the provisions must be transposed in such a way that they address perception of, as well as the existence of, separate 'racial' groups. This is not helped by the fact that the Commission states that Member States do not have to define race in their national law.[125] Moreover, it could be contended that the acceptance of a difference in treatment based on a characteristic related to 'racial origin' contained in the provision covering genuine occupational qualifications, supports the argument that the EU impliedly accepts the notion of separate 'racial' groups. This may be further reinforced by the concept of positive action in Article 5.[126] This provision does not prevent Member States from using' … specific measures to prevent or compensate for disadvantage linked to racial … origin'.[127] The obscurity may compound difficulties in the transposition of the Race Directive into the legal system of Member States that is likely to have negative consequences for victims of racial discrimination because a number of Member States do not use the concept of race in their national legislation.[128] Here there would clearly be a failure to provide a service based on race and this constitutes institutional racism. This could occur in former slave trading and colonial nations such as Portugal who do not believe there is a 'race' problem. They have been involved with black people since the fifteenth century but refuse the term 'black-Portuguese'. Rather they use terms such as 'immigrants' or 'new Portuguese'.[129]

Problems regarding racism that have surfaced in Northern Ireland, Germany and Greece serve as timely reminders of these difficulties. A series of reports on Northern Ireland consider that characteristically the principal trigger for racially discriminatory behaviour is 'skin colour racism'.[130] That is the use of the colour of a person's skin as grounds for discriminatory and offensive behaviour. In Northern Ireland discriminators do not generally know the ethnic or national background of victims. The tendency is to discriminate on the basis of 'visible' characteristics. Similar problems have arisen with people in Austria (whether or not they are native born).[131] These problems suggest that the failure to define 'race' to include discrimination on the basis of skin colour will present a problem for those seeking to rely on the transposition arrangements to protect them from racial discrimination.

'Rasse' the German word for 'race' tends to be perceived of as a quintessential category in Germany. Discourse on racism in Germany manifests itself in the stigma attached to Colonialism and the Holocaust and thus is rarely discussed outside those terms. This makes it difficult to consider contemporary forms of racism and how that might impact on integration.[132] By contrast, it is suggested that in Greece, where the Christian Orthodox Church considers all children derive from 'Adam and Eve' and that to talk of racial ideas is heresy, a very low profile may be given to the question of 'race'. This poses difficulties since there is little in the public sphere to challenge the widely held notion that integration of 'races' may lead to degeneration.[133]

This problem indicates that if the question of 'race' is not part of public discourse because it does not 'exist' on that level in Member States, it will not be taken seriously.

Yet it was precisely the use of race to denigrate black people during slavery that has led to institutional racism today. Moreover, a failure to define race in the Race Directive compounds this problem since Member States will not have a duty to acknowledge something that they can deny exists at the conceptual level. Further, victims will not have an instrument they can point to that is clear and precise in defining discrimination on the basis of racial origin, causing complaints to be harder to make and raising the issue of an effective remedy.

This ambiguity in the Race Directive is likely to have an impact across a range of public services that are covered by its scope, such as housing, education and health, since it fails to challenge racial discrimination along 'skin colour' lines for instance. This failure points to the problem identified as institutional racism. Institutional racism is the failure to provide a service to people because of, for instance, the colour of their skin. This failure is not one based on conscious racism; rather it arises from unconscious and unwitting racism that results in racial discrimination. It is suggested that in this respect at least the EU has failed to provide an adequate service to people subject to racial discrimination in the internal market. The Race Directive would have been a more comprehensive instrument and useful weapon in combating race discrimination had it incorporated a concept of race that was derived from the effects of the slave trade and has become an integral part of the ideology of institutions.

'Ethnicity'

The Race Directive prohibits both direct and indirect discrimination on the basis of 'ethnic' origin.[134] This prohibition includes harassment and an instruction to discriminate.[135] The converse is true where the question of genuine occupational qualification or positive action is the object of the discriminating factor. Here the Directive does not prohibit provisions that seek to provide for a difference of treatment 'related to ethnic origin'.[136] However, it does not provide a definition of 'ethnic' origin. This omission is likely to raise issues regarding the question of what is an 'ethnic' group. Further, this may have implications for monitoring the effectiveness of the transposition arrangements for those subject to this form of discrimination.

A recent report from the EU Commission tells us that there is still scarcity of data collection on the part of Member States which makes for difficulty in targeting legislation based on the Directive.[137] It has been argued that the paucity of the collection of data in this area is to do with data protection laws but the Commission suggests that there are safeguards set out that would mean Member States would not breach data protection laws by collection information on ethnicity.[138] It is suggested that this problem with the collection of data on ethnicity is also an instance of institutional racism because it constitutes a failure to provide a service based on ethnicity.

In British case law the question of whether or not a person is a member of an ethnic group is problematic.[139] In *Mandla (Sewa Singh) v Dowell Lee and Others*[140] the House of Lords has held that for the purposes of the Race Relations Act 1976 (RRA), an ethnic group is one defined by reference to a long shared history and a cultural tradition of its own.[141] This definition has been criticised as being overly restrictive since certain groups are unable to take advantage of it in order to seek legal redress under the Act in cases of discrimination. Thus in *Cooper v British Rail*,[142] *CRE v Precision Manufacturing Services Ltd*[143] and *Dawkins v Department of the Environment*[144] the courts have consistently decided that certain groups such as Muslims and Rastafarians[145] are not ethnic groups. By contrast, groups such as Jews[146] and gypsies[147] have been afforded the benefit of the *Mandla* definition enabling them to seek legal redress under the RRA. Given the racism that Rastafarians and Muslims face, commentators have argued that it is illogical not to extend anti-racist legislation to them.[148] The Race Directive might have resolved this anomaly had a comprehensive definition of ethnicity been provided, one that took account of the slave trade and its consequences. It would also have provided another avenue for black people as descendants of slave trading to seek legal redress.

Although the Framework Directive[149] now covers religion and belief its scope only applies to employment and occupation. Under UK law religion and belief is now covered by section 10 of the Equality Act 2010 when dealing with goods and services and not just employment and occupation which is the focus of the Framework Directive.

In a number of Member States, ethnic minorities are often discriminated against in the internal market for jobs, good and services. African ethnic minorities are particularly vulnerable because they are subject to 'latent racism'. That is embedded, racial stereotypes, racist assumptions and racial profiling.[150] However, an evaluation of the legal jurisprudence related to this suggests a lacuna.[151] Discrimination is not dealt with by reference to 'ethnicity' rather issues are framed in terms of 'working' and 'living' conditions. This means that who is within and who without these parameters, in terms of ethnic groups, is difficult to decipher. Without a working definition of what an ethnic group might be, it is difficult to assess to what extent the transposition arrangements will effectively deal with discrimination against ethnic groups. By way of contrast, Austrian legal jurisprudence is familiar with the term 'ethnic origin'. This is dealt with through the Austrian Constitution's equality clause and takes its language from the International Convention on the Elimination of all Forms of Racial Discrimination (ICERD): 'any distinction, exclusion, restriction or preference based on ... ethnic origin ... '.[152] However, there is no definition of what is meant by ethnic origin. This means that the potential exists for certain groups to be excluded and thus not afforded protection from racial or ethnic discrimination. An added complication in the Austrian context is the existence of 'special measures' for protected national minorities. Some groups of national minorities in Austria are so defined under the *Volksgruppengesetz* (National Minorities Act). This defines 'a national minority as one that comprises groups of Austrian citizens with a non-German mother tongue and a common autonomous cultural heritage who have their residence and home in a part of the Austrian Federal territory'.[153] Whilst anyone can affiliate to an ethnic group,[154] given the prevalence of skin colour racism in Austria[155] it seems highly unlikely that Austrian born people of African descent could do so in the context of how national minorities are defined. The Race Directive might have been better served in terms of its desire to protect people from ethnic discrimination had it provided a way of dealing with the issues raised here, with particular reference to the continued victimisation of people of African descent.

Recent events in relation to 'September 11' have brought to the fore the question of 'cultural racism'.[156] It has been argued that racism cannot be understood as based only on colour[157] nor can the racism experienced by Muslims be side-stepped by construing the victimisation process as one based on religion or indeed ethnicity.[158] There are developing sets of 'cultural racisms' that use cultural difference to denigrate or 'demand cultural assimilation from groups who also suffer colour racism'.[159] The Directive fails to provide a mechanism whereby this problem is both understood and dealt with in terms of national anti-race discrimination legislation.

It is argued that the issues raised in this section demonstrate the 'fractured' approach to the prohibition of racial or ethnic discrimination at national level, using the Race Directive as a device to combat racism. Whilst well-meaning, such a strategy indicates that the Directive reflects a failure to provide a service to a significant proportion of people of the EU who are black. This failure indicates the process of institutional racism because this blinkered approach tends to impact on people on the basis of ethnicity. A far more comprehensive approach to the breadth of the problem is to be welcomed. It is argued here that such an approach should also take into account the transatlantic slave trade and chattel slavery that has caused institutional racism.

Third-country nationals

The Race Directive expressly excludes a

> difference of treatment based on nationality and is without prejudice to provisions and conditions relating to the entry into and residence of third-country nationals and stateless persons on the territory of Member States, and to any treatment which arises from the legal status of the third-country nationals and stateless persons concerned.[160]

Third-country nationals[161] have been the victims of institutional racism in a number of Member States of the EU.[162] This phenomena is understood as

> the collective failure of an organisation to provide an appropriate and professional service to people because of their colour, culture, or ethnic origin ... it can be seen or detected in processes, attitudes and behaviour which amount to discrimination through unwitting prejudice, ignorance, thoughtlessness and racist stereotyping which disadvantage minority ethnic people.[163]

This chapter argues that this legislation does not go far enough in meeting the European unions' concern to combat racism in the market and related areas. Rather the measure tends to perpetuate double standards in relation to third-country nationals. This may be a travesty if a more purposive interpretation of the directive is not developed in the transposition and/or application of this essential measure.

Third-country nationals as victims of institutional racism

The term 'third country national' is used in a variety of ways at national level depending on the particular circumstances. Thus 'alien',[164] 'Other'[165] and 'undesirable immigrants'[166] are words used to describe those people who are subject to a process proliferated by Member States in their dealings with third-country nationals that tends to produce varieties of economic and political exclusion and poor social integration.[167] This works against Community policy geared towards the racial desegregation of markets in labour, services and goods. Within this process institutional racism tends to be perpetuated. The plight of third-country nationals has been the subject matter of much scholarly work[168] however there has been insufficient analysis of the impact of institutional racism in this area.

It has been argued that this form of racism can be seen or detected in processes.[169] It is also argued that institutional racism can be seen in attitudes and behaviour which amount to discrimination.[170] These attitudes and type of behaviour impinge on third-country nationals and have implications for the operation of the Race Directive. It is contended that the Race Directive would have to be amended to take account of the racial discrimination that third-country nationals face because at present they are excluded from its remit. It would take a proposal from the European Commission that is accepted by the European Parliament stating that third-country nationals should be covered by the Race Directive. For people of

African descent it could be argued that this amendment would be based on a reparations policy, a policy that gives treatment to those that are the victims of institutional racism today.

Institutional racism as detected in process

The allocation of public services in Member States such as housing, education and health are areas of concern to the EU in relation to its commitment to equality in the field of race relations. This is indicated by the preamble to the Race Directive that states the need for '... specific action in the field of ... areas such as education ... and access to the supply of goods and services'.[171] To this end Article 3 of the Directive provides that the concept of discrimination[172] 'shall apply to ... public bodies ... '[173] in relation to education[174] and 'access to and supply of goods and services which are available to the public, including housing'.[175] The EU appears to have taken account of international human rights obligations[176] in relation to these areas recognising that equality before the law cannot come about if areas where racial discrimination is manifest, but are beyond traditional notions of the discrimination in the employment market, are not simultaneously addressed.[177] This is an area of great concern especially given the presence of racism and prejudices in public institutions that the European Commission against Racism and Intolerance (ECRI) has deplored and has expressed regret that not enough energy has been invested in combating this area of racism.[178] Although there is nothing explicit in the Race Directive in regard to dealing with institutional racism, it is argued that the focus on public institutions is an important step in developing mechanisms to tackle this phenomenon.[179] This is because institutional racism may be endemic in an organisation in terms of its policies and practices, and, more critically, appear as a 'normal' part of institutional culture. This type of racism cannot be adequately handled by focusing on individual fault primarily because it takes little account of the fact that individuals are 'clothed with the attributes of the dominant culture ...'.[180] This means that individual discriminatory behaviour may be a manifestation of discriminatory processes at work in institutions.[181] A form of racism that Africans and Afro-Caribbeans have been subject to as a result of slavery.

Access to public housing for third-country nationals may be an area where institutional racism can be detected in the processes. For instance, the process of public housing allocation in some Member States may serve to keep people '... locked in dilapidated slum [housing]',[182] and subject to the dangers that arise from being placed in residential areas where third-country nationals may fall prey to racist attacks and general hostility.[183] This may be due to a policy that specifically allocates housing for vulnerable groups or it may arise from a lack of awareness of the impact on third-country nationals of placing them in particular areas. This type of process has been termed 'unwitting' racism[184] because there is little evidence to suggest that conscious racism is at play, rather, it can be argued that this type or racism operates in 'respected and established forces in the society, and thus receives far less ...'.[185] attention. Disproportionately high numbers of immigrants and people of immigrant origin live in disadvantaged areas and in inadequate private and public accommodation. Although this is partially due to a lack of resources, which are often more modest among this category of persons, racial discrimination also contributes to this situation.

In France, the ECRI has urged the French authorities to strengthen their efforts to combat discrimination in this field. Furthermore, although ECRI realises that housing policies are primarily designed to help those who are economically disadvantaged, it suggests that the needs of immigrants could be better met by making provision for the additional obstacles they encounter.[186] Whilst in Denmark it is reported that the dispersal system where third-country nationals are sent to live in various areas on the basis of a quota system is problematic. Penalties are imposed if the person dispersed moves from the area for which they are designated, further, they are expected to 'become Danish' without any acknowledgement by state municipalities of the need to be housed in areas where they would obtain strength from being able to identify with cultural, linguistic and religious communities similar to their own.[187] Similar articles describe the German situation where cases of discrimination are not taken seriously – which may account for the dearth of reported cases in this area and where those who do complain are seen as either 'hypersensitive' or 'psychotic'.[188] In the UK, housing patterns show that third-country nationals tend to live in the most deprived areas compared to their 'white' counterparts with 'the mixed and black ethnic groups having worse labour market outcomes whether they live in better-off or deprived neighbourhoods'.[189]

More recently, access to *decent* housing has been an issue of concern for the global community.[190] In international human rights terms poor access to this resource raises questions of state commitment to non-discrimination and equality in housing provision,[191] which is of particular importance given state commitment to international human rights legal instruments such as Article 25 of the Universal Declaration of Human Rights[192] and Article 11(1) of the International Covenant on Economic, Social and Cultural Rights.[193] In the context of the Race Directive the focus on areas such as housing that go beyond discrimination in the employment market demonstrates that the EU takes human rights obligations seriously and is committed to ensuring Member States meet their international legal obligations, but the failure to deal with third-country nationals is a travesty.

Some of these third-country nationals, specifically Africans and Afro-Caribbeans, are the people who have suffered as a result of the consequences of the transatlantic slave trade and chattel slavery. They suffer skin colour racism – a trait that marked out the chattel slave trade as unique in the histories of slave trade regimes.[194] Third-country nationals of this kind find access to public and private services just as difficult as their national black minorities. There is no difference in the institutionalised problems wrought on them as people of African descent. Their forebears were victims of the transatlantic slave trade and chattel slavery. Africans and Afro-Caribbeans were chattel, a notion underpinned by a racialised regime reinforced by 'code noir'.[195] The fact is that the EU institutions that brought into effect the Race Directive missed the opportunity to address this problem. They could have made a distinction in the status of black people who share similar slave histories, and who continue to suffer the effects of this history in terms of institutional racism.

The Race Directive could and should ensure that institutions examine their internal processes and cultural practices with a view to eradicating this form of racism. However, the provision as it stands presents difficulties for third-country nationals to challenge institutional racism. If one considers the concept of discrimination as defined in Article 2(2) of the Race Directive, the measure states that:

> Direct discrimination shall be taken to occur where one person is treated less favourably than another is, has been or would be treated in a comparable situation on grounds of racial or ethnic origin.[196]

It is not improbable that public institutions will have to take account of institutionally racist processes in relation to matters such as access to housing and education. Indeed, Article 3(1) makes particular reference to the public sector and public bodies as coming within the area of the Directive.[197]

Furthermore, the instrument covers indirect discrimination '... where an apparently neutral provision, criterion or practice would put persons of a racial or ethnic origin at a particular disadvantage, compared with other persons ...'[198] and harassment which is stated to relate to '... any unwanted conduct related to racial or ethnic origin ... with the purpose or effect of violating the dignity of a person and of creating an intimidating, hostile, degrading, humiliating or offensive environment'.[199] The same argument would apply to public institutions in relation to this form of discrimination. What is problematic is the fact that unless a third-country national could show that the institutional process was racially discriminatory (and not based on nationality) they would not be able to rely on the provision.

Article 3(2) of the Race Directive states that 'the Directive does not cover differences of treatment based on nationality ...'.[200] As scholars have pointed out this is likely to be a troublesome area because it is difficult to determine whether discrimination occurred on the basis of nationality or race or indeed ethnicity.[201] Since the three are often intertwined some Member States have encompassed discrimination on the grounds of nationality as a ground of racial discrimination.[202] It is argued that such inclusive analysis might avoid the kind of problems that have plagued the American courts where the question of motivation is difficult to prove.[203] Taking the Dutch example, it would be hard for an African[204] subject to the dispersal system for residential purposes to establish (even as a prima facie case)[205] that they have been treated less favourably on the grounds of racial discrimination by the Dutch municipality in comparison with other persons. This is likely to be because the process of dispersal is geared to third-country nationals who have narrowly defined rights of residence. It is not explicitly based on race but has a disproportionate impact on third-country nationals who are not Danish. Furthermore, since the Race Directive does not rely on motivation but can determine racial discrimination on the basis of indirect discrimination, not to include third-country nationals is a missed opportunity to hold institutions to account.

Institutional racism as detected in attitude and behaviour

One particular intellectual discourse on institutional racism has raised the issue of institutional attitude or behaviour towards ethnic minorities.[206] Such behaviour is replicated in institutional dealings with third-country nationals more generally,[207] reflecting a disturbing pattern of 'deep-seated discriminatory structures'[208] that domestic legislation has, hitherto, found hard to address.[209] The type of attitude or behaviour may be discernible in the manner, for instance, in which police forces in many Member States 'handle' certain categories of persons perceived by the institutional culture as lacking the credentials that would entitle them to fair and just treatment.[210] Employing institutions may unwittingly adopt an employment culture that favours 'home' nationals compared to those from third countries. For example, the presumption that third-country nationals do not want to work for organisations, or that they are an unknown quantity and thus a potential economic risk, that their loyalties might not lie with the organisation or that employing them may lead to a cultural clash within the organisation may result in them not being employed. None of this conjecture is borne out with hard fact, rather it would seem to be the result of institutional habit. These sorts of opinions seem to be based on historical notions of 'outsiders' as being inferior to the dominant group. This is particularly so for descendants of the transatlantic slave trade and chattel slavery. Such a sense of group position '... guides, incites and coerces ... '[211] individual behaviour. Yet, recent reports show that this institutional attitude defies logic. In labour market terms there is often a shortage of people with the skills that third-country nationals may possess. The problem is national control over the immigration of third-country nationals both in terms of who is let in and who is kept out of 'fortress Europe'.[212]

Institutional attitudes are also reinforced by 'blindness' to structural and historical inequalities, the creation of which they may have been involved in. When patterns of inequality are detected where there are disproportionate numbers of third-country nationals occupying the lowest rungs in terms of employment, and poor access to education and health services, it is often the individual that is blamed.[213] However, it can be argued that 'blaming the victim'[214] loses sight of some of the institutional attitudes that are really the source of the problem. Moreover, it is difficult to make complaints that will be taken seriously if the pathogen is perceived by institutions at the level of the individual psyche.[215] A relevant example can be seen in the case of *Hakunila*[216] where the defendant (a Somalian) fleeing an attack by several Finnish youths wielding baseball bats, was forced to reverse his car, injuring one of them. The perpetrators had attacked the windscreen of the car with an axe and had also completely smashed the side windows. The defendant unsuccessfully pleaded that his conduct was caused by a 'forced situation, in which he was in panic because of the threatening attack, and was therefore unable to do anything, but to escape from the scene by all means necessary'.[217] He was found guilty of attempted assault, sentenced to a term of imprisonment of four years and required to pay an indemnity.[218] Equally critical of *Hakunila*'s response to the situation he faced were the Local Court of Vantaa and the Court of Appeal of Helsinki.

The local court focused on what it saw as lack of pity and deliberate and cruel motive on the part of the defendant, whilst the Court of Appeal thought there were no circumstances that warranted the defendant's behaviour.[219] The decision raised public disquiet because of the judiciary's apparent failure to recognise the general racist and xenophobic context as well as the particular circumstances within which Hakunila reacted.[220] It is argued that where justice fails to pierce the veil of 'colour blindness'[221] it compounds the institutional attitude that determines matters according to the dominant cultural norm. This colour blindness now requires understanding in the context of xeno-racism, a 'natural fear' of 'strangers which goes beyond black skin colour because racism is ... meted out to impoverished strangers even if they are white'.[222] This '... new racism ... marries up the worst practices throughout the Western World'.[223] This is one way in which ... 'racism continue[s] to evolve ... post-equality ... legislation, across ... geographic, temporal and political distance'.[224]

The need for institutional activism

The extent to which the Race Directive will be able to tackle institutional racism in terms of process, attitude and behaviour, raises some concern about the effectiveness of the measure. Whilst the concept of discrimination can take account of individual conduct and the conduct of a group for instance, this is unlikely to penetrate racism at the institutional level.

Reading the spirit of the provision

There are a number of ways in which a more effective approach to the eradication of institutional racism in relation to the protection of third-country nationals could be afforded through the Race Directive. One is to read the provisions when transposed at the national level as if they covered all persons including those defined by nationality. The Race Directive provides a level playing field. A perusal of the text shows that 'Member States may introduce or maintain provisions that are more favourable to the protection of the principle of equal treatment than those laid down …'.[225] The strength in this approach lies in breaking the hypocrisy that would otherwise be maintained if people of similar nationalities were treated differently on the basis of nationality for the purpose of the Directive. For instance, the British Race Relations Act 1976 (Amendment) Regulations 2003, includes reference to discrimination on the basis of national origins as a prohibited ground of discrimination (the inclusion of third-country nationals is not new since the Race Relations Act 1976 included nationality). Thus if an applicant applies for credit from an institution, and as a condition of the loan, the applicant is required to be registered on the electoral roll, so that the institution can carry out credit checks, this may discriminate indirectly against non-UK nationals who are not eligible to vote.[226] The British approach may be used as an example of 'good practice' that other Member States might be persuaded to follow, particularly, the judiciary in determining whether or not a third-country national should, as a matter of the principle of equality and fairness, be able to rely on the transposed provisions.

A more purposive approach might also meet the concerns of the Khan Commission, a body that recommended the use of EU law in combating racism in the EU. According to the Commission, this law should preserve international principles that, 'all individuals, regardless of their colour, race, nationality, ethnic or national origin, or religion, should have the right of equal access to employment, equal pay and fair treatment'.[227] Furthermore, the Khan Commission was adamant that the right to equal treatment should apply whether or not a person was an EU citizen.[228] Unfortunately, this is likely to be a slow process. As things stand the rate of progress in Member States' implementation of the Race Directive, given the 19 July 2003 deadline, was deplorable. Political commentators have said, 'This foot-dragging is a betrayal of one of the most progressive and essential steps forward in anti-discrimination taken by the European Union in recent years. It's clear that many governments are only prepared to pay lip service to their basic obligation to protect millions of their citizens from racism'.[229] In 2005 the European Court of Justice (ECJ) ruled that a number of EU Member States including Finland and Austria had failed to honour their obligations in implementing the Race Directive.[230] Fourteen Member States were subject to infringement proceedings by the EU Commission for failure to implement the Directive properly.[231]

Nevertheless, slothfulness in the implementation of instruments concerning social law is not uncommon. The argument remains that third-country nationals should be protected by the provisions of the Directive. This would give more meaning to the human rights framework to tackle racism addressed in the preamble to the Directive. This approach would also give better meaning to the idea that the Race Directive is a mechanism for transposing international anti-racist human rights obligations that states have signed up to but which fail to adequately protect individuals particularly those of African descent.

Linking nationality to institutional racism through positive action

Another area where change is possible is in relation to Article 5 which covers positive action. According to this article:

> With a view to ensuring full equality in practice, the principle of equal treatment shall not prevent any Member State from maintaining or adopting specific measures to prevent or compensate for disadvantages linked to racial or ethnic origin.[232]

This could prove to be a very useful provision because it prepares the legislature and those key actors seized with the duty to implement the Race Directive, with an opportunity to 'ensure full equality in practice'. A principle that should not be applied in an ad hoc manner based on race or ethnicity (rather than nationality) but determined despite it. The possibility lies in the language of Article 5 itself: to 'adopt specific measures to prevent or compensate for disadvantage linked to racial or ethnic origin'. The key word here is 'linked'. This word may be ambiguous in that it is unclear what is meant but herein lies its strength. It could be argued that not using the words 'of a racial or ethnic group' which is found elsewhere in the directive,[233] but instead importing the term 'linked to racial or ethnic origin'[234] makes the use of the Race Directive as a weapon in the fight against institutional racism in relation to third-country nationals potentially strong. Article 5 states that 'the principle of equal treatment shall not prevent any Member State from maintaining or adopting specific measures … '[235] such measures are recommended as a way of addressing '… structural and institutional discrimination based on race'.[236]

UK law

The Race Directive has had most effect in relation to domestic legislation[237] that has been implemented through the Equality Act 2010. The primary provision that deals with race and ethnic[238] discrimination in the UK is section 9(1) of the Equality Act 2010, formerly section 3 of the Race Relations Act 1976. Sections 9(1)–(4) provide for the prohibited grounds of racial discrimination including colour, nationality, ethnic or national origins and also refers to racial groups.[239] Furthermore reference to racial discrimination can be found in section 13 which deals with direct discrimination, section 14 that deals with combined discrimination (such as race and sex) along with section 19 which covers indirect discrimination. Harassment[240] and victimisation,[241] section 26 and 27 respectively, are also provided for by the Equality Act. One of the key changes is that the Equality Act has sought to bring all discrimination legislation together. Prior to the 1 October 2010 the Race Relations Act was a stand-alone provision, together with the Sex Equality Act and the Disability Act. With the Race discrimination provisions, if the act or omission that is complained about occurred before the 1 October 2010 the complainant has to rely on the Race Relations Act 1976.[242] The Equality Act and its forerunners have not dealt with the legacy of the transatlantic slave trade or chattel slavery but have seen fit to react to racial discrimination and racism as 'modern' phenomena. It is argued that this failure has meant that institutional racism has not been addressed.

One of the main changes to race equality law that occurred before the Race Directive was the Race Equality Duty (RED). The RED came into force through the Race Relations (Amendment) Act 2000. This provision came about because of the Stephen Lawrence Inquiry. That Inquiry stated that all public bodies, not just the police, were institutionally racist and that public bodies should take action to address it. Parliament legislated that from December 2000 such bodies should outlaw racist practices within their organisations. This includes the general duty which comprises three elements: to eliminate unlawful discrimination; promote equality of opportunity; and to promote good race relations between people of different racial groups.[243] There are in addition specific duties that pertain to organisations depending on the functions they perform.[244] The Equality Act has expanded the concept of the Race Equality Duty to a Public Sector Duty (section 149 (1)-(7)).[245] Under this duty when a public authority exercises its functions (or a person who is not a public authority exercises public functions)[246] it must have *due regard* to the need to eliminate discrimination, harassment and victimisation; to advance equality of opportunity and foster good relations between persons.[247] To have 'due regard' is a slippery term bound to raise argument as to whether such has been given in a particular instance. However, the Equality and Human Rights Commission (ECHR)[248] give guidance which involves removing disadvantage, taking steps to meet need and encouraging participation in public life.[249] What the public sector equality duty does not is to contextualise itself in terms of the transatlantic slave trade, chattel slavery and its consequences.

Compliance and institutional racism

The United Kingdom's compliance with EU law as far as the Race Directive is concerned has been an issue.[250] Along with other Member States, the UK was sent a 'reasoned opinion'[251] Infringement No 2005/ 2363 from the Commission for failure to show complete and correct transposition of the Race Directive. This reasoned opinion was sent on 7 June 2007.[252] One of the problem areas was the definition of indirect discrimination provided by the Race Directive had not been implemented correctly by the UK. This was despite the UK legislation inserting a new definition into section 1 of the Race Relations Act 1976 by the Race Relations Act (Amendment) Regulations 2003 (SI 2003/1626). The next attempt to transpose the Race Directive's definition of indirect discrimination was by the Race Relations Act (Amendment) 2008, SI 2008/3008 where further amendments were made. In the Commission's Annual Report for 2011[253] the Commission reported that it was able to stop further infringement proceedings because the UK developed new anti-discrimination laws.[254] Indirect discrimination is now defined in Section 19 (1) and (2) of the Equality Act 2010:

> (1)A person (A) discriminates against another (B) if A applies to B a provision, criterion or practice which is discriminatory in relation to a relevant protected characteristic of B's. (2)For the purposes of subsection (1), a provision, criterion or practice is discriminatory in relation to a relevant protected characteristic of B's if – (a)A applies, or would apply, it to persons with whom B does not share the characteristic, (b)it puts, or would put, persons with whom B shares the characteristic at a particular disadvantage when compared with persons with whom B does not share it,(c)it puts, or would put, B at that disadvantage, and (d)A cannot show it to be a proportionate means of achieving a legitimate aim.[255]

From the Race Directive indirect discrimination reads:

> indirect discrimination shall be taken to occur where an apparently neutral provision, criterion or practice would put persons of a racial or ethnic origin at a particular disadvantage compared with other persons, unless that provision, criterion or practice is objectively justified by a legitimate aim and the means of achieving that aim are appropriate and necessary.[256]

The concept of indirect discrimination under British law refers to 'a person' and a person can either be a human being or an artificial person such as an organisation or a company.[257] It is difficult to know, however, whether by 'person' section 19 refers to an artificial person. There is no mention of an organisation or organisational failure. Article 2 of the Race Directive is more vague. The Directive refers to provision, criterion or practice which would fit in well with the notion of how organisations work in the Macpherson definition of institutional racism but it is not clear whether these criteria or practices can emanate from organisations as well as from humans. Nevertheless Recital 16 of the Race Directive reads:

> It is important to protect all natural persons against discrimination on grounds of racial or ethnic origin. Member States should also provide, where appropriate and in accordance with their national traditions and practice, protection for 'legal persons' where they suffer discrimination on grounds of the racial or ethnic origin of their members.

This statement refers to legal persons as victims of racial or ethnic discrimination on account of their membership in terms of race or ethnicity. So whilst it is unclear whether organisations are aimed at as perpetrators it is quite clear that they should be protected as victims of racial discrimination. At this juncture then we do not have sufficient clarity as to whether organisations in terms of institutional racism are seen as perpetrators in the Race Directive. This clarification is needed and it is suggested that the Directive should be amended in this regard.

Conclusion

This chapter argues that whilst the Race Directive is welcomed it comes with problems in terms of interpretation, ambiguity, as well as the failure to protect third-country nationals. Howard suggests that on the question of institutional racism the 'term does not appear to have played a role in discussions on anti-discrimination law within the EU at the time the Race Directive was negotiated'.[258] This is strange since the Race Directive evolved in the context of the Stephen Lawrence Inquiry in 1999[259] which was a watershed in British race relations policy and law. The European Commission was alive to the Report and its recommendations if one goes by one of its integration programmes called SLES.[260] It is contended that a purposive reading of the Race Directive might encompass the concept of institutional racism. It is argued that whether the problem is textual, or to do with the scope or a purposive reading of the Directive the failure to address institutional racism comprehensively is a major lacuna. The result will possibly constitute organisational failure on the part of the entities of Member States as 'organisations to provide a professional service to people because of their colour, culture or ethnic origin. This can be seen or detected in processes, attitudes and behaviour which amount to discrimination through unwitting prejudice, ignorance, thoughtlessness and racist stereotyping which disadvantage minority ethnic people'.[261] According to Gearty[262] the 'evil of racism ... if left alone this seed will grow'.[263] In the European context, this applies not only to those influenced by the racist ideology of the Far Right, but also to the failure of some Member States to recognise the racist legacy manifested in institutional racism as a result of their involvement in the transatlantic slave trade. This is particularly difficult where a number of Member States do not even want to implement the Race Directive itself.[264] Moreover, there is evidence of considerable under-reporting of incidents of racial discrimination.[265] Solanke[266] argues that the infringement proceedings taken against several Member States by the Commission for failure to take action to ensure the Race Directive is part of their domestic law is a positive action since it highlights the importance of human rights within the European Union.[267] Nonetheless, the failure to explicitly address the concept of institutional racism within the Race Directive has been a missed opportunity. It could have provided a valuable tool in the effort to remove this toxic legacy from some Member States.

Notes

1 Hieronymous Seiler and Heinrich Ehinger from Konstanz are recorded as the first Germans to be involved in the slave trade. 'Slavery in Europe'. Available at: www.histclo.com (accessed 3 December 2015).
2 Stephen Lawrence Education Standard, 01 01 2000. Available at: http://ec.europa.eu/ewsi/en/practice/details.cfm?ID_ITEMS=9110 (accessed 11 April 2014).
3 European Commission, Report from the Commission to the European Parliament and the Council, Brussels, 17. 1. 2014 COM (2014) 2 final.
4 Directives are binding on Member States to whom they are addressed, Article 254(3) EC.
5 Official Journal L 180, 19/07/2000 pp. 0022-0026.
6 See preamble 2, 3 and 4 Council Dir 2000/43/EC where reference to international legal obligations are made.
7 Council Directive 2000/43/EC, Article 1.
8 Ibid.
9 Ibid., Article 14.
10 The directive does not cover difference of treatment of third-country nationals where their legal status has not been resolved at the level of national law. See Article 3(2) of Council Directive 2000/43/EC.
11 Article 13 Treaty of Amsterdam amending the EC Treaty. F. Brennan, 'European Race Directive: A Bridge So Far?' In Raphael Walden (ed.), *Racism and Human Rights* (Leiden: Martinus Nijhoff, 2004).
12 See Article 249(2) EC Treaty and Case 148/78. *Publico Ministero v Tullio Ratti* [1979] ECR I629.
13 Article 249(2) EC Treaty.
14 Once they are implemented, individuals can rely on the rights that they confer as against those who flout those rights. Individuals may rely on an unimplemented directive under the doctrine of 'direct effect', Case 41/74 *Van Duyn v Home Office* [1974] ECR 1337, [1975] I CMLR I, and 'indirect effect' Case 14 /83 *Von Colson and Kaman v Land Nordrhein-Westfalen* [1984] ECR 1891, [1986] 2 CMLR 430. They may also bring an action in damages against a Member State that fails to implement a directive Cases C-6/ 90 and C-9/ 90 *Francovich and Bonifaci v Italy* [1991] ECR I-5357, [1993] 2 CMLR 66.
15 Article 16 Council Directive 2000/43/EC.
16 E. Howard, *The EU Race Directive: Developing the Protection against Racial Discrimination within the EU* (London: Routledge, 2010), p. 33.
17 See M. O'Brien, 'The European Race Directive – Our plans for implementation', *European Lookout* 3 (2000): 2.
18 Art 14 Council Directive 2000/43/EC.
19 C. Dandeker and D. Mason, 'Diversity in the British Armed Forces: The Debate over Ethnic Minority Representation', paper presented to a conference on 'Redefining Society-Military Relations: From Vancouver to Valdistock, at the University of Birmingham, 16–18 April 1999.
20 W. Macpherson, *The Stephen Lawrence Inquiry* (London: Home Office, 1999).
21 Set up in accordance with Council Regulation No 1035/97 2 June 1997 to monitor and report on racism and xenophobia in the Member States of the European Community.
22 European Monitoring Centre, *Looking Reality in the Face.* Annual Report 1998 (Vienna: EUMC, 1998) p. 4.
23 The CRE is now part of the British Equality and Human Rights Commission.
24 See CRE, 'What is Discrimination?'. Available at: www.cre.uk/legaladv/rra_discrim.html. This Commission has been replaced by the Equality and Human Rights Commission.
25 Ibid., p. 3.
26 S. Fredman, *Discrimination Law* (Oxford: Oxford University Press, 2002).
27 Ibid., pp. 4–5.
28 Ibid., p. 6.
29 There were several race relations Acts passed beginning in the 1960s with the Race Relations Act 1965, then 1976 and 2000.
30 Ibid.

31 G. Singh, 'Race Discrimination in the 21st Century: The Need for Action', 7 December 2000. See www.bihr.org.uk/sites/default/files/Lecture-Singh.pdf (accessed 6 June 2014).
32 Black graduates with the same qualifications find it three or four times harder to get a job than their peers. Unemployment is 14 per cent for black and Asian people but 6 per cent for whites. Singh, *Race Discrimination in the 21st Century.*
33 It was found that black Caribbean pupils were over three times more likely to be permanently excluded than the school population as a whole, for the period 2014/5 Department of Education 21 July 2016. See https://www.gov.uk/government/uploads/system/uploads/attachment_data/file/449433/SFR27_2015_Text.pdf (accessed 21 July 2016). In 2013 it was found that a high number of school exclusions occurred with black children. www.voice-online.co.uk (accessed 21 July 2016). Black Caribbean pupils are four times more likely to be permanently excluded from school than their white counterparts in the UK according to The Poverty Site www.poverty.org.uk (accessed 21 July 2016). Afro Caribbean school leavers leave school having progressed less well than other school leavers. Singh, *Race Discrimination in the 21st Century.*
34 There are patterns of inequality in health patterns amongst ethnic minorities. Singh, 'Race Discrimination in the 21st Century'.
35 Fifteen per cent of the male prison population is drawn from Afro Caribbean and Asian people compared with their representation of 7 per cent in the general population. Singh, 'Race Discrimination in the 21st Century'.
36 Ibid.
37 G. Ford, *Report Drawn up on Behalf of the Committee of Inquiry into Racism and Xenophobia* (Luxembourg: Office of Official Publication of EC, 1991).
38 Ibid., p. 57.
39 Ibid., pp. 61–64.
40 See Chapter 2.
41 European Union Open Data Portal. Available at: www.data-europa.eu (accessed 12 October 2016).
42 'The Transatlantic Slave Trade, Understanding Slavery'. Available at: www.understandingslavery.com (accessed 4 December 2015).
43 International influence on racial discrimination has tended to come from the jurisprudence of the European Court of Human Rights in interpreting the ECHR; however, racial discrimination is not an autonomous right and the remedy relies on the willingness of Member States' governments to comply with court rulings.
44 I. Forbes and G. Mead, 'Measure for Measure: A Comparative Analysis of Measures to Combat Racial Discrimination in the Member Countries of the European Community', Equal Opportunities Study Group, University of Southampton, 1992, Research Series No 1 (London: Department of Employment).
45 UN Centre for Human Rights (1996) 'Model National Legislation for the Guidance of Governments in the Enactment of Further Legislation against Racial Discrimination'.
46 See M. Bell, 'Beyond European Labour Law? Reflections on the EU Racial Equality Directive', 8 (2002) European Law Journal 384. Also see Forbes & Mead above.
47 Non-EC nationals in any EC country who have been legally admitted as residents. These include all residents from outside the EC, citizens of Commonwealth countries (if they have not registered or naturalised as British citizens), British nationals but not British citizens, see A. Dummett, *Citizens, Minorities and Foreigners* (London: CRE 1994).
48 W. Duncan, 'Racism and Xenophobia in Europe', in G. Barrett (ed.), *Justice and Cooperation in the European Union* (Dublin: Institute of European Affairs 1997), p. 183. Also see *European Monitoring Centre on Racism and Xenophobia, Looking Reality in the Face*, Annual Report 1998, part 2 (Vienna: EUMC, 1998).
49 For analysis of the 'business case model' in relation to ethnic minorities and the armed services see Dandeker and Mason above.
50 Ibid., at 3.
51 EU Anti-discrimination Policy. 'From Equal Opportunities between Men and Women to Combating Racism, Working Documents', Public Liberties Series LIBE 102 EN, 3.
52 Prior to the Khan Commission, the Starting Line Group (1994) suggested that the European Community Treaty should be amended to cover discrimination including on the grounds of race, colour or ethnic origin. See E. Howard, *The EU Race Directive: Developing the Protection against Racial Discrimination within the EU* (London: Routledge, 2010), p. 12.

53 European Council Consultative Commission (1995) Final Report, Ref 6906/1/95 Rev 1 Limite RAXEN 24.
54 Ibid., p. 59.
55 The European Commission is the executive body of the EU responsible for proposing law.
56 Para 15, Resolution on the Communication from the Commission on Racism and Xenophobia and Anti-semitism, 9 May 1996 (OJ 1996 C 152/57).
57 J. Wench, 'Mechanisms of Exclusion: Ethnic Minorities and Labour Markets', *Nordic Labour Journal* 1 (1997): 16, 17
58 The European Parliament, Council, Representatives of Member States and the Commission agreed the 1986 Declaration Against Racism and Xenophobia. A number of organisations have been actively engaged in compiling draft instruments aimed at the enhancement of the EC's competence in dealing with racial discrimination on a Community-wide basis. These have included the former Commission for Racial Equality, the Dutch National Bureau against Racism, Belgian Centre for Equal Opportunities, Churches Commission for Migrants in Europe, the Migrants Forum and Starting Line.
59 Now Article 19 of the Consolidated Version of the Treaty on the Functioning of the European Union, Official Journal of the European Union, 9. 5. 2008, C115/47.
60 It has been unsuccessfully argued that the Community already had competence in this area under the old Art 235 of the Treaty of Rome. See Dummett above.
61 After consulting the European Parliament, Art 13 EC Treaty.
62 Additional grounds of discrimination in the Article included sex, religion or belief, disability, age and sexual orientation. Contrast this with the equal treatment of men and women in relation to pay for instance under Art 141, formerly Art 119. Another difficulty is the requirement that the Council act unanimously in any appropriate action. It could lead to inaction or limited action. This was a problem that the CRE hoped to avoid in its proposal in the early 1990s that the Council act by qualified majority. See Dummett above pp. 12–13.
63 Article 19 of the Consolidated Version of the Treaty on the Functioning of the European Union, Official Journal of the European Union, 9. 5. 2008, C115/47.
64 The extent to which this article can deal with racial discrimination wherever it may arise is questionable.
65 On 2 June 1997 the Council of Ministers adopted regulation (EU No 1035/97) to set up this centre. For a critique of the limited objectives of the Centre, see F. Brennan, 'Can the Institutions of the European Community Transcend Liberal Limitations in the Pursuit of Racial Equality?' in B. Brecher, J. Halliday and K. Kolinska (eds), *Nationalism, Racism and the Liberal Order* (Aldershot: Ashgate, 1998) p. 108.
66 See Decision of the Representatives of the Governments of the Member States of the 2 June 1997, published in Official Journal C 194, 25. 06. 97. Available at: http://europa.eu/legislation_summaries/other/c10411_en.htm (accessed 3 May 2014).
67 Available at: http://europa.eu/legislation_summaries/other/c10411_en.htm (accessed 3 May 2014).
68 M. Harrison, I. Law and D. Phillips, *Migrants, Minorities and Housing: Exclusion, Discrimination and Anti-Discrimination in 15 Member States of the European Union*, EUMC, December 2005. Available at: http://fra.europa.eu/sites/default/files/fra_uploads/188-CS-Housing-en.pdf (accessed 3 May 2014).
69 Ibid., p. 3.
70 Ibid.
71 The Annual Report on the Situation regarding Racism and Xenophobia in the Member States of the EU – (EUMC 2006). Available at: http://fra.europa.eu/en/publication/2006/annual-report-2006-inadequacy-data-racist-crime-2006 (accessed 3 May 2014).
72 The EUMC's activities were established in 1998 and finished on the 28 February 2007. Available at: http://fra.europa.eu/en/about-fra/who-we-are (accessed 3 May 2014).
73 Also known as the European Union Agency for Fundamental Rights. See http://fra.europa.eu/en/theme/racism-related-intolerances (accessed 8 May 2014).
74 FRA, 'Racism, Football and the Internet (Thematic Report)', 7 July 2001. Available at: www.fra.europa.eu (accessed 21 July 2016).
75 C. Balestri, *Racism, Football and the Internet* (Vienna: EUMC, 2002). Available at: http://fra.europa.eu/sites/default/files/fra_uploads/154-Football.pdf (accessed 8 May 2014).

76 Ibid.

77 For instance, Ya Ya Toure and Emmanuel Frimpong are football players who have been subject to monkey chants in 2015. See www.edition.cnn.comyaya-toure-racism-fifa and www.theguardian.com2015jul respectively (accessed 21 July 2016).

78 The other instrument is the Council Framework Decision 2008/913/JHA of the 28 November 2008 on combating certain forms and expressions of racism and xenophobia by means of criminal law. See http://fra.europa.eu/en/theme/racism-related-intolerances?page=key-texts-and-policy-documents (accessed 8 May 2014).

79 Council Dir 2000/43/EC adopted on 29 June 2000 implementing the principle of equal treatment between persons irrespective of racial or ethnic origin, above n 2. It may be useful to add that this directive was rushed through, precipitated by fears over the human rights situation in Austria due to the rise of the Far Right Freedom Party in 2000. See Douglas-Scott, S Constitutional Law of the European Union (Longman 2002) 435 and M. Bell, 'Beyond European Labour Law? Reflections on the EU Racial Equality Directive' 8 (2002) European Law Journal 384, 385. As part of the package of measures, provisions to deal with discrimination on the grounds of religion were adopted through Council Dir 2000/78/EC, establishing a general framework for equal treatment in employment and occupation, Official Journal L303/16.

80 The Council of Ministers consists of representatives of each Member State at ministerial level imbued with authority to commit the government of that State.

81 Art 249 EC Treaty provides that a Directive shall be binding as to the results to be achieved.

82 Art 16 of the Race Directive.

83 Ibid.

84 Ibid., Art 13.

85 Ibid., Art 15.

86 Ibid.

87 For analysis of the Race Directive as a model for worldwide mechanisms to combat racial discrimination see F. Brennan, *The European Race Directive: A Bridge So Far?* (London: Consultative Council of Jewish Organisations, 2001) discussion paper produced for the World Conference Against Racism, 2001.

88 Art 7(1) of the Race Directive.

89 Ibid., Art 2(1) (a) and (b).

90 Ibid., Art 2(4).

91 Ibid., Art 9.

92 Article 3(1) of the Race Directive.

93 Ibid., Art 3(1).

94 Ibid., Art 12.

95 Ibid., Art 8.

96 Ibid., Art 10.

97 See European Commission on the application of EU Law, 'What are Directives?'. Available at: http://ec.europa.eu/eu_law/introduction/what_directive_en.htm (accessed 31 May 2014).

98 For instance, whilst Britain, the Netherlands and France have laws against discrimination, in other EC countries such protection amounts to a pittance.

99 See European Commission on the application of EU Law, 'What are Regulations?' Available at: http://ec.europa.eu/eu_law/introduction/what_regulation_en.htm (accessed 31 May 2014).

100 Ibid.

101 Member States may introduce more favourable provisions, but they cannot reduce levels of protection that were already afforded by them prior to the Directive, Art 6 of the Race Directive.

102 Individuals may rely on an unimplemented directive under the doctrine of 'direct effect', Case 41/74 *VanDuyn v Home Office* [1974] ECR 1337, [1975]1 CMLR, and 'indirect effect', Case 4/83 *Von Colson and Kaman v Nordrhein- Westfalen* [1984] ECR 1891, [1986]2 CMLR 430.

103 Between individuals or an individual.

104 Between an individual and the state.

105 Art 1 Council Dir 2000/4 3/EC. Joined cases C-6/90 and C-9/90 *Francovich and Bonifaci v Italian State* [1991] ECR 1–5357.

106 As a set of beliefs or dogma that is used to justify the existence of groups, i.e. natural and fixed biological criteria, inferior culture or religion. See B. Bowling and C. Phillips, *Racism, Crime and Justice* (Harlow: Pearson, 2002), p. 21.

107 A type of cleansing of the process of decision-making on behalf of the individual complainant, see C. McCrudden, D. Smith and C. Brown, *Racial Justice at Work: The Enforcement of the Race Relations Act 1976 in Employment* (London: PSI, 1991) pp. 5–6.
108 Art 2(2)(b) of the Race Directive.
109 See McCrudden, Smith and Brown above pp. 6–7.
110 Article 1 of the Race Directive 2000.
111 Article 2(2)(a) and (b) of the Race Directive 2000.
112 Article 2(2)(b) of the Race Directive 2000.
113 S. Fredman, *Discrimination Law* (Oxford: Oxford University Press, 2002), p. 1.
114 Ibid.
115 M. Connolly, *Discrimination Law* (London: Sweet and Maxwell, 2006).
116 [1986] I.C.R. 514 CA. This was a case allegedly based on direct discrimination.
117 [2002] 1 W.L.R. 1947.
118 [2003] UKHL 34.
119 [1997] I.C.R. 1, EAT.
120 [2003] UKHL 34.
121 Now the Supreme Court.
122 Para 6 of Preamble Council Directive 2000/43/EC.
123 P. Fitzpatrick and J. Bergeron, *Europe's Other: European Law between Modernity and Post-modernity* (Aldershot: Ashgate 1998).
124 See C. Gearty, 'The Internal and External "Other" in the Union Legal Order: Racism, Religious Intolerance and Xenophobia' in P. Alston (ed.) *The EU and Human Rights* (Oxford: Oxford University Press 1999), p. 327.
125 European Commission, Report from the Commission to the European Parliament and the Council, Brussels, 17. 1. 2014 COM (2014) 2 final, 5.1.
126 The Race Directive.
127 Ibid.
128 European Commission, Report from the Commission to the European Parliament and the Council, Brussels, 17. 1. 2014 COM (2014) 2 final, 5.1.
129 J.G. Henriques, 'Portugal is Race Blind, but not for the Right Reasons', *The Guardian*, 12 September 2011.
130 NICEM, Submission to the OFMDFM in Response to the Draft Race Regulations in Implementing EU Equality Obligations in Northern Ireland, 31 March 2003, Belfast. Also see ECRI, Second Report on Ireland Adopted 22 June 2001, 23 April 2003 where it is reported that people generally reject the idea that a person may be Irish and black, para 55.
131 See ECRI, Second Report on Austria, 3 April 2001.
132 A. Hieronymus and M. Moses, *ENAR, Shadow Report 2002, Talking 'Race' in Germany* (Hamburg: Institut fur Migrations-und Rassismusforschung, 2003), para 1.1.
133 See generally N. Roubani, *ENAR Shadow Report-2001, for Greece.*
134 Art 2 of the Race Directive above.
135 The Race Directive, above n 2, Arts 2(3) and (4) respectively.
136 Ibid., Arts 4 and 5.
137 European Commission, Report from the Commission to the European Parliament and the Council, Brussels, 17. 1. 2014 COM (2014) 2 final.
138 Ibid., 3.2.
139 See K. Dobe and S. Chhokar, 'Muslims, Ethnicity and the Law' 4 (2000) International Journal of Discrimination and the Law 369, and S. Poulter, *Ethnicity, Law and Human Rights: The English Experience* (Oxford: Oxford University Press, 1998), ch. 9.
140 [1983] 2 AC 548.
141 [1983] 2 AC 548 at 562.
142 Unreported, Independent 27 November 1986.
143 Case No 4106/91 where it was alleged that an instruction to discriminate against Muslims fell outside the Race Relations Act because Muslims did not constitute an ethnic group because the tribunal believed that Islam was a spread of faith rather than a group of people who could trace their descent from a common geographical origin. Also see *Nyazi v Ryamans*, EAT, 10 May 1998 (unreported), *Tariq v Young, Birmingham* IT, 19 April 1989 (unreported); *J H Walker Ltd v Hussain* [1996] IRLR 11.

144 [1993] IRLR 284.
145 Muslims and Rastafarians may now be protected because of the Framework Directive 2000/78/EC but this measure is strictly related to employment and occupation.
146 *Seide v Gillette Industries Ltd* [1980] IRLR 427.
147 *Commission for Racial Equality v Dutton* [1989] 1 All ER 306.
148 See C. Gearty, 'The Internal and External "Other" in the Union Legal Order: Racism, Religious Intolerance and Xenophobia' in Alston above pp. 335–339 at 327 (in relation to Rastafarians and Muslims); K. Dobe, S. Chhokar, 'Muslims, Ethnicity and the Law' 4 (2000) *International Journal of Discrimination and the Law*, 369 (regarding Muslims).
149 Council Directive 2000/78/EC of 27 November establishing a general framework for equal treatment in employment and occupation. Official Journal L 303, 02/12/2000 pp. 0016-0022.
150 L. Dennis, 'Addressing Latent Racism and Blatant Discrimination in America', *Chicago Monitor*, 4 April 2013. Available at: http://chicagomonitor.com/2013/04/addressing-latent-racism-and-blatant-discrimination-in-america/ (accessed 17 June 2014).
151 J. Niessen and I. Chopin (eds), *Anti-discrimination Legislation in EU Member States: A Comparison of National Anti-discrimination Legislation on the Grounds of Racial or Ethnic Origin, Religion or Belief with the Council Directives, Austria* (Vienna: EUMC, 2002).
152 Art 1, para 1 of ICERD.
153 Niessen and Chopin, p. 20.
154 Ibid.
155 See ZARA, *Racism Report 2001: Case Reports on Racist Excesses in Structures in Austria* (Vienna: 2001).
156 See F. Brennan, 'Punishing Islamophobic Hostility: Are Any Lessons to be Learned from Racially Hostile Crimes?', *The Journal of Civil Liberties* 8(1) (2004).
157 T. Modood *et al., Ethnic Minorities in Britain: Diversity and Disadvantage.* The Fourth National Survey of Ethnic Minorities in Britain (London: Policy Studies Institute, 1997).
158 Religious discrimination is dealt with by the Framework Directive on Employment and Occupation.
159 S. Fredman, *Discrimination Law* (Oxford: Oxford University Press, 2002).
160 Article 3(2) Race Directive 2000/43/EC.
161 There is a proposal for a Directive on the entry and residence of third-country nationals for the purposes of research, studies, pupil exchange, training, voluntary training and au pairing. See Brussels, 25.3.2013COM (2013) 151 Final, aimed at common migration flows and fair treatment of third-country nationals.
162 M. Kamali, 'Conceptualising the "Other", Institutionalized Discrimination and Cultural Racism', European Commission, Improving Human Research Potential and the Socio-economic Knowledge Base, Socio-Economic Research, Racism and Xenophobia: Key Issues, Mechanisms and Policy Opportunities, 5–6 April 2001, (Centre Brochette, Rue Froissart 36, Brussels). Also see I.F. Haney Lopez, 'Institutional Racism: Judicial Conduct and a New Theory of Racial Discrimination', (2000) 109 Yale Law Journal.
163 See Macpherson, *The Stephen Lawrence Inquiry*, para 6.34.
164 Blanca Vila Costa, 'The Quest for a Consistent Set of Rules Governing the Status of non-Community Nationals', in P, Alston (ed.), *The EU and Human Rights* (Oxford: Oxford University Press, 1999) pp. 411–12.
165 S. Douglas-Scott, 'The Common Foreign and Security Policy of the EU: Reinforcing the European Identity?', in P. Fitzpatrick and J.H. Bergeron (eds), *Europe's Other: European Law Between Modernity and Postmodernity* (Aldershot: Ashgate, 1998), pp. 131–33.
166 A. Geddes, *Immigration and European Integration: Towards Fortress Europe?* (Manchester: Manchester University Press, 2000), p. 6.
167 Ibid., 21–27; Douglas-Scott above, pp. 132–133.
168 Fitzpatrick and Bergeron above, and Douglas-Scott above.
169 See Macpherson above.
170 Ibid.
171 Preamble 12 Council Dir 2000/43/EC.
172 Defined in Art 2 Council Dir 2000/43/EC.
173 Art 3(1) Council Dir 2000/43/EC.
174 Art 3(1)(g) Council Dir 2000/43/EC.

175 Art 3(1)(h) Council Dir 2000/43/EC.

176 Thus Preamble 2 and 3 of Council Dir 2000/43/EC refers to human rights, the Universal Declaration of Human Rights, the International Covenant on the Elimination of all forms of Racial Discrimination, the United Nations Covenants on Civil and Political Rights and Economic, Social and Cultural Rights and the European Convention for the Protection of Human Rights and Fundamental Freedoms.

177 See Preamble recital 12 Council Dir 2000/43/EC.

178 CRI (2003) 23 Annual report on ECRI'S activities covering the period from 1January to 31 December 2002 Strasbourg, 20 March 2003.

179 In Britain the Race Relations (Amendment) Act 2000 has imposed legal obligations on public bodies to promote equality of opportunity. Further, it is unlawful for such bodies to discriminate whilst carrying out their functions and it is a duty that such bodies promote equality of opportunity and good race relations.

180 Fredman, *Discrimination Law*, p. 16.

181 Macpherson above n 16; also see Hieronymus and Moses, *ENAR Shadow Report 2002*, part 3, p. 14.

182 S. Carmichael and C.V. Hamilton, *Black Power: The Politics of Liberation* (New York: Vintage Books, 1967) p. 4.

183 See EUMC Annual Report 1998, pp. 7–17.

184 Macpherson above para. 6.34.

185 Carmichael and Hamilton above.

186 CRI (2000) 31 Second Report on France, adopted on 10 December 1999.

187 B. Qurashy, ENAR Shadow Report 2002, *Racism and Discriminatory Practices in Denmark.*

188 Hieronymus and Moses above.

189 Joseph Rowntree Foundation, 'Ethnicity and Deprivation in England. Dynamics of Diversity, Evidence from the 2011 Census'. Available at: www.ethnicity.ac.uk (accessed 3 December 2015).

190 United Nations Centre for Human Settlements, *Cities in a Globalising World: Global Report on Human Settlements* 2001 (UN-HABITAT, 2001).

191 B. Thiele and M. Gomez, 'Non-discrimination and Equality in the Cities: Applying Internationals Human Rights and Housing Rights Standards', *Human Rights Tribune* 8(3) (2002).

192 Art 25 of the Universal Declaration of Human Rights reads that 'Everyone has the right to a standard of living adequate for the health and well-being of himself and of his family, including food, clothing, housing and medical care and necessary social services, and the right to security in the event of unemployment, sickness, disability, widowhood, old age or other lack of livelihood in circumstances beyond his control'.

193 Art 11 (1) of the International Covenant on Economic, Social and Cultural Rights provides: 'The States Parties to the present Covenant recognize the right of every one to an adequate standard of living for himself and his family, including adequate food, clothing and housing, and to the continuous improvement of living conditions. The States Parties will take appropriate steps to ensure the realization of this right, recognizing to this effect the essential importance of international co-operation ...'.

194 See Chapters 1 and 2.

195 See Chapter 1.

196 Art 2(2) Council Dir 2000/43/EC.

197 Art 3(1) Council Dir 2000/43/EC dealing with the scope of the provisions states that, 'Within the limits of the powers conferred upon the Community, this directive shall apply to all persons, as regards both the public and private sectors, including public bodies ...'.

198 Art 2(2)(b) Council Dir 2000/43/EC which also further states' ... unless that provision, criterion or practice is objectively justified by a legitimate aim and the means of achieving that aim are appropriate and necessary'.

199 Art 2(3) Council Dir 2000/43/EC.

200 Art 3(2) Council Directive 2000/43/EC.

201 J.A. Goldston, 'The European Union Race Directive', *Open Society Justice Initiative, 2003.* Available at: www.justiceinitiative.org/publications/russia_ec/moscow_workshop/goldston_ (accessed 15 December 2015).

202 For instance Section 3(1) Race Relations Act 1976 refers to 'racial grounds' as including colour, race or national group and 'racial group' as persons defined by reference to colour, race, nationality or ethnic or national origins.

203 See Goldston above n 191.
204 There are 38,000 Africans in Denmark; the highest proportions are Somalian followed by Moroccans. See Qurashy, 'Racism and Discriminatory Practices in Denmark', 5.
205 Art 8 Council Dir 2000/43/EC dealing with the burden of proof affords a lesser burden of proof on the complainant. Providing a prima facie case is made out the burden shifts to the respondent to prove that there has been no breach of the equal treatment principle.
206 See Macpherson above para. 6.34. Also see Carmichael and Hamilton above, and P.J. Williams, *Seeing a Colour-Blind Future: The Paradox of Race. The 1997 Reith Lecture* (London: Virago, 1997).
207 See ECRI Second Report on Spain, CRI (2003) 40, para J and M, ECRI Second Report on France, CRI (2000) 31,2000, para M, ECRI Second Report on Germany, CRI (2001) 36, para K and M, 2001, ECRI Second Report on Italy, CRI (2002) 4, para I and ECRI Second Report on the UK, CRI (2001) 6, 2000, para K.
208 Fredman, *Discrimination Law*, p. 6.
209 Ibid.
210 See ECRI Second Report on Spain, CRI (2003) p. 40, ECRI Second Report on France, CRI (2000) p. 31, 2000, ECRI Second Report on Germany, CRI (2001) p. 36, 2001, ECRI Second Report on Italy, CRI (2002) p. 4, and ECRI Second Report on the UK, CRI (2001) p. 6.
211 H. Blumer, 'Race Prejudice as a Sense of Group Position' (1958) *Pacific Sociological Review*.
212 J. Hagen-Zanker and R. Mallett, 'Migration Policy: Three Things to Know about Fortress Europe'. Available at: https://www.odi.org/comment/9995-migration-policy-three-things-know-about-fortress-europe (accessed 12 October 2016).
213 S. Isal, *Racism and Race Relations in the UK*, ENAR Shadow Report, April 2002.
214 S. Pinto, 'Padded Walls' , *Connections* (Autumn 2002).
215 This clinical approach to racism has been discussed in relation to perpetrators; see F Brennan, 'Can the Institutions of the EC Transcend Liberal Tendencies in the Pursuit of Racial Equality?', in B. Brecher, J. Halliday and K. Kolinska (eds), *Nationalism and Racism and the Liberal Order* (Aldershot: Ashgate, 1998), pp. 108–23.
216 Vantaa Local Court R 00/3085, p. 16.
217 Ibid.
218 The sentence was reduced on appeal to two and a half years imprisonment.
219 For a full account of this case see ENAR Shadow Report for Finland 2001, March 2002.
220 ENAR Shadow Report for Finland 2001, March 2002, p. 8.
221 Williams above.
222 A. Sivinandan, IRR *European Race Bulletin* (No. 37, June 2001) from a workshop paper for the Institute of Race Relations.
223 L. Fekete, 'The Emergence of Xeno-Racism', in *The Three Faces of British Racism: A Special Report, Race and Class* 43 (2001): 23–40.
224 Williams above, p. 13.
225 Art 6 Council Dir 2000/43/EC.
226 See CRE at www.cre.gov.uk/legaladv/rra_regs_indirect.html (accessed 15 December 2015).
227 European Council Consultative Commission (1995) Final Report, Ref. 6906/1/95 Rev 1 Limite RAXEN 24.
228 Ibid., 59.
229 Mel Read and Phillip Whitehead, East Midlands Labour MEPs, the site for European, National & Local Government and Politics, 11 June 2003. Available at: www.labmeps-emids.fsnet.co.uk/index.htm (accessed 15 December 2015).
230 European Commission Press Releases IP/04/1512, 20 December 2994; 28 April 2005; IP/05/543, 4 May 2005.
231 'Commission acts to close gaps in racial equality rules' IP/07/928, Brussels, 27 June 2007.
232 Art 5 of Council Dir 2000/43/EC.
233 For instance, see Art 2 Council Dir 2000/43/EC.
234 Art 5 of Council Dir 2000/43/EC.
235 Council Dir 2000/43/EC.
236 Martiniello, 'Affirmative Action and Racism: Affirmation Action as a Tool or Hinder', Socio-Economic Research, Racism and Xenophobia, Key Issues, Mechanisms and Policy Opportunities

Socio-economic Research, Racism and Xenophobia as Challenges to the European Integration Process, 5–6 April 2001 (Centre Borchette, Rue Froissart 36, Brussels).

237 Equality Act 2010 Explanatory Notes. Available at:www.legislation.gov.uk (accessed 4 December 2015).

238 In fact this measure deals with wider matters such as nationality, colour and national origins.

239 Section 9(2)-(4) of the Equality Act 2010.

240 Harassment and racist abuse are forms of direct discrimination according to the Equality and Human Rights Commission. Available at: www.equalityhumanrights.com/advice-and-guidance/your-rights/race/what-is-race-discrimination/what-forms-does-racial-discrimination-take/ (accessed 4 June 2014).

241 Victimisation is also a form of racial discrimination. See www.equalityhumanrights.com/advice-and-guidance/your-rights/race/what-is-race-discrimination/what-forms-does-racial-discrimination-take/ (accessed 4 June 2014).

242 Department of Culture Media and Sport, Equality Act 2010: Guidance. Available at: www.gov.uk/equality-act-2010-guidance (accessed 4 June 2014).

243 Department of Health, Chief Inspectors Letters, the National Archives. Available at: http://webarchive.nationalarchives.gov.uk/+/www.dh.gov.uk/en/Publicationsandstatistics/Lettersandcirculars/Chiefinspectorletters/DH_4003911(accessed 4 June 2014).

244 Gurbux Singh, former Chair, Commission for Racial Equality. Available at: www.fbu.me.uk/newspress/ffmag/2002/0102/0102raceact.pdf (accessed 4 June 2014).

245 That came into force on 6 April 2011.

246 Section 149(2). Available at: www.legislation.gov.uk/ukpga/2010/15/section/149 (accessed 5 June 2014).

247 Sections 149 (1) (a)-(c) of the Equality Act 2010. See www.legislation.gov.uk/ukpga/2010/15/section/149 (accessed 5 June 2014).

248 Equality and Human Rights Commission, *The Essential Guide to the Public Sector Equality Duty*, vol. 1 of 5, January 2011. Available at: www.equalityandhumanrights.com (accessed 4 November 2015).

249 Ibid., p. 5.

250 This did just not only apply to the UK, other Member States such as Germany, Austria and Finland had failed to comply with the directive and it was found that this was in breach of EU law, I. Solanke, *Making Anti-Racial Discrimination Law* (London: Routledge, 2009), p. 184.

251 A reasoned opinion is the second out of three stages where the Commission can raise issues with Member States over their failure to comply with Community law – called infringement. The Commission's power is derived from article 258 of the Treaty on the Functioning of the European Union.

252 E. Howard, *The EU Race Directive: Developing the Protection against Racial Discrimination within the EU* (London: Routledge, 2010), p. 34.

253 Report from the Commission, 29 Annual Report on Monitoring the Application of EU Law, 2011.

254 Ibid., p. 43.

255 S19 of the Equality Act 2010.

256 Article 2(2) (b) of the Race Directive.

257 In Brief, Legal Personality. Available at: www.inbrief.co.uk/legal-system/english-law.htm (accessed 29 May 2014).

258 Howard, *The EU Race Directive*, p. 74.

259 Macpherson, *The Stephen Lawrence Inquiry*.

260 Stephen Lawrence Education Standard, 01 01 2000. Available at: http://ec.europa.eu/ewsi/en/practice/details.cfm?ID_ITEMS=9110 (accessed 11 April 2014).

261 Macpherson, *The Stephen Lawrence Inquiry*, para. 6.34.

262 Gearty, 'The Internal and External "Other" in the Union Legal Order'.

263 Ibid., p. 327.

264 Solanke, *Making Anti-Racial Discrimination Law*.

265 European Commission, Report from the Commission to the European Parliament and the Council, Brussels, 17. 1. 2014 COM (2014) 2 final.

266 Ibid.

267 Ibid., p. 184.

Bibliography

Bell, M., 'Beyond European Labour Law? Reflections on the EU Racial Equality Directive', *European Law Journal* 8 (2002).

Blumer, H., 'Race Prejudice as a Sense of Group Position', *Pacific Sociological Review* (1958): 3–7.

Brennan, F., 'Can the Institutions of the European Community Transcend Liberal Limitations in the Pursuit of Racial Equality?', in B. Brecher, J. Halliday and K. Kolinska (eds), *Nationalism, Racism and the Liberal Order* (Aldershot: Ashgate, 1998).

Brennan, F., 'European Race Directive: A Bridge So Far?', in Raphael Walden (ed.), *Racism and Human Rights* (Leiden: Martinus Nijhoff, 2004).

Brennan, F., 'Punishing Islamophobic Hostility: Are Any Lessons to be Learned from Racially Hostile Crimes?', *The Journal of Civil Liberties* 8(1) (2004): 28–50.

Carmichael, S. and C.V. Hamilton, *Black Power: The Politics of Liberation* (New York: Vintage Books, 1967).

Connolly, M., *Discrimination Law* (London: Sweet and Maxwell, 2006).

CRI (2000) 31 Second Report on France, adopted on 10 December 1999. Available at: http://www.coe.int (accessed 16 February 2017).

Dandeker, C. and D. Mason, 'The British Armed Services and the Participation of Minority Ethnic Communities: From Equal opportunities to Diversity?', *The Sociological Review*, 49(2) (2001): 219–235.

Dennis, L., 'Addressing Latent Racism and Blatant Discrimination in America', *Chicago Monitor*, 4 April 2013.

Directive 8*European Law Journal* 384 (2002).

Dobe, K. and S. Chhokar, 'Muslims, Ethnicity and the Law', *International Journal of Discrimination and the Law* 4 (2000): 369.

Douglas-Scott, S., 'The Common Foreign and Security Policy of the EU: Reinforcing the European Identity?', in P. Fitzpatrick and J.H. Bergeron (eds), *Europe's Other: European Law Between Modernity and Postmodernity* (Aldershot: Ashgate, 1998), 131–133.

Dummett, A., *Citizens, Minorities and Foreigners* (London: CRE, 1994).

Duncan, W., 'Racism and Xenophobia in Europe', in G. Barrett (ed.), *Justice and Cooperation in the European Union* (Dublin: Institute of European Affairs 1997), 183.

European Commission, 'European Social Policy – A Way Forward for the Union' COM (94) 333 final, 27. 7. 94, ch VI.

European Commission, Report from the Commission to the European Parliament and the Council, Brussels, 17. 1. 2014 COM (2014) 2 final.

European CouncilConsultative Commission, (1995) Final Report, Ref 6906/1/95 Rev 1 Limite RAXEN 24.

European Monitoring Centre, *Looking Reality in the Face.* Annual Report 1998 (Vienna: EUMC, 1998).

Fekete, L., 'The Emergence of Xeno-Racism', in *Race and Class* 43 (2001): 87–91.

Fitzpatrick, P. and J. Bergeron, *Europe's Other: European Law between Modernity and Postmodernity* (Aldershot: Ashgate1998).

Forbes, I. and G. Mead, 'Measure for Measure: A Comparative Analysis of Measures to Combat Racial Discrimination in the Member Countries of the European Community', Equal Opportunities Study Group, University of Southampton, 1992, Research Series No 1 (London: Department of Employment).

Ford, G., *Report Drawn up on Behalf of the Committee of Inquiry into Racism and Xenophobia* (Luxembourg: Office of Official Publication of EC, 1991).

Fredman, S., *Discrimination Law* (Oxford: Oxford University Press, 2002).

Gearty, C., 'The Internal and External "Other" in the Union Legal Order: Racism, Religious Intolerance and Xenophobia', in P. Alston (ed.), *The EU and Human Rights* (Oxford: Oxford University Press, 1999).

Geddes, A., *Immigration and European Integration: Towards Fortress Europe?* (Manchester: Manchester University Press, 2000).

Goldston, J.A., The European Union Race Directive, Open Society Justice Initiative (2003). Available at: www.justiceinitiative.org/publications/russia_ec/moscow_workshop/goldston (accessed 16 February 2017).

Haney Lopez, I.F., 'Institutional Racism: Judicial Conduct and a New Theory of Racial Discrimination', *Yale Law Journal* 109 (2000): 1717–1884.

Harrison, M., I. Law and D. Phillips, *Migrants, Minorities and Housing: Exclusion, Discrimination and Anti-Discrimination in 15 Member States of the European Union* (EUMC, 2005).

Hieronymus, A. and M. Moses, *ENAR, Shadow Report 2002, Talking 'Race' in Germany* (Hamburg: Institut fur Migrations- und Rassismusforschung, 2003).

Howard, E., *The EU Race Directive: Developing the Protection against Racial Discrimination within the EU* (London: Routledge, 2010).

Isal, S., *Racism and Race Relations in the UK*, ENAR Shadow Report, April 2002. Available at: www.cms.horus.be.files.MediaArchive.pdf (accessed 16 February 2017).

Kamali, M., 'Conceptualising the "Other", Institutionalized Discrimination and Cultural Racism', European Commission, Improving Human Research Potential and the Socio-economic Knowledge Base, Socio-Economic Research, Racism and Xenophobia: Key Issues, Mechanisms and Policy Opportunities, 5–6 April 2001 (Centre Brochette, Rue Froissart 36, Brussels).

McCrudden, C., D. Smith and C. Brown, *Racial Justice at Work: The Enforcement of the Race Relations Act 1976 in Employment* (London: Policy Studies Institute, 1991).

Macpherson, W., *The Stephen Lawrence Inquiry* (London: Home Office, 1999).

Martiniello, M., *Affirmative Action and Racism: Affirmation Action as a Tool or Hinder.* Available at: https://cordis.europa.eu.improving.docs (accessed 16 February 2017).

Modood, T. et al., *Ethnic Minorities in Britain: Diversity and Disadvantage* (London: Policy Studies Institute, 1997).

Moon, G., ENAR Shadow Report 2002, *Racism and Race Relations in the UK.* Available at: www.enar-eu.org (accessed 16 February 2017).

Niessen, J. and I. Chopin (eds), *Anti-discrimination Legislation in EU Member States: A Comparison of National Anti-discrimination Legislation on the Grounds of Racial or Ethnic Origin, Religion or Belief with the Council Directives, Austria* (Vienna: EUMC, 2002).

O'Brien, M., 'The European Race Directive – Our Plans for Implementation', *European Lookout* 3 (2000): 2.

Pinto, S., 'Padded Walls', *Connections* (2002).

Poulter, S., *Ethnicity, Law and Human Rights: The English Experience* (Oxford: Oxford University Press, 1998).

Qurashy, B., *ENAR Shadow Report 2002, Racism and Discriminatory Practices in Denmark.* Available at: www.mirror.unhabitat.org (accessed 16 February 2017).

Global Report on Human Settlements 2001 (UN-HABITAT, 2001). Available at: www.mirror.unhabitat.org (accessed 16 February 2017).

Roubani, N., *ENAR Shadow Report-2001 for Greece.* Available at: www.enar-eu.org.Shadow-Reports-on-racism-in-europe (accessed 16 February 2017).

Singh, G., *Race Discrimination in the 21st Century: The Need for Action*, 7 December 2000. Available at: www.chester.ac.uk.launch-2014 (accessed 16 February 2017).

Sivinandan, A., *IRR European Race Bulletin* (No. 37, June 2001) from a workshop paper for the Institute of Race Relations. Available at: http://www.books.google.co.uk (accessed 16 February 2017).

Socio-Economic Research, Racism and Xenophobia, Key Issues, Mechanisms and Policy Opportunities Socio-economic Research, Racism and Xenophobia as Challenges to the European Integration Process, 5–6 April 2001 (Centre Borchette, Rue Froissart 36, Brussels).

Solanke, L., *Making Anti-Racial Discrimination Law* (London: Routledge, 2009).

Thiele, B. and M. Gomez, 'Non-discrimination and Equality in the Cities. Applying Inter nationals Human Rights and Housing Rights Standards', *Human Rights Tribune* 8(3) (2002).

Thomas, H., *The Slave Trade: The History of the Atlantic Slave Trade 1440–1870* (London: Papermac, 1997).

UN Centre for Human Rights, (1996) 'Model National Legislation for the Guidance of Governments in the Enactment of Further Legislation Against Racial Discrimination'. Available at: https://searchworks.stanford.edu.view (accessed 16 February 2017).

United Nations Centre for Human Settlements, Cities in a Globalising World. Global. Available at: www.un.org.events.pastevents.pdfs (accessed 16 February 2017).

Vila Costa, Blanca., 'The Quest for a Consistent Set of Rules Governing the Status of non-Community Nationals', in P. Alston (ed.), *The EU and Human Rights* (Oxford: Oxford University Press, 1999).

Wench, J., 'Mechanisms of Exclusion: Ethnic Minorities and Labour Markets', *Nordic Labour Journal* 1(1997): 16, 17.

ZARA, *Racism Report 2001: Case Reports on Racist Excesses in Structures in Austria* (Vienna: 2001).

6 Black custodial deaths as an instance of institutional racism

Introduction

The House of Commons Home Affairs Select Committee (Committee) in its Inquiry on Young Black People and the Criminal Justice System (CJS), found that they were over-represented due to discriminatory factors.[1] Furthermore, there have been patterns of persecution of people of African descent stemming from chattel slavery over 400 years. It is argued that the two are linked. There has been the an historical desire by the state to control black men, for instance witnessed in Britain,[2] the USA[3] and apartheid South Africa.[4] Slavery, colonialism, apartheid and institutional racism tend to be divorced from each other as separate and distinct episodes in history, but it is argued here that they form a tapestry in which the race relations between primarily black men and state and non-state actors interconnect when it comes to highly dangerous discriminatory practices. This chapter considers controversial deaths in custody of black people which arise from the use of lethal force[5] or from the failure of a duty of care by state actors and private actors carrying out state functions in order to detain black people by the police, prison and mental health services and private security firms.[6] It also focuses on the failure on the part of the Crown Prosecution Service (CPS) to prosecute state and non-state actors involved in these deaths. INQUEST, a campaign group concerned with custodial deaths, shows that a disproportionate number of those who die following police custody where the use of physical restraint is employed are from the black and minority ethnic communities (BAME).[7] This chapter aims to situate these controversial black deaths in custody as an instance of the racism that has come down from chattel slavery times to its culmination in institutional racism.

Institutional racism has been defined as the collective failure to provide a service to people because of their colour, culture or ethnic origin and this can be seen in processes, attitudes and behaviour which amounts to discrimination through unwitting prejudice, ignorance, thoughtlessness and racist stereotyping which disadvantage minority ethnic people (Macpherson).[8] It has been suggested that black people are racially stereotyped as being aggressive and violent and because of this they are more likely than whites to die in custody through the use of physical constraints that cause asphyxia or lack of a duty of care and death occurs.[9] Moreover, Hannon and others suggest that people of 'BAME groups were significantly more likely to be restrained than white people'.[10]

It is argued that state and private actors carrying out state work deal aggressively with black people on the basis of a canteen culture[11] of racist assumptions that black people are aggressive and violent and that violence is the only language they understand.[12] The presumption stems from the ideology of chattel slavery where it was assumed that black people were little more than animals, that they were monsters, naturally inferior to whites.[13]

Given the public concern on the over-representation of black deaths in custody, this chapter will consider the case of the death of Alder and others, the Independent Inquiry into the death of David Bennett,[14] the Sainsbury's Report on Mental Health and black People and the report from Black Mental Health UK. The Butler Report[15] will be discussed as will the Code for Crown Prosecutors and the Independent Police Complaints Commission (IPCC) in the wake of concerns over institutional racism as the context within which these reports have been written and the problem of institutional racism ignored. Few of these investigations have examined the place that institutional racism has to play in the attitudes and behaviour meted out by state actors and non-state actors to black people because of racial stereotyping. Chattel slavery was a racial stereotyping system from at least the seventeenth century where it was believed black people were descended from apes and in the nineteenth century where science decided from skull measurements that black people were inferior to whites and made to serve white people.[16] Remnants of this racist ideology still hold sway and it is critical that this phenomenon be acknowledged and accorded its weight in the fight against the provision of racially delivered services.

Background

From 2002 to 2012 the majority of deaths where black and ethnic minority people have come into contact with the police have been deaths in custody (INQUEST).[17] In 2011 38 per cent of those who died in custody were from black or ethnic minority communities.[18] Moreover, black and Asian people dying in police custody had risen by 50 per cent.[19] Afro-Caribbean people were six times more likely to die in the custody of the police than would be expected from their numbers in the population.[20] Afro-Caribbeans form 2.9 per cent of the general population but constitute 20 per cent of those who die in police custody.[21] There is, to put it mildly, an issue when it comes to custodial deaths and black people because of the restraint techniques or the failure to provide a duty of care to black people in custody. Some of the cases make for gruesome reading and it is worth looking at them and the consequences when the question of black deaths comes into contact with the criminal justice system.

Alder was picked up from a nightclub after a brawl. He was first taken to hospital and then moved to a police station custody suite. He was placed face down for 11 minutes and died in a pool of blood and his own urine and excrement with his trousers pulled down around his knees. Police were heard to say that Alder was 'faking it' and monkey noises were heard on an audio tape.[22] These monkey noises are a throw-back from the times when black people were considered to be descended from apes.[23] In 2002 five police officers went on trial accused of manslaughter and misconduct in public office. All were cleared on the orders of the judge. An internal disciplinary inquiry cleared the officers of any wrong doing. The IPCC said that four of the officers were guilty of the most serious neglect of duty but still the officers walked free.[24] Similarly whites have escaped punishment for the cruelty they inflicted on black people during the times of racialised chattel slavery. The state did not hold whites responsible for slavery then and today the police are not held to account.

Sey was a case reported on by INQUEST in 1997. His family found that Sey had a mental health problem and his family called the police after he had been acting strangely. Once Sey was in the rear yard of the police station, the police tied his hands behind his back. They also sprayed him with CS gas and he was held down for at least 15 minutes. The mode of death was positional asphyxia.[25] The Coroner's jury returned a verdict of unlawful killing in 2007.[26]

Douglas was stopped by police officers and in an unprovoked attack he was hit on his head by a policeman with a police baton[27] and died after that incident. Police said they were acting in self-defence. A verdict of misadventure was recorded at the Coroner's court.[28]

Lapite was stopped by police officers in 1994. They thought he was acting suspiciously. Within half an hour he was killed. The evidence showed that the cause of death was asphyxia from compression of the neck consistent with the application of a neck-hold.[29] The Director of Prosecution (DPP) at the time said that it could no longer defend the decision not to prosecute the officers implicated in Lapite's death.[30] However, although the inquest found that he was unlawfully killed, the CPS decided not to prosecute.[31]

Rose died in 1981 when he was being conveyed in a police van. He was restrained in the police van and died in the vehicle.[32] The inquest into his death found for an unlawful killing at the hands of the police. No prosecution was brought.[33]

In the case of Burrell-Brown, he called on the police for help when out with his little son, after he saw a local gang 'tooled up' to attack him. Instead of helping him, the police arrested him and beat him up in front of his son. He died three days later in 2011.[34] Two officers were arrested and bailed on suspicion of manslaughter and a further four police officers were arrested and interviewed by the IPCC under criminal caution.

Rigg died after unsuitable force was used on him. He was held down in a 'V' shaped prone position for 8 minutes which brought on a cardiac arrest.[35] An inquest jury found in 2012 that police actions had contributed to his death. The CPS decided that the police officers implicated in Rigg's death would not be prosecuted on the basis that they did not have sufficient evidence.[36]

The treatment of black people by the G4S (a private security firm) has also been called into question. Mubenga's jury in the Coroner's court found that he had been unlawfully killed by G4S, a private security firm contracted by the Home Office to carry out deportations.[37] The killing took place when Mubenga was physically restrained using the 'carpet karaoke' method where a person's head is forced down so that they cannot breathe properly. During the time Mubenga was restrained, it was later found that there were racist jokes on the mobile phones of two of the guards.[38] The security guards were acquitted of the killing of Mubenga in December 2014.

Myatt was the first child to die at the hands of G4S.[39] These security guards held the boy in a seated double embrace which involved holding his upper body and pushing his torso towards his knees whilst holding his head. He died.[40] He choked on his own vomit. The inquest into his death returned a verdict of accident but also found that he might still be alive if the Youth Justice Board, which oversees privately run centres, had carried out adequate safety checks into the type of restraints staff were being trained to use on children in their care. This type of restraint has now been withdrawn from use within juvenile custody but it took the death of a little mixed heritage boy to do it.[41]

Gardner was seized by immigration officers and restrained. She ended up in hospital on life support and eventually died.[42] She was restrained by a body belt and was wrapped with 13 feet of tape around her head. This led to suffocation and she fell into a coma[43] and died. Gardner, a third-country national, died as the result of the execution of a deportation order that was carried out in a racist way.[44] The CPS brought a case against the officers but the officers were acquitted.

The concern

These are a sample only of the restraint based cases caused by state and non-state actors where a black person is the victim.[45] Furthermore, the government is alive to this issue given the report of the Independent Advisory Panel on Deaths in Custody (IAP) held in May 2010 to which the Ministry, Home Office and Department of Health were parties. The IAP said that there needs to be a focus on de-escalation techniques.[46] The IAP recognised that there were a disproportionate number of restraint incidents involving BAME prisoners and that this group were consistently more likely than white British prisoners to have force used against them.[47]

Therefore there are three related problems. The first is at the beginning of the process where state and non-state actors go in hard to restrain black people based on racially constructed myths about black people and how they will respond to authority. These racially constructed myths include the notion that black people are big, black and dangerous.[48] The second is the difference between the Coroner's inquest that tends to find unlawful killing and the failure of the CPS to prosecute and the third is the acquittal rate by the jury in the Crown Court. In none of these scenarios was the issue of institutional racism brought out as a problem by the criminal justice system as one of the strands that interplay thus making it hard to gain access to justice.

The relative failure to prosecute state actors who kill shows why there is concern that the response of the criminal justice system remains colour blind (in a bad way). This colour blindness means that the problems black people face at the hands of the criminal justice system are not perceived as a problem first and foremost when they are in the hands of state and non-state actors and second when they are killed by the same groups. The criminal justice system should be colour conscious[49] if it is to deal with those who cause racial harm to black people so that black people can be provided with an appropriate service. The problem is that the criminal justice system has not evolved to recognise that blacks are more vulnerable in the hands of state and non-state actors. Instead there is 'non-recognition'[50] which is part of the ideology of colour blindness.[51] There is a commitment to colour blindness as a symbol and as a message.[52] This runs throughout the criminal justice system even whilst black people are dying at the hands of state actors. This ideology, symbol, message needs to be exposed so that it can lift the institutional veil behind which restraint led deaths or lack of duty of care occur and the fact that no one is held to account.

Several comments and reports have appeared as a result of concern regarding suspicious related deaths in custody and black people. Internationally the UN Committee on the Elimination of Racial Discrimination (CERD) 57 Session commented that there had been a number of deaths in police and prison custody of members of ethnic minority communities in which no officers of the police or prison service have been prosecuted, and recommended investigations be taken on to inspire confidence among the ethnic minority communities.[53] The problem with CERD's comments is that they are political in their impact, and while negative comments may bring embarrassment to a government, they are not legally binding[54] and therefore easy to ignore, at least in this instance.

The Independent Inquiry into the death of David Bennett[55]

Mental health institutions have also been called into question in the context of restraint related death. Bennett was held in a secure mental health institution. Following an altercation with another patient Bennett was moved within the same institution and later on he assaulted a nurse. First five and then four nurses were used to restrain him for 25 minutes. He was restrained 'across his upper body and by his arms and ankles'[56] and he died 25 minutes later.[57] There was an independent inquiry that found that 'staff treated Mr Bennett as a lesser being who should be ordered about'.[58] It is argued that this treatment was like that of chattel slaves where black people were seen as less than human beings. Furthermore, black and minority ethnic (BAME) groups are not getting the service they are entitled to from the mental health service. The inquiry called on the Department of Health to 'cure this festering abscess [racism] which is at present a blot upon the good name of the NHS'.[59]

The inquiry was published on 12 February 2004 and pointed out the problems with the mental health part of the National Health Service (NHS) and its relationship with ethnic minority groups as institutionally racist. 'The report … found that at present people from the black and minority ethnic communities, who are involved in the mental health services, are not getting the service they are entitled to. Putting it bluntly, this is a disgrace'.[60] The reaction to the report was varied as far as the government was concerned but they did not go as far as accepting institutional racism to be the root cause, (despite the report findings to the contrary) that needed to be cut out of mental health service delivery. Indeed John Reid, then Secretary of State for Health, in a statement to the Commons avoided an acceptance of institutional racism. He merely said, 'I accept that there is discrimination in the NHS, both direct and indirect'.[61] More crucially, he failed to concur with a key recommendation in the report – that a three minute time limit be set for restraining people in a prone position. On this, his response was, 'The National Institute for Clinical Excellence (NICE) will shortly publish guidance in this area'.[62] The NICE report presented that 'black and particularly African Caribbean users are over-represented within the mental health services in the UK[63] – [the] variety of reasons [come from the] prevalence of schizophrenia amongst African Caribbean users [and] institutional racism'.[64] Young Afro-Caribbean men were stereotyped as big, black and dangerous and this affected the treatment of them as service users in a racially discriminatory way.[65] One of the recommendations of NICE was that if force is going to be applied it should be so 'for the minimum time possible'.[66] However, this is surely what those inflicting force would argue if asked to account for their actions so this statement is rather ineffectual. The three minute maximum rule was not recommended. This poses the question of why not? Institutional racism was mentioned in passing in the report but a lot more could have been done to explain this link with the Black user experience and delivery of services. The report into the David Bennet case had been preceded by another investigation of Black deaths in custody entitled *Big, Black and Dangerous?* Report of the Committee of Inquiry into the Death in Broadmoor Hospital of Orville Blackwood and a Review of the Deaths of two other Afro-Caribbean Patients in 1993. Thomas[67] tells us that the inquiry commented on 'organisational racism'[68] in the mental health system and that staff were blind to it in terms of its operation as a subtle form of racism.[69] It is argued that this form of racism is institutional racism handed down from the treatment of slaves during chattel slavery, and meted out when black people are at their most vulnerable in the hands of the state apparatus.

The Sainsbury's Report

Nationally there have been several relevant reports regarding black deaths in custody.This includes the Sainsbury's Centre for Mental Health (SCMH) (2002),[70] and a report by Black Mental Health UK (2013) (BMH).[71] Let us look first at the SCMH. It was argued in that report that 'stereotypical views of black people, cultural ignorance, and the stigma and anxiety associated with mental illness often combine to undermine the way in which mental health services assess and respond to the needs of Black and African Caribbean communities'.[72] Black people are over-represented in mental health services and are the largest group to which fear is associated in society and within the mental health service.[73] This fear is based on the idea of being threatened by racial differences that cause racial prejudice based on ancient myths about black people widely believed to be the primary function of cultural and psychological racial prejudice.[74] Racism remains evident within mental health services and racial stereotyping of dangerousness influences the management of Black patients.[75] Fear plays a major role in how black people are perceived as the 'Other' in mental health services as well as how black service users experience the services. Black service users fear the more coercive services such as police or prison and their association with mental health. This is particularly pertinent when it comes to deaths in custody where there is a link between custody deaths and the black people viewed and treated with 'suspicion, hostility and anger'.[76] This report supports the argument that institutional racism thrives in the mental health setting.

Black Mental Health UK

Suspicious black deaths in custody have also been raised by Black Mental Health UK (BMH). In terms of black deaths in police custody since 2004, in England and Wales, a disproportionate number were of black people.[77] BMH are a body set up in 2006 to conduct awareness raising and to deal with the stigma caused by people's biased views of the mental health system. They aim to make access to services fairer for African and Caribbean people. They also have as their objective to improve the black service user experience and decrease the use of the coercive end of mental health care. BMH submitted evidence to the House of Commons, Home Affairs Select Committee inquiry into the Independent Police Complaints Commission regarding deaths in custody with respect to mental health services and African Caribbean users.[78] This evidence that was submitted in January 2013 concerned the way black people with mental health problems were treated by state actors. BMH wanted a judicial inquiry into how all deaths in custodial settings were handled starting with Winston Rose in 1981 and ending with Kingsley Burrell-Brown in 2011. The concern so far has been the role racism plays in causing deaths of black people in custody in the first place and the Sainsbury Report was particularly helpful in this regard. The second concern has been the relative failure to bring the perpetrators to justice. Again this report by the BMH lends itself to the problem that institutional racism is at play in the way that mental health services are delivered to black and ethnic minority people.

The Butler Inquiry

Cases involving black and mixed ethnicity form a greater proportion of those restrained and this has the danger that it could lead to lethal restraint.[79] The background to the Butler Inquiry was the fact that there were three successful challenges to the discretion of the Director of Public Prosecution (DPP) and that of the Police Complaints Authority (PCA) that officers implicated in the deaths of Lapite[80] and O'Brien[81] and the torture of Treadaway[82] were neither prosecuted and/or disciplined for the unlawful killings and the torture of Treadaway. The importance of this background is that it constituted 'the first … instances of successful challenges to the exercise of the DPP's prosecutorial discretion, resulting in a judicial inquiry, called the Butler Inquiry and, at least in part, the decision of the then DPP to resign'.[83]

On 28 July 1997, His Honour Gerald Butler QC was appointed by the government to conduct an, 'Inquiry into Crown Prosecution Decision-Making in Relation to Deaths in Custody and Related Matters'.[84] The report acknowledged that there was a failure of the CPS to prosecute officers implicated in deaths in police and prison custody. The terms of reference required that the inquiry consider the Lapite and O'Brien[85] cases; to examine the Treadaway case (all were BAME); to consider how these cases were prepared for the Divisional Court, to look at the process and quality of casework decision-making in death in custody cases and to consider changes and make appropriate recommendations.[86]

The inquiry focused on the three cases of Lapite, O'Brien and Treadaway where the CPS's decision not to prosecute police officers implicated in criminal wrongdoing had been challenged by way of an application for judicial review. The inquiry found that there were a number of mistakes in the way the decision not to prosecute was reached that did not instil confidence in the decision-making process.[87] It was argued that many of the decisions were caused by systemic failure. The system for taking decisions was 'inefficient and fundamentally unsound.'[88] There was confusion over who took the decision not to prosecute in the Lapite and O'Brien cases yet such a decision was made. The inquiry considered whether there was any unfair bias in the decisions not to prosecute and decided that although the decisions not to prosecute were not flawless, they were reached honestly and without unfair bias.[89] If any blame was to be levelled for the inadequacy in the way the cases were handled that should be laid at the door of the CPS itself and not at individual prosecutors. It was the system that failed. For Butler, the CPS, (in the form of Central Casework), had formed a pessimistic view of a reasonable prospect of conviction.[90] This was particularly so as a result of the acquittal of officers after the death in custody of Joy Gardner. Such pessimisim was perhaps not necessary since each case, according to Butler, '... depends very much on its own facts'.[91]

The recommendations broadly speaking were that the CPS pay attention to the lack of transparency regarding the decision-maker, that the CPS pay consideration to the lack of transparency in decision-making and that there was a need for compulsory training. As regards the decision-maker the inquiry recommended that this person should be higher than the Branch Crown Prosecutor and that it should be the Assistant Chief Crown Prosecutor (ACCP) who should receive papers from the police and decide whether or not to prosecute state and non-state actors involved in deaths in custody. The ACCP should read and consider all the evidence and prepare a note stating the decision and the reason for the decision.[92] Putting the responsibility for dealing with deaths in custody higher up the chain of command responded to the criticism that this area was not being treated sufficiently seriously by staff with the commensurate expertise.

The second area covered by the recommendations was that there should be transparency in the decision-making process. It should be clear who takes the decision whether or not to prosecute and reasons for such decisions should be made in writing.[93] The advice of Senior Treasury Counsel[94] should be sought where the decision was that there was not a realistic prospect of conviction.[95] The ACCP should reconsider the matter if Senior Treasury Counsel disagreed. The requirement that cases should be sent to Senior Treasury Counsel appeared to relate to the concern that there was not sufficient independent advice sought. Where decisions not to prosecute were reached prior to an inquest, they should be reviewed following the conclusion of the inquest.[96] The obligation to seek advice from a source 'independent' of Central Casework might allay some of the criticism levelled at the CPS that decisions not to prosecute police officers in death in custody cases was consequent upon the close working relationship between the CPS and the police[97] that showed there was no independence between the two elements of the state.

To deal with the concerns raised in the inquiry several recommendations were made. These were contained in section 11 of the report and generally covered the three areas already discussed. The CPS responded positively to the Butler Inquiry recommendations taking all of them on board.[98] However the findings and the recommendations fell far short of what one would expect given the public concern about controversial Black deaths in custody. For instance the IPCC stated about deaths in custody that they impact on trust and confidence in the police particularly Black and ethnic minority communities.[99] This aspect was not brought out in the report.

Transparency and the veil behind which institutional racism operates

The Butler Inquiry raised the issue of the lack of transparency in terms of the decision-making process of the CPS when it came to whether there was a case for prosecution, and recommended that such decisions should be taken at a higher level. Transparency means something that is easily seen through. Keir Starmer QC, then Director of Public Prosecutions said that his 'vision is of a transparent, contemporary CPS which engages in an open and honest way with the communities it serves'.[100] How would a higher level of decision-making combat the problem that a professional service such as the CPS failed to provide a service that did not potentially discriminate on the basis of ethnic origins?[101] Both Jones (aka Lapite) and O'Brien were ethnic minorities and it seems as though the unsuccessful prosecution of Gardner[102] (another ethnic minority) may have laid heavily on the 'mind' of the CPS when considering a scenario where the victim was an ethnic minority and the defendant was a state actor. But there is precedent to show that the police can be successfully prosecuted. David Oluywale[103] was the first Black man to die in custody where officers were convicted of the crimes committed on him.[104] Butler also reported that the lack of transparency meant that the system had failed rather than there being an individual officer at whom blame should be levelled but it is difficult to know what was meant by 'the system'. Furthermore the prosecutor in the Lapite and O'Brien case was the same person who had decided that there was sufficient evidence to go to the jury in the unsuccessful Gardner case.[105] Was this prosecutor working in a kind of 'canteen culture' of the CPS pointed out in the Macpherson Report with respect to the police?[106] Racism can unconsciously influence performance.[107] More work should have been undertaken by the inquiry on the notion of systemic failure meaning a 'complex whole, set of connected things or parts, organised body of material or immaterial things'.[108] For instance, what was the relationship between the police, the evidence, the CPS and the failure to prosecute officers? Clearly they were part of the system but how did that relationship work in terms of lack of prosecutions? This matter is precisely the sort of thing the Macpherson Report concerned itself with when considering how services 'unwittingly' discriminate against ethnic minorities when they fail to provide a professional service.[109] This failure to provide a professional service is institutional racism, a racism that is rooted in the complex relationship of chattel slavery and its racist justification that are not seen as part of the system but perceived as divorced from it.

The need for training

In a number of places the Butler Inquiry raised concern that there was no requirement for compulsory training in the Central Casework[110] team. It recommended that there should be formal compulsory training that would incorporate an understanding and consistency of application of the 'realistic prospect of conviction' test[111] especially in relation to the type of work undertaken by Central Casework.[112] Furthermore, the inquiry pointed out that there should be training on the developments and changes in the law and the structuring and drafting of review notes. What was absent was any mention of training as regards racial inequality especially given that Butler had discovered bias (although not unfair bias) in the system and the CPS was itself concerned with bias in the system.[113] Moreover, Butler acknowledged that the inquiry was concerned with the perceptions of favourable treatment shown to the police by CPS in the decision not to prosecute officers for ethnic minority deaths in custody. All Butler did in this regard was to assert that '... I do not believe this to be a justified perception'.[114] But it has been argued that there may be prosecutorial bias at work in decision-making that is not itself governed by the Code for Crown Prosecutors.[115] For instance Ashworth and Fionda[116] argue that unconscious creeping in of bias may have an effect on the ultimate outcome of whether or not to prosecute.[117] There is the possibility of the 'predictive approach' where the prosecutor gives weight to the disposition of the local court where the court history plays a disproportionate role in determining the prosecutor's decision and this may reflect the reality of the situation.[118] Alternatively there is the 'intrinsic merits' paradigm where the law is prioritised over the whims of magistrates and juries.[119]

Furthermore, it has been argued that the CPS are police-dependent, uncritical and lacking in independent evaluation, there is 'undue reliance upon the police version of events'.[120] It is argued that the evidence utilised by the CPS is itself highly police-oriented since the police are the source of the supply such that information dependency cases are police products and CPS decisions are police driven.[121] Given the public concern about racial discrimination, the killings of black people and the failure to prosecute state actors for deaths in custody, it is hard to see why there would not be a suggestion of training on the role that racial discrimination and institutional racism in terms of a canteen culture can play in terms of potential 'racialised' assumptions regarding the decision not to prosecute. As the CPS itself reported '... a death in custody ... takes on an added significance when the person who has died belongs to a group which considers itself as having had historically strained relationships with the police and other institutions of the criminal justice system'.[122]

Code for Crown Prosecutors and institutional racism

It is argued that the failure to prosecute state actors for deaths in custody demonstrates the failure of the state system to hold state and non-state actors accountable for their involvement in these deaths. But what about the Code for Crown Prosecuters (the Code) whose use is to bring perpetrators to justice through the exercise of the Code for Crown Prosecutors? We have seen with the Butler Inquiry that the CPS have been investigated for failure to bring prosecutions in three cases but what of the Code? Whether or not to bring a prosection for a death in custody is based on the use of the Code for Crown Prosecutors. This Code provides that before a prosecution can be brought two things must satisfy the prosecutor. The first is whether there is '... enough evidence to provide a realistic prospect of conviction ...'[123] the evidential test. According to the Code this is an objective test which means that '... a jury or bench of magistrates, properly directed in accordance with the law, is more likely than not to convict the defendant of the charge alleged'.[124] According to the Code, if evidence is not sufficient the case cannot proceed 'no matter how serious or sensitive it may be.'[125] It is argued controversial black custodial deaths are serious and that the use of lethal force should be sufficient to provide the type of evidence necessary to bring a prosecution. For the sake of justice in these cases the evidential test should be changed and made more flexible. This is so that the cases are heard and the defendants prosecuted.

The second matter that must be assured in the Code is whether it is in the 'public interest' to prosecute.[126] The Attorney General (2003)[127] cited the Butler Inquiry stating that 'there is a powerful public interest in the prosecution of police officers who have committed an offence of such gravity'.[128] Moreover, in the House of Commons[129] where the issue of the lack of prosecutions in these circumstances was raised, it was said that there are 'certain classes of cases which excite such public interest that even if the evidence is not quite as strong as it is for the common run of cases, there is an argument for saying that it should be put in front of the court'.[130] So the argument might be that both the evidential test and the public interest test should have a paradigm that takes into account the type of defendant that could potentially be put before a jury, where conduct could expect to be of a higher standard than usual precisely because the defendants are who they are. And the offences might be misconduct in public office[131] or gross negligence manslaughter if not reckless manslaughter or murder. Gross negligence requires a duty in law, a breach of duty, the conduct of the defendant was the cause of the breach and the breach was so bad, so criminal in nature, as to be grossly negligent.[132] Reckless manslaughter relies on the defendant foreseeing a risk and taking it in any event, whilst murder is the unlawful killing of the victim with intention. It is contended that in these cases of lethal restraint at least gross negligence or reckless manslaughter charges should be brought against the defendants. There is the need to understand that the brutalisation used on black people stems from a racist ideology that marks them off as big, black and dangerous. This ideology is one stemming from chattel slavery days that has become locked in the institutions that concern the criminal justice system. An understanding of this by the CPS would warrant the prosecution of these defendants.

The problem is that the exercise of the use of the Code is only part of the picture. There appears to be not only a general reluctance on the part of the CPS to prosecute state and non-state actors involved in black death in custody cases,[133] but also a specific reluctance to prosecute them where there has been a perceived element of justification (or believed justification) in the use of force.[134] The law is vague in this area and its limits unclear, but this is only to be expected given the paucity of prosecution material. The problem is also compounded when there is a disproportionate reliance on the police version of events[135] since the victim is not there to speak for themselves and the evidence is police driven and therefore there is an imbalance. Furthermore, the prosecutor may be influenced by stereotypical views of black people as being aggressive and thus warranting the reaction received at the hands of the state actors.[136] Indeed the *Denman Report*[137] suggests that the CPS is institutionally racist in the way staff are treated and that is part of a culture.

> Culture makes the world meaningful for the people in it, by selecting from a potentially infinite number of objects and concerns in the noumenal world a finite set of things, and directing people's attention towards them and not to others. This is how the world comes to have meaning for us and how we come to feel ... secure, that is, feel reality is patterned and orderly.[138]

This culture has institutional racism as an ingredient which has meaning but for which there is no conscious recognition and this racism may inadvertently feed into prosecutorial decision-making.[139] Particularly where the victim is black and the perpetrator is a state or non-state actor dealing with an intense set of circumstances. Moreover, there is support for the argument that this culture within which the Code exists drowns out the decision-making that is supposed to be determined by the Code. Hoyano *et al.*[140] suggest that the Code does not affect the decision-making at all. Whilst Baldwin's[141] research argues that the paradigm of the CPS is police-dependent, uncritical and lacking in independent evaluation.[142] Sanders[143] contends that this dependency on police evidence means that the evidence utilised by the CPS becomes police products and CPS decisions are police driven. This is dangerous territory since the independence of the CPS and the utility of the Code are then brought into question, and it raises the issue of to what extent the evidence is filtered so that it gives the police an unfair advantage, due to an unconscious creeping in of bias[144] when the CPS are considering sufficient evidence and public interest issues with respect to controversial black deaths in custody.

For instance in the Lapite case the police officer gave contradictory evidence about the relationship between his arm and the victim's throat during what he claimed was a struggle. In his incident report book the officer acknowledged that his arm was tightening around Lapite's throat yet he denied that his arm was in such contact at the inquest.[145] If the CPS and the Code for Crown Prosecutors are not working with respect to black deaths in custody perhaps we should adopt a system where the evidence is considered by judges properly trained on the effects of institutional racism in decision-making and the case dealt with by them from indictment to trial. The Crown Prosecutors should also be trained in the workings of institutional racism and its role in lethal restraint of black people. Both judges and prosecutors should also be educated in the chattel slavery context that has brought about institutional racism. This educational process would seek to ensure independence and confidence in BAME communities. It is also argued that state and non-state actors should go through a similar educational process so that it might also encourage them to reflect on how they treat BAME individuals in controversial situations and ultimately avoid killings. The training could be taken on by the Equality and Human Rights Commission (EHRC) together with suitable NGOs.

The Independent Police Complaints Commission

As its name tells us there is an Independent Police Complaints Commission (IPCC) set up to deal with complaints about the police in England and Wales. The state has granted the police wide ranging powers such as the right to deprive citizens of their liberty, the IPCC is there to ensure that those powers are not misused. When there is a death in custody the IPCC is expected 'to investigate intelligently, robustly, fearlessly and effectively all the circumstances surrounding the death. The investigation must give an honest and clear-sighted account of what happened, including whether any crime or disciplinary offence occurred or any other actions or omissions not meeting the threshold of a crime or disciplinary matter but nonetheless of public concern'.[146]

In July 2013 the IPCC produced a document dealing with racism and the police in London.[147] The IPCC found that complaints about racism are not taken seriously by the Metropolitan Police Service, whether the racism was overt or covert, and there was a resistance to dealing and learning from past practice to a position of positive reinforcement of non-racist practice.[148] This tells us that institutional racism is not taken seriously by the police despite the Macpherson Report in 1999 that found this form of racism in the police service, and it does not bode well for BAMEs caught in intense situations with the police where the police and other state actors use restraint.

Whilst the IPCC oversees complaints against the police as a body they have come in for serious criticism regarding their investigation into deaths in custody and black people. A black man named Sean Rigg was restrained and arrested by police in London and died whilst in police custody in 2008. A death in custody is automatically referred to the IPCC.[149] The original investigation by the IPCC found that 'officers had acted reasonably and proportionately'.[150] Following an inquest where the jury found that positional asphyxia and lack of care to Sean Rigg contributed to his death an independent review[151] (the Casale Report)[152] was set up with a mandate:

- to examine the IPCC investigation in light of both the evidence given at the Coroner's Inquest and the verdict of the Inquest;
- to consider whether any further investigation is required, with a view to misconduct or criminal proceedings against any member of the police service;
- to identify any lessons to be learnt or broader issues for both the IPCC and the overall system for investigating deaths following police contact;
- to take account of the Rigg family's concerns; and
- to take account of parallel reviews relating to policing, mental health and deaths in custody.

The Casale Report found that there were many holes in the investigation by the IPCC regarding the Sean Rigg story, including allowing officers to confer with each other before they were interviewed. The Casale Report 'criticised the IPCC for accepting accounts from officers that were "improbable" and "implausible"'.[153] The IPCC accepted the review and said that it could no longer support its original findings and 'would consider reopening its investigation to examine misconduct issues'.[154] INQUEST[155] has argued that the wrongdoing around the case of Rigg's is not a one-off. The problem represents a broader concern of systemic issues in the IPCC that need to be addressed. This problem with systemic issues is one that was raised in the Stephen Lawrence Inquiry[156] where it was held that public services fail to provide a professional service, unwittingly, and this leads to institutional racism. Here we have the IPCC, an independent body whose job it is to investigate possible police wrongdoing, finding itself in the 'dock'.

What were these systemic issues? According to the Casale Report there was a failure to 'adopt basic investigative practices'.[157] There were possible breaches of a duty of care to Sean Rigg including the use of the type of restraint 'rear stack'[158] position and the duration of restraint (which took approximately eight minutes)[159] as possible misconduct by officers. There was poor police performance, including an implausible failure to recognise that Sean Rigg had a mental health problem.[160] The same notion that Sean Rigg was violent and not unwell determined by the police was also adopted by the IPCC's view of the police conduct as being reasonable and proportionate.[161] More generally, the IPCC should draw on mental health expertise in cases like that of Rigg,[162] particularly as it turned out there were culturally sensitive issues that meant services took a more relaxed approach, rather than an assertive one, to the relapse of Rigg.[163]

Race came up as a general issue in the Casale Report. The report stated there was a lack of reference to race throughout the IPCC investigation which should have been picked up, particularly when one of the officers questioned said of people with Rigg's conduct who came from Brixton[164] that this was typical 'especially with people you come across in Brixton,'[165] Again, a stereotype with no foundation, rather misperception, a misperception that led to lack of a duty of care and ultimately the death of Rigg. It is argued that just like the police, there is a 'canteen culture' of institutional racism in the IPCC as is demonstrated in the Rigg case. This partly comes from the fact that a large proportion of IPCC staff are themselves ex-police officers, that there is a willingness on the part of the IPCC to be influenced by the police version of events and there is a failure to retain independence from the police.[166]

The IPCC mentioned the case of Sean Rigg in their Annual Report 2012/13. They said they were going to look at the evidence from the inquest to see whether further action should be taken[167] and more generally to tighten up procedures but there was no acknowledgement of institutional racism and the role it had to play in the way Sean Rigg's case was handled.[168][169] Here is another example of an organisation in need of training in both institutional racism and its chattelised context.

The work done by the IPCC on racism and the Metropolitan Police Service, as pointed out above, and the fact that the IPCC have accepted all the Casale Report recommendations may demonstrate that the IPCC is willing to learn from its mistakes and not allow itself in terms of its framework in death in custody cases to be driven somewhat by a police perspective. However, it does not inspire confidence that 11 per cent of staff, 33 per cent of investigators and 90 per cent of Senior Investigators are former police officers, a matter that has raised concern.[170] How can the important element of independence and objectivity when investigating the police be retained when it seems as though the police are investigating themselves? Furthermore, Doreen Lawrence[171] has said that she has no confidence in the IPCC.[172] There was a similar comment from the Rigg family regarding investigation into Sean Rigg's death in custody.[173] Moreover, the IPCC 'is not yet capable of delivering the kind of powerful, objective scrutiny that is needed to inspire … confidence'.[174] The IPCC has also come in for criticism from the Newham Monitoring Project[175] and the Police Action Lawyers Group[176] both of whom argue that the IPCC falls down in terms of independence, accessibility and moral support.[177] It would appear that there needs to be a thorough root and branch change of the IPCC with staff versed in institutional racism and its chattelised context.

Conclusion

'Violence is the only language they understand'[178] is a strong stereotype because it gives state and non-state actors an excuse for 'going in mob handed' when dealing with black people. This stereotype is also a dangerous one with respect to black people, particularly young black men, because it can lead to the use of lethal force. This stereotype is part of the material of institutional racism spread throughout institutions that state and non-state actors unwittingly work through without any consciousness that it has become part of their armoury. Quite what is it about skin colour that makes the victims of state actor conduct vulnerable? It is more than coincidence and it is more than a 'few rotten apples' as Lord Scarman[179] would have us believe. Rather there have been hundreds of years of racist ideology stemming from the transatlantic slave trade where black people were seen as nothing more than inhuman, chattel to be treated in anyway their owners chose. That essential racism did not disappear upon emancipation but rather it had time over hundreds of years to be woven into the institutional fabric of societal institutions. Whilst legislation in the twentieth century tackled direct and indirect racial discrimination, it failed to come to terms with the phenomenon of institutional racism. State and non-state actors who work in coercive institutions reinforce the racism by carrying out the day to day work that continues to degrade and belittle the Other. In this case black and Asian people. It is like the conversation overheard by a black officer whilst sitting in the back of a police car and 'a female white officer on seeing a black person driving a very nice car just said "I wonder who he robbed to get that?" and she then realised she was actually voicing an unconscious assumption'.[180]

It is argued that there is a common thread in identifying institutional racism and deaths in custody and that is the failure to prosecute state actors and non-state actors for their role in black deaths in custody. The big players here are the CPS and the IPCC. The CPS because of the way the Code for Crown Prosecutors militates against prosecution when dealing with deaths in custody and the IPCC due to the fact that they appear not to hold the police responsible for these deaths (a clear example being the death of Sean Rigg). The Casale Report laid open the problem with the Sean Rigg case and it was hoped that since the IPCC had agreed to review the case there would be a stepping stone to the identification and prosecution of officers, in other words, that event would have a cascading effect on the other services who would recognise institutional racism as part of the problem, and come up with a solution to counter it. This did not happen. Instead the IPCC said that there were lessons to be learned from the investigation.[181] Further, that an external investigation would be commenced to consider areas of improvement.

The solution is that where there is a controversial black death in custody the procedure from prosecution to trial should be left to judges with a proviso that they are suitably trained in the way institutional racism works. There would not be a jury in the early stages nor a prosecutor or defence lawyer. This is a radical move from the adversarial system that we have now. It is argued that the issue is too critical to leave to the current sytem. It should be handled by a system where we have judges who act as instructing magistrates as is the case in some civil law jurisdictions. As instructing magistrates the judges will be in charge of investigating the crime, the circumstances, the perpetrators and other relevant matters. The judge would be independent of the office of Public Prosecutor as is the case in France where it is the judge who investigate homicides.[182] It is the judge who questions witnesses and interrogates suspects. Although judges would have to rely on the evidence from the police, they would also have the inquest evidence. The latter would be used as the package of materials that a judge would consider with respect to the guilt or otherwise of the defendant. If a prima facie case was made out by the judge as to the responsibility of the defendant/s then the case would be submitted for trial before a judge with a prosecutor, defence lawyer and a jury. It would need to be ensured that the parties were educated in institutional racism, chattelised slavery and its role in the criminal justice system. With the judge, prosecutor and defence and jury training in institutional racism and its chattelised context would be carried out by the Equality and Human Rights Commission.

There is the issue that too much faith is put in a judicial system that is mostly, white, male and middle to upper class. To counter that argument it is contended that, unlike the CPS, the judiciary is more transparent as a public body and it is easier to see what it is doing. Moreover the judges would be working in the knowledge that the process was public from beginning to end. At that point it is argued that the jury direction should include a reference to institutional racism and chattel slavery.

These extra layers in the prosecution of state and non-state actors where there is a controversial death in custody might instil more confidence in the criminal justice system that is so badly required from the point of view of the black and minority ethnic community.[183]

Notes

1 The House of Commons Home Affairs Select Committee. Available at: www.statewatch.org (accessed 7 December 2015).
2 A. Sivanandan, *Deadly Silence: Black Deaths in Custody* (London: Institute of Race Relations, 1991).
3 Available at: www.washingtonsblog.com2015/01 (accessed 25 May 2016).
4 Available at: www.gohistorygo.com (accessed 25 May 2016).
5 It was pointed out in the *Guardian* that a black man was shot in the back by a white policeman whilst running away from him (8 April 2015). Furthermore a Sheriff's reserve officer shot and killed a black man on the 13 April 2015 (*Guardian*, 14 April 2015). Both incidents occurred in the USA.
6 A death in custody occurs when those in the custody of the State die. See *Crown Prosecution Service* (CPS), 'What is a Death in Custody?' Available at: www.cps.gov.uk/legal/d_to_g/deaths_in_custody/. (26 September 2014). There is also the gendered nature of these deaths that tend to occur with black men.
7 INQUEST, 'BAME Deaths in Custody 2004–2013', 3 January 2015. Available at: www.inquest.org.uk/statistics/bame-deaths-in-police-custody (accessed 14 January 2015).
8 W. Macpherson, *The Stephen Lawrence Inquiry*(London: Home Office, 1999), para. 6.34.
9 Sivanandan, *Deadly Silence*, Introduction.
10 M. Hannan, I. Hearnden, K. Grace and T. Bucke, 'Deaths in or following Police Custody: An Examination of the Cases 1998/99–2008/9', IPCC Research Series Paper: 17, Executive Summary.
11 This is defined as 'a set of conservative and discriminatory attitudes said to exist within the police force'. Available at: www.oxforddictionaries.com.
12 Sivanandan, *Deadly Silence.*
13 'Port Cities, Bristol, Racist Ideas'. Available at: www.dicoveringbristol.org.uk (accessed 7 December 2015).
14 H. Athwal and R. Bennett, 'Rocky Bennett – Killed by Institutional Racism', *Institution of Race Relations*, 18 February 2004. Available at: www.irr.org.uk/news/rocky-bennett-killed-by-institutional-racism/ (accessed 25 September 2014).
15 His Honour Gerald Butler QC, *Inquiry into Crown Prosecution Service Decision-Making in Relation to Deaths in Custody and Related Matters* (London: Stationery Office, 1999) (hereafter Butler Inquiry).
16 Port Cities, Bristol, Racist Ideas.
17 INQUEST was founded in 1981 and it provides a service into controversial deaths in England and Wales. Available at: www.inquest.org.uk/ (accessed 23 September 2013).
18 House of Commons Home Affairs Committee, *Independent Police Complaints Commission, Eleventh Report of Session 2012–13*, 1 February 2013, p. 3. Available at: www.publications.parliament.uk/pa/cm201213/cmselect/cmhaff/494/494.pdf (accessed 23 July 2014).
19 *Electronic Telegraph*, issue 1625, 6 November 1999, based on Home Office figures.
20 B. Bowling and C. Phillips, *Racism, Crime and Justice* (Harlow: Longman, 2002), p. 135.
21 Office of National Statistics (ONS), *2001 Census*, Office of National Statitics.
22 INQUEST 'Death in Police Custody', Report on the Death of Ibrahima Sey 1997, London. Available at: http://inquest.gn.apc.org/pdf/Ibrahima%20Sey%20briefing.pdf.
23 P. Fryer, *Staying Power: The History of Black People in Britain* (London: Pluto Press, 1985), pp. 165–167.
24 K. Couvee, 'Deaths in British Police Custody: No Convicted Officers since 1969', *Open Security and Peace Building*, 9 August 2013. Available at: www.opendemocracy.net (accessed 14 January 2015).
25 S. Cape, 'No Charges after CS Spray Death', *BBC News*, 1 October 1998. Available at: http://news.bbc.co.uk/1/hi/uk/184410.stm (accessed 25 September 2014).
26 Bhatt Murphy Solicitors, 'Deaths in Custody'. Available at: www.bhattmurphy.co.uk/bhatt-murphy-91.html (accessed 14 January 2015).
27 S. Hattenstone, 'Why? Special Report Deaths in Police Custody', *guardian.co.uk*, March 2001. Available at: www.theguardian.com/celldeaths/article/0,465301,00.html (accessed 25 September 2014).

28 'Relatives Protest at Custody Deaths', BBC News, 30 October 1999. Available at: http://newsbbc.co.uk/1/hi/uk/106733.stm.

29 Hattenstone, 'Why?'.

30 Bhatt Murphy Solicitors, 'Deaths in Custody'.

31 BBC News, 30 October 1999. Available at: http://newsbbc.co.uk (accessed 15 June 2015).

32 Athwal, 'Black Deaths in Custody'.

33 Ibid.

34 L. Jasper, 'Kingsley Burrell: British Justice', *Operation Black Vote*, 9 June 2011. Available at: www.obv.org.uk/news-blogs/kingsley-burrell-british-justice (accessed 26 September 2014).

35 S. Morrisson, 'IPCC to Re-examine Custody Death of Sean Rigg as Review Criticises Initial Investigation', *The Independent*, 17 May 2013. Available at: www.independent.co.uk/news/uk/home-news/ipcc-to-reexamine-custody-death-of-sean-rigg-as-review-criticises-initial-investiga tion-8619815.html (accessed 27 September 2014).

36 V. Dodd, 'Police Officers in Sean Rigg Death in Custody will not be Prosecuted', *The Guardian*, 7 October 2014. Available at: www.the guardian.com (accessed 15 January 2015).

37 J. Haughton, 'Pervasive Racism among G4S, says Jimmy Mubenga Coroner', *The Voice*, 7 August 2013.

38 Ibid.

39 G4S are an international security firm that deal with security issues and create safe environments for their clients. Available at: www.g4s.com/en/Who%20we%20are/Our%20Business/ (accessed 25 September 2014).

40 C. Sambrook, 'G4S Guard Fatally Restrains 15 year old – Gets Promoted', *OurKingdom power and liberty in Britain*, 2 July 2013 (accessed 25 September 2013).

41 L. Smith, 'Nobody Can Hurt Him Now', *The Guardian*, 4 July 2007 (accessed 20 January 2015).

42 J. Torode, 'When Deportation Means death: Joy Gardner Died after Police Raided Her Home: John Torode Sifts Facts from Prejudice'. *The Independent*, 3 August 1993. Available at: www.independent.co.uk/voices/when-deportation-means-death-joy-gardner-died-after-police-raided-her-home-john-torode-sifts-fact-from-prejudice-1458919.html (accessed 27 September 2014).

43 R. Pryor, 'No Justice No Peace Racial Justice in Britain', *The Black Presence in Britain*. Available at: www.blackpresence.co.uk/tag/black-deaths-in-custody/ (accessed 27 September 2013).

44 Bowling and Phillips, *Racism, Crime and Justice*, p. 132.

45 Institute of Race Relations, *Deadly Silence: Black Deaths in Custody* (1991). Also see Athwal, 'Black Deaths in Custody'.

46 Independent Advisory Panel on Deaths in Custody,*Report of the Cross-Sector Restraint Workshop*, May 2010 (London: Ministry of Justice, Home Office and Department of Health, 2010), p. 28.

47 Ibid., pp. 28–29.

48 L. Nelstrop, J. Chandler-Oatts, J. Cowl *et al.*, NICE Clinical Guidelines, no. 25S (London: Royal College of Nursing, 2005). H. Prins, 'Big, Black and Dangerous? Report of the Committee of Inquiry into the Death in Broadmoor Hospital of Orville Blackwood and a Review of the Deaths of Two Other Afro-Caribbean Patients, 1993'. Available at: www.ncbi.nlm.nih.gov/books/NBK55910/ (accessed 23 January 2015).

49 J. Skelly Wright, 'Colour – Blind Theories and Color – Conscious Remedies', *The University of Chicago Law Review* 47(92) (1980).

50 R. Richard Banks, 'Race Consciousness, Color Blindness and Antidiscrimination Doctrine', p. 4. Available at: www.law.virginia.edu/pdf/workshops/0708/banks.pdf (accessed 30 September 2014).

51 Ibid.

52 Ibid.

53 See United Nations Committee on the Elimination of Racial Discrimination (CERD) 57 Session, Concluding Observations of the CERD: United Kingdom and Northern Ireland 18/08/2000, A/5518, paras 346–372.

54 Leaflet No. 4: 'Human Rights Treaty Bodies and Indigenous Peoples: The Treaty-based System and How to Use it'. Available at: www.ohchr.org/Documents/Publications/GuideIPleaflet4en.pdf (accessed 30 September 2014).

55 Athwal and Bennett, 'Rocky Bennett – Killed by Institutional Racism'.

56 Ibid.

57 Ibid.
58 J. Carvel, 'How the Death of One Black Patient Treated as a 'Lesser Being' Showed up Race Bias', *The Guardian*, 6 February 2004.
59 Athwal, 'Rocky Bennett – killed by Institutional Racism'.
60 Ibid.
61 Ibid.
62 Ibid.
63 NACRO have also stated that Black people are disproportionately over-represented in the mental health service. See NACRO, *Black Communities, Mental Health and the Criminal Justice System*, NACRO Mental Health and Crime Briefing, 2007.
64 NICE, *Disturbed/Violent Behaviour In-Patient Psychiatric Settings and Emergency Departments*, published by the Royal College of Nursing, London, February 2005, p. 24.
65 Ibid.
66 Ibid., p. 98.
67 P. Thomas, 'Black and Mad'. Available at: www.schizophreniainquiry.org/news/black-and-mad (accessed 20 November 2014).
68 Ibid.
69 Ibid.
70 The Sainsbury's Centre for Mental Health, *Breaking the Circles of Fear: A Review of the Relationship between Mental Health Services and African and Caribbean Communities* (London: SCMH, 2002).
71 Home Affairs, written evidence submitted by Black Mental Health UK (IPCC) 31 January 2013. Available at: www.publications.parliament.uk/pa/cm201213/cmselect/cmhaff/494/494we06.htm (accessed 16 July 2014).
72 The Sainsbury's Centre for Mental Health, *Breaking the Circles of Fear*, p. 8.
73 Ibid., p. 13.
74 P. Fryer, *Staying Power: The History of Black People in Britain* (London: Pluto Press, 1985), pp. 133–134.
75 The Sainsbury's Centre for Mental Health, *Breaking the Circles of Fear: A Review of the Relationship between Mental Health Services and African and Caribbean Communities* (SCMH, London, 2002), p. 14.
76 Ibid., p. 21.
77 Written evidence submitted by Black Mental Health UK [IPCC]. Available at: www.parliament.uk (accessed 6 December 2015).
78 Home Affairs, Written evidence submitted by Black Mental Health UK (IPCC) 31 January 2013. Available at: www.publications.parliament.uk/pa/cm201213/cmselect/cmhaff/494/494we06.htm (accessed 16 July 2014).
79 Ibid.
80 *R vDPP ex parte Jones (aka Lapite)* (unreported) Divisional Court transcript 6 June 1997.
81 *R vDPP ex parte O'Brien* (unreported) Divisional Court transcript 6 June 1997.
82 *R vDPP ex parte Treadaway* (unreported) Divisional Court transcript 6 June 1997.
83 Bhatt Murphy Solicitors. Available at: www.bhattmurphy.co.uk/bhatt-murphy-68.html (accessed 8 October 2014).
84 Butler Inquiry.
85 O'Brien was an ethnic minority not Black.
86 Butler Inquiry section 1.1 (i)-(v).
87 Butler Inquiry section 8.2(iv).
88 Butler Inquiry section 8.2.
89 Butler Inquiry section 8.6.
90 Butler Inquiry section 8.7(v).
91 Butler Inquiry section 8.7(v).
92 Butler Inquiry section 11 recommendation 2.
93 Ibid.
94 They prosecute some of the most serious cases for the CPS.
95 Butler Inquiry section 11 recommendation 3.
96 Butler Inquiry section 11 recommendation 4.
97 Butler Inquiry section 9.4(iii).

98 CPS, Press Release, 11 August 1999. 131/99.
99 Independent Police Complaints Commission, 'Deaths in Custody Study, August 2011'. Available at: www.ipcc.gov.uk/page/deaths-custody-study (accessed 31 October 2014).
100 K. Starmer, QC, 'CPS Speech – A Prosecution Service for the 21st Century'. Available at: www.cps.gov.uk (accessed 7 December 2015).
101 W. Macpherson, *The Stephen Lawrence Inquiry*, para. 6.34.
102 A. Kleebauer, 'Joy Gardner Police Death: Mum Vows to Continue Fight for Justice 20 Years after Losing Daughter', *Tottenham and Woodgreen Journal*, 17 October 2013. The officers involved in the restraint of Joy Gardner were acquitted of her manslaughter in 1995.
103 David Oluwale died on the 17 April 1969 having been chased by police officers to a river following a series of bullying, assaults and harassments. Harmit Athwal comments on a book entitled *The Hounding of David Oluwale*. This book traces the life of Oluwale from his entry into this country as a stowaway to his many altercations with the police and his eventual death at their hands.
104 Hattenstone, 'Why?'.
105 Butler Inquiry section 8.7(v).
106 Macpherson, *The Stephen Lawrence Inquiry*, para. 6.11.
107 Ibid., 6.5.
108 *The Concise Oxford Dictionary* (Oxford: Oxford University Press, 1964).
109 Macpherson, *The Stephen Lawrence Inquiry*, para. 6.34.
110 Looking at the CPS website this team appears as a Special Crime Division that deals with a number of matters including deaths in custody. Available at: www.cps.gov.uk/your_cps/our_organisation/sc_and_ctd.html#a04 (accessed 10 October 2014).
111 Butler Inquiry section 11 recommendation 6(i).
112 Ibid.
113 The Rt Hon The Lord Goldsmith QC, Her Majesty's Attorney General, 15 July 2003, CPS, *A Review of the Role and Practices of the Crown Prosecution Service in Cases Arising from a Death in Custody*, paragraph 1.5. Available at: www.cps.gov.uk/publications/others/agdeathscust.html (accessed 30 October 2014).
114 Butler Inquiry section 9.4(iii).
115 A. Hoyano *et al.*, 'A Study of the Impact of the Revised Code for Crown Prosecutors', [1997] Crim L.R.556.
116 A. Ashworth and J. Fionda, 'The New Code for Crown Prosecutors: (1) Prosecution, Accountability and the Public Interest', [1994] Crim LR 894.
117 Ibid.
118 A. Ashworth, *The Criminal Process: An Evaluative Study*, 2nd edition (Oxford: Oxford University Press, 1998).
119 Ibid., p. 183.
120 J. Baldwin, 'Understanding Judge Ordered and Directed Acquittals in the Crown Court', [1997] Crim L.R. 536.
121 A. Sanders and R. Young, *Criminal Justice*, 2nd edition (London: Butterworths, 2000).
122 Goldsmith, *A Review of the Role and Practices of the Crown Prosecution Service in Cases Arising from a Death in Custody.*
123 The Code paragraph 4.4. Available at: www.cps.gov.uk/ublications/docs/code2013english_v2.pdf (accessed 28 November 2014).
124 The Code paragraph 4.5.
125 The Code paragraph 4.4.
126 The Code paragraph 6.
127 A Review of the Role and Practices of the Crown Prosecution Service in Cases Arising from a Death in Custody. Available at: www.cps.gov.uk/publications/others/agdeathscust.html (accessed 28 November 2014).
128 Ibid, paragraph 1.4.
129 The House of Commons Select Committee on Home Affairs, Minutes of Evidence Questions 1–19, Tuesday 9 May 2000.
130 Ibid., p. 6.
131 *R v Dytham* [1979] QB 722.
132 *R v Adomako* [1995] 1 AC 171.

133 NGOs held a vigil on the 6 December outside the CPS on this issue. Available at: www.irr.org.uk/wp-content/uploads/2013/11/CPS_Crisis_v3.pdf. (accessed 9 December 2014).
134 Ibid.
135 J. Baldwin, 'Understanding Judge Ordered and Directed Acquittals in the Crown Court', [1997] Crim LR 536.
136 Butler Inquiry section 5.2. where the assumption was made about the victim as being violent.
137 S. Denman, *The Denman Report – Race Discrimination in the CPS* (CPS, July 2001).
138 D. Inglis, *An Invitation to Social Theory* (Cambridge: Polity Press, 2012), p. 17.
139 Denman, *The Denman Report.*
140 A. Hoyano, L. Hoyano, G. Davis and S. Goldie, 'A Study of the Impact of the Revised Code for Crown Prosecutors', [1997] Crim. LR 556.
141 J. Baldwin, 'Understanding Judge Ordered and Directed Acquittals in the Crown Court', [1997] Crim LR 536.
142 Ibid.
143 Sanders and Young, *Criminal Justice.*
144 A. Ashworth and J. Fionda, 'The New Code for Crown Prosecutors:(1) Prosecution Accountability and the Public Interest'[1994] Crim LR 894.
145 Butler Inquiry section 5.5.
146 Casale *et al., Report of the Independent External Review of the IPCC Investigation into the Death of Sean Rigg*. Available at: www.seanriggjusticeandchange.com/Review%20Report%20FINAL.pdf (accessed 19 July 2014).
147 Independent Police Complaints Commission, *IPCC Report Concludes the Metropolitan Police Service is failing to Deal Effectively with Race Complaints*, 17 July 2013. Available at: www.ipcc.gov.uk/news/Pages/pr_170713_mps_race_complaints.aspx (accessed 17 July 2014).
148 Ibid.
149 Casale *et al., Report … into the Death of Sean Rigg.*
150 V. Dodd, 'Police Watchdog Criticised for Errors in Investigation into Death in Custody', *The Guardian*, 17 May 2013.
151 'The review was ordered after an inquest jury [2012] found that police used unsuitable and unnecessary force against Rigg, with officers failing to uphold the detained man's basic rights, and with police actions contributing to his death'. V. Dodd, Police Watchdog Criticised for Errors in Investigation into Death in Custody, *The Guardian*, 17 May 2013.
152 Casale *et al., Report … into the Death of Sean Rigg.*
153 Dodd, 'Police Watchdog Criticised for Errors in Investigation into Death in Custody'.
154 Ibid.
155 Ibid.
156 Macpherson, *The Stephen Lawrence Inquiry*, para. 6.34.
157 Editorial, *The Observer*, 19 May 2013.
158 'The stack positions (front or rear) are those where the wrists pass through the cuffs in opposite directions (rather than in the palm to palm or back to back positions). This is the standard secure position, producing the greatest degree of immobilisation. The Review understands that the rigid cuffs used were standard issue'. Casale *et al., Report … into the Death of Sean Rigg*, p. 3.
159 H. Athwal, 'Jury Applauded for Critical Inquest Verdict', *Institute of Race Relations*, 2 August 2012. Available at: www.irr.org.uk/news/jury-applauded-for-critical-inquest-verdict/ (accessed 22 July 2014).
160 Casale *et al., Report … into the Death of Sean Rigg*, pp. 1–6.
161 Dodd, 'Police Watchdog Criticised for Errors in Investigation into Death in Custody'.
162 Casale *et al., Report … into the Death of Sean Rigg*, p. 47.
163 Ibid.
164 Brixton is an area in London with a high proportion of black people who reside and work there.
165 Casale *et al., Report … into the Death of Sean Rigg*, pp. 70–71.
166 House of Commons Home Affairs Committee, *Independent Police Complaints Commission*, Eleventh Report of Session 2012–13, 1 February 2013, paras 7–16. Available at: www.publications.parliament.uk/pa/cm201213/cmselect/cmhaff/494/494.pdf (accessed 29 July 2014).
167 Independent Police Complaints Commission, *Annual Report and Statement of Accounts 2012/13.* Available at: www.ipcc.gov.uk/sites/default/files/Documents/publications/annual_report_IPCC_2013_web.pdf (accessed 17 December 2014).

168 On the 9 December 2013 the IPCC announced that it would reinvestigate Sean Rigg's case to see whether any criminal charges should lie against officers involved in Rigg's detention, R. Blundy, *London Evening Standard*. Available at: www.standard.co.uk/news/london/police-reopen-investigation-into-death-of-balham-man-in-custody-8993414.html (accessed 17 December 2014).

169 The CPS informed the IPCC that it would not be bringing a prosecution against officers implicated in the death of Sean Rigg (15 September 2016). Available at: www.ipcc.gov.uk (accessed 13 October 2016).

170 House of Commons Home Affairs Committee, *Independent Police Complaints Commission*, Eleventh Report of Session 2012–13, 1 February 2013, para. 13.2. Available at: www.publications.parliament.uk/pa/cm201213/cmselect/cmhaff/494/494.pdf (accessed 23 July 2014).

171 The mother of Stephen Lawrence. His death by a group of racists became the subject matter of a report that found institutional racism in terms of police conduct in the Stephen Lawrence Inquiry by Sir Macpherson in W. Macpherson, *The Stephen Lawrence Inquiry*.

172 House of Commons Home Affairs Committee, *Independent Police Complaints Commission*, Eleventh Report of Session 2012–13, 1 February 2013, para. 9. The mother of Stephen Lawrence who was killed and was the subject matter of the Macpherson Inquiry.

173 Ibid., para. 22.

174 Ibid. Part of this is due to lack of resources and the other is that the IPCC does not have binding authority.

175 The project is an anti-racist, independent community based project that aims to keep an eye on racist attacks and the statutory responses to them. Available at: www.nmp.org.uk/p/about-nmp.html (accessed 29 July 2014).

176 This is a national organisation of lawyers who represent victims of police harm. Available at: www.palg.org.uk/ (accessed on July 2013).

177 House of Commons Home Affairs Committee, *Independent Police Complaints Commission*, Eleventh Report of Session 2012–13, 1 February 2013, paras 9–10.

178 Sivanandan, *Deadly Silence*.

179 M. Rowe,*Policing Race and Racism* (Cullompton: Willan Publishing, 2004); Scarman, 1981, 4.62 and 4.63.

180 Macpherson, *The Stephen Lawrence Inquiry*, para. 6.11.

181 IPCC, 'IPCC Publishes Report into death of Sean Rigg', 15 August 2012. Available at: www.ipcc.gov.uk/news/ipcc-publishes-report-death-sean-rigg (accessed 23 January 2015).

182 G. Harris, 'Investigating Homicide Investigation in France', *Policing and Society*, 23(3) (2013): 328–345.

183 The Institute of Race Relations reported in the *Guardian* that 500 black and ethnic minority individuals have died in suspicious circumstances in custody over the last 24 years. *The Guardian*, 21 March 2015. Available at: www.theguardian.com (accessed 13 October 2016).

Bibliography

Ashworth, A. and J. Fionda, 'The New Code for Crown Prosecutors: (1) Prosecution, Accountability and the Public Interest', [1994] *Crim LR* 894.

Ashworth, A., *The Criminal Process: An Evaluative Study*, 2nd edition (Oxford: Oxford University Press, 1998).

Athwal, H., 'Black Deaths in Custody', *Institute of Race Relations* (2002). Available at: www.irr.org.uk (accessed 15 December 2016).

Athwal, H. and R. Bennett, 'Rocky Bennett – Killed by Institutional Racism', Institution of Race Relations, 18 February 2004. Available at: www.irr.org.uk/news/rocky-bennett (accessed 12 February 2017).

Baldwin, J., 'Understanding Judge Ordered and Directed Acquittals in the Crown Court', [1997] *Crim L.R.* 536.

Bowling, B. and C. Phillips, *Racism, Crime and Justice* (Harlow: Longman, 2002).

Butler, Gerald, *Inquiry into Crown Prosecution Service Decision-Making in Relation to Deaths in Custody and Related Matters* (London: Stationery Office, 1999).

Denman, S., *The Denman Report – Race Discrimination in the CPS* (London: CPS, 2001).
Dodd, V., 'Police Watchdog Criticised for Errors in Investigation into Death in Custody', *The Guardian*, 17 May 2013.
Hannan, M., I. Hearnden, K. Grace and T. Bucke, 'Deaths in or Following Police Custody: An Examination of the Cases 1998/99–2008/9', IPCC Research Series Paper: 17, Executive Summary. Available at: www.ipcc.gov.uk/sites/default…2010-swpf.org (accessed 12 February 2017).
House of Commons Home Affairs Committee, Independent Police Complaints Commission, Eleventh Report of Session 2012–2013, 1 February 2013.
Hoyano, A.*et al.*, 'A Study of the Impact of the Revised Code for Crown Prosecutors', [1997] *Crim L.R.* 556.
Independent Advisory Panel on Deaths in Custody, *Report of the Cross-Sector Restraint Workshop* (London: Ministry of Justice, Home Office and Department of Health, 2010).
Inglis, D., *An Invitation to Social Theory* (Cambridge: Polity Press, 2012).
Institute of Race Relations, *Deadly Silence: Black Deaths in Custody* (London: IRR, 1991).
Haughton, J., 'Pervasive Racism among G4S, says Jimmy Mubenga Coroner', *The Voice*, 7 August 2013.
Macpherson, W., *The Stephen Lawrence Inquiry* (London: Home Office, 1999).
NACRO, *Black Communities, Mental Health and the Criminal Justice System* (NACRO Mental Health and Crime Briefing, 2007).
Nelstrop, L., J. Chandler-Oatts, J. Cowl *et al., NICE Clinical Guidelines, No. 25S* (London: Royal College of Nursing, 2005).
NICE, *Disturbed/Violent Behaviour In-Patient Psychiatric Settings and Emergency Departments* (London: Royal College of Nursing, 2005).
Office of National Statistics (ONS), *2001 Census* (London: Office of National Statistics).
Prins, H., 'Dangerous Offenders: Some Problems of Management', *International Review of Law, Computers and Technology* 12(2) (1998): 299–313.
Rowe, M., *Policing Race and Racism* (Cullompton: Willan Publishing, 2004).
Sambrook, C., 'G4S Guard Fatally Restrains 15 Year Old – Gets Promoted', *Our Kingdom power and liberty in Britain*, 2 July 2013. Available at: www.opendemocray.net>clare-sambrock (accessed 12 February 2017).
Sanders, A. and R. Young, *Criminal Justice*, 2nd edition (London: Butterworths, 2000).
Sivanandan, A., *Deadly Silence: Black Deaths in Custody* (London: Institute of Race Relations, 1991).
Skelly Wright, J., 'Colour – Blind Theories and Color – Conscious Remedies', *The University of Chicago Law Review* 47(92) (1980).
Smith, L., 'Nobody Can Hurt Him Now', *The Guardian*, 4 July 2007.
Stacey, A., 'Protest March over Kingsly Burrell Custody Death', *The Voice*, 1 June 2014.
The House of Commons Select Committee on Home Affairs, Minutes of Evidence Questions 1–19, Tuesday 9 May 2000.
The Sainsbury's Centre for Mental Health, *Breaking the Circles of Fear: A Review of the Relationship between Mental Health Services and African and Caribbean Communities* (London: SCMH, 2002).
United Nations Committee on the Elimination of Racial Discrimination (CERD), 57th Session, Concluding Observations of the CERD: United Kingdom and Northern Ireland 18/08/2000, A/5518. Available at: www.ohchr.org (accessed 12 February 2017).

7 Institutional racism as a current and continuing legacy of the transatlantic slave trade

Skin bleaching and hair-straightening

Introduction

This chapter argues that current forms of the legacy of the slave trade such as institutional racism can be found in black women's skin bleaching and hair straightening. Skin bleaching is a process by which darker-skinned black women lighten their skin through the use of skin whitening or lightening products. Hair straightening is a procedure whereby black women use chemicals to straighten what is sometimes called 'nappy' hair or hair that has tight curls also known as afro-hair. At times this natural hair is plaited in corn rows and human or synthetic straight hair sewn into the corn rows so that the hair looks 'natural' i.e. straight.

It is argued that skin bleaching and the desire not to wear natural hair is a sign of the idea that to reach optimal beauty or even just to look good is premised on the notion that white imagery is the 'norm' and natural black features are to be shunned as lacking in these qualities of white/light skin and straight hair. Even more problematic is the issue that this skin bleaching/hair straightening whilst a complex phenomenon in terms of the reasons it exists, is also an indication of self-hatred. This hatred of black imagery is founded in chattel slavery where black women suffered racial discrimination and racism. They were treated as property to rape, beat and put to labour in the fields or domesticity and child rearing in the house of white folks. Black women were seen and treated as animals. Black women have suffered in the intersection wrought by race and gender discrimination. Centuries of the reinforcement of this white/straight hair normality situation was bound to take its toll in the flight to get away from what has been seen as the 'curse' of darker skin[1] and curly hair. It is the legacy of chattel slavery that has been blamed for poor social relations and for not being able to succeed in life.

Although this relationship between race/gender and the white norm has not been explicitly referred to at the international level it has been noted in the United Nation's production of the Declaration and Programme of Action,[2] the World Conference Against Racism, Racial Discrimination, Xenophobia and Related Intolerance, Durban South Africa, 2001(WCAR) that 'the transatlantic slave trade [is] among the major sources and manifestations of racism, racial discrimination … and that Africans and people of African descent … continue to be victims of their consequences'.[3] As a result of that nefarious trade black women have suffered through the ages of slavery, colonialism and post-colonialism[4] in terms of the status associated with skin and hair type.

It has been argued by Alonge[5] that it is fine for millions of African women to skin lighten and it is not a matter of betraying race. Maybe not but it surely shows that skin continues to be an issue for millions of black women who happen to be born with dark skin.[6] This chapter argues that skin-lightening and hair straightening is more than just a fashion statement or a question of preference, and it is not in the least bit offensive to argue that subconsciously there is a desire to emulate the 'norm' of white beauty. The bleaching of skin and straightening of afro-hair is a sign of self-hatred that is played on by businesses that profit from the chattel slavery mind set internalised by some black women. It is argued that there is a critical relationship between skin-lightening, hair straightening and institutional racism. Businesses that sell products to achieve the white norm buy into the 'canteen culture' of racism that is alive in the social relations of societies. This culture helps to shape attitudes and beliefs that black women are inferior to white. There is a failure on the part of these agencies to recognise this form of unwitting racism that survives in post-colonial societies, and a failure on the part of the state to hold these businesses to account.

Background

There was great complexity in the role of the black woman as a chattel slave. There was, and continues to be, an intersection of race and gender. It has been argued that they had a binary position being that of forced productive labour in the fields and domestic work and forced reproductive labour being raped by their masters to produce part of the future labour force.[7] Furthermore it was the lighter skinned black women that tended to carry out household domestic chores, whilst the darker-skinned black women worked outside in the fields picking sugar, tobacco leaves and cotton.

The institution of slavery was secured or justified by racist ideas that enabled slavers to treat their slaves as property. As Shyllon[8] argues the exact date that private property in black people became the norm is difficult to ascertain but between 1621 which was the indication that black people were subjects of commerce and 1698 when 'free trade in black slaves was recognised as a fundamental and natural right of Englishmen',[9] the inferiority of black people was established. Discriminatory colourism and shadism against black women in Britain continues to exist despite 200 years of abolition of slavery and the existence of legislation to prohibit racial discrimination. This colourism infects the Western world generally, the USA and the Caribbean to name but a few.[10] It is argued that whilst the Slave Emancipation Act of 1833[11] abolished slavery[12] it did not remove, nor was it aimed at disposing with, racial discrimination or racism on the grounds of skin colour or hair texture. There have been several Acts[13] aimed at dealing with the problem of discrimination on the grounds of skin colour the latest of these being the 1976 Race Relations Act and the 2010 Equality Act.[14] Racism continues to perpetuate itself and has become so problematic[15] that it has been dealt with in British criminal legislation primarily through sections 28 to 32 of the Crime and Disorder Act 1998.[16] The fact that these provisions exist at all is a testament to the hold that racial discrimination and racism has in British society. On top of this what we do not have is specific legislation that identifies and aims to eradicate institutional racism[17] which should be recognised as another form of racial harm whose context covers black women and discriminatory colourism or shadism and hair straightening. The entities that reinforce this problem – multinationals and the media – should be held to account under legislation that should be amended where necessary to deal with the institutional racism harboured in these businesses.

The United Nations (UN) recognises the 'elephant in the room' has something to do with structures and processes and that this throws up the problem of racism and racial discrimination. However, it does not go far enough in its analysis in order to incorporate the problem of institutional racism and its relationship to the problems that darker-skinned and natural haired women face. Nonetheless, the UN was quite clear that historic abuse can have an impact on victims in the present in a way that is detrimental to those victims, and that Africans and African descendants should be seen as victims of the consequences of the past – but what are those consequences? In terms of victims they can work in at least two critical ways. The first way is where the victim is loathed by other groups and the second is where the victim loathes themselves. This loathed/self-loathing has a detrimental impact on how black women are/are not portrayed. Both of these positions encapsulate institutional racism because there is here unwitting and unconscious bias by the beauty industry and the media who perpetuate and maintain this problem.

In 'Fear of the Dark', Young[18] argues that colonialism denied people, subject to it, human agency, Africans were constituted as a primitive stage of development and texts show that the African was associated with 'darkness' 'blackness, dirtiness, ignorance, evil'.[19] Darker-skinned women in particular suffered from this imagery. On the other hand white [women] were imbued with light, white and privilege which affect many aspects of their lives from what is predominantly shown in the media to not being asked to speak for their race.[20] Why? It is argued that '... white [women] are systematically privileged in Western society [and] enjoy unearned advantage and conferred dominance'[21] relative to their darker-skinned counterparts – black women – and this is a sign of institutional racism.

Loathing of the 'Other'

There is no question regarding the white skin which is in fact symbolic and a taken for granted signature of individuality, privilege and power. Through this position the Other is a '... construction of stereotypes ... [that is] crucial to the imperialist hegemonic[22] project'.[23] According to Kant,[24] in his attempt to explain the classification of what he determined were four races, he said of negroes, due to climate they have developed a 'thick snub-nose and tumid lips'[25] and due to acids of phosphorus 'all Negroes stink'.[26] Kant went on to say that 'in short, the Negro is produced, well suited to his climate; that is, strong, fleshy, supple ... lazy, soft and dawdling'.[27] Furthermore, Kant stated that the 'Negroes of Africa had feelings that were only "trifling" no talents and nothing to contribute in terms of arts or science, there is a wide gap between white and Negro which is based on mental capacity as well as colour'.[28]

It should come as no surprise that Kant read black people the way he did. The 'spectacles' through which black people were perceived, argues Fanon,[29] was based on the total disruption of cultural life, the replacement of legal systems through the negation of the nation, 'the banishment of natives and their customs to outlying districts'[30] and the 'enslaving of men and women'.[31] This problem of how black people were seen and treated did not only occur during slavery but also post emancipation. A social system was constructed following slavery in the Caribbean that rested on superiority and inferiority of race[32] black women were particularly vulnerable to this because they did not explicitly count as part of the social system, they were just there.

Self-loathing

The UK Parliament produced a report on skin-lightening treatments where it considered the motivation for changing skin colour. It acknowledged that 'colonialism established a racial hierarchy within which dark-skinned native Africans were considered "primitive" and inferior compared to light-skinned Europeans'.[33] Furthermore Parliament went on to say that 'increasingly the global ideal of beauty links with light skin and with this the idea of success, modernity, sophistication and desirability, which is perpetuated and reinforced by mass media'.[34] Moreover, some people have surmised that there is a type of social hierarchy linked to 'status … attractiveness …'[35] job security and fashion when it comes to skin colour.

'Black self – loathing [resides] in the abuse of one's body to make it white'.[36] Such self-loathing stems from low self-esteem and loss of hope and self-respect.[37] For some time, long and straight hair worn by black women and lighter skin colour were seen as the ideal by both the black community and dominant communities. This perception was challenged by the Civil Rights 'Black Power' movement in the 1960s where the focus was on accentuating African characteristics. Hair texture in particular became the grounds on which political discourse was carried out. Deloch-Hughes[38] tells us that about 50 years ago the 'Black is Beautiful' movement was launched in the USA to counter the belief that black people's features were inherently unattractive. This slogan had a positive impact on black people throughout the Diaspora, especially the USA to challenge white aesthetics. This movement consisted of 'showing off natural textured hair, full features and no make-up'.[39] The Civil Rights Movement of the 1960s helped push the 'Black is Beautiful' action into the mainstream in the USA at least. The media and advertising picked up on this discourse and soon 'natural' black was seen in major outlets. This black imagery has died off and it is difficult to know the reasons, it could be integration, assimilation or/and multiculturalism. Black people have held onto the 'black' but some have ditched the 'beautiful'. This has been witnessed in, for example, the 'upsurge in weaves'.

Hair straightening by chemicals or through weaving by black women has been discussed in several forums. In 'Weave vs. Natural' the Politics of Afro Hair'[40] several black women discussed their 'hair journeys'. This included a discussion of the experimentation with hair straightening products that in some cases left bald patches in the head or led to hair thinning and breaking. The panel agreed that hair was a big part of their lives and that in modern times the many hair styles that involved natural/weave/straightening was a multiplicity of ways of expressing themselves. Some commented on the inability to wear natural hair in the corporate environment, others believed this to be an issue that is non-negotiable. Panellists thought that the notion of 'good hair' equated with the 'n' word that sends a chill and which should be consigned to history. The panel discussed Michelle Obama's hair and whether had she worn afro-hair it would have damaged her husband's chances of the Presidency. Some believed that she would not be free to wear afro-hair and that such was a serious statement about the state of race/gender relations. The panel also discussed the idea of turning up to an interview with braids or dreadlocks and agreed that this was probably still something one would not do if one wanted the job.

Donaldson[41] argues that the hair journey is a complex one and that it is 'erroneous to believe that hair straightening is a reflection of self-hatred and an attempt to be white in all cases'.[42] No evidence is produced to show in how many cases this is or is not a factor but Donaldson argues that the matter is quite complex. It involves slavery and the internalisation of white standards of beauty, media and advertising of straight hair as the norm, assimilation and economic security based on the belief that there is a need on some level to 'normalise' to the white norm based on the idea that black women would otherwise be negatively affected. There is also the fact that afro-hair is difficult to manage and that straightening makes for an easier and quicker job, so hair straightening is a matter of personal preference. Furthermore, this process becomes a cultural script whereby hair alteration is part of a 'strict and powerful cultural norm'.[43] Hair alteration is based, Donaldson contends, on a multiplicity of factors not all related to wanting to emulate white women. However, whilst it is accepted that hair alteration is a complex factor it is still argued that there is a problem with self-hatred.[44]

Although less obvious today hair texture and skin colour still play a role in how black women see themselves and other black women.[45] There is a kind of internalised stratification going on which still holds some characteristics of the beautiful white woman as superior. This in turn relates to a legacy in which the history and culture of black women in the Diaspora are not accentuated but played down according to Lago.[46] Rather the history that black women have inherited has led to self-loathing and self-hatred spawned from the slave history and its psychological effects still felt today.[47] 'Slavery stripped Africans, and African women in particular, of their true heritage',[48] lumping them together as chattel with no acknowledgement of their separate ethnic identities and cultures and labelling them as 'niggers'[49] growing up or acclimatising themselves to a culture where the lighter the skin colour the better life chances were afforded them[50] in the Diaspora. It is argued that this has led to the development of institutional racism as a culture where skin colour becomes the embodiment of the failure to provide professional services to black women such as healthcare programmes that counter skin bleaching by promoting skin health care. The National Health Service, as cash strapped as it is, should be allocated monies to run a race awareness campaign surrounding the dangers associated with skin whitening and hair straightening.

In *Perceptions of and Preferences for Skin Colour, Black Racial Identity, and Self Esteem among African Americans,*[51] Coard *et al.*[52] argue that skin colour has been the subject matter of much controversy as to its role in life. There is a correlation between dark and light skin colour and self-esteem. This is due in some part to the way in which white society in the times of slavery treated those of lighter skin to preferential treatment compared to darker skin slaves.[53] The abolition of slavery did nothing to alleviate this obsession with lighter skin and people were able to usurp better socio-economic positions because of their lighter skin colour.[54]

What of the experiences in the Caribbean with British slavery and its abolition? According to Lago[55] 'Caribbean heritage is one of self-loathing. Self-hatred is a destructive byproduct of hundreds of years of enslavement where the black body was simultaneously an instrument of torture and a receptacle of European projection'.[56] Today the Caribbean is still plagued with this problem. Research conducted by Robinson[57] suggests that in Jamaica 'bleachers' (people who bleach their skin in order to achieve a lighter colour) use bleach as a form of social capital. Not only to enhance the chance of getting mates but also to increase opportunities in the job market.

The cause of bleaching is multifaceted but its history has developed since the slave trade and colonisation where lighter skinned people were given preferential treatment. Today those behind the skin-lightening/whitening industry (Unilever for instance) stand to gain from this self-loathing to the tune of billions of dollars – 10 billion by 2015 says Sayeed[58] talking in the context of the effect of this billion dollar industry on India. In Western countries and the United States there is a growth in the use of skin-lightening products by African women.[59] 'If you go to the ghettoes, you will see people with their faces white from the applications of these bleach preparations. You see this every day in Jamaica'.[60] The preparations are dangerous and can lead to skin cancer.[61] A recent article in *The Guardian*[62] reported that the products include steroids and other chemicals[63] banned by the European Union but not all skin bleaching products fall under this regime. Skin bleaching, to give it the medical name, is not just a fashion statement, it is tied up with the colonial and chattel slavery past. More positively, in Senegal there are NGOs such as Nuul Kukk (which means 'pitch black')[64] and some evidence that the public are fighting back. Following an advert on a billboard pitching 'Khess Petch' (all white) to the female population promising 'extreme skin-whitening after 15 days'[65] there was a campaign against the advert and product. And in

Britain? Southwark Council trading standards report that skin-lightening creams remains a critical problem amongst African-Caribbean women who use them. Some of the creams are illegal in the UK because they have dangerous chemicals in them that can cause permanent skin damage such as hydroquinone and steroids. These latter are banned from products made in the UK[66] but there is the global reach of the market in these products so that those products containing these chemicals are still accessible, particularly via the Internet.

The desire to use these creams is multifaceted but this includes 'complex social, cultural and historical factors'.[67] The matter has been raised in the House of Commons by Mr Roger Godsiff, MP.[68] The concern was the illegal sale of toxic substances. It was reported that the Medicines and Healthcare products Regulatory Agency (MHRA) were aware of this practice and pursued offenders but 'suitcase trade' persisted.[69]

There is clearly demand for the product despite it being illegal unless it is a prescription drug. The main problem is the inculcation of what it means to be beautiful. The comparison with white people who tan their skin ends when contextually it is not only the deep scars left by slavery and colonisation,[70] but the problem that darker-skinned black women want to look as Caucasian as possible in order to emulate some dominant notion of beauty, no doubt inspired by the media industry.[71] So it is not just the traders that need to be tackled for selling illegal skin whitening creams but the media who press home the image that lighter skin is better. The media are to take their share of the blame in failing to provide a professional service to black women based on their darker hue.

Institutional wrongdoers

Multinationals – constructing and maintaining the ideal woman

Some African women are buying into the bleaching skin colour image leaving devastation in its wake 'Twi as nansoben' (who told you to do it?).[72] Indeed it is big business in West African countries such as Ghana[73] despite moves by governments to ban it.[74] Skin-lightening is promoted by multinational companies[75] such as L'Oreal Paris[76] under the guise of 'Brighten your skin into the Light' and 'True Match Foundation'.[77] The colouring ranges from white to brown, moreover there are hardly any dark coloured models or products for dark/black skinned people in sight, although L'Oreal claims to ascribe to the basic value of diversity[78] at the same time they promote skin whitening cream.[79] Christian Dior promotes 'the most complete lightening program by Dior'[80] and Guerlain promises 'an exceptional whitening power' to reduce dark spots.[81] Others can be mentioned but the picture is clear, white is 'right'. It is not only that the multinationals are causing racial harm unwittingly or otherwise to darker-skinned black women, but skin whitening products should come with a health warning. The World Health Organisation names skin-lightening products and cosmetics amongst those products that contain mercury and are a danger to health.[82] A Dermatologist suggests that there is demand for 'not off the shelf' skin whitening products amongst poorer communities such as the black female community. Such products contain mercury[83] which is a poison that causes insomnia, depression and weight loss amongst other side effects.[84] Olumide[85] argues that these products are toxic because they 'alter the chemical structure of the skin by inhibiting the synthesis of melanin and should be treated as drugs not as cosmetics'.[86] Moreover, Lamkin[87] suggests that whilst poorer health outcomes are associated with darker skin, skin-lightening is likely to make racial factors worse because this is negative and would promote racial disparities. Indeed Karnani[88] points out that in terms of corporate social responsibility multinationals such as Unilever may be 'doing well' but not 'doing good' in terms of the 'negative implications for public welfare'[89] their skin whitening products have in the in terms of white and black perceptions of beauty. These multinationals should be made to take their social responsibilities more seriously since they fail to provide a service to the black woman in that they pursue the image that white or light-skinned as the perfect way to be if you want to succeed in society.

It is argued that the way through this myriad of problems is to develop a package of measures to tackle the problem of the white norm and its inculcation by black women. One thing that could be pursued is that a legal case could be brought against some of the multinationals on the basis of racial/gender discrimination. This would be a powerful public tool. The cause of action would be based on the tort of negligence. Negligence requires that there be a duty of care between the plaintiff and the defendant, that the defendant breach the duty of care (did the standard fall below that of a reasonable man), that injury or loss was suffered by the plaintiff and that the injury or loss was caused by a direct breach of the defendant's duty and that it is fair and reasonable to impose liability on the defendant. It is argued that there is a duty to take care on the part of multinationals. That duty is to portray dark-skinned natural hair imagery of black women. The failure to comply with this duty is a breach of the duty of care and has constituted injury to the plaintiff in that she has suffered low self-esteem and self-loathing. That self-hatred is caused by the defendant's failure to portray natural black imagery which is a direct breach and it would be fair and reasonable to hold the defendant legally responsible.

The case would initially have to be brought in domestic courts, the complainant would be an individual/NGO representing the black Diaspora (financially backed by the Equality and Human Rights Commission). The remedy sought would be damages against the defendant by way of financial compensation and injunctive relief by way of specific performance which is to make the multinationals change their focus on white imagery. It is appreciated that suing multinationals is a complex affair and a lot of obstacles would have to be overcome to get one into court.[90]

Whether or not the case was successful it would constitute a powerful educational tool. This education should be at least on three levels, one is to do more to teach people about the dangers of the products they use on their skin and in their hair. This would involve governments working with NGO's to get the message across to those who use these products that they are unhealthy. Indeed, the World Health Organisation (WHO) expresses concern about the availability of skin-lightening products and their use in Mali, Nigeria, Senegal, South Africa and Togo. There is common use in Africa and in Europe and North America among dark-skinned women.[91] The second approach would be to educate employers that the value of skin colour and hair texture is a worthless criterion when it comes to appointing people for jobs. The third approach is to use the media to get the message across that the promotion of lighter skin is an irresponsible thing to do, that serves to reinforce skin colour prejudice harking back to the days of slavery where some lighter skinned slaves were house slaves and the darker-skinned slaves worked in the fields.

The media

So why do these attitudes persist so long after independence in the twenty-first century? Academics studying these trends say it is because of globalisation and the emergence of 'international beauty' prototypes, based on the looks you see in fashion magazines and films.[92] Halle Berry, Rhianna and Beyoncé are three examples of this global notion of beautiful black people, the prototype that all black women should look up to and all black men desire[93] – light skin and straight soft hair. But Cohen[94] tells us that 'race' … is an ideological construct, not an empirical social category, as such it signifies a set of imaginary properties'.[95] Therefore it must be asked why do we buy into these imaginary properties when it comes to skin and hair type? This is because 'these properties of inheritance … fix and legitimate real positions of domination or subordination in terms of genealogies of generic difference'.[96] Skin colour has become a signifier of difference according to Young[97] and the media have reinforced and played on this by a reliance on stereotypes of beauty very much relying on black women who look almost white. These stereotypes have been challenged by writers such as Toni Morrison who argue that the negative presentation of black women and fitting a particular framework have to be challenged and destroyed.[98] This is difficult as Heidi Mirza tells us in relation to black women in Britain, 'We can't talk about Jim Crow or Apartheid. But like blacks globally we are both visible and invisible … we are let into desegregated spaces and constantly watched. We remain totally ignored and excluded'.[99] When we are 'recognised' it is through a Eurocentric view of 'self' portrayed by the media and reinforced by things like the lack of beauty products to suit anything other than light honey,[100] or recognised as not clever and over-sexualised. Mostly mainstream media is clearly institutionally racist and must take its share of the blame in failing to provide an adequate service to black women both by promoting the lighter skinned black female and mainly ignoring darker-skinned/natural hair females.

In the UK, the media could be held to account by the Advertising Standards Authority (ASA) that is a complaints-led entity that monitors the implementation of a Code of Conduct for broadcasting (e.g. TV and radio) and non-broadcasting (e.g. online sales, telesales and emails) advertising. Rule 4.1. states that 'Marketing communications must not contain anything that is likely to cause serious or widespread offence. Particular care must be taken to avoid causing offence on the grounds of race … or gender'.[101]

The rule deals with a serious offence on the grounds of race/gender. It is argued that the the targeting of light/white/straight hair and the omission of darker hue, curly hair advertising is sufficiently serious and offensive to black women and should be banned or amended. The latter remedies lie in the hands of the ASA. The media can always take voluntary steps to change where a complaint is upheld. A search of the ASA rulings does not reveal any complaints based on racial discrimination. That does not mean that black women are satisfied with the way they are/are not portrayed in advertising. One thing that could be done is to run a campaign in the media on the existence of the ASA, its powers and its remit focusing on Rule 4.1. The campaign would be run and funded by the ASA in collaboration with the Equality and Human Rights Commission (EHRC). This work is likely to get the complaints system moving and get the advertising businesses to think seriously about the underlying messages in their ads that are, it is submitted, racially offensive.

Changes could easily be made by banning skin whitening and hair straightening products altogether and through the monitoring of advertising by the ASA in the UK. This would be with a view to banning or amending the adverts that reinforce white dominance on the basis that they are misleading or offensive to black women in the Diaspora, whose ancestors have been in the UK since Hadrian's Wall was built in AD 122.[102] I argue that these businesses are institutional wrongdoers who should be held to account by the law and other organisations. They should have in place social/ethical policies that are aimed at them working in a colour conscious manner so that they remove racial bias. These social/ethical policies would cover the well-being of black women in society, specifically they would promote the range of black skin and natural hair types in their products and would be banned from promoting skin-lightening and hair straightening items. Together with this these businesses would have a strap line supporting racial awareness campaigns. A strap line such as 'Black is Beautiful' would be an example. These race awareness campaigns should be run to deal with the chattel slavery mentality of self-hatred and the abuse concomitant with the use of skin whitening and hair straightening products. Furthermore, involvement by the businesses would be aimed at changing their institutionally racist ideology. The race awareness campaign would be run and financed in collaboration with the EHRC and Anti-Slavery International and trading standards councils[103] in the UK. It is the EHRC whose job it is to monitor and deal with racial discrimination and the promotion of human rights under the Equality Act 2010. The EHRC have the power to ensure that the Public Sector Equality Duty (PSED) is carried out so that public bodies have 'due regard' to the need to eliminate racial discrimination. It is argued that the PSED be amended to a more general 'Equality Duty' that would then include the private sector and so catch multinational advertising and the selling of products based on white/light skin and straight hair.

Another entity that might prove fruitful is the office of the Anti-Slavery Commissioner that monitors the Modern Slavery Act 2015. The Act contains reparations for justice mechanisms which shows that the government has already accepted reparations when it comes to remedies for the trafficking of people as slaves. The Act would require an amendment so that reparations could be made available where a multinational or a business refused to make changes to their advertising and/or sales. Here financial compensation would be payable. That compensation could be earmarked for racism awareness campaigns. The Commissioner would have the job of overseeing the complaint and coming up with a suitable outcome.

Multinationals would do well to take a leaf out of the book of Procter and Gamble (P&G) who are a multinational company running a campaign entitled 'My Black is Beautiful'.[104] This is a 'long-term, community-building programme … to spark a broader dialogue around black beauty'.[105] P&G are focused on the US where they aim to teach a million girls to believe that their black is beautiful. Reaching a million girls is probably a small number by US standards since P&G serve 5 billion people around the world[106] but this initiative shows what can be done when corporate minds and the black community work together. Such a programme would be welcomed in the UK.

Conclusion

The triangular slave trade was a complex format linking African people as chattels to industrial development. At its heart were profits on the one hand and the brutalisation of Africans on the other. African human beings were constructed as beasts of burden and it was easy to use skin colour and hair type as the dividing point between the civilised white and the chattelised black. The racism that pervaded the chattelised black became a construct that was racially institutionalised so that its ideology became the norm long after the economic reasons for it had all but vanished. Two hundred years post the abolition of the slave trade 'skin' and 'hair' is still a divisive matter.

The perspective is that society is to adorn white/light skin and straight hair as the dominant norm. Dark skin/natural hair is to be shunned. This has had a detrimental impact on the confidence and self-esteem of the darker-skinned black female. This problem is part of the process of institutional racism and can be seen in the way globalised industries project the norm of white/light/straight and the products meant to enhance this construction, a creation that can be seen from at least the eighteenth century. Some dark-skinned women go to the lengths of bleaching their skin to get away from the stigma dark skin attracts, without the realisation that they are buying into an institutionally racist construction of how a woman's skin should be. This problem has bitten into the black community where 'the fair-skinned black woman who most nearly resembled white women were seen as the 'lady' and placed on a pedestal while darker-skinned women were seen as bitches and whores'[107] Whilst the skin colour/straight hair of white carries with it a 'sense of moral and also aesthetic superiority',[108] it is part of the status quo that requires challenging starting with multinationals. The multinationals could lead the way by realising that there is financial gain to be made since dark-skinned black women wear make-up too and wear products in their hair that are nothing to do with straightening. Thus the portrayal of white dominance is not necessary. Skin whitening and hair straightening products should just be banned. Work will need to be done to deal with access to these products on the Internet. The transformative strategies mentioned in this chapter are just part of a wider reparations package for people of African and Afro-Caribbean descent in the Diaspora and around the world.

Notes

1 M. Hunter, *Race, Gender and the Politics of Skin Tone* (New York: Routledge, 2005).
2 U.N. *World Conference against Racism, Racial Discrimination, Xenophobia and Related Intolerance Declaration and Programme of Action* (New York: United Nations, 2002).
3 Ibid., para. 13, p. 16.
4 R.E. Howard-Hassmann, *Reparations to Africa* (Philadelphia: University of Pennsylvania Press, 2008).
5 S. Alonge, 'Not All African Women Believe "Black is Beautiful". And that's OK', *The Telegraph*, July 2014.
6 P. Thacker, 'Another African Nation Bans Popular Skin-Whitening Creams', tells us that 'skin-lightening or bleaching is a common practice not only in Africa but in parts of Asia and the Middle East', *Women in the World*, 5 December 2015. Available at: www.nytlive.nytimes.com (accessed 5 April 2016).
7 C. LaFleur, J.K. Nishikawa, K. Thomas and S. Tillman, 'Enslaved Women and Rebellion', *Comparative Slave Rebellions*, Winter 2011. Available at: http://www.hebrewvisionnews.blogspot.co.uk (accessed 5 April 2016).
8 F. Shyllon, *Black People in Britain 1555–1833* (London: Oxford University Press, 1977).
9 Ibid., p. 7.
10 E. Zadeh, 'Light Skin v Dark Skin: Where it All Started', *The Voice*, 2014.
11 This Act came into force on the 1 August 1834. See the National Archives at www.nationalarchives.gov.uk/pathways/blackhistory/rights/emancipation.htm (accessed 1 October 2014).
12 The Slavery Emancipation Act 1833 introduced the 'apprenticeship' system for slaves on the pretext that complete freedom would not be good for slaves they would not be able to cope with it. It was only on the 1 August 1838 that 'freedom without apprenticeship' was gained. See the National Archives at http://discoveringbristol.org.uk/slavery/against-slavery/freedom-from-slavery/apprenticeship/slavery-end/ (accessed 1 October 2014).
13 The 1965 and 1968 Race Relations Acts set up the Race Relations Board and Community Relations Council respectively to monitor racial discrimination on the grounds of skin colour in public places. The 1976 Act was wider in scope and set up the Commission for Racial Equality to deal with racial discrimination. See Museum of London, 'Exploring 20th Century London' at www.museumoflondon.org.uk/Collections-Research/Research/Your-Research/X20L/Themes/1380/1203/ (accessed 1 October 2014).
14 The material scope of these Acts is wider than skin colour discrimination and the latter provision also focuses on institutional discrimination.
15 R. Leng, R. Taylor and M. Wasik, *Blackstone's Guide to the Crime and Disorder Act 1998* (London: Blackstone Press, 1998), chapter 3.
16 This came into effect on the 30 September 1998.
17 There is legislation under the Equality Act 2010 that deals with the prohibition of forms of discrimination including 'race' in terms of public services provision, and to give due regard to racial discrimination but it is argued that this is a watered down version of the Stephen Lawrence Inquiry

since the term institutional racism is not referred to. Moreover, in terms of implementation what little there is being whittled away because racism is not on the government agenda according to Doreen Lawrence, the mother of Stephen Lawrence, *The Guardian*, 19 December 2012.

18 L. Young, *Fear of the Dark* (London: Routledge, 1996), chapter 3.
19 Ibid., p. 57.
20 R. Dyer, *White* (London: Routledge, 1997), p. 8.
21 Ibid., p. 9.
22 Domination of a state over others. See the Free Dictionary at: www.thefreedictionary.com/hegemony (accessed 3 October 2012).
23 L. Young, *Fear of the Dark* (London: Routledge, 1996), pp. 58–59.
24 I. Kant, 'This Fellow was quite black … a clear proof that what he said was stupid', in E.C. Eze (ed.), *Race and the Enlightenment* (Oxford: Blackwell Publishers, 1997).
25 Ibid.
26 Ibid.
27 Ibid.
28 Ibid., p. 55.
29 F. Fanon, *The Wretched of the Earth* (Harmondsworth: Penguin Books, 1978).
30 Ibid., p. 190.
31 Ibid.
32 P. Bryan, *A Celebration of Emancipation* (Jamaican Information Service, 2009).
33 Houses of Parliament, 'Skin Lightening Treatments', Parliamentary Office of Science & Technology, Postbox. Available at: www.parliament.uk (accessed 25 November 2015).
34 Ibid.
35 Ibid.
36 C. Sartwell, *Act Like You Know: African American Autobiography and White Identity* (London: University of Chicago Press, 1998), p. 116.
37 House of Commons, Home Affairs Committee, *Young Black People and the Criminal Justice System: Second Report of Session 2006–2007, vol. 2: Oral and Written Evidence* (London: Stationery Office, 2007).
38 E. Deloch-Hughes, '"Black is Beautiful", 50 Year Anniversary: A Movement that went Viral before Digital Technology', March 2012. Available at: www.eldhughes.com (accessed 24 November 2015).
39 Ibid.
40 A conference held at the Southbank Centre 10 March 2013, chaired by Hannah Pool that can be viewed on YouTube.
41 C. Donaldson, 'Hair Alteration Practices amongst Black Women and the Assumption of Self Hatred', New York University, Department of Applied Psychology. Available at: www.steinhardt.nyu.edu (accessed 24 November 2015).
42 Ibid.
43 Ibid.
44 I. Banks, *Hair Matters: Beauty, Power and Black Women's Consciousness* (New York: New York University Press, 2000); C. Thompson, 'Black Women, Beauty, and Hair as a Matter of Being', *Women's Studies* 38(8) (2009): 831–856; C.L. Robinson, 'Hair as Race: Why "Good Hair" may be Bad for Black Females', *Howard Journal of Communications* 22(4) (2011): 358–376.
45 L.C. Jackson and B. Greene (eds), *Psychotherapy with African-American Women* (New York: The Guilford Press, 2000), p. 172.
46 C. Lago, *The Handbook of Transcultural Counselling and Psychotherapy* (McGraw-Hill International, 2011), p. 233.
47 Ibid., pp. 233–234.
48 Y. Danieli, *International Handbook of Multigenerational Legacies of Trauma* (New York: Springer, 1998), p. 394.
49 The word 'nigger' is a racial insult when used in an offensive manner. See R. Kennedy, *Nigger: The Strange Career of a Troublesome Word* (New York: Pantheon Books, 2002).
50 Danieli, *International Handbook of Multigenerational Legacies of Trauma*, p. 394.
51 S.I. Coard, A.M. Breland and P. Raskin, 'Perceptions of and Preferences for Skin Colour, Black Racial Identity, and Self Esteem among African Americans', *Journal of Applied Social Psychology* 31(11) (2001): 2256–2274.

52 Ibid., p. 2256.
53 Ibid., pp. 2256–2274.
54 M.S. Harrison and K.M. Thomas, 'The Hidden Prejudice in Selection: A Research Investigation on Skin Color Bias', *Journal of Applied Social Psychology* 39(1) (2009): 134–168, at p. 135.
55 Lago, *The Handbook of Transcultural Counselling and Psychotherapy.*
56 Ibid., p. 234.
57 P.A. Robinson, 'Perceptions of Beauty and Identity: The Skin Bleaching Phenomenon in Jamaica'. Available at: www.adulterc.org/proceedings/2011/papers/robinson.pdf (accessed 27 October 2014).
58 L. Sayeed, 'Stand up to Unilever's Hypocrisy over Skin-Lightening', *The Guardian*, 16 July 2010. Available at: www.guardian.co.uk/commentisfree/2010/jul/16/unilever-hypocritical-promoting-skin-lightening (accessed 27 October 2014).
59 Skin Inc, *Global Skin Lighteners Market to Reach $10 Billion by 2015*, 23 June 2009. Available at: www.skininc.com/spabusiness/global/48898927.html (accessed 30 October 2014).
60 Dr N. Persadsingh, 'Women Bleach at their Peril', BBC Caribbean.com, 6 September 2004. Available at: www.bbc.co.uk/caribbean/news/story/2004/09/040906_bleaching.shtml (accessed 30 October 2014).
61 Ibid.
62 A. Hirsch, 'Fury at Senegal Ads for Cream to Lighten Skin', *The Guardian*, 15 November 2012, p. 25.
63 Such as hydroquinone which is a potentially carcinogenic chemical.
64 Hirsch, 'Fury at Senegal Ads for Cream to Lighten Skin', p. 25.
65 Ibid.
66 Houses of Parliament, 'Skin Lightening Treatments', Parliamentary Office of Science & Technology, Postbox. Available at: www.parliament.uk (accessed 25 November 2015).
67 Southwark Council Trading Standards, *Illegal Skin Lighteners.* Available at: www.southwark.gov.uk/info/200098/trading_standards/215/illegal_skin_lighteners/1 (accessed 30 October 2014).
68 'Skin Whitening Creams', Hansard, House Commons, 2 November 2005: Column 1157W. Available at: www.publications.parliament.uk/pa/cm200506/cmhansrd/vo051102/text/51102w34.htm (accessed 16 November 2014).
69 Jane Kennedy, 'Skin Whitening Creams' Hansard, House Commons, 2 November 2005: Column 1157W. Available at: www.publications.parliament.uk/pa/cm200506/cmhansrd/vo051102/text/51102w34.htm (accessed 16 November 2014).
70 L. Al Mubarak, 'Black becomes White', Sudan Vision. Available at: www.sudanvisiondaily.com/modules.php?name=News&file=article&sid=47175 (accessed 16 November 2014), darker slaves worked in the fields whilst the lighter skinned ones worked in the house.
71 Ibid.
72 N. Adae-Amoakoh, 'Skin Whitening is a Self-Denying Legacy of Colonialism', *Think Africa Press*, 14 March 2012. Available at: http://thinkafricapress.com/culture/skin-whitening-light-and-fair (accessed 27 November 2014).
73 There have been calls in Ghana to take robust measures to highlight the use of certain chemicals in skin whitening creams, some of which cause cancer; GNA, 'Publish List of Unsafe Bleaching Creams', 29 April 2004. Available at: www.modernghana.com/news/54244/1/publish-list-of-unsafe-bleaching-creams-researcher.html (accessed 27 November 2014).
74 Hydroquinone is a cancer causing agent used in skin-lightening products. This chemical has been banned in countries such as Ghana, South Africa, the Ghambia, Kenya, Zambia and Senegal but the market continues to be saturated with skin bleaching products, N. Adae-Amoakoh, 'Skin Whitening is a Self-Denying Legacy of Colonialism', *Think Africa Press*, 14 March 2012. Available at: http://thinkafricapress.com/culture/skin-whitening-light-and-fair (accessed 3 December 2014).
75 According to Sayeed a Facebook app has been created and promoted by a sub-brand of Unilever called Vaseline. The app promotes a variety of whitening creams to 'transform your face on Facebook with Vaseline'. The skin lightening industry is predicted to reach $10bn by 2015. L. Sayeed, 'Stand up to Unilever's Hypocrisy over Skin-Lightening', *The Guardian*, 16 July 2010.
76 L'Oreal Paris is a division of L'Oreal (UK) Limited.
77 Available at: www.loreal-paris.co.uk/skincare/face-care/derma-genesis.aspx (accessed 27 November 2014).

78 Available at: www.loreal-paris.co.uk/_en/_gb/navigation/diversity.aspx (accessed 27 November 2014).
79 Available at: www.loreal-paris.co.in/skincare/face-care/pearl-perfect/day-cream-spf15.aspx (accessed 27 November 2014).
80 Available at: www.dior.com/beauty/gbr/en/skincare/faceskincare/discover_diorsnow/td131-22.html (accessed 28 November 2014).
81 Available at: www.selfridges.com/en/Beauty/Brand-rooms/Designer/GUERLAIN/Skincare/Treatments/Blanc-de-Perle-Whitening-essence_397-77002296-G060949/?cm_mmc=PPC-_-Google-_-PlusBox-_-Guerlain&_%24ja%3Dkw%3A{keyword}%7Ccgn%3Apla%C2%AC16249783%7Ctsid%3A33956%7Ccn%3Apla%C2%AC16249783%7Cmt%3A{MatchType}%7Ccrid%3A19879381294&gclid=CMv6-uGW8rMCFe7MtAodylcAUA.
82 World Health Organisation, 'Mercury and Health', Fact Sheet No 361, April 2012. Available at: www.who.int/mediacentre/factsheets/fs361/en/index.html (accessed 3 December 2014).
83 Mercury in skin products are banned by a European Directive. And the use of mercury has been banned in many countries; however, products containing mercury can be trafficked through the Internet. 'Mercury in Skin-Lightening Products', *The Ghanaian Journal*, June 2012. Available at: www.theghanaianjournal.com/2012/06/13/mercury-in-skin-lightening-products/ (accessed 3 December 2014).
84 Dr S. Taylor (dermatologist, clinical researcher and expert of treating skin of colour), 'The Continued Danger of Skin Lightening Creams', *Huff Post, Black Voices*, 23 March 2012. Available at: www.huffingtonpost.com/dr-susan-taylor/the-continued-dangers-of-_b_1371524.html (accessed 28 November 2014).
85 Y.M. Olumide, professor of medicine, 'Use of Skin Lightening Creams', *British Medical Journal*, 2010; 341:c6102.
86 Ibid.
87 M. Lamkin, 'Racist Appearance Standards and the Enhancements that Love Them: Norman Daniels and Skin-Lightening Cosmetics', *Bioethics* 25(4) (2011).
88 A.G. Karnani, 'Doing Well by Doing Good – Case Study: "Fair and Lovely" Whitening Cream', Ross School of Business Working Paper no. 1063; *Strategic Management Journal* 28 (13) (2007).
89 Ibid.
90 J. Dine, *Companies, International Trade and Human Rights* (Cambridge: Cambridge University Press, 2007).
91 World Health Organisation, Preventing Disease through Healthy Environments, Mercury in Skin Lightening Products. Available at: www.who.int/ipcs/assessment/public-health/mecury_flyer.pdf (accessed 14 December 2014).
92 Y. Alibi-Brown, 'Why I Believe Beyoncé is betraying all Black and Asian Women', *The Mail*, 18 February 2011. Available at: www.dailymail.co.uk/debate/article-1358119/Beyonce-Knowles-Why-I-believe-betraying-black-Asian-Women.html (accessed 27 November 2014).
93 'Nor did it help that all the best-looking black boys would only date a girl if they were light-skinned', P. Bracchi, 'Dying to be Whiter: The Black Women who Risk their Lives for Lighter Skin', *The Daily Mail*, 12 January 2007. Available at: www.dailymail.co.uk/femail/article-428541/Dying-whiter-The-black-women-risk-lives-lighter-skin.html (accessed 3 December 2014).
94 P. Cohen, 'Tarzan and the Jungle Bunnies: Class, Race and Sex in Popular Culture', in *New Formations*, 5 (1988): 25–30, at p. 23.
95 Ibid.
96 Ibid.
97 L. Young, *Fear of the Dark, 'Race', Gender and Sexuality in the Cinema* (London: Routledge, 1996), p. 39.
98 K. Qasim, M. Hayat and U. Asmat, 'Black Women and Racial Stereotypes: A Black Feminist Reading of Morrisson's Novels', *Language in India, Strength for Today and Bright Hope for Tomorrow*, vol. 12, 5 May 2012. Available at: www.languageinindia.com/may2012/khamsamorrison.pdf (accessed 17 December 2014).
99 L. Membis, Invisible Women: Black Britons Struggle to be Heard, *CNN* 14 October 2011. Available at: http://edition.cnn.com/2011/10/14/world/europe/black-british-women/index.html (accessed 17 December 2014).

100 Ibid.

101 Marketing and Advertising: the Law. Available at: www.gov.uk (accessed 22 November 2015).

102 B. Adewunmi, 'Black Women in Britain – from Romans to Windrush', 6 October 2014. Available at: www.theguardian.com (accessed 25 November 2015).

103 The UK Trading Standards Council of Southwark has dealt with some businesses that have sold illegal skin-lightening products. Hackney Council Trading Standards seeks to adopt a coordinated approach amongst trading standards councils to stop the trade. It is argued that this is not sufficient and that these councils need to run campaigns in collaboration with the mass media.

104 P & G Corporate Announcement, Procter and Gamble's 'My Black is Beautiful Celebrates Beauty in Action for Essence Festival's 20 Anniversary', 1 July 2014. Available at: www.news.pg.com (accessed 24 November 2015.

105 Ibid.

106 Ibid.

107 b. hooks, *Ain't I a Woman: Black Women and Feminism* (Boston: South End Press, 1982), p. 110.

108 R. Dyer, *White* (London: Routledge, 1997), p. 70.

Bibliography

Abbott, E., *Sugar: A Bitter Sweet History* (London: Duckworth, 2010).

Blackburn, R., *The Making of New World Slavery from the Baroque to the Modern 1492–1800* (London: Verso, 1998).

Bridges, R., 'Letter in the Guardian', *The Guardian*, 11 October 2012.

Choudry, I., 'The Elephant in the Room – Campaigners Want Answers over Policy Custody Deaths', *Eastern Eye*, 5 January 2015.

Coard, S.I., A.M. Breland and P. Raskin, 'Perceptions of and Preferences for Skin Colour, Black Racial Identity, and Self Esteem among African Americans', *Journal of Applied Social Psychology* 31(11) (2001): 2256–2274.

Cohen, P., 'Tarzan and the Jungle Bunnies: Class, Race and Sex in Popular Culture', in *New Formations* 5(1988): 25–30.

Danieli, Y., *International Handbook of Multigenerational Legacies of Trauma* (New York: Springer, 1998).

Dyer, R., *White* (London: Routledge, 1997).

Equiano, O., *The Interesting Narrative of the Life of Olaudah Equiano or Gustavus Vassa. The African. Written by Himself*, Vol. 1, edited by Paul Edwards (Oxford: Heinemann, 1969 [1789]).

Fanon, F., *Black Skin: White Masks* (London: Pluto Press, 1967).

House of Commons, Home Affairs Committee, *Young Black People and the Criminal Justice System: Second Report of Session 2006–2007*, Vol. 2: *Oral and Written Evidence* (London: Stationery Office, 2007).

Harrison, M.S. and K.M. Thomas, 'The Hidden Prejudice in Selection: A Research Investigation on Skin Color Bias', *Journal of Applied Social Psychology* 39(1) (2009): 134–168.

Hirsch, A., 'Fury at Senegal Ads for Cream to Lighten Skin', *The Guardian*, 15 November 2012.

hooks, b., *Ain't I a Woman: Black Women and Feminism* (Boston: South End Press, 1982).

Howard-Hassmann, R.E., *Reparations to Africa* (Philadelphia: University of Pennsylvania Press, 2008).

Hume, D., 'Negroes … Naturally Inferior to the Whites', in E.C. Eze (ed.), *Race and the Enlightenment: A Reader* (Oxford: Blackwell, 1997).

Jackson, L.C. and B. Greene (eds), *Psychotherapy with African-American Women* (New York: The Guilford Press, 2000).

Kant, I., 'This Fellow was Quite Black … a Clear Proof that What he said was Stupid', in E.C. Eze (ed.), *Race and the Enlightenment* (Oxford: Blackwell, 1997).

Karnani, A.G., 'Doing Well by Doing Good – Case Study: "Fair and Lovely" Whitening Cream', Ross School of Business Working Paper No. 1063, *Strategic Management Journal* 28(13) (2007): 1351–1357.

Kennedy, R., *Nigger: The Strange Career of a Troublesome Word* (New York: Pantheon Books, 2002).
Krikler, J., 'The Zong and the Lord Chief Justice', *Hist Workshop J* 64(1) (2007): 29.
Lago, C., *The Handbook of Transcultural Counselling and Psychotherapy* (McGraw-Hill International, 2011).
Lamkin, M., 'Racist Appearance Standards and the Enhancements that Love Them: Norman Daniels and Skin-Lightening Cosmetics', *Bioethics* 25(4) (2011): 185–191.
Leng, R., R. Taylor and M. Wasik, *Blackstone's Guide to the Crime and Disorder Act 1998* (London: Blackstone Press, 1998).
Macpherson, W., *The Stephen Lawrence Inquiry* (London: Home Office, 1999).
Olumide, Y.M., 'Use of Skin Lightening Creams', *British Medical Journal* 341(c6102) (2010).
Ormerod, D., *Smith and Hogan Criminal Law*, 12th edition (Oxford: Oxford University Press, 2008).
Phillips, C., 'Institutional Racism and Ethnic Inequalities: An Expanded Multilevel Framework', *Jnl Soc. Pol.* 40(1) (2011): 173–192.
Redman, R.C. and P. Finkelman, 'Legal Aspects of Slavery', in *Encyclopaedia of Genocide and Crimes Against Humanity*, edited by D. Shelton (Washington: Thomson, Gale, 2005).
Rodney, W., *How Europe Underdeveloped Africa* (London: Bogle-L'Ouverture Publications, 1978).
Salih, S., *The History of Mary Prince: A West Indian Slave* (London: Penguin, 2004 [1831]).
Sartwell, C., *Act Like You Know: African American Autobiography and White Identity* (London: University of Chicago Press, 1998).
Sayeed, L., 'Stand up to Unilever's Hypocrisy over Skin-lightening', *The Guardian*, 16 July 2010.
Sherwood, M., 'The Trade in Enslaved Africans and Slavery after 1807', in F. Brennan and J. Packer (eds.), *Colonialism, Slavery, Reparations and Trade: Remedying the Past?* (Abingdon: Routledge, 2012).
Shyllon, F., *Black People in Britain 1555–1833* (London: Oxford University Press, 1977).
Sweney, M., 'Beyoncé Knowles: L'Oreal Accused of "Whitening" Singer in Cosmetics Ad', *The Guardian*, 8 August 2008.
Thomas, H., *The Slave Trade: The History of the Atlantic Slave Trade 1440–1870* (London: Papermac, 1998).
Thomson, J., 'Summer, Complete Works', in H. Thomas, *The Slave Trade: The History of the Atlantic Slave Trade 1440–1870* (London: Papermac, 1998).
Transitional Racial Justice Initiative, 'The Persistence of White Privilege and Institutional Racism in US Policy. A Report on Government Compliance with the International Convention on the Elimination of All Forms of Racial Discrimination' (California, 2001). Available at: www.raceforward.org/files/pdf (accessed 12 February 2017).
Tuitt, P., *Race, Law, Resistance* (London: Glass House Press, 2004).
U.N. *World Conference against Racism, Racial Discrimination, Xenophobia and Related Intolerance Declaration and Programme of Action* (New York: United Nations, 2002).
Virey, J.J., 'Natural History of the Negroes Particularly', in H.F. Augstein (ed.), *Race: The Origins of an Idea 1760–1850* (London: Thoemmes Press, 1996).
Walvin, J., *The Trader, The Owner, The Slave* (London: Vintage Books, 2007).
Williams, E., *Capitalism and Slavery* (Chapel Hill: The University of North Carolina Press, 1994).
Young, L., *Fear of the Dark* (London: Routledge, 1996).

8 The moral, legal and political case for reparations for the legacy of the transatlantic slave trade and chattel slavery

Introduction

Reparations consist of the recognition of gross violation of human rights that should be put right by material and other measures. Reparations are well recognised in international law and have been used to ameliorate the damage done in some of the most painful of circumstances, the Holocaust survivors being one. Recently we have seen that victims of the Mau Mau torture incident are to sue the British government for compensation due to the outrageous cases of torture inflicted on them during the rebellion against British rule in the 1950s.[1] However although the horrors of the transatlantic slave trade and chattel slavery have been recognised, no reparations have been made. It is argued here that institutional racism has been the main reason for the failure to make reparations because institutional racism is a culture that thrives on denial of the source of the legacy[2] and of the legacy itself. It is founded on the 'uniqueness'[3] of the transatlantic slave trade. Unique because it 'fuelled the world economy'[4] in the eighteenth century and also due to the 'racial nature'[5] with whites at the top of the ladder and blacks at the bottom. It is argued that in institutional racism this ideology of racism persists.

Van Boven and Bassioni developed guidelines on the right to an effective remedy and reparations which were adopted by the General Assembly of the United Nations on 16 December 2005.[6] The scope of reparations include restitution which 'restore[s] the victim to the original situation before the gross violations of humanitarian law occurred',[7] compensation for damage that is economically assessable,[8] rehabilitation which consists of 'medical and psychological care, as well as legal and social services',[9] satisfaction including public apology[10] and guarantees of non-repetition.[11] However none of these types of reparations have been made available to those who suffer racial harm today as a consequence of the transatlantic slave trade and chattel slavery.

This chapter will consider the moral, legal and political case for reparations claims for this legacy. The moral case for reparations will be assessed in particular compared to reparations claims satisfied elsewhere. It will be argued that the utility in reparations is that it could help to heal the social divide – it could atone for 'original sin' according to Curtis.[12] The legal case for reparations will be considered, in particular issues of jurisdiction, time limits, who the claimants and respondents might be and the possible demands that might be made in a claim. Even if the legal case falters Shelton[13] argues that litigation is a reparative device that has a special role since it makes the legacy of chattel slavery visible in public discourse, and is a way of educating the public. The question of official apology raises the political case for reparations and then finally the legacies themselves are discussed, that is the African legacy, the Caribbean legacy, the European legacy and the institutional legacy.

This chapter argues that the refusal of those Western Europeans who were involved in the slave trade to make reparations for the legacy of the transatlantic slave trade and chattel slavery is another instance of institutional racism where hurdles are unwittingly raised, and eyes averted to refuse access to justice for reparations for Africans, Caribbeans and Afro-Caribbeans in the Diaspora. It is argued that whilst Britain used legislation to abolish the slave trade and slavery, it has not used legislation to abolish institutional racism which now requires reparative justice. As Corlett,[14] Feagin[15] and Thompson[16] argue barriers are raised against claims for dealing with contemporary racial harm. It is advanced that racial harm is sourced in a history that has not taken seriously the continuing problems of institutional racism. Having weighed up the arguments it will be concluded that reparations has the power to play a fundamental role in the fight for justice for those who still suffer from the legacy of the slave trade and chattel slavery, that is institutional racism.

Background: History, the core of reparations and the moral case for reparations

History

Early demands from black people for reparations can be identified with the Pan-African movement through people such as Edward Wilmot Blyden (1832–1912). Blyden was known as the father of Pan-Africanism. He argued for black equality and against the notion that black people were inferior to whites that was current around Europe and North America, and 'he called for the emigration of skilled and intelligent black West Indians and African Americans to Liberia'.[17] Other equally important people in the quest for reparations were Marcus Garvey who developed a Pan-Africanist Black Star Liner movement for back to Africa and he also founded the Universal Negro Improvement Association (UNIA).[18] There was also Martin Luther King who led the Montgomery, Alabama, bus boycott in the States.[19] He argued that 'both segregation in America and colonialism in Africa were based on the same thing – white supremacy and contempt for life'.[20] The Rastafarian movement[21] and the Nation of Islam[22] have also argued that the essence of the provision of 'economic, political, social and cultural progress of the descendants of the formerly enslaved'[23] depends on reparations.[24] It was not only black Americans that demanded reparations but white Americans too such as Thomas Jefferson and the American Colonisation Society (ACS).[25] Jefferson proposed to set black people up as a 'free and independent people'[26] in his quest to have the freed slaves deported from the country and the desire to not unsettle the un-freed slaves. The ACS was founded in 1817 by 'Quakers and powerful American slaveholders'.[27] According to the Quakers those African Americans that wanted to leave America should be financed to go to Liberia – a country free from the type of discrimination they experienced in the States.[28] However this was not so much a case of reparations such as one of repatriation.

In terms of international and national agendas there was little heard about reparations. Then was the build-up to the 1990s and the successful campaigns for reparations for the Jewish Holocaust victims, the internment of Japanese people in the US during the Second World War and successes for indigenous people in Canada, New Zealand, USA and Australia. These triumphs were the driving force behind the push for Diaspora Africans to develop the fight for reparations.

The 1990s also saw the Organisation of African Unity (OAU) appoint a Group of Eminent Persons (GEP) to consider a paper by Gifford[29] for an organisation to work on behalf of Africans that would continue to suffer from the transatlantic slave trade and chattel slavery in terms of the quest for reparations. There was a Pan-African Conference based in Nigeria where a public statement was made regarding the moral debt and debt of compensation that remained unsettled within the context of those who profited from transatlantic slavery, colonialism and neo-colonialism. Around the same time, Bernie Grant MP developed the African Reparations Movement in the UK. He addressed the House of Commons on the issue of reparations.

> On the floor of the House of Commons he was outspoken in the cause of eliminating racism both in Britain and the world. He campaigned against racist policing methods, and deaths in custody, on institutionalised racism in health, housing and education, for refugees, and for greater resources for inner city areas. Internationally he fought for the elimination of overseas debt for poor nations, and for the recognition of the past injustices of colonisation and enslavement.[30]

The twenty-first century brought the issue of reparations to the forefront as raised at the World Conference against Racism, Racial Discrimination, Xenophobia and Related Intolerance held in Durban, South Africa. Former slave owning powers refused to entertain the call for reparations, arguing that it was not a crime at the time so there were no legal grounds for pursuing reparations. Instead of quietening calls for justice this denial only raised activism at the grass roots and national levels. This was evident in the focus in Barbados in 2002 on a conference entitled 'the African and African Descendants World Conference against racism'.[31] The 200th anniversary of the abolition of the slave trade in 2007 produced a lot of action, and a renewed impetus in the discussion of the role of reparations in the context of colonialism and post-colonialism.

To bring us up to present times, on a visit to Jamaica in 2015, the British prime minister was asked to address the call for reparations. David Cameron bypassed any discussion about reparations by stating that his visit was about future bilateral relations with Jamaica, so the call for reparations was put on the back burner by Cameron.

There are several scholars who have argued about reparations such as Brophy[32] who contends that in the USA reparations and apologies are some of the most controversial debates that have groups divided along racial lines. White taxpayers do not want to pay out for something that they view as having happened centuries ago. Brophy argues that reparations look both to address past harm and improve matters for the future.[33] Howard-Hassmann[34] tells us that there should be symbolic reparations to Africa from the West. This means to acknowledge the truth about what happened to their society and economy and who was responsible for it. Furthermore, Torpey[35] argues that in terms of reparations, financial claims are merely symbolic. This comes to represent historical injury and perpetrate regret.

At the time of writing there is a political movement in the West Indies by the Caribbean Community (CARICOM)[36] to make demands of the Western European governments regarding reparations for the slave trade and chattel slavery.[37] In particular the issues that are to be raised include six fundamental ones – public health, education, cultural institutions, cultural deprivation, psychological trauma and scientific and technological backwardness.[38] As a human rights issue of the twenty-first century reparations tops the list for 'Africans across the Diaspora'.[39]

The core of reparations

Having considered the context in which the call for reparations has arisen, it would be a good idea to look at what the core of reparations is.

> The essential principle contained in the actual notion of an illegal act is that reparation must, as far as possible, wipe out all the consequences of the illegal act and re-establish the situation which would, in all probability, have existed if that act had not been committed.[40]

It is a form of restitution which under the UN Basic Principles and Guidelines[41] includes such matters as enjoyment of human rights, identity and return of property. Thus one of the things reparations relates to is a clean sweep in terms of the *consequences* of illegal acts. It is to brush away those consequences as if they had never occurred.

An example of this would be the eradication of type 2 diabetes. This disease is said to affect black people in the Caribbean and the Diaspora more than whites.[42] According to the World Health Organisation (WHO) type 2 Diabetes is up to three times more common among those of African and African-Caribbean origin.[43] It is claimed that this disease has its roots in the slave 'masters manipulation of slaves' diets by adding fats to increase energy for maximum labour output, [that] has impacted the dietary habits and soul food cuisine of slaves' descendants today as social inheritance'.[44] According to Tull and Roseman[45] the 'rates of diabetes are higher for African Americans relative to whites, even after controlling for age ... and socio-economic status'.[46] Furthermore, 'western hemisphere blacks are descendants of a highly selected group of Africans who were able to survive the long sea voyages from Africa by efficiently retaining salt'[47] this is now a problem in terms of hypertension and diabetes and Tull and Roseman argue that poor management strategies amongst this group needs to be looked at in terms of 'socio-economic and psychological factors'.[48] An educational programme aimed at educating black people about type 2 Diabetes, and resources for organisations that work in this area to understand how to work with black people with type 2 Diabetes, should be one of the top priorities on public health agendas in the Caribbean, Africa and the Diaspora. Thus reparations in this context would perform the clean sweep in terms of dealing with the consequences of the illegal act of slavery and the slave trade.

Rehabilitation is another form of reparation that 'should include medical and psychological care as well as legal and social services'.[49] Satisfaction is another form of reparation that includes a number of matters including the 'cessation of continuing violations',[50] 'public disclosure of the truth',[51] a 'public apology',[52] 'judicial and administrative sanctions against persons liable for the violations,'[53] 'commemorations and tributes to the victims'[54] and 'inclusion of an accurate account of the violations that occurred in international human rights law and international humanitarian law training and in educational material at all levels'.[55] These examples of reparations are mainly directed towards governments since it is they that have the power to put measures in place to deal with public disclosure and apology for instance. Moreover,

> compensation should be provided for any economically assessable damage, as appropriate and proportional to the gravity of the violation and the circumstances of each case, resulting from gross violations of international human rights law and serious violations of international humanitarian law, such as: (*a*) physical or mental harm; (*b*) lost opportunities, including employment, education and social benefits; (*c*) material damages and loss of earnings, including loss of earning potential; (*d*) moral damage; (*e*) costs required for legal or expert assistance, medicine and medical services, and psychological and social services.[56]

The moral case

Reparations involve facing up to institutional racism that is itself based on the wrong that was committed by perpetrators in terms of the transatlantic slave trade and chattel slavery, the creation of a system of 'exploited and exploiters'.[57] The wrong is reducing people into chattel slaves, divesting African human beings of their own sense of self-worth and turning them into property,[58] to be herded like cattle in the market place for the slave holders.

To the argument that the current incumbents of governments in Europe were not around at the time of the atrocities so did not cause the harm and should not carry the blame, there are several points. There are precedents of governments taking responsibility for what their previous incumbents have done. For instance, the U.S. government has actively pressured the German government since World War II to make large-scale reparations to victims of the Holocaust, although those making reparations were not part of the Nazi governments. This is known as inter-generational justice where current incumbents are considered to have inherited the wrongs committed by their forebears and held to account for the injuries caused. The Holocaust reparations is seen by some Reparationists and others as 'the gold standard of reparations claims'.[59] 'The Jewish Agency submitted to the governments of the US, USSR, UK and France, a memorandum demanding reparations ... due to the Jewish people from Germany for its involvement in the Holocaust'.[60] In 1951 the West German government agreed to compensate Israel to the tune of $1.5 billion that was reduced to $1billion by the time the Claims Conference was set up whose job it was to distribute the money to claimants. In 1988 $125 million was given by the German government for reparations that allowed Holocaust survivors to have payment of monthly sums for the duration of their lives and in 1999, the German government and German industry agreed to allocate reparations funds of $5 billion for slave and forced labour on the understanding that there would not be any litigation on this issue and the last payment was made in September 2006.[61] It may be argued that the Holocaust was within living memory. That makes it different from the call for slave trade and chattel reparations. This chapter contends that reparations is for the continuing legacy of the slave trade and that is institutional racism. In that sense this call for reparations is no different from the call for reparations regarding the Holocaust because the slave trade is the basis of the current harm suffered by black people and reparations needs to be made. For instance, just as organisations that deal with Jewish Holocaust have been given funds to build educational institutions to educate the public about the Holocaust,[62] so funds should be afforded for Africans to inform the public regarding the role played by institutional racism in the continuing discrimination black people face.

It is not only the Holocaust claim that has been successful in obtaining reparations from governments that were not around when the particular atrocities occurred and whom have made reparations. The Waikato peoples of New Zealand, the Japanese internees of the US and the disenfranchised Native American Indians have also successfully raised the issue of reparations. In 1995 the Waikato peoples were able to get the 'Crown of New Zealand [to announce] an official apology, [to restore] ... lost lands and [to give] financial compensation through the Waikato Raupatu Claims Settlement Act 1995'.[63] In the case of the American Japanese, these were people who were interned in the USA during the Second World War as enemies of the state, on the basis of Executive Order 9066.[64] Racial identity was used to intern them and although some of the victims saw reparations as ineffective they were spurred on by the precedent set by the Jewish Holocaust survivors' example. The Act that brought reparations into play for the interned Japanese was the Japanese American Evacuation Claims Act 1948. This Act resulted in the US government paying out $37 million amongst the 26,500 claims.[65] Finally, but by no means the least,[66] the Native American Indians where, due to the invasion of their lands that were taken over by the government, several treaties were made with the Native American Indians; however, as Muhammad[67] contends, 'The irony of these treaties was that they did not give any substantial restitution to the Native Americans. The treaties declared the Native Americans to be contained in specific segments of the United States, in a country that was originally their own'.[68] So it is quite clear that some governments have taken responsibility for some of the wrongs that their predecessors have done. As such the argument that a current incumbent government cannot be held responsible for the wrongs committed by their predecessors does not stand up to scrutiny. Given the examples above, the notion of inter-generational governmental responsibility is clear. The problem is that the government chooses not to engage in reparation discussions when it comes to the legacy for the slave trade and chattel slavery, not that it cannot do so.

A point in the government's favour is that reparations are paid out to survivors and it may be argued that as far as the African, African-Caribbean and Diasporas' reparations claims are concerned there are no 'survivors'. It is argued here that this is incorrect. It is not the past that looks to reparations but current institutionally racist problems sourced in the past of slavery, in that sense there continue to be survivors. For instance, Caribbean peoples still feel like 'second class citizens in the world'.[69] This is a legacy of the slave trade and chattel slavery, that legacy is in the form of institutional racism where institutions still treat Africans and African-Caribbeans in racist ways. There is a failure to locate current forms of racism, such as institutional racism, in a history bedevilled by the historically inhuman treatment meted out to Africans and African-Caribbean people in the Diaspora, the racist ideology that went with it and that racist thought that continues. The failure of the British government, for instance, to entertain any political discussion in terms of a claim for reparations for this group represents a deficiency in providing professional services to black people.[70]

It is also countered that blacks owned slaves and that African monarchs participated in the slave trade[71] so would they have to provide reparations also?[72] To that claim it is argued that in systems where there are crimes against humanity there will also be found collaborators. This does not take away from the main emphasis that there are victims who still need to be healed from a current system of racial wrong. Furthermore, it is said consideration should be taken concerning the fact that some whites helped to free slaves, is there no credit for that? William Wilberforce and Thomas Clarkson amongst others have been given credit. Indeed there is a centre dedicated to Wilberforce at Hull University, for example.[73] But there is a problem in the UK where the focus in schools is on the liberators to the expense of the perpetrators of the transatlantic slave trade and chattel slavery. In schools and public education that story still needs to be told in a way that makes the connection between chattel slavery and institutional racism. These arguments only serve to take us away from the main focal point in which institutional racism is an obstinate problem. It is a predicament that originated in the slave trade and chattel slavery, was maintained in colonialism and continuously reinforced in postmodern society. If institutional racism is accepted as a phenomenon of modern society the relationship between it and transatlantic slavery is arguably not straight forward. It begins with the desire to produce plantation products like sugar, rum, tobacco and rice[74] by designing a regime that constituted a crime against humanity,[75] that crime against humanity was built on racism. Institutional racism continues with institutional blindness to the racism in the services within which black people are engaged[76] such as the criminal justice system, education, health and trade.

The moral case is that slavery and slave trading were a crime against humanity argues Beckles[77] and the ideology of racism in institutions stems from this crime. Not only was chattel slavery a wrong committed by states, institutional racism is a wrong perpetrated by public and private entities today which is an injustice against Africans and those of Afro-Caribbean descent. Institutional racism is a wrong because it is based on an ideology that came from the oppression of black people in Africa and the Diaspora. This ideology came along with the 'theft of labour and lives'[78] carried out by whites and by the state for which there has never been any compensation. States and 'national institutions'[79] have become wealthy on 'slave-derived wealth'[80] and remain wealthy today on the basis of this wealth. These national institutions include the Church of England, merchant houses, insurance companies and banks.[81] The figure in terms of wealth regarding the US is estimated at $24 trillion for stolen black labour.[82] Following slave emancipation British slave owners received £20 million, an estimated £16 billion in today's money,[83] as compensation for their financial loss. There is at least a case for arguing that this amount should be sought to deal with the ravages of institutional racism built on the back of transatlantic slavery.

The legal case

Jurisdiction

There are three options when it comes to the appropriate jurisdiction: a special international tribunal, the International Court of Justice or the national court system. The jurisdiction within which to bring a claim has been raised as an issue by Gifford.[84] In which jurisdiction should a claim for reparations be brought? Should the claim be raised in each jurisdiction where the state and others can be said to have had a role in the slave trade and chattel slavery and institutional racism today or should the claimaints seek an international forum? Although Gifford does not discuss institutional wrong-doing, he suggests that the claim for reparations could 'be determined by a special international tribunal recognised by all parties'.[85] Special international tribunals have been established for Yugoslavia and Rwanda for grave atrocities. The 'doctrine of universal jurisdiction allows national courts to try cases of the greatest crimes against humanity'.[86] In the UK courts could try the government for crimes against humanity committed by its forebears. A claim could also be considered by the International Court of Justice (ICJ). However, there are several reasons why this forum might be difficult to use. Some former slave owning countries, such as France, do not recognise its authority, and the UK does not accept its jurisdiction for crimes committed before 1974. Furthermore the ICJ does not accept historical cases although it is argued that the claim would be brought on the basis of the current problem of institutional racism resulting from the transatlantic slave trade. Martyn Day, the legal firm leading CARICOM's claim, have suggested that the claim would be based on racism today that is sourced in the slave trade thereby dispensing with the 1974 time limit and the concern over historical cases.[87] However, Martyn Day does not raise the spectre of institutional racism that is a major concern of this book, that argues that it must be dismantled if there is going to be real change to the status quo, if we are going to clear away the consequences of the transatlantic slave trade.

It is also possible that a claim could be brought in a national court based on restitution. This constitutes a legal remedy that is available in civil and criminal cases. Bracegirdle[88] contends that restitution could be used against a defendant to get him to give up

> his gain to a successful claimant … [moreover] a claim for restitution may be preferable to claimants seeking reparations for historic slavery, as it might be easier to establish an identifiable gain made by the defendant than a loss suffered by the claimant who will … not be the person actually enslaved.[89]

The cause of action for a restitution remedy is unjust enrichment where no person is to profit from another's expense. It is argued that the £16 billion identified above is the amount that would be sought by a claimant. That claimant would represent the Africans and Afro-Caribbeans in the UK that have suffered loss in terms of institutional racism that is a result of the transatlantic slave trade.

Timing issues

This claim for reparations is likely to be denied on the basis that the British government argues that 200 years is too long a timeframe through which to capture fault and they will not be held responsible for their predecessors conduct over that period of time. However, it is argued that if the issue about time limits is not a smoke screen it constitutes a form of unwitting racism because it denies a path to a possible legal remedy that affects people of African and African -Caribbean descent in the Diaspora. A time limit would be sure to block any claim. The limitation period to bring a case can prove difficult and most of the domestic law of the states that would be subject to a reparations claim will have limitation periods,[90] although it has been argued by Bracegirdle that in the context of Britain at least

> there is sufficient ambiguity [in terms of the application of limitation periods] here that a case could be argued on behalf of the claimants of restitution for historic slavery that no limitation period would be applicable to those who make a claim for reparations under the heading of unjust enrichment.[91]

Moreover, as Gifford tells us 'there is no limitation period in international law'.[92] In any event the argument is that time limits should not apply because the claim is for current harm in terms of institutional racism that is itself sourced in the past but whose consequences present a contemporary problem. Beckles tells us that 'some persons living in the Caribbean today had grandparents and great- grandparents who were enslaved. Families continue to live with the memory of slavery and to experience life as the victims of slavery'.[93] For some in the Caribbean then the slave trade and chattel slavery was not so long ago, it is still in living memory. Even if it were not in living memory, the consequences including institutional racism certainly are.

Not a wrong at the time?

Another issue regarding time is that of illegality. It is argued that reparations should not be made because chattel slavery was not a wrong at the time. Though it was morally wrong[94] it was not legally wrong on English soil at least[95] and in the Caribbean too.[96] However, this may not be as straightforward as it appears. In Britain in the seventeenth and eighteenth centuries there was judicial controversy over whether a slaver could have property in a slave[97], leaving the whole question of whether chattel slavery was legal or not in a judicial quandary. Apart from the more general position that slaves knew it was wrong to own them and treat them like animals,[98] the English judiciary gave conflicting opinions about the status of slaves as to whether they constituted property of their masters or not.[99] In cases such as *Butts v Penny*[100] and *Chamberlain v Harvey*[101] there was no doubt that slaves were property whereas in the latter case slaves could be freed from their status with a Christian baptism. Similarly it was said in *Smith v Gould*[102] that blacks are like any other men, as in *Smith v Brown and Cooper*,[103] they were free on English soil. Clarification was given in the English Yorke/Talbot decision of 1729 that stated the slave does not become free by entering English soil from the West Indies or becoming a Christian but this was not a judicial decision, rather an *opinion* of the Advocate General and the Solicitor-General at the time. However, this was an opinion that received judicial approval in *Pearne v Lisle*.[104]

Wittmann[105] questions the assumption of ownership. Wittmann asks the question: chattel slavery was legal by whose standards? Europeans as a global minority could not decide that it was legal.[106] According to Wittmann the fundamentals of international law existed in Europe, the Middle East, India and China and some international law was observed by African states at the time.[107] Historical evidence shows that European officials recognised African states as equals but they did abandon treaties of African states on the grounds that they considered the treaties as non-binding.[108]

Wittmann argues that 'chattel slavery, such as practiced in the transatlantic system was not legal under the national laws of the European slaver nations'.[109] England is used as an example, in the form of the *Somerset* case.[110] In that case, Lord Mansfield released a slave from his master's ship under the writ of habeas corpus and said that slaves could not be forcibly returned to another country once they were on English soil, thereby recognising some *human agency* in a slave. This case did not free slaves but it gave them some rights against their masters. It is argued here that whether black people were legally chattel or not they were generally treated as such in the transatlantic slave trade. This treatment has had its repercussions down the ages, so much so, that the racism that they face in contemporary times has become institutionalised. The question that occupies the mind is that of causation. How to link the transatlantic slave trade and chattel slavery to the current racial harm[111] of institutional racism.

The cause

The term causation has not one meaning but several and in its modern sense Nagel contends that it 'has a wide spectrum of uses [which] rules out the possibility that there is just one correct and privileged explanation for it'.[112] Causation in law is drawn very narrowly meaning but for or factual causation in that X must be shown to produce Y and legal or proximate causation showing that the law holds X or another responsible for Y. So, for example, in a case where a Jehovah's Witness was stabbed by the accused, the victim refused to receive blood based on religious belief. The accused then argued that the victim was responsible for the death that followed because of her refusal of a blood transfusion and this refusal did break the chain of causation between his stabbing of her and her death. The court held the accused liable for the death on the basis that it did not lie in the mouth of the defendant to say who was responsible, the defendant was to take the victim as he found her, religious beliefs and all.[113]

If we were to deal with this call for reparations as based on a crime against humanity or the tort of negligence factual and legal causation would be required under English law. Factual causation requires that the wrong was actually committed by the defendant. Legal causation holds that the defendant was morally responsible. This narrow way of considering causation that the law employs makes a claim for reparations for the legacy of the transatlantic slave trade a perilous task. How can it be proved that the transatlantic slave trade is a 'but for' or factual cause of institutional racism? Who should be held legally and morally responsible for this legacy?

It is argued that for the law to provide a professional service to black people a wider notion of causation should be used. One that can accommodate the claim that institutional racism is the legacy of the transatlantic slave trade and chattel slavery which is damaging black people today. That wider notion would be that if certain conditions are satisfied a claim would lie. In terms of facts the law should stretch back its hands in time and consider the conditions and ideology under which the system of chattel slavery operated, it should then consider that same ideology – racism – under which contemporary black people are made subject. Furthermore, the law should consider the system of racism from the slave trade as one internalised by institutions that make the treatment of black people institutionally racist rather than believe that all that is being argued for is compensation for an old wrong.

What is the relationship between what may be argued are historic crimes and institutional racism? In other words how can we draw a link between the transatlantic slave trade and institutional racism? The link is not linear nor is it clearly visible. It consists of a tapestry of events leading from slavery, to emancipation, from colonialism through to modernity. The concept of causation being worked with is based on the theory called NESS (necessary element in a sufficient set) test of causation, coined by Hart and Honoré.[114] In this theory one does not have to accept 'causation in terms of a uniform sequence'.[115] Hart and Honoré argue that 'uniform sequences in nature … are not … simple … [and that] an occurrence of a given kind … follows when a complex set of conditions is satisfied'.[116] Hart and Honoré give as an example the tossing of a lighted cigarette into a waste paper basket that has caused a fire, but this leads to a fire only if other matters are also present such as oxygen and materials that burn.[117]

The transatlantic slave trade, chattel slavery and colonialism were a complex set of conditions that have led to the existence of institutional racism in contemporary times. Hart and Honoré go on to state that there may be a 'cluster of related concepts'[118] of causation that relate to a particular event. This chapter argues that social actors and institutions, racism and racial discrimination have their causative elements that have led to the event of institutional racism. Furthermore, in their analysis of Mill's[119] work, Hart and Honoré say that 'there may be several independent causes of an event'.[120] It is argued that the causes of institutional racism are not independent but interdependent with historical racism as an ideology that has become institutionalised in the organs of society, such an event having been 'produced by different causes'.[121] As Hart and Honoré ask; 'would Y have occurred if X had not occurred? It is argued that had the transatlantic slave trade and chattel slavery not happened nor would institutional racism. Institutional racism is an event which has come about through the network of successive stages of racism. These stages were not linear but interdependent in a tapestry of events which is often just taken for granted in that it is supposed racism is a product of the twentieth and twenty-first centuries – de-coupled from its history. Institutional racism is caused by the 'careless provision of opportunities for others to do harm'.[122] in this case the careless provision of services that allow social actors to do harm. For example, the multinational manufacture of skin whitening products, sold by outlets that do 'harm' to women of a darker hue.

During these episodes black people were discriminated against not only because they were worked like mules and oxen on plantations and this was economically cheap for plantation owners,[123] but because of the colour of their skin.[124] Emancipation made of slave labour free labour but this was under an unsuccessful apprenticeship system. There was still no difference in their racialised status and they were still seen as nothing better than chattel – being of animal-like quality.

Fryer,[125] in his chapter on the rise of English racism, discusses its development. He argues that the relationship between white and black existed well before black people were seen in England. 'Blackness, in England, traditionally stood for death, mourning, baseness, evil, sin, and danger'.[126] Why even 'the devil himself was black'.[127] Black people then slotted into an already racialised ideology reinforced by the control of white people over their bodies. Beckles tells us that during slavery black women were frequently raped and used to breed children, the system was a 'socio-sexual'[128] service enterprise. This view of black women did not change overnight just because they were emancipated. In a number of West Indian islands they were kept as prostitutes and distinctions were made between 'coloured' women and black, the former being more favoured than the latter.[129]

In this tapestry of assumed superiority of white people over black people it was taken for granted that black people were there to serve whites, 'just as the black ants are made on purpose to serve the red'.[130] By the 1850s the ideology of some of the greatest thinkers was that Britain was the most superior race. Africans were generally seen as unwashed and sinful,[131] childlike and non-inventive.[132]

Fryer argues that it is critical to understand the racist ideology that was left behind after the material means for it had long since gone.[133] It is argued that this ideology has racially infected the institutions of society of modernity such as health,[134] education[135] and policing.[136] It is these factors that should be considered when taking account of legal action to deal with institutional racism.

The legal cause

Turning Africans into chattel slaves was a crime against humanity.[137] According to Gifford[138] the transatlantic slave trade was a crime against humanity so it was a crime under international law. These were 'acts which are so reprehensible as to offend the conscience of mankind directed against civilian populations, are crimes in international law and always have been. The criterion is the conscience of decent human beings … not the standards of those who perpetrated the crimes'.[139] What follows from the notion that the chattel slavery was illegal under international law is 'the concept that reparations are payable where a crime against humanity has been committed by one people against another (and this) is well established in international law and practice'.[140] The problem is how to frame the cause of action so that it reflects institutional racism rather than relying on an action which is focused on an ancient wrong. We do not want to be focused on an ancient wrong because that is not the problem that is faced currently. The ancient wrong is the cause of institutional racism. A cause of action is a fact or set of facts that gives a person the right to seek judicial redress or relief against another. It is argued that institutional racism constitutes a set of facts because it operates to reinforce racism against black people in unwitting ways and that gives black people the right to take a case to court. What would be requested to satisfy the claim would be reparations for economic damage, cultural damage, social damage and psychological damage,[141] as well as an undertaking of non-repetition.

Corlett,[142] Feagin[143] and Thompson[144] inform us that barriers are raised against claims for dealing with contemporary harm. It is argued that these barriers are sourced in a history that has not taken seriously the continuing problems of institutional racism. The claim for damages as part of a package of reparation claims for institutional racism needs to be taken seriously to stop black oppression[145] caused by this form of harm.

Defendant beneficiaries and claimants

Defendant beneficiaries

Closely connected to the idea of inter-governmental responsibility is that of beneficiary. For instance, Beckles[146] tells us that 'the British state had its own specific financial interest in defending the sanctity of property rights in blacks as a paramount legal principle. It was a major direct investor in enslaved Africans ...'[147] and unjustly enriched from slave trade profits,[148] unjust enrichment being the state's wrongful profit at the expense of slaves. It is argued that the transatlantic slave trade was itself an instance of unjust enrichment.[149] But it is difficult to know how far to take this concept of unjust enrichment because it is contended that 'there is no public international legal foundation for such a claim'[150] only domestic law relates to unjust enrichment that 'exists in virtually every modern legal system'.[151] Nevertheless, Vohryzek[152] argues that unjust enrichment is not only a general principle of international law but also a principle of customary international law.[153] These mean there are grounds for making a claim based on unjust enrichment. It is another matter when it comes to corporations. There are several corporations as well as the churches in existence today whose wealth was built on the slave trade as well as the £20 million[154] granted by the British government to compensate slave owners for the loss of property in their slaves when slaves were 'freed'[155] in 1833 in the British Caribbean, such as Lloyds Banking Company Ltd and the Bank of London.[156] Moreover, Marryat of Lloyds marine insurance was awarded compensation of £15,000 'in 1837 for 391 slaves in Trinidad and Jamaica'.[157] The Church of England was given over £8,000 which is about £500,000 currently and the Bishop of Exeter received £13,000,[158] both these sums were compensation for loss of property in slaves. To take law suits against corporations would be similar to the trend in the US where several corporations have been found to have had their hands in the historical barrel of slavery, such as Tiffany and Co, Aetna, Brooks Brothers and Bank of America,[159] and law suits have been taken against some of them.[160] The cause of action, that is, the legal basis of the claim in these cases, was to hold the defendants liable for the commercial activities of their predecessors involved in the institution of slavery. What is claimed is that on the basis of the 'moral principle of fairness, and the fundamental legal principle that parties must repay their debts, this justifies reparations'.[161] Unfortunately, the claims have not been successful with one court seeing the issue as a political one and the US Supreme Court denying to hear the claim altogether.[162] Nevertheless this should not prevent those in the Diaspora and the Caribbean from pursuing a claim for legal restitution (for instance) for the harm that institutional racism has caused to black people precisely because they are black.

Another potential beneficiary (and therefore defendants) of the legacy of the transatlantic slave trade are the power brokers in the WTO. These are some of the developed countries who made their wealth on the back of the transatlantic slave trade such as the UK, the USA and many other West European countries like France and the Netherlands. They would be joined as parties to a reparation claim because they continue through the WTO to further their economic interests at the expense of the Caribbean nations[163] particularly in the preferential agreements wars between the EU, the Caribbean countries and the US operating as multinationals out of Latin American countries – such as Chiquita[164] It is hoped that rather than litigation a political solution could be reached where the Western European nations would support a claim for Caribbean trade and service preferences as part of a reparations package. This preferential agreement would last until the Caribbean was in an economically stable position to trade in the global market for goods and services.

Further defendants would be the European Union on the basis that they have failed to provide an appropriate service to black people concerning the Race Directive. This Directive has not only harboured interpretational difficulties in terms of race and ethnicity but has also excluded third-country nationals from its protection. It would be expected that the directive would be amended to provide for definitions of race and ethnicity and also to be extended to cover third-country nationals.

Claimants

One of the issues is who would be a claimant in court. It has been argued that there are no existing survivors or immediate descendants who could stand in the place of the claimant to bring a case[165] because they are not direct victims. Yet for those in Africa, the Caribbean and the European Diaspora the legacy of the slave trade and slavery continues to have consequences. Thackeray and Findling[166] argue that Africans contend that the slave trade has impacted on their economic development. Moreover, 'racial prejudice and economic inequality'[167] continue to plague societies.[168]

The notion of access to justice demands that there be some way in which these issues are resolved. Gifford raises this matter and answers it by stating that 'in law, the descendants who still suffer from the consequences of the crime have the right to restitution as much as the immediate victims'.[169] Bracegirdle suggests that 'the direct victims may not necessarily be as remote in time and by generation as might be supposed'.[170] There may be living descendants of slaves in the Diaspora and the Caribbean that are able to qualify for locus standi in order for a case to be brought before the courts on the basis that they are descended from slaves. Certainly, Beckles tells us that in the Caribbean at least there are descendants of slaves.

However, the argument against individuals bringing claims is that, were they to be successful, it would be unjust for them to receive a windfall whilst other black people continue to suffer and it would do nothing to challenge the status quo that is institutional racism. Bracegirdle says we might follow the US litigation model where claimants brought litigation on behalf of themselves and 'on behalf of all formerly enslaved Africans and their descendants and all living former enslaved African-Americans and their descendants'.[171] In any event the body to bring a claim would have to be one that was trustworthy and representative.[172] Reparationists would have to work out what that body was. If the court were to award damages on the basis of unjust enrichment, the money could be applied to those structures where institutional racism needed to be dismantled such as health care, education, policing and trade.

If litigation were to occur with respect to Africans and those of African descent in the Diaspora the same pattern might emerge, that of applying compensation to infrastructural projects such as better health provision, better housing and educational opportunities. These provisions would be delivered without the racism that often accompanies them. An example in Britain is in the private housing sector where racial discrimination is said to be rife in terms of landlords not wanting to let their accommodation to black people and lettings agents supporting this by telling Afro-Caribbean people who approach them for rented housing that the property is gone or under offer already, when it is not.

The Runnymede Trust found that of 750 adults about 29% of black people had experienced racial discrimination compared to 1% of white people.[173] This occurs despite legislation[174] to prevent it and a Property Ombudsman to whom complaints can be made about such practices. This discrimination is a 'culture'[175] that needs further exposure, challenge and to be changed. Maybe some of the compensation secured from successful litigation could be used to bring a focus on the licence of every lettings agent. The latter could be required to advertise that they do not provide a racially discriminatory service. Where the practice of racial discrimination is found their licence to practice could be rescinded, the work to bring this about funded by compensation from litigation or from the housing budget. Having adverts that are anti-discriminatory and publication of rulings from the Property Ombudsman may deter landlords from racially discriminating in the first place. This could have an impact on the institutionally racist practice that is said to exist in this area.[176] Information on anti-racially discriminatory lettings and house sales could be run online, in the property section of newspapers and property magazines as well as in letting and sales agents shops. The cost of adjusting the information to reflect anti-discriminatory practices would be minimal. The transformation could be overseen by the office of the Property Ombudsman in collaboration with the Equality and Human Rights Commission.

In terms of health provision, the Afiya Trust states that mainstream mental health provision is doing a dis-service to black and minority ethnic young people (BAME). The trust argues that there is no breakdown of disorders associated with this group and there is a failure 'to include racism, racial harassment or racist bullying'[177] which are amongst the risk factors that cause mental health problems in black and minority potential health users. Often the intervention of mental health services is at the crisis point after much of the damage has been done. Afiya tells us that 'specific culturally sensitive support'[178] is needed but is sparse in mainstream provision. There is also the issue of lack of confidence and trust that black people are concerned about when it comes to accessing the service. It is not only young BAME groups that have problems with mental health services.

Fernando[179] suggests that there are racial disparities in mental health services that impact on black people which are being ignored by the government and need to be on the health agenda. He argues 'that the health service could be institutionally racist'[180] due to the inheritance of 'ideas about racial stereotypes among mental health professionals – such as the 'perceived dangerousness' of black men'.[181] This perception in turn has 'produced a skewed diagnostic and treatment system'.[182] The King's Fund Briefing in February 2006 also pointed out that health services need to cater for the varying lifestyles of ethnic minority groups and that some of this group 'experience poorer access to services and poor quality of service'.[183] In order to change this position service providers need to be educated in institutional racism and how it impacts on service delivery when it comes to the BAME community. In particular the problem that lies in labelling black men as schizophrenic.[184] This stigmatises them and undermines their humanity where the diagnosis is racially contrived. Work can be done through the government running seminars in local boroughs and centrally dealing with the issues of institutionally racist service delivery. The Care Quality Commission could target the monitoring of service provision of mental and other health services with respect to racially sensitive provision. To increase awareness for users campaigns could be run on the internet, in schools and universities and GP services aimed at providing knowledge of this targeted provision and how to access it. In terms of education Kiely[185] focuses on university education. Kiely argues that lower university grades are obtained by minority ethnic students with the same A-level results as their white counterparts who fare better in terms of university grades; 72% of white students obtain a first or upper second compared to 53% of black students. Hillman, director of the Higher Education Policy Institute suggests that 'Universities need to think very carefully about how they can best support their students with different ethnic backgrounds, as many are underperforming against their classmates'.[186] The National Student's Union said that more help needed to be given to those from diverse backgrounds without stating what kind of help. Diane Abbott MP campaigns in Parliament to bring attention to the fact that 'black pupils face specific challenges in education and often do less well compared to their peers'.[187] Abbott suggests that government, schools and parents need to work together to ensure positive educational outcomes for young people of African and African-Caribbean descent.[188] One reform that could be made is to fund the supplementary schools, first set up to counter 'blatant racism'[189] in mainstream education. There has been a call that black businesses fund these Saturday schools but it is argued that here these schools should be funded by the Education budget as part of a transformative reparations package.

One issue that arises with regard to reparations claims is that other groups can also be victims of institutional racism. For example, Asian groups may also suffer from institutional racism although their history may not be based on the slave trade but other forms of colonial exploitation. To this it is said that their suffering is not denied nor their problems with institutional racism overlooked but this book is about the African, Caribbean and Afro-Caribbean Diaspora experience and how they could pursue a claim for reparations.

Political case

The political position should start with an apology and acceptance that a wrong was done, that wrong continues to cause racial harm in the form of institutional racism and that the state will primarily take responsibility for that wrong.[190] Local councils such as Liverpool apologised for their part in the slave trade, Bristol (which benefited tremendously from trade) refuses,[191] as does the UK government.[192] But what is an apology and what would it entail? Making an apology is a complex matter. For instance, it is not just about the British government's reluctance to make an apology[193] on the basis that this going down such a road might open the door to litigation and ultimately financial reparations. Apologies by the state and other institutions are complex phenomenon seen as 'the remedial work which serves the crucial function of repairing relationships after injury'.[194] They can be viewed as an 'acknowledgement and painful embracement of our deeds, coupled with a declaration of regret … In its purest expression, an apology clearly announces that "I have no excuses for what I did or did not do or say. I am sorry and regretful. I care. Forgive me."'[195] They can also be seen as the context within which the victim can recover from the harm done by the perpetrator.[196] Perceived as having a civilising mission and a humanising one on society generally.[197] This last point is particularly pertinent in the context of institutional racism because it serves as a willingness for institutions to cleanse themselves of the racist culture that is so destructive to the lives of black people.

Engerman[198] suggests that it has seemed to become politically acceptable that apologies are made without what would appear to be the inevitable claim for compensation. Brooks[199] contends that this is an age of apology if we look at the remorseful words that have come from many parts of the world on behalf of governments. The Maori people received an apology from Queen Elizabeth II, the American government apologised to the victim survivors of the Tuskegee experiment, and Polish, French and Czechs apologised for the Second World War atrocities committed during that era.[200] Brooks says that 'the apologies offered today can be described as 'a matrix of guilt and mourning, atonement and national revival."'[201] Close to this it would appear that apology requires political pressure to be brought upon the political regime more generally. This pressure can come from civil society as well as influence civil society. Furthermore, to gain this support for an apology as far as the consequences of the slave trade and chattel slavery are concerned another element that is required is that black people generally support the claim for reparations.[202]

According to Matsuda[203] for a meritorious claim, what must have been committed is a human injustice, this human injustice must have a detailed recording, there must be a distinct group of individual victims, 'the current members of the group must continue to suffer harm'[204] and the past injustice must have caused the harm. Some proponents of reparations like Anderson,[205] argue that it is reparations that is required and not so much an apology, whilst others argue that a formal apology is the start of the process rather than an end in itself.[206] For the legacy of the slave trade then it is not enough to rely on apologies. There needs to be recognition that the institutional infrastructure must be changed so that institutional racism is completely removed from the system, and this may well depend on raising reparations claims against states.

The African legacy

Many parts of Africa are still dominated by white culture – a form of institutional racism. This form of institutional racism in South Africa, for instance, serves to perpetuate division along economic, geographical and linguistic lines. Slaves were not taken from every part of Africa. The focus was on the West coast. In many of the countries where African people were captured, the disruption left its mark. Economic damage otherwise known as economic underdevelopment according to Rodney[207] occurred because of the 'exploitation of one country by another'.[208] In some countries on the African continent chattel enslavement, colonial and the early capitalist periods were witnesses to the taking of the strongest and most valuable in terms of labour and natural and other resources or the benefit of the stronger powers, who exploited them in many ways, so that skilled people are still scarce, land is impoverished and there is disruption in the socio- economic system as well as in families. African countries that suffered in these periods have not fully recovered.[209]

Those of the labour force that do exist in some of the African countries do not occupy sufficient income-generating jobs – such as 'civil servants, merchants [and] soldiers',[210] – to secure the funds needed to build viable infrastructure. But the main reason for Africa's underdevelopment is the exploitation of it by developed countries. This can be traced back to the transatlantic slave period where the healthiest captives were obtained through 'warfare, trickery, banditry and kidnapping',[211] as well as being bought and sold in slave markets. In the colonial period the exploitation of some of the African working class persisted with the very low wages per head compared to that of the working classes of Europe, meaning less money to invest in infrastructural projects.[212]

Rodney[213] also contends that

> The massive loss to the African labour force was made more critical because it was composed of able-bodied young men and young women. Slave buyers preferred their victims between the ages of 15 and 35, and preferably in the early twenties; the sex ratio being about two men to one woman. Europeans often accepted younger African children, but rarely any older person. They shipped the most healthy where- ever possible, taking the trouble to get those who had already survived an attack of smallpox, and who were therefore immune from further attacks of that disease, which was then one of the world's great killer diseases.[214]

Cultural damage

What does it mean to ask for cultural damage to be restored? Cultural damage consists of 'ruptures in the cultural fabric of society by damaging heritage structures, movable cultural properties and cultural practices'.[215] One could also talk of 'civilisation' or 'cultures' as Rodney[216] puts it. These were there before the Europeans engaged with Africa. Culture, argues Rodney, embraces a number of things. It relates to the social mores around dance and music with respect to birth, initiation, marriage and death and recreation.[217] Drums, percussion and a religious world view were fundamental to the cultural structure of some African countries and Christianity and Islam easily found a home in these societies.[218] In some African countries religion was used as a way of organising society and the way the world was viewed long before the Europeans came with their particular view of society. What was critical to the cultural and social order was the way society was organised. Some societies were organised along matriarchal lines whilst others were arranged in ways that underpinned patriarchy. What was clear is that in many African countries everybody tended to have their place in a communal social order based on family and kinship.[219]

Land was also critical to the culture of some African communities with the labour to work the land generally kept in-house through the family. In some African societies family was dominant and there are many examples of where it was family that worked the land and enjoyed the spoils as well as examples where if disaster struck the land of one part of the kin another part would help out.[220] Age was a very important factor in some societies and the older you were the more you were respected and seen as a wise elder.[221] In parts of Africa there were Africans captured and turned into slaves as a result of war for instance but this was not the norm and such people were generally integrated into the society.[222] They were not chattellised.

The point is Africa had a cultural history long before the Europeans came along and caused a rupture in the cultural way of doing things.[223] The view that Africa was without 'manufacture … arts … science'[224] as Hume put it, 'Africa [was] … no historical part of the world'.[225] These are racist views that even today hold Africa in an inferior position as often being the victim and of having no agency. 'Not only was transatlantic slavery of demographic significance, in the aggregate population losses but also in the profound changes to settlement patterns, epidemiological exposure and reproductive and social development potential'.[226]

Language is critical to the culture of a society and it is important to be able to think and speak in a country's language – this relates to African languages as to any other. Unfortunately the experience of colonialism means that those Africans exposed to colonial systems have to think and speak in French or English for example. In fact there is competition between the language spoken in the public intellectual space and that spoken at home.[227]

The Caribbean legacy

The British empire profited hugely from goods produced in the West Indies, in particular sugar and cotton. The slaves were made to work without payment whilst the slavers accumulated that money were enabled to invest in infrastructure in Britain not in the West Indies.[228] The slaves and the infrastructure were exploited for gain and not for reinvestment. Even after the abolition of chattel slavery in the West Indies there was no programme of economic development for the benefit of the Caribbean, rather;

> only children under six would be immediately free; the rest being regarded as 'apprentices' who would, in exchange for free board and lodging, have to work for their 'owners' 40 and a half hours for no pay until 1840. Several large disturbances meant that the deadline was brought forward and so, in 1838, 700,000 slaves in the West Indies ... were finally liberated.[229]

With this liberation came a certain kind of economic freedom where now freedmen would not necessarily work on the plantations. 'The choices that the freedmen made resulted in more personal freedom, but at the same time in a decline in their standard of living, their life expectancy, and their educational progress'.[230] However, freedmen preferred to work their own land rather than that of the planters and the higher the wage the less likely were freedmen to engage in the long hours of plantation work and its restrictive life,[231] where up until the 1930s plantation life remained highly labour intensive in terms of the harvesting of sugar cane.[232] To stay economically viable the Caribbean planters had to reduce the cost of their labour force despite this 'plantation work remained the most secure source of income for the freedmen and most alternative employment caused a substantial decline in their living standards'.[233]

During the world wars and following the Second World War many young Caribbean men and women came to Britain to work in the war effort[234] and in the post-war reconstruction of Britain,[235] not being able to find work in their own countries. This must also have had an effect on the ability of the Caribbean nations to increase their gross domestic product and reinvest in the infrastructure; for sure Chamberlain[236] contends that the post-colonial economies were poor.[237] The region was in a poor state which the Caribbeans inherited when they received independence from the British and other colonial rulers. This followed the centuries of neglect and abuse which preceded national rule.[238]

The Department for International Development (DFID) has identified that the Caribbean today suffers from 'high levels of debt, slow economic growth and having to adjust to the loss of historical trade preferences'.[239] It suffers from climate change and the effects of natural disasters as well as concern over organised crime.[240] DFID proposes £75 million worth of aid to spend on employment projects and other infrastructural projects[241] whilst Reparationists argue that as a bare minimum £7.5 trillion would be the sum that Britain should pay to the Caribbean. It is clear then that a realistic programme of economic infrastructural development would be needed as part of a reparations package. In modern times the West Indies is a melting pot of many cultures and sometimes politically it is described as one culture.

> However, the positive strengths which have emerged out of this adversity can be swamped through lack of self-esteem; created through the force-fed consumption of negative stereotyping to West Indians by the colonial masters and pseudo-historians. This stereotyping still continues today in a diluted form. It is perhaps for these reasons West Indians are sometimes perceived as having no positive culture of their own. We often hear talk of 'lack of identity' a search for 'roots' and 'lack of culture', sometimes from people of West Indian or in today's terminology 'African Caribbean' people.[242]

It is important then that such negative stereotypes that are institutionally racist be addressed through education and public intellectual discourse. In terms of the Diaspora there has been the development of an inferiority complex that has to be understood and removed in order to go forward, in the context of medical and psychological care. The moral wrong is the system of racism that has consequences for black people in terms of racial harm. That racial harm consists of the existence of an inferiority complex[243] and the perception by white people that this inferiority complex is not justified.[244] This inferiority complex is reinforced by the way black people are perceived by white people broadly speaking.[245] So in the case of *Alexander v Home Office*[246] where an inmate complained that he was passed over for more desirable work in the kitchen, the prison authorities wrongly stereotyped him as showing 'the usual traits associated with people of his ethnic background being arrogant, suspicious of staff, anti-authority, devious and possessing a very large chip on his shoulder … common in most coloured inmates'.[247]

Black men, in particular, are feared according to Johnson[248] and this is another stereotype that needs to be removed from the psychological spectacles through which black men are viewed. What needs to happen to resolve this problem is for the mediums through which black people are negatively portrayed to reconstruct the message in order to send positive messages in public spaces through education, the media and similar organisations.

Other matters include access to legal services to put the reparations claim. Access is critical for if there is none then a large number of people will be disappointed. So far there has been no access to the law on the basis that in the public space it is not believed that there is a case to answer regarding those who controlled and benefited from the legacy of the transatlantic slave trade and chattel slavery. The view seems to be that if there is no case to answer then there is no need for legal resources to be provided.

There is a push for the legal domain to be opened up to a reparations claim by the Caribbean Community (CARICOM). CARICOM has a focus to improve socio-economic conditions for its people in the Caribbean.[249] CARICOM is seeking involvement in legal negotiations with Western countries in terms of their participation in the slave trade such as 'Britain, France, Spain, Portugal, the Netherlands, Norway, Sweden and Denmark'.[250] So far only Sweden has made a positive move by stating that they will consider the claim and respect the process.[251] However, Britain whilst regretting and condemning 'the iniquities of the historic slave trade, [argues that] these shameful activities belong to the past [and] [g] overnments' today cannot take responsibility for what happened over 200 years ago'.[252]

The European legacy

Psychological damage

For black people 'the first encounter with a white man oppresses [them] with the whole weight of …'[253] their blackness. Their 'view of the world is white because no black voice exists'.[254] Here Fanon is discussing the way racism works on the unconscious world of the black person. It is damaging. Psychological damage then consists of a type of trauma 'to the psyche that occurs as a result of a traumatic event'.[255] The trauma can consist of several events which result in a dysfunctioning of the mind in terms of how a person thinks, feels and behaves and it causes mental distress. It could be argued that another name for this kind of injury is 'post traumatic slave syndrome' (PTSS).[256] DeGruy has named this kind of psychological racial harm because the harm is repeated over generations by white society so much so that it has become, it can be argued, institutionalised.

DeGruy asks what is the impact on people of generations of slavery?[257] It is trauma, and the question then becomes 'what does the trauma look like? How does the trauma manifest itself?'[258] There are patterns of behaviour in terms of three categories, 'vacant esteem, ever present anger and racist socialisation'.[259] We are more familiar with Post Traumatic Stress

Disorder (PTSD). MIND[260] suggests that PTSD consists of a number of symptoms that might cause a delayed reaction in terms of its effect on the human mind but can have a lasting effect on the person subject to the trauma. This trauma may make a person feel emotionally numb followed by mental distress and then a range of symptoms might follow such as the ease with which a person is upset or angry, taking on activities to avoid reliving the memory or memories and going through 'aspects of the trauma'.[261] The Diagnostic Statistical Manual of Mental Disorders IV[262] says that elements of PTSD can arise from 'a serious threat or harm to one's life or physical integrity, a threat or harm to one's children, spouse or close relative, sudden destruction of one's home or community, the stressor is experienced with intense fear, terror and helplessness, the stressor and disorder is considered to be more serious and will last longer when the stressor is of human design'.[263] But what about slavery and PTSS – what considerations should be taken into account for those who have had to suffer a lifetime of the effects of slavery? As DeGruy puts it there were no centres established to deal with the trauma of slavery,[264] nor where there any centres to deal with the aftermath of slavery, such as the experience of freedom, which in the West Indies meant apprenticeship, or the experience of colonialism, which meant the continuation of racial harm against black people. Currently in Britain, Western Europe and the West Indies there are no health services specifically dedicated to PTSS. Yet black people continue to suffer the effects that are similar to those of their slave past. For example, some black women straighten their hair and lighten their skin to adopt white European features. It is argued that this is a based on the social construct during slavery times that white people were superior to black. The most important matter about PTSS is that it has had an impact on self-esteem.[265] Those black people who suffer from this have no expectations from society and do not feel a member of it in the sense that they do not think the society has anything to offer them. There is no sense of self-worth. As far as black people in the Diaspora[266] and America are concerned, the negative interactions with public and private services only act to reinforce these feelings.[267]

Some scholars[268] have labelled this syndrome Post Traumatic Slavery Disorder (PTSD) and have defined the disorder as 'a condition that exists when a population has experienced multigenerational trauma resulting from centuries of slavery and continues to experience oppression and institutional racism today'.[269] This definition is certainly more all-encompassing and could easily apply to black people in the West Indies who could be said to suffer from this syndrome, although Mims *et al.* relate the disorder to the African experience.

There are scholars who reject the theory of Post Traumatic Slave Syndrome. Robinson-Aberdeen[270] argues that concern over PTSS may detract from other causes of mental illness and the biggest problem is that mental health services do not take the racial dimension of mental health sufficiently serious enough.[271] Whilst Neil[272] contends that PTSS might avoid the problem as he sees it of poor decision making. There are at least eight generations of freed persons, he argues, who have not experienced slavery and that is long enough to make good decisions about life and improve positive life chances. Vernon,[273] on the other hand, suggests, 'The emotional legacy of our enslaved past impacts us today in terms of our behaviour, cultural norms, parenting, relationships, lifestyle choices and in how we project our identity'.

Moreover, DeGruy describes the condition of PTSS as 'a consequence of multi-generational oppression of Africans and their descendants resulting from centuries of chattel slavery – a form of slavery predicated on the belief that African Americans [and black people more generally][274] were inherently/genetically inferior to whites. This was then followed by institutionalised racism which continues to perpetuate injury'.[275] The institutional legacy institutional racism has survived colonialism and modernity and has been identified as a phenomenon that is deeply hidden in the culture of institutions meant to serve all people but from which black people are disadvantaged. Gillborn argues that this is so in the education system[276] and, according to Gilroy,[277] it is at the very centre of British politics.[278] Institutional racism is in short the legacy of the slave trade and its emergence and survival is now to which we will turn. How is it then that the African moved from being a free person, to a captive to a slave[279] and then to a victim of racism?[280] The answer lies in the conversion of a free people to that of chattels. Chattel slavery constitutes the *complete* control of a person for the benefit of another[281] over the duration of their lives. Institutional racism covers the failure to see the destruction of black lives through lack of delivery of appropriate and professional services whether those services are delivered by institutions in the public or private sector.

Conclusion

The West Indian call for reparations for the legacy of the slave trade and chattel slavery sometimes gets mixed up with the notion of monetary compensation. Whilst financial compensation should not be ruled out it is not the central issue as can be seen from the above discussion. Economic, cultural and psychological damage require deep analysis and carefully planned programmes to deal with the problems that endure today and that is institutional racism in its various guises such as the problem with the type of access to public and private services. In the light of these issues problems with lack of self-esteem are deep routed and can cause inter or multi-generational trauma as DeGruy points out. CARICOM want to bring the question of reparations to the negotiation table when dealing with Western powers involved in the transatlantic slave trade and its aftermath but it is important that CARICOM spell out in fine detail exactly what is meant by matters such as economic and psychological damage for example. It is also critical that CARICOM have the backing of NGOs and civil society so that they become part of the process of reparations, after all it is civil society in particular that CARICOM are representing, and it is important that this dealing with reparations should not be a top down exercise. However, as things stand CARICOM is going to sue Britain, Holland and France at the International Court of Justice if it gets no satisfaction at the negotiation table.

At the heart of this chapter stands the argument that reparations are required for the legacy of the slave trade and slavery – institutional racism. Reparatory justice however is difficult to build. It is possible to consider restitution but that has several hurdles and may in the end not prove as fruitful as one would hope. Litigation could be considered as a general strategy but as with restitution it is not an easy or straightforward process.

There is a quasi-political argument that the pursuance of reparations is a separatist and racist action and that we do not need to consider this in multi-cultural societies, where the burden of payment will fall on tax payers including black people. However, this view cheapens the debate since it is argued that it is not only financial compensation that is looked to but reparations in the wider sense of the meaning of the word, and it starts with an apology. Few if any want to pursue costly litigation in court. The Caribbean in the form of CARICOM would rather sit around a table and discuss what is needed to put things right.

However, the discussion will be stinted unless institutional racism is raised as major issue. This hidden form of racism is one that needs to be brought out of its hiding place and discussed in the public domain as a reason why reparations should be made. It is argued that the role of institutional racism in maintaining racial harm can be raised as part of the litigation process or/and as a major concern in the political negotiations that CARICOM want to raise with those Western governments involved in the slave trade and chattel slavery. However, the work that bodies like CARICOM want to pursue may require a ground swell of support in the form of a social movement. This is where we turn to in the next chapter.

Notes

1 BBC News, 'Mau Mau Torture Victims to Receive Compensation – Hague', BBC News, 6 April 2013. Available at: www.bbc.co.uk/news/uk-22790037 (accessed 24 June 2014).
2 A. Moore, '12 Ways Neo-Racists Deny Responsibility for Slavery and How to Respond', Atlantablackstar, 2014. Available at: www.atlantablackstar.com (accessed 1 December 2015).
3 UNESCO, 'Slavery and Racism', UNESCO Press. Available at: www.unesco.org (accessed 1 December 2015).
4 Ibid.
5 Ibid.
6 Basic Principles and Guidelines on the Right to a Remedy and Reparation for Gross Violations of International Human Rights Law and Serious Violations of International Humanitarian Law, GA Res. 60/147, 16 December 2005, A/RES/60/147; 13 IHRR 907 (2006), hereinafter, Basic Principles.
7 Principle 19 of the Basic Principles.
8 Principle 20 of the Basic Principles.
9 Principle 21 of the Basic Principles.
10 Principle 22 of the Basic Principles.
11 Principle 23 of the Basic Principles.
12 J. Curtis, 'Arguments for Slavery Reparations', in *Humanities 360*, 13 March 2009. Available at: www.humanities360.com/index.php/arguments-for-slavery-reparations-2-45293/ (accessed 11 June 2014).
13 D. Shelton, 'Litigation and Political Action to Address Historic Injustices in the United States: Problems and Prospects', in F. Brennan and J. Packer (eds), *Colonialism, Slavery, Reparations and Trade: Remedying the Past?* (Abingdon: Routledge, 2012).
14 J.A. Corlett, *Race, Racism and Reparations* (Ithaca: Cornell University Press, 2003).
15 J.R. Feagin, 'Documenting the Costs of Slavery, Segregation and Contemporary Racism: Why Reparations are in Order for African Americans', *Harvard Black Letter Law Journal* 20 (2004).
16 J. Thompson, 'Taking Responsibility for the Past: Reparation and Historical Justice', *Restorative Justice Online*. Available at: www.restorativejustice.org/articlesdb/articles/2980 (accessed 11 June 2014).
17 Black past. org, 'Remembered and Reclaimed'. Available at: www.blackpast.org/gah/edward-wilmot-blyden-1832-1912 (accessed 11 June 2014).
18 J.K. Dagnini and Marcus Garvey: 'A Controversial Figure in the History of Pan-Africanism', *The Journal of Pan-African Studies* 2(3) (2008).
19 L. Sustar, 'The Origins of Pan-Africanism', *Socialistworker.org*, 5 October 2012. Available at: http://socialistworker.org/2012/10/05/origins-of-pan-africanism (accessed 11 June 2014).
20 Ibid.
21 Rastafarianism is a religion that is African-centred and evolved in Jamaica in the 1930s. Their head is Haile Selassie I who was king of Ethiopia. Rastafarians believe he is God who will bring back to Africa those of the black community exiled because of colonisation and slavery, 'Rastafari at a Glance', *BBC Religions*, 10 February 2009.
22 The Nation of Islam teaches black people that they are equals and should be independent through God, NOI History. Available at: www.noi.org/noi-history/ (accessed 13 June 2014).
23 C. Jones, 'Focus: Righting Historical Wrongs: The Case for Reparations', *Discover Society*, 6 May 2014, Focus Issue 8.
24 The formerly enslaved were used to build the wealth of slavers and the wealth of Western economies. See E. Williams, *Capitalism and Slavery* (London: The University of North Carolina Press, 1994).

25 'Black Reparations', *Stanford Encyclopaedia of Philosophy*, 14 December 2010. Available at: http://plato.stanford.edu/entries/black-reparations/ (accessed 13 December 2014).
26 Ibid.
27 Ibid.
28 'Black Reparations', *Stanford Encyclopaedia of Philosophy.*
29 Lord Anthony Gifford is a human rights lawyer who practises in Jamaica and Britain.
30 The National Archives, Bernie Grant Collection.
31 African and African Descendants WCR: IAAR response to expulsion of non-blacks from Barbados, Choike.org, 11 October 2002. Available at: www.choike.org/nuevo_eng/informes/621.html (accessed 16 June 2014).
32 A.L. Brophy, *Reparations Pro and Con* (Oxford: Oxford University Press, 2006).
33 Ibid., p. 9.
34 R.E. Howard-Hassmann, *Reparations to Africa* (Philadelphia: University of Pennsylvania Press, 2008).
35 J.C. Torpey, *Making Whole What Has Been Smashed: On Reparations Politics* (Cambridge, MA: Harvard University Press, 2006).
36 CARICOM consists of the Heads of Government of the West Indies who work for a number of things including a 'fully integrated and liberalised internal market', preamble of the Revised Treaty of Chaguaramas Establishing the Caribbean Community including the CARICOM Single Market and Economy.
37 CARICOM Reparations Commission Press Statement, delivered by Professor Sir Hilary Beckles (Chairman) on behalf of the CARICOM Reparations Commission Press Conference, Regional Headquarters, the University of the West Indies (UWI), 10 December 2013, http://caricom.org/jsp/pressreleases/press_releases_2013/pres285_13.jsp (accessed 13 June 2014).
38 Ibid.
39 C. Jones, 'Focus: Writing Historical Wrongs, the Case for Reparations' *Discover Society*, 6 May 2014, Focus Issue 8. Available at: www.discoversociety.org/2014/05/06/focus-righting-historical-wrongs-the-case-for-reparations/ (accessed 16 June 2014).
40 H. MCD. Beckles, *Britain's Black Debt* (Kingston: University of the West Indies Press 2013), p. 13. Also see T. Van Boven, *Victims' Rights to a Remedy and Reparation: The New United Nations Principles and Guidelines*, p. 24. Available at: www.corteidh.or.cr/tablas/r26214.pdf (accessed 25 June 2014).
41 Basic Principles and Guidelines on the Right to a Remedy and Reparation for Victims of Gross Violations of International Human Rights Law and Serious Violations of International Humanitarian Law. Adopted and proclaimed by General Assembly resolution 60/147 of 16 December 2005.
42 CARICOM Reparations Commission Press Statement Delivered by Professor Sir Hilary Beckles (Chairman) on behalf of the CARICOM Reparations Commission Press Conference Commission Regional Headquarters, UWI 10 December 2013.
43 World Health Organisation/Europe. Available at: www.euro.who.int/en/health-topics/noncommunicable-diseases/diabetes/data-and-statistics (accessed 21 October 2014).
44 J.P.P. Robinson, 'Socio-cultural Risk Factors of Non-Insulin Diabetes Mellitus among Middle Class African Americans in Central Ohio', electronic thesis or dissertation, Ohio State University, 2003, *OhioLINK Electronic Theses and Dissertations Center*. Available at: https://etd.ohiolink.edu/ (accessed 16 June 2014).
45 E.S. Tull and J.M. Roseman, 'Diabetes in African Americans'. Available at: www.diabetes.niddk.nih.gov/dm/pubs/america/pdf/chapter31.pdf (accessed 18 June 2014).
46 Ibid.
47 Ibid., p. 623.
48 Ibid., p. 625.
49 Paragraph 21 of the Basic Principles and Guidelines.
50 Paragraph 22(a) of Basic Principles and Guidelines.
51 Paragraph 22(b) of Basic Principles and Guidelines.
52 Paragraph 22(e) of Basic Principles and Guidelines.
53 Paragraph 22(f) of Basic Principles and Guidelines.
54 Paragraph 22(g) of Basic Principles and Guidelines.
55 Paragraph 22(h) of Basic Principles and Guidelines.

56 Paragraphs 20(a) to (e) of Basic Principles and Guidelines.
57 Williams, *Capitalism and Slavery*, p. 23.
58 'The psychological trauma of slavery lingers on, the commission says: "For over 400 years Africans were classified in law as non-human, chattel, property and real estate. They were denied recognition as members of the human family by laws and practices derived from the parliaments and policies of Europe."' O. Bowcott and I. Cobain, 'UK Sternly Resists Paying Reparations for Slave Trade Atrocities and Injustices', *theguardian.com*, 24 February 2014.
59 Howard-Hassmann, *Reparations to Africa*, p. 43.
60 American Jewish Historical Society, 'Holocaust Restitution: German Reparations', Jewish Virtual Library (The Philip Leff Group, 1999). Available at: www.jewishvirtuallibrary.org/jsource/Holocaust/reparations.html (accessed 30 June 2014).
61 Ibid.
62 S. Hira, *20 Questions and Answers about Reparations for Colonialism.*
63 P.M. Muhammad 'The Transatlantic Slave Trade: A Legacy Establishing a Case for International Reparations', *Columbian Journal of Race and Law* 3(2) (2013): 14.
64 'Issued by President Franklin Roosevelt on 19 February 1942, this order authorized the evacuation of all persons deemed a threat to national security from the West Coast to relocation centers further inland. In the next 6 months, over 100,000 men, women, and children of Japanese ancestry were moved to assembly centers. They were then evacuated to and confined in isolated, fenced, and guarded relocation centers, known as internment camps.' From the American National Archives. Available at: www.archives.gov/historical-docs/todays-doc/?dod-date=219 (accessed 1 July 2014).
65 Japanese American Cases. Available at: http://legal-dictionary.thefreedictionary.com/Japanese+American+Evacuation+Cases.
66 For example the 'stolen generations' of Aborigines in Australia. The government has agreed to compensate them to the tune of £2.2 million and has expressed its sorrow for the fact that on the basis of race children were removed from their families. B. Macmahon, 'Tasmania to pay "stolen generation" of Aborigines £2.2 million in reparations', *The Guardian*, 23 January 2008.
67 Muhammad, 'The Transatlantic Slave Trade'.
68 Ibid., p. 7.
69 *theguardian.com*, 24 February 2014. Also see B. Edmonson, *Caribbean Middlebrow, Leisure, Culture and the Middle Class* (Ithaca: Cornell University, 2009), p. 72. Also see M. Cervantes-Rodriguez, R. Grosfoguel and E. Mielants, *Caribbean Migration to Western Europe and the United States* (Philadelphia: Temple University Press, 2009), p. 7.
70 W. Macpherson, *The Stephen Lawrence Inquiry*(London: Home Office, 1999), para. 6.34.
71 The National Legal and Policy Centre, 'The Case against Slave Reparations' (2004) U.S. Newswire.
72 Muhammad, 'The Transatlantic Slave Trade', p. 47.
73 Wilberforce Institute for the Study of Slavery and Emancipation.
74 P. Fryer, *Staying Power: The History of Black People in Britain* (London: Pluto Press, 1985), p. 17.
75 A. Gifford, *The Passionate Advocate* (Kingston: Arawak Publications, 2007), p. 246.
76 Macpherson, *The Stephen Lawrence Inquiry*, chapter 6.
77 Beckles, *Britain's Black Debt.*
78 J. Feagin, 'A Legal and Moral basis for Reparations', *Time* 28 May 2014. Available at: www.time.com (accessed 27 November 2015).
79 Beckles, *Britain's Black Debt*, p. 163.
80 Ibid.
81 Ibid.
82 Feagin, 'A Legal and Moral basis for Reparations'.
83 D. Olusoga, 'The History of British Slave Ownership has been Buried: Now its Scale can be revealed', *The Guardian*, 12 July 2015.
84 Lord Anthony Gifford, 'Formulating the Case for Reparations', in F. Brennan and J. Packer (eds), *Colonialism, Slavery, Reparations and Trade: Remedying the Past?* (Abingdon: Routledge, 2012), p. 84.
85 Ibid.
86 Global Policy Forum, 'Universal Jurisdiction'. Available at: www.globalpolicy.org (accessed 1 December 2015).

87 Bowcott and Cobain, 'UK Sternly Resists Paying Reparations for Slave Trade Atrocities and Injustices'.
88 K. Bracegirdle, 'Restitution after Slavery', in F. Brennan and J. Packer (eds), *Colonialism, Slavery, Reparations and Trade: Remedying the Past?* (Abingdon: Routledge, 2012).
89 Ibid., p. 147.
90 Howard-Hassmann, *Reparations to Africa*, p. 67.
91 Bracegirdle, 'Restitution after Slavery', p. 150.
92 Lord Anthony Gifford, *The Passionate Advocate* (Kingston: Arawak Publications, 2007), p. 249.
93 Beckles, *Britain's Black Debt* (Kingston: University of the West Indies Press 2013), p. 169.
94 M.K. Asante, 'The Ideological Origins of Chattel Slavery in the British World', Slavery Remembrance Day Memorial Lecture 2007. Available at: www.liverpoolmuseums.org.uk/ism/resources/origins_chattel_slavery.aspx# (accessed 25 November 2014).
95 The Yorke/Talbot Opinion of 1729.
96 S. Dziobon, 'Judge, Jurisprudence and Slavery in England 1729–1807', in F. Brennan and J. Packer (eds), *Colonialism, Slavery, Reparations and Trade: Remedying the Past?* (Abingdon: Routledge, 2012).
97 Ibid.
98 M. Prince, *The History of Mary Prince: A West Indian Slave*, edited by S. Salih (London: Penguin Books, 2004), p. 7.
99 Dziobon, 'Judge, Jurisprudence and Slavery in England 1729–1807', pp. 170–171.
100 (1677) 83 ER.
101 (1679) 5 Mod. 182 K.B.
102 (1706) 2 Salk, 666.
103 F.O. Shyllon, *Black Slaves in Britain* (Oxford: Oxford University Press, 1974).
104 (1749) Ambler 77.
105 N. Wittmann, 'International Legal Responsibility and Reparations for Transatlantic Slavery', in F. Brennan and J. Packer (eds), *Colonialism, Slavery, Reparations and Trade: Remedying the Past?* (Abingdon: Routledge, 2012).
106 Ibid., p. 3.
107 Ibid., p. 5.
108 Ibid., p. 8.
109 Ibid., p. 15.
110 King's Bench, 12 George III A. D.[1771–72].
111 M. du Plessis and S. Pete (eds), *Repairing the Past?: International Perspectives on Reparations for Gross Human Rights* Abuses (Oxford: Intersentia, 2007).
112 M. Kistler, *Causation and the Laws of Nature*(London: Routledge, 2010), P. 4.
113 *R v Blaue* [1975] 3 All ER 446 CA.
114 H.L.A. Hart and T. Honoré, 2nd edition, *Causation in the Law* (Oxford: Oxford University Press, 1985).
115 Ibid., p. 16.
116 Ibid., p. 17.
117 Ibid.
118 Ibid., p. 19.
119 J.S. Mill, *A System of Logic Ratiocinative and Inductive*, 8th edition (London: 1886).
120 Hart and Honoré, *Causation in the Law*, p. 19.
121 Ibid., p. 20.
122 Ibid., p. 127.
123 Williams, *Capitalism and Slavery*, p. 10.
124 Shyllon, *Black People in Britain 1555–1833* .
125 Fryer, *Staying Power*.
126 Ibid., p. 135.
127 Ibid.
128 Beckles, *Britain's Black Debt*, p. 76.
129 Ibid., p. 81.
130 *Spectator*, no. 1942 (16 September 1865), 1035.
131 Fryer, *Staying Power*, pp. 184–185.
132 G.A. Henty,*By Sheer Pluck: A Tale of the Ashanti War* (Blackie & Son, 1884), p. 118.

133 Fryer, *Staying Power*, p. 190.
134 H. Jones, *Health and Society in Twentieth-Century Britain* (Abingdon: Routledge, 2013).
135 D. Gillborn, *Education and Institutional Racism* (London: Institute of Education, 2002).
136 Bowling and Phillips, *Racism, Crime and Justice.*
137 Gifford, 'Formulating the Case for Reparations'.
138 Ibid.
139 Ibid., pp. 80–81.
140 Muhammad, 'The Transatlantic Slave Trade', p. 5.
141 Gifford, *The Passionate Advocate*, p. 250.
142 Corlett, *Race, Racism and Reparations*, p. 1.
143 Feagin, 'Documenting the Costs of Slavery, Segregation and Contemporary Racism'.
144 Thompson, 'Taking Responsibility for the Past: Reparation and Historical Justice'.
145 Feagin, 'Documenting the Costs of Slavery, Segregation and Contemporary Racism', p. 49.
146 Beckles, *Britain's Black Debt.*
147 Ibid., p. 145.
148 Bracegirdle, 'Restitution after Slavery', p. 149.
149 R. Dibie and J. Njoju, 'Cultural Perceptions of Africans in Diaspora and in Africa on Atlantic Slave Trade and Reparations,' *African and Asian Studies* 4(3) (2005): 410.
150 Howard-Hassmann, *Reparations to Africa*, p. 67.
151 C.M. Fombad, 'The Principle of Unjust Enrichment in International Law', *The Comparative Law Journal of South Africa* 30(2) (1997): 120.
152 A. Vohryzek, 'Unjust Enrichment Unjustly Ignored: Opportunities and Pitfalls in Bringing Unjust Enrichment Claims Under ICSID', *Yale Law School*, 2008. Available at: http://digitalcommons.law.yale.edu/cgi/viewcontent.cgi?article=1072&context=student_papers, p. 5 (accessed 2 July 2014).
153 Ibid.
154 This amounted to £200 billion in today's money. See Beckles, *Britain's Black Debt*, p. 144.
155 British slaves were not entirely freed in 1833 but tied to an unsuccessful apprenticeship system.
156 'Legacies of British Slave-Ownership', UCL. Available at: www.ucl.ac.uk/lbs/commercial/ (accessed 3 July 2014).
157 Williams, *Capitalism and Slavery* , p. 105.
158 S. Bates, 'Church Apologises for Benefiting from the Slave Trade'. Available at: www.theguardian.com/uk/2006/feb/09/religion.world (accessed 22 October 2014).
159 'Shocking List of 10 Companies that Profited from the Slave Trade', *Your Black World*, 3 July 2014. Available at: www.yourblackworld.net/2013/08/black-news/shocking-list-of-10-companies-that-profited-from-the-slave-trade/ (accessed 3 July 2014).
160 'Law Suit Chases Companies tied to Slavery', Fox News. Available at: www.foxnews.com/story/2002/03/27/lawsuit-chases-companies-tied-to-slavery/ (accessed 3 July 2014).
161 *In re African-American Slave Descendants Litigation*, United States District Court, 6 July 2005, p. 1.
162 'Business and Human Rights Resource Centre', *Slavery Reparations Law Suit (re USA)*, 18 February 2014. Available at: http://business-humanrights.org/en/slavery-reparations-lawsuit-re-usa#c9314 (accessed 17 December 2014).
163 C. Barnett, 'The Caribbean Community: Preparing for and Adjusting to the New Rules of the International Trading System, Caribbean Community Secretariat, 2011'. Available at: www.caricom.org (accessed 18 November 2015).
164 S. Meunier, 'Banana Splits: Nested and Overlapping Regimes in the Transatlantic Banana Trade Dispute (2006)', in K. Alter (ed.), *The European Court's Political Power* (Oxford: Oxford University Press, 2010), p. 223.
165 Muhammad, 'The Transatlantic Slave Trade', p. 35.
166 F.W. Thackeray and J.E. Findling (eds), *Events that Formed the Modern World: From the European Renaissance through the War on Terror* (Santa Barbara: ABC-CLIO, LLC, 2012).
167 Ibid., p. 271.
168 Ibid.
169 Gifford, *The Passionate Advocate*, p. 249.
170 Bracegirdle, 'Restitution after Slavery', p. 155.
171 Ibid., p. 156.

172 Gifford, 'Formulating the Case for Reparations', p. 83.
173 G. Lynn and E. Davey, 'London Letting Agents Refuse Black Tenants', BBC News London, 14 October 2013. Available at: www.bbc.co.uk/news/uk-england-london-24372509 (accessed 8 July 2014).
174 Under sections 33 and 34 of the Equality Act 2010.
175 Lynn and Davey, 'London Letting Agents Refuse Black Tenants'.
176 Ibid.
177 M. Malek, 'Mental Health Provision is Failing Black and Minority Ethnic Young People', *The Guardian*, 7 July 2011.
178 Ibid.
179 M. O'Hara, 'Black and Minority Ethnic Mental Health Patients' "Marginalised" under Coalition', *The Guardian*, 17 April 2012. Surman Fernando is a Psychiatrist.
180 Ibid.
181 Ibid.
182 Ibid.
183 King's Fund, Briefing, 'Access to Health Care and Minority Ethnic Groups', February 2006. Available at: www.kingsfund.org.uk (accessed 26 November 2006).
184 P. Thomas, 'Black and Mad', where he argues that 'Schizophrenia is emblematic of the oppression and mistreatment of black people by psychiatry'. In 2012 an independent inquiry was launched into the labelling of schizophrenia. Available at: www.schizophreniainquiry.orgnews (accessed 25 May 2016).
185 A. Kiely, 'Why are Britain's Universities still Failing Black and Asian Students?' *The Guardian* 28 March 2014.
186 Ibid.
187 D. Abbott, 'London Schools and the Black Child'. Available at: www.blackeducation.info (accessed 26 November 2015).
188 Ibid.
189 N. Duncan, 'All Black Children Should Attend Supplementary Schools', *The Voice*, 10 November 2013.
190 Beckles, *Britain's Black Debt*, p. 169.
191 C. Milmo, 'Slavery: Is it Time for an Apology?' *The Independent*, 11 May 2006.
192 Gifford, *The Passionate Advocate*, p. 250.
193 'Blair "sorrow" over Slave Trade', BBC News, 27 November 2006. Available at: http://news.bbc.co.uk/1/hi/6185176.stm (accessed 29 October 2014).
194 C. Jenkins, 'Taking Apology Seriously', in M. Du Plessis and S. Pete (eds), *Repairing the Past? International Perspectives on Reparations for Gross Human Rights Abuses* (Oxford: Intersentia, 2007), p. 57.
195 N. Tavuchis, *Mea Culpa: A Sociology of Apology and Reconciliation* (Stanford: Stanford University Press, 1991), p. 19.
196 Jenkins, 'Taking Apology Seriously', p. 58.
197 Ibid., p. 59.
198 S.L. Engerman, 'Apologies, Regrets and Reparations', *European Review* 17(3–4) (2009).
199 R.L. Brooks, *When Sorry isn't Enough: The Controversy over Apologies and Reparations for Human Injustice* (New York: New York University Press, 1999).
200 Ibid., p. 1.
201 Ibid.
202 CARICOM Nations Unanimously Approve 10 Point Plan for Slavery Reparations, *CARICOM*, 11 March 2014. Available at: www.leighday.co.uk/News/2014/March-2014/CARICOM-nations-unanimously-approve-10-point-plan- (accessed 29 October 2014).
203 Brooks, *When Sorry isn't Enough*, p. 7.
204 Ibid.
205 J. Lieberson, 'Slavery May Have Ended, but Leaders of the African Community Insist its Effects are Still Being Felt. Is Money the Answer?' *Slave Routes: the Long Memory*. Available at: http://journalism.nyu.edu/publishing/archives/slave_routes/4_payback.htm (accessed 9 July 2014).
206 Beckles,*Britain's Black Debt*, chapter 14.
207 W. Rodney, *How Europe Underdeveloped Africa* (London: Bogle-L'Ouverure, 1978).
208 Ibid., p. 22.

209 Ibid.
210 Ibid., p. 27.
211 Ibid., p. 104.
212 N. Nunn, 'Historical Legacies: A Model Linking Africa's Past to its Current Underdevelopment', *Journal of Development Economics* 83 (2007): 157–175, at pp. 157–158.
213 Rodney, *How Europe Underdeveloped Africa*.
214 Ibid., p. 105.
215 Business World on Line. Available at: www.bworldonline.com/content.php?section=Arts&Leisure&title=Assessing-the-cultural-damage&id=80919 (accessed 11 July 2014).
216 Rodney, *How Europe Underdeveloped Africa*, p. 41.
217 Ibid.
218 Ibid., p. 42.
219 Ibid., p. 43.
220 Ibid., p. 44.
221 M. Ampin, 'African Studies: The Five Major African Initiation Rites (2003)'. Available at: www.manuampim.com/AfricanInitiationRites.htm (accessed 2 November 2014).
222 Rodney, *How Europe Underdeveloped Africa*.
223 Ibid., p. 45. 008. Available at: www.africanholocaust.net/news_ah/africa%20before%20slavery.htm (accessed 14 July 2014).
224 Ibid.
225 Ibid.
226 Ibid.
227 Ibid.
228 D. Randal, 'Britain's Colonial Shame: Slave-owners Given Huge Payouts after Abolition', *The Independent*, 24 February 2014.
229 Ibid.
230 E.C. Emmer, 'The Big Disappointment: The Economic Consequences of the Abolition of Slavery in the Caribbean, 1833–1888', *History in Focus*, Issue 12, 'Slavery'.
231 Hence Asians were brought in as indentured labour to take over the role of the freed slaves, Emmer, 'The Big Disappointment'.
232 Ibid.
233 Ibid.
234 'Caribbean Migration to Britain during the First World War', *Black History Month*, 2014. Available at: www.blackhistorymonth.org.uk/caribbean-migration-to-britain/4567455752 (accessed 11 July 2014).
235 'Post-war Migration, Brave New World', the *National Archives*. Available at: www.nationalarchives.gov.uk/pathways/citizenship/brave_new_world/immigration.htm (accessed 11 July 2014).
236 M. Chamberlain, 'Migration and Post-Colonialism: The Commonwealth Caribbean', *Migration Citizenship Education*, 2008.
237 Ibid.
238 Chamberlain, 'Migration and Post-Colonialism: The Commonwealth Caribbean'.
239 H. Walker, 'DFID Caribbean'. Available at: www.gov.uk/government/world/organisations/dfid-caribbean (accessed 11 July 2014).
240 Ibid.
241 Ibid.
242 West Indian culture, 'Out of Many People, One Culture' – West Indian Culture – A Way of Life'. Available at: www.onespace.org.uk/your-roots/west-indian-culture (13 July 2014).
243 Fanon, *Black Skin White Masks*, pp. 100, 109.
244 'Where some books have portrayed black people as having done well through slavery because that has exposed them to the white man's civilization', C.G. Woodson (Clear Words.org 2009) 7.
245 L. Frohne, 'Why Do People Stereotype Black Men? Ask Your Brain' (Open Society Foundations 2013). Available at: www.opensocietyfoundations.org/voices/why-do-people-stereotype-black-men-ask-your-brain (accessed 25 June 2014).
246 [1988] 2 All ER 118, CA.
247 M. Connolly, *Townshend-Smith on Discrimination Law: Text, Cases and Materials*, 2nd edition (London: Cavendish Publishing, 2004), p. 171. In this case the Court of Appeal found this treatment to be discriminatory.

248 Frohne, 'Why Do People Stereotype Black Men? Ask Your Brain'.
249 See the objectives of the Community. Available at: www.caricom.org/jsp/community/objectives.jsp?menu=community (accessed 21 October 2014).
250 *theguardian.com*, 24 February 2014.
251 Ibid.
252 *theguardian.com*, 24 February 2014. Also see Foreign Office spokesperson on this point, European Parliamentary Research Service. Available at: http://epthinktank.eu/2014/06/04/caribbean-slavery-reparation-claims-against-some-european-countries/ (accessed 21 October 2014).
253 Fanon, *Black Skin, White Masks*, p. 150.
254 Ibid., pp. 152–153.
255 'Psychological Trauma', *Science Daily*. Available at: www.sciencedaily.com/articles/p/psychological_trauma.htm (accessed 13 July 2014).
256 J. DeGruy, *Post Traumatic Slave Syndrome: America's Legacy of Enduring Injury and Healing* (Portland: Joy DeGruy Publications, 2005).
257 Ibid., p. 113.
258 Ibid., p. 113. Racist socialisation is the inculcation of racist barriers that prohibit successful life chances.
259 Ibid., p. 121.
260 MIND supports anyone with a mental health problem.
261 Available at: MIND www.mind.org.uk/about-us/ (accessed 15 July 2014).
262 DeGruy, *Post Traumatic Slave Syndrome*, p. 114.
263 Ibid.
264 Ibid., p. 115.
265 Ibid., p. 117.
266 G.D. Howe, 'A White Man's War? The First World War and the West Indies', *BBC History*, 2011. Available at: www.bbc.co.uk/history/worldwars/wwone/west_indies_01.shtml (accessed 17 July 2014).
267 Macpherson, *The Stephen Lawrence Inquiry*.
268 S. Mims, L. Higginbottom and O. Reid, *Post Traumatic Slavery Disorder* (Dorchester: Pyramid Builders). Available at: www.pyramidbuilders.org/pdfs/PTSD_Manuscript.pdf (accessed 17 July 2014).
269 Ibid., p. 121.
270 N. Duncan, 'Are we suffering from post-traumatic slave syndrome? Experts debate whether the racist theory that enslaved Africans were 'subhuman' has had a powerful impact on present-day self-esteem', *The Voice*, 16 February 2014.
271 Ibid.
272 Ibid.
273 Ibid.
274 My emphasis.
275 Duncan, *The Voice*, 16 February 2014.
276 D. Gillborn, *Education and Institutional Racism* (London: Institute of Education, 2002), p. 2.
277 P. Gilroy, 'The End of Antiracism', in J. Donald and A. Rattansi (eds), *'Race', Culture and Difference* (London: Sage, 1992).
278 Ibid., p. 51.
279 Rodney, *How Europe Underdeveloped Africa*, p. 103.
280 In the US there is concern from the descendants of enslaved Africans and slavers surrounding 'the racial nature of slavery of the slave system and the persistence of institutional racism that emerged from it'. See H. McDonald Beckles, *Slave Voyages: The Transatlantic Trade in Enslaved Africans* (Paris: United Nations Education, Scientific and Cultural Organisation Slave Trade Education Project, 2001).
281 The Free Dictionary. Available at: http://legal-dictionary.thefreedictionary.com/Chattel+slavery (accessed 8 August 2014).

Bibliography

Basic Principles and Guidelines on the Right to a Remedy and Reparation for Gross Violations of International Human Rights Law and Serious Violations of International Humanitarian Law, *GA Res.* 60/147, 16 December 2005, *A/RES*/60/147; 13*IHRR* 907(2006).

Beckles, H. McDonald, *Slave Voyages: The Transatlantic Trade in Enslaved Africans* (Paris: United Nations Education, Scientific and Cultural Organisation Slave Trade Education Project, 2001).

Beckles, H. McDonald, *Britain's Black Debt* (Kingston: University of the West Indies Press, 2013).

Blackburn, R., *The Making of New World Slavery from the Baroque to the Modern 1492–1800* (London: Verso, 1998).

Bowcott, O. and I. Cobain, 'UK Sternly Resists Paying Reparations for Slave Trade Atrocities and Injustices', *The Guardian*, 24 February 2014.

Bowling, B. and C. Phillips, *Racism, Crime and Justice* (Harlow: Pearson Education, 2002).

Bracegirdle, K., 'Restitution after Slavery', in F. Brennan and J. Packer (eds), *Colonialism, Slavery, Reparations and Trade: Remedying the Past?* (Abingdon: Routledge, 2012).

Brooks, R.L., *When Sorry isn't Enough: The Controversy over Apologies and Reparations for Human Injustice* (New York: New York University Press, 1999).

Brophy, A.L., *Reparations Pro and Con* (Oxford: Oxford University Press, 2006).

CARICOM, *Reparations Commission Press Statement Delivered by Professor Sir Hilary Beckles (Chairman) on behalf of the CARICOM Reparations Commission Press Conference Commission Regional Headquarters*, UWI 10 December 2013. Available at: http://www.caricom.org/communications view (accessed 12 February 2017).

Cervantes-Rodriguez, M., R. Grosfoguel and E. Mielants, *Caribbean Migration to Western Europe and the United States* (Philadelphia: Temple University Press, 2009).

Chamberlain, M., 'Migration and Post-Colonialism: The Commonwealth Caribbean', *Migration Citizenship Education* (2008). Available at: http://www.migrationeducation.org (accessed 12 February 2017).

Connolly, M., *Townshend-Smith on Discrimination Law: Text, Cases and Materials*, 2nd edition (London: Cavendish Publishing, 2004).

Corlett, J.A., *Race, Racism and Reparations* (Ithaca: Cornell University Press, 2003).

Dagnini, J.K. and Marcus Garvey, 'A Controversial Figure in the History of Pan-Africanism', *The Journal of Pan-African Studies* 2(3) (2008): 198–208.

DeGruy, J., *Post Traumatic Slave Syndrome: America's Legacy of Enduring Injury and Healing* (Portland: Joy DeGruy Publications, 2005).

Dibie, R. and J. Njoju, 'Cultural Perceptions of Africans in Diaspora and in Africa on Atlantic Slave Trade and Reparations', *African and Asian Studies* 4(3) (2005): 410.

Duncan, N., 'Are We Suffering from Post-traumatic Slave Syndrome? Experts Debate whether the Racist Theory that Enslaved Africans were "subhuman" has had a Powerful Impact on Present-day Self-esteem', *The Voice*, 16 February 2014. Available at: www.voice-online.co.uk/article/are-we-suffering-post-traumatic-slave-syndrome (accessed 12 February 2017).

Dziobon, S., 'Judge, Jurisprudence and Slavery in England 1729–1807', in F. Brennan and J. Packer (eds), *Colonialism, Slavery, Reparations and Trade: Remedying the Past?* (Abingdon: Routledge, 2012).

Edmonson, B., *Caribbean Middlebrow, Leisure, Culture and the Middle Class* (New York: Cornell University, 2009).

Edwards, P. (ed.), *Equiano's Travels* (Oxford: Heinemann Educational, 1969 [1789]).

Elkins, C., *Britain's Gulag: The Brutal End of Empire in Kenya* (London: Pimlico, 2005).

Emmer, E.C., 'The Big Disappointment: The Economic Consequences of the Abolition of Slavery in the Caribbean, 1833–1888', *History in Focus* 12. Available at: www.history.ac.uk/ihr/Focus/Sla very/articles/emmer.html (accessed 12 February 2017).

Engerman, S.L., 'Apologies, Regrets and Reparations', *European Review* 17(3–4) (2009): 593–610.

Fanon, F., *Black Skin, White Masks* (London: Pluto Press 1986).

Feagin, J.R., 'Documenting the Costs of Slavery, Segregation and Contemporary Racism: Why Reparations are in Order for African Americans', *Harvard Black Letter Law Journal* 20(2004): 49–81.

Fryer, P., *Staying Power: The History of Black People in Britain* (London: Pluto Press, 1985).

Gifford, A., *The Passionate Advocate* (Kingston: Arawak Publications, 2007).

Gifford, Anthony, 'Formulating the Case for Reparations', in F. Brennan and J. Packer (eds), *Colonialism, Slavery, Reparations and Trade: Remedying the Past?* (Abingdon: Routledge, 2012).

Gillborn, D., *Education and Institutional Racism* (London: Institute of Education, 2002).

Gilroy, P., 'The End of Antiracism', in J. Donald and A. Rattansi (eds), *'Race', Culture and Difference* (London: Sage, 1992).

Henty, G.A., *By Sheer Pluck: A Tale of the Ashanti War* (London: Blackie & Son, 1884).

Howard-Hassmann, R.E., *Reparations to Africa* (Philadelphia: University of Pennsylvania Press, 2008).

Jenkins, C., 'Taking Apology Seriously', in M. Du Plessis and S. Pete (eds), *Repairing the Past? International Perspectives on Reparations for Gross Human Rights Abuses* (Oxford: Intersentia, 2007).

Jones, C., 'Focus: Righting Historical Wrongs: The Case for Reparations', *Discover Society*, 6 May 2014, Focus Issue 8. Available at: http://www.discoversociety.org/2014/05/06/focus-righting-historical-wrongs-the-case-for-reparations (accessed 12 February 2017).

Jones, H., *Health and Society in Twentieth-Century Britain* (Abingdon: Routledge, 2013).

Krikler, J., 'The Zong and the Lord Chief', *History Workshop Journal* 64(1) (2007): 29–47.

Loveless, J., *Criminal Law: Text, Cases and Materials* (Oxford: Oxford University Press, 2014).

Macpherson, W., *The Stephen Lawrence Inquiry* (London: Home Office, 1999).

Milmo, C., 'Slavery: Is it Time for an Apology?' *The Independent*, 11 May 2006.

Muhammad, P.M., 'The Transatlantic Slave Trade: A Legacy Establishing a Case for International Reparations', *Columbian Journal of Race and Law* 3(2) (2013): 147–202.

Nunn, N., 'Historical Legacies: A Model Linking Africa's Past to its Current Underdevelopment', *Journal of Development Economics*, 83(2007): 157–175.

Plessis, M. du, and S. Pete (eds), *Repairing the Past?: International Perspectives on Reparations for Gross Human Rights Abuses* (Oxford: Intersentia, 2007).

Prince, M., *The History of Mary Prince: A West Indian Slave*, edited by S. Salih (London: Penguin Books, 2004).

Randal, D., 'Britain's Colonial Shame: Slave-owners Given Huge Payouts after Abolition', *The Independent*, 24 February 2014.

Rodney, W., *How Europe Underdeveloped Africa* (London: Bogle-L'Ouverure, 1978).

Salih, S., *Mary Prince: The History of Mary Prince* (London: Penguin, 2004 [1831]).

Shelton, D., 'Litigation and Political Action to Address Historic Injustices in the United States: Problems and Prospects', in F. Brennan and J. Packer (eds), *Colonialism, Slavery, Reparations and Trade: Remedying the Past?* (Abingdon: Routledge, 2012).

Shyllon, F.O., *Black Slaves in Britain* (Oxford: Oxford University Press, 1974).

Spectator, no. 1942 (16 September 1865), 1035.

Tavuchis, N., *Mea Culpa: A Sociology of Apology and Reconciliation* (Stanford: Stanford University Press, 1991).

Thackeray, F.W. and J.E. Findling (eds), *Events that Formed the Modern World: From the European Renaissance through the War on Terror* (Santa Barbara: ABC-CLIO, LLC, 2012).

The National Legal and Policy Centre, 'The Case against Slave Reparations' (2004) *U.S. Newswire*. Available at: www.nipc.org/wp-content/uploads/files/Reparationsbook.pdf (accessed 12 February 2017).

Torpey, J.C., *Making Whole What Has Been Smashed: On Reparations Politics* (Cambridge, MA: Harvard University Press, 2006).

Usherwood, S., 'The Black Must be Discharged: The Abolitionists' Debt to Lord Mansfield', *History Today* 31(3) (1981). Available at: www.historytoday.com/stephen-usherwood/black-must-be-discharged-abolitionist (accessed 12 February 2017).

Williams, E., *Capitalism and Slavery* (London: The University of North Carolina Press, 1994).

Wittmann, N., 'International Legal Responsibility and Reparations for Transatlantic Slavery', in F. Brennan and J. Packer (eds), *Colonialism, Slavery, Reparations and Trade: Remedying the Past?* (Abingdon: Routledge, 2012).

9 Social movements to global movements

This chapter argues that there is a global reparations movement but the model this movement consists of is not like the traditional social movements model described by social movement theorists. As social movements go, Howard-Hassmann[1] defines them as 'a collection of formal organisations, informal networks, and unaffiliated individuals engaged in a more or less coherent struggle for change'.[2] Moreover, Tarrow, cited in Staggenborg,[3] argues that the definition of social movements is 'as collective challenges, based on common purposes and social solidarities, in sustained interaction with elites, opponents, and authorities'.[4] This 'blue print' for a social movement is arguably not one that exists as far as reparations for Africa, the Diaspora and the Caribbean is concerned. In the context of reparations for people of African descent we are witnessing a revolution in terms of how this global movement is evolving. That revolution has seen West Indian government backed movements in the Caribbean region. There is a reparations movement in the Caribbean headed up by an academic, Beckles[5] following the call from the Caribbean Community (CARICOM)[6] for reparations for the slave trade from those European states that were enriched by the trade – including Great Britain There are also movements in America and Britain that call for reparations for people of African descent. It is argued that these movements are global in the sense that they are transnational in nature, although they do not sit squarely within the traditional model of social movements. We need to consider whether this global movement has the means to sustain it such as like-minded people, that it has a goal, has tactics, has activists and has policies. In the light of this we will also consider positive reparations, the consideration of a charter for the movement and a rolling programme of reparatory measures in the context of Britain.

Background

In 2009 I had the opportunity to attend Durban II.[7] This followed a world conference against racism organised by the United Nations in 2001 entitled Durban I.[8] The purpose of the Durban II conference was to 'Review [the] progress and assessment of implementation of the Durban Declaration and Programme of action by all stakeholders at the national, regional and international levels, including the assessment of contemporary manifestations of racism, racial discrimination, xenophobia and related intolerance'.[9] At Durban II I met leaders of the Durban 400 mainly from the USA and individuals from the UK all of whom were reparation activists. They saw the key to reparations as managed 'through their lobbying efforts [to make sure that] the issue of reparations was placed squarely before an international governmental body, including countries directly involved in the slave trade'.[10]

The Durban 400 see themselves as a 'grassroots coalition of political activists, educators and students'.[11] They claim to represent 'the aspirations of millions of African people around the world'[12] and their goals are to have the transatlantic slave trade and colonialism declared as crimes against humanity and to 'keep the pressure on, ensuring that someday soon reparations will be a reality'.[13] The Durban 400 asked for a press interview at the UN but only one reporter turned up who had no sympathy for the issue of reparations raised by the group.[14]

Staggenborg suggests that social movements need the media in order to get their messages across to the wider public but the use of the media is often difficult. Although not all media are the same and have the same values, such a large institutions can ignore developments and/or distort messages thus it can be difficult to ensure that the message gets out to the wider public and that it is accurate. At the conclusion of the Durban II conference the Drammeh Institute, which produced the *Durban 400* DVD[15] was given the opportunity to make a presentation. Claudette Perry of the Drammeh Institute said she represented millions of Africans who support the call for reparations. She commented that there was disappointment that the final UN document had diluted the issue of reparations in order to appease the perpetrators of crimes against humanity. Furthermore, in contemporary times racism manifested itself in factors such as black people being 12 per cent of the American population but 80 per cent of the prison population (in England and Wales 'black prisoners make up 15% of the prison population compared to.2.2% of the general population'.)[16] This, she said constituted proof of the re-enslavement of black people by the criminal justice system in the States (and it could be argued in England and Wales also). It could also be argued that this is a manifestation of institutional racism, a point on which the group was silent.[17] A group often held up as a classic example of a social movement is the Civil Rights movement in the US[18] in the 1960s which led to major legislative[19] and other changes[20] that focused on the abolition of racist policies that black people had to endure because of the colour of their skin.[21] The Durban 400 does not command that support in terms of numbers in its membership. However, it has a moderate base from which it has launched the call for reparations for the consequences of the slave trade. Another movement is in the Caribbean region where the CARICOM Reparations Commission (CRC) has grown into a regional movement, and is a creature of Caribbean governments. The CRC calls for reparations to the descendants of African slaves in the Caribbean. Together with this is the Jamaican Reparations Commission, a creature of government that has involved civil society in the call for reparations this movement has been taken over by the National Council on Reparations (Jamaica) (NCR).

What is a social movement?

As has already been said social movements are critical to changing the status quo but one needs to know what a social movement is. What are the constituent parts? Having read through some of the voluminous literature on the subject of social movements it seems clear that there is not one homogeneous definition.[22] Rather there are key indicators of what those parts are that one would expect to see a social movement contain and these are 'vehicles for social and political change'.[23] An example was the abolition movement in Britain organised around a single issue: to liberate the slaves in the Caribbean. They organised 'a boycott of sugar grown with slave labour [and sent] petitions signed by a large number of supporters to the British Parliament'.[24]

Presence of a group of like-minded people

Accordingly, one indicator is the presence of a group of people who are not generally part of the elite of society.[25] This group of people remain largely invisible in society, unless they come from the elite.[26] Several members of the group tend to be poor and unrepresented by unions and political parties.[27] The group is in a conflictual relationship with a 'clearly identified opponent'[28] according to Porta and Diana[29] and may have several leaders in the social movement's life time depending on the issue at stake.[30] The group requires a 'pre-existing communications or infrastructure within a social base'[31] in order to generate 'spontaneous activity'.[32] What this means is that 'the movement needs to consist of 'like-minded' people whose background, experiences or location in the social structure makes them receptive to the ideas of a specific ... movement'.[33]

The leadership needs to be skilful in galvanising people or there needs to be people who are 'tuned in'[34] to the problem even if they are not co-ordinated.[35] Typically the group will be fighting for resources, argues Touraine,[36] particularly as they are unlikely to have any themselves apart from their representation in numbers, although there may be some who come from the elite and are well resourced. Diani[37] suggests that a social movement is a 'network of informal interactions between a plurality of individuals, groups or organisations with a shared collective identity'.[38] Social movements, argue Snow and Soule,[39] happen under the 'radar of the various media'[40] and act collectively rather than individually.[41] Howard- Hassmann[42] contends that a social movement consists of 'a collection of formal organisations, informal networks and unaffiliated individuals'.[43] Essentially then when it comes to the elements that make up a social movement, we are looking for a group of like-minded people who make up a network of formal and informal relations, driven by a leader/ leaders.

The reparations movement is formed of some of these elements. There is broadly a group of like-minded people. There is the CARICOM Reparations Commission (CRC) that was established by heads of government of the West Indies in 2013.[44] CRC pledges to deal with reconciliation, truth and justice for the victims of slavery and their descendants. The National Commission on Reparations, Jamaica (NCRJ) was set up by the Jamaican Government in 2009.[45] The NCRJ was tasked to 'recommend the form or forms which reparations may take, and to receive testimony from the public and from experts, with the aim of guiding a national approach to reparations'.[46] The NCRJ has become the National Council on Reparations (NCR). Established in 2016 it will be working closely with the CARICOM Reparations Commission.[47]

There are non-governmental organisations (NGOs) such as the Pan-African Reparations Coalition of Europe (PARCOE) based in the UK. PARCOE is a grassroots alliance of organisations, groups and campaigns that have forged a global alliance that focuses on building a unity of First Nations Peoples affected by colonisation. PARCOE push for reparations in the form of repairs in the realm of mental, psychological, cultural, organisational, social, institutional, technological, economic, political and educational repairs.[48] There is also the African Reparations Movement (UK) (ARM). This body seeks reparations from countries that benefited from the slave trade, and colonialism. The reparations are asked for the loss of human life in the slave trade,[49] the loss of over 400 years of wages not paid to slaves and an apology for slavery and exploitation.[50] The Durban 400 (D400) in the USA was formed out of the 12 December Movement and the National Black United Front (NBUF). D400 lobbied the World Conference Against Racism (2001) to have slavery and the transatlantic slave trade declared a crime against humanity,[51] and that reparations are owed to people of African descent. The declaration was successful.[52] However, the claim for reparations to be part of the programme of action was not a success. In the USA there is a United Nation Group of Experts that has gathered evidence from officials, activists, and families of people killed by police in major American cities. The group state that the killings are reminiscent of the 'racial terror lynching in the past'.[53] The group have stated that the slave trade was a crime against humanity.[54]

There are also a number of scholar activists such as Lord Anthony Gifford,[55] Professor Sir Hilary Beckles,[56] Nathaniel Coleman[57] and the author[58] of this book. So there are a number of formal groups, NGOs and individuals who are working on the same theme – reparations for people of African descent. They do not, necessarily, work together but they co-exist within a global terrain such that they constitute a network which has culminated in a global movement on reparations. What these do have in common is their claim to represent a group wider than themselves. They work on behalf of people of African descent in Africa and the Diaspora on the issue of reparatory justice.

The goal as a factor in social movements

The question here is how does a global movement on reparations define its aims so that it can function in the social complex?[59] Zirakzedeh suggests that the goal of a social movement may be to 'build a radically new social order',[60] the aim may also be one where the participants seek 'immediate gratification and private benefits'.[61] The objective of a social movement may be to 'challenge the reproduction of current patterns of inequality in status, wealth and power'[62] determined by the elite. The focus of social movements may be to 'seek changes from the state in the regulation, financing and distribution of … resources'.[63] It is argued that the various calls for reparations is in some way the argument over how the financing and distribution of resources is organised in the fight to counter racism, which is the legacy of the transatlantic slave trade. This area receives very little in the form of resources from the state. It is argued here that these calls for reparations should be aimed at a range of institutions including the state, the church (such as the Church of England and the Catholic Church) and commercial organisations who benefited from the transatlantic slave trade, and continue to benefit.[64]

Depending on the nature of the goal they pursue, social movements may look to challenge 'issues of law and order'.[65] The goal may be to challenge laws or decisions that are considered unjust and so the social movement challenges the established norms.[66] A social movement that had monumental affects in the social sphere was the Civil Rights movement in the 1960s in the USA, which was resolute that segregation of public facilities on the basis of skin colour was unjust. As Blumberg[67] pointed out, following the undivided decision in the *Brown*[68] case, the court was of the opinion that segregation 'generates a feeling of inferiority'[69] for 'colored children'[70] 'that may affect their hearts and minds in a way unlikely ever to be undone'.[71]

The substance of the aspirations of a social movement may require some understanding of history and culture in terms of deprivation and the argument for justice. The goal of the women's movement could/cannot be understood without addressing the issues arising from the historical and cultural context.[72] Similarly, the goal of the global movement on reparations cannot be understood outside its historical and cultural context. That is that a debt is due to people of African descent who are descendants of those who were enslaved. These people suffer from the legacy of that trade and chattel slavery. The kernel of the argument had to be constructed in a historical and cultural fashion to understand the 'now' according to Susser.[73] The central core of the goal of a social movement then is to struggle for change or to maintain the status quo. One can see the global reparations movement as a struggle for change, and as a movement that counters those critics who argue that reparations are not due on legal or moral grounds because, it is argued, there are no direct survivors, it was not illegal at the time to own slaves, or it was too long ago and there is no valid claim.[74] The global movement on reparations states the reverse. That on moral, if not legal grounds, reparations are due to descendants of the transatlantic slave trade and chattel slavery. Each of the following Caribbean countries have committed to reparations for the legacy of the slave trade and slavery, namely, Antigua/Barbuda, the Bahamas, Barbados, Belize, Dominica, Guyana, Jamaica, St Kitts and Nevis, Saint Lucia, St Vincent and the Grenadines, Suriname and Trinidad and Tobago.[75] These 12 countries have developed national reparations committees[76] that liaise with the CRC.

What tactics do social movements use to get their message across?

There appear to be several tactics pursued by social movements. These include litigation, negotiation the use of social media and symbolism. Litigation was used in the Mau Mau case from 2009, pursued by Leigh Day Solicitors. In the British courts it was held that the British state could be sued in damages for the horrific treatment of the Mau Mau in Kenya whilst it was under British occupation in the 1950s – 1960s. Victims of the Mau Mau rebellion won the right to sue for compensation from Britain for the abuse of their human rights.[77]

After a lengthy battle between victims of the Mau Mau group and the Foreign and Commonwealth Office[78] the British government settled the case. The government agreed to pay £19.9 million in damages to 5,228 claimants identified by Leigh Day Solicitors, including legal costs.[79] The then Foreign Secretary made a statement to the House of Commons full of regret for the abuses that took place, that 'marred Kenyan progress towards independence'.[80] The final part of the settlement 'was the construction of a permanent memorial in Nairobi'[81] which was unveiled in 2015.

Instructed by Leigh Day Solicitors, the Caribbean Community and Common Market (CARICOM), seek to sue Britain, France and the Netherlands in damages 'for the lingering effect of slavery',[82] if they cannot reach a negotiated settlement with the three European countries. Negotiation is another tactic used by social movements to get their message across to the wider public. The CARICOM wish to negotiate a settlement with Britain, France and the Netherlands for 'the impact of slavery on their communities today'.[83] The CARICOM Reparations Commission want to negotiate a ten-point plan with Britain, France and the Netherlands that includes a full formal apology, repatriation, dealing with public health issues, the eradication of illiteracy, psychological rehabilitation, technology transfer and debt cancellation.[84]

Then there is the use of social media that can be galvanised to give exposure of the movement and the cause. Shelton[85] argues that with litigation you may not win the battle but you might win the war in terms of getting the message or messages out into the public domain with the result that one might win some public support. The CRC, in seeking to boost support for its cause, plans to roll out a new website and new social media platforms via Facebook, Twitter and Instagram.[86] The aim here is to show the public that a global reparations movement has emerged through the CRC. Furthermore, the use of social media via the Internet, will be used to educate the young in the Caribbean and around the world about the ongoing conversations in the call for reparatory justice.

Somehow social movements need to find the key messages that would entice what is essentially a neo-colonial Western press to publicise their concerns. This can be done through press release statements that convey the message about reparations and the use of the Internet. The CRC have announced on their website the establishment of a CARICOM Reparations Justice Program (CRJP). The CRJP seeks to be a necessary path towards progress on the issue of reparatory justice.[87] Another tactic is the use of symbols to get the main message across. The Caribbean countries that have committed to reparations have a symbol of reparations which is a baton that is passed to different Caribbean countries through the Reparations Relay Initiative (RRI). The RRI, when held by a Caribbean country, sees a number of activities hosted by the state connected to days of historical significance to do with the slave trade, slavery and native genocide. So far the baton has been passed to Barbados (April), Guyana (May) Suriname (August) and Antigua/Barbuda (October), 2016.

Leaders

Charismatic leader/leaders may also be vital to a social movement but it is argued that they are not fatal. Whitaker[88] looked at the top ten social movements that could be said to have transformed society. He compiled these movements according to web page hits, news stories and people's votes.[89] Whitaker found that with some of these movements the prime actors were individuals or groups. The Iranian Revolution of 1979 was started by Ayatollah Khomeni who led the opposition to the reigning leader in Iran by sending cassette tapes from where he was exiled in France. The message in these cassettes were copied and spread all over Iran and led to a groundswell that the incumbent leadership could not control. The Salt Satyagraha (Salt Movement) was led by Ghandi[90] in 1930. Ghandi started a 200-mile journey to challenge the state monopoly of salt which was a precious commodity whose extraction of it was tightly curtailed by legislation.[91] Martin Luther King[92] was a key figure in the social movement in the States in the 1960s against racial discrimination. Not every leader has to be charismatic or even a leader – sometimes, as Whitaker argues, 'what can start out as something very minor can turn into something incredibly effective'.[93] Rosa Parks would not take her racially designated seat at the back of a bus, where a person's seating was determined by skin colour. If you were Black, you sat at the back. This was the spark that started events culminating in the Montgomery Bus Boycott of 1955. This embargo led to desegregation of the buses in parts of the US. There are social movements where there is no leader as such but a group of people who have an impact on how a movement evolves. An example is the Egypt Protest of 2011 where groups of people rallied against the 30-year regime of President Hosni Mubarak. For nigh on two weeks protestors occupied Tahrir Square.

With the reparations development it is difficult to identify a leader or a group that leads. Rather it is Caribbean states that are leading the call for reparations through the efforts of the CRC. 'You must be the change you want to see in the world'[94] is a famous quote by Ghandi. Effective rhetoric and peaceful protest provides another pathway used by social movements to 'exercise their right to peaceably assemble'.[95] Ghandi and Martin Luther King were both leaders of non-violent social movements. Their inspiration was wrapped up in 'sites of contestation in which bodies, symbols, identities, practices and discourse [were] used to pursue … changes in institutional power relations'.[96] These changes in institutional power relations may include targeting the legal system. This happened in *Brown v Board of Education*[97] where the U.S. Supreme Court overturned its previous ruling[98] that separate but equal educational facilities were legitimate. Behind this movement to bring change was the National Association for the Advancement of Colored People (NAACP).[99]

Therefore, social movements require the deployment of tactics such as use of the media, in its broadest sense, leaders or a group who will act as a catalyst for change and to be clearly focused on the message aimed at the 'opposition'. If we take this paradigm, then the reparations movement is not only a kind of social movement, but is a global movement. There is no Ghandi or Martin Luther King but there is a group strong enough to get changes made to institutional power, and that is the CARICOM Reparations Commission.

Does a social movement on reparations for the legacy of the transatlantic slave trade exist?

If we take the traditional model then the short answer appears to be that the global movement on reparations does not follow the traditional model. The essential features of a social movement on reparations for the transatlantic slave trade would be a group of 'complainants' who are like-minded, who may or may not be operating under the media's radar depending on how that is defined. This group forms a network of informal relations, is driven by a leader or leaders and the group is receptive to the ideas of the leader. There is some kind of communications infrastructure and the focus of the group is on a particular goal. That goal would be to acquire reparations for the legacy of the slave trade, and that goal is targeted in a specific way, at the state, churches and multinationals who are beneficiaries of the transatlantic slave trade.[100] And who in Britain were paid compensation for the loss of their property post emancipation. Furthermore, the goal is to pursue, in my estimation, forward-looking positive reparations, as opposed to negative, backward-looking reparations.[101]

Who are the complainants/reparations activists?

Let us consider the Durban 400 (D400) as an example. They are made up of 12 December Movement International Secretariat (D12) and the National Black United Front (NBUF).[102] In the DVD about this group they claim to represent 'the aspirations of millions of African people around the world'.[103] There is some evidence that the debate has also arisen in African states. In the 1990s there was the Pan-African Conference on Reparations,[104] the first of its kind. This was held in the capital of Nigeria, Abuja. The purpose of the conference was to bring together many eminent people to discuss reparations and Lord Anthony Gifford was tasked with setting out the legal case for reparations.[105] There was also a group of experts on reparations to Africa and Africans in the Diaspora (those persons of African descent who reside outside Africa) set up in the 1990s.[106] The National Commission on Reparations Jamaica has been involved in considering the issue of reparations. This Reparations Commission covered Jamaican descendants and Jamaicans in the Diaspora,[107] not Africans per se. The Jamaican Reparations Commission is a creation of government. The Commission was set up to 'recommend the form or forms that reparations may take, and to receive testimony from the public and from experts, with the aim of guiding a *national* approach to reparations'.[108] This commission has now become the National Council on Reparations (NCR). The Caribbean region has a reparations commission which comes out of the formation of member states of CARICOM.

Human Rights Watch (HRW),[109] a Non-Governmental Organisation (NGO) has raised the issue of reparations in an article entitled *An Approach to Reparations.*[110] This NGO suggests the setting up of national and international panels in order to examine racist practices.[111] There are a number of NGOs, individual activists,[112] academics[113] and scholars[114] who have pursued the subject of reparations. But what distinguishes the reparations movement is the large element of government based group activity in the Caribbean region focused on obtaining reparations for the legacy of the slave trade.

Some have claimed that 'there is no large base of activists',[115] but it is argued here that there is and it is this lack of co-ordination that means the true size is concealed. This apparent lack of co-ordination need not necessarily prove a barrier to the establishment of a global movement on reparations. Indeed, as has already been said, 'like-mindedness' is a factor in the establishment of social movements and it could be argued that in the case of reparations this exists in a broad sense.

In search of a common goal

'I, young in life, by seeming cruel fate, was snatched from Afric's fancyd happy seat; What pangs excruciating must molest, what sorrows labor in my parent's breast'.[116] This poem illustrates the wrong that reparation activists and others sympathetic to the cause tend to seek to address. This relates to a historical analysis and a backward-looking claim that focuses on past injustices without much reference to the problem by which 'African descendants still suffer from racism inculcated in the days of slavery'.[117] For some the issue is historical redress for the transatlantic slave trade,[118] for others the matter is to combat the legacy of the transatlantic slave trade.[119] Others, the author included, would redefine this further as the need to deal with institution racism.[120]

Human Rights Watch suggest that for 'practical reasons, when addressing relatively old wrongs, we would not base claims of reparations on past abuse itself but on its contemporary effects'.[121] The World Conference Against Racism Xenophobia and Related Intolerances (Durban I) Programme of Action was certainly of the opinion that the transatlantic slave trade has been the cause of contemporary racism.[122] The dominant focus in Britain has been the production of historically based scholarly works such as Blackburn, *The Making of the New World of Slavery*,[123] Hochschild, *Bury the Chains*[124] and Prince, *The History of Mary Prince*.[125] Some public discourse has also appeared on social media websites.

For example, African Holocaust is an NGO that provides education on what it calls the African Holocaust. UNESCO have produced a website dedicated to education concerning the transatlantic slave trade and a UNESCO project, set up in 2002, entitled 'Breaking the Silence Surrounding the Slave Trade'[126] continues to push for education around the slave trade in schools, raising awareness as another part of the package of measures to deal with public awareness.

The N'Cobra International Affairs Commission (NIAC) with other organisations put together a conference on reparations in 2006. Their intention was to produce a deeper understanding of the international reparations movement, a dialogue on international capital and to support return to Africa projects[127] where people of African descent who live outside Africa could reside in Africa. Nimako and Small[128] write that there are other projects being led by what may loosely be termed social movements or sometimes named 'reparations movements' in Britain and the Netherlands, the focus of which is mainly financial reparations. However, the main reparations movement led by Caribbean governments ask for other resources, not only financial compensation.

Positive reparations

One of the differences is positive reparations. Positive reparations are policies that seek to make good the racial harm done by the legacy of the slave trade, through programmes of action that are beneficial to people of African descent. Here it is argued that positive reparations hinge on two issues: whether reparations are due at all (the moral issue), and, if reparations are due, what type of reparations should be focused on (the policy issue).[129]

The moral issue

'She used to lead me about by the hand, and call me her little nigger'.[130] Mary Prince, from whose book this excerpt is taken, represents an example of how the dehumanisation of people came about because of the colour of their skin. She continues to tell us that this was the 'happiest period of her life'[131] so oblivious was she to what slavery was and its consequences for her as she grew older. These consequences, suggests Fanon[132] led to a conclusion, 'what a disgrace it is to be Black in this world!'[133] Yet no one had been given the moral right[134] to dehumanise and re-categorise part of the human race through the mechanism of slavery and its association with skin colour, with the inevitable shortening of life. Given this situation, the moral question is whether the justice system should recognise the legacy of racism that has haunted the arguments about whether reparations are due to people of African descent. This is not only because of the peculiar history[135] that has placed them in an inferior position, materially[136] and psychologically,[137] but also because of the continuing manifestation of this atypical position for black human beings which, to paraphrase Rawls[138] this is not 'justice as fairness',[139] is not the original position and is not part of the social contract between people. It is not just everyday racism that keeps the arguments about reparations under the radar of public discourse, it is reinforced by institutional racism. Institutional racism is so embedded in the policies and practices of established institutions that it is almost invisible. It is woven into the policies and practices of institutions, as part of the institutional scripting of the way social actors go about their daily business, reinforcing institutional racism in matters such as policing, health care, education and trade.

Arguably, in terms of morality, we need to adopt a common position that starts, as Rawls would say, as the 'original position', as the social contract between black and white people. A moral social contract that recognises and makes compensation for the fact that some human beings (people of African descent in this case) were left out of the social contract. In order to be just and fair, the social contract would need to recognise and address the historical wrongs so that blacks and whites would be treated equally in the arena of social relations. The moral case has been made for reparations in the vast literature on the subject, in particular Gifford[140] and Corlett.[141] Gifford argues,

> so it is with the claim for Reparations. Indeed, once you accept … the truth of three propositions: (a) that the mass kidnapping and enslavement of Africans was the most wicked criminal enterprise in recorded human history; (b) that no compensation was ever paid by any of the perpetrators to any of the sufferers; and (c) that the consequences of the crime continue to be massive, both in terms of the enrichment of the descendants of the perpetrators, and in terms of the impoverishment of Africans and the descendants of Africans; then the justice of the claim for reparations is proved beyond reasonable doubt.[142]

Corlett suggests that, in the US context at least, reparations are due for the physical and psychological brutality of slavery as well as its wrongful gain by means of coerced free labour power 'and the value that it brings illicitly to slaveholders in particular, and to an entire U.S. economy more generally, and the incessant refusal over generations of the U.S. government to rectify its injustices against blacks by way of slavery'.[143] The general and underlying problem we have is one of guilt. The underlying notion is that the Western European powers, and their peoples, should make reparations on the basis of guilt and shame. Perhaps this explains why there is much resistance even to making an apology.

What if the underlying message was different? Could reparations be requested in a positive way? This would involve not using shame or guilt as an underlying theme but rather emphasising what we share in common as a people. It would mean identifying where the blocks are and working together as a people to remove them. The argument is that it is in all our interests to make positive reparations because we would all benefit. In the UK, one example would be a reconsideration of the history curriculum taught in secondary schools. English schools have a choice on whether to teach the British transatlantic slave trade, its effects and its eventual abolition in history modules.[144] That history could be made a compulsory part of the national curriculum, revamped in such a way as to include how countries were involved and benefited from the slave trade, colonialism and neo- colonialism and migration. It would mean the shifting of attention from 'them' and 'us' in the world to 'us' in the world. This would help to avoid the underlying guilt and shame and replace it with knowledge and understanding. Peace, not guilt or shame, as an underlying strategy on the moral case is likely to obtain more sympathisers.

The policy issue

Here the question is what type of reparations should be focused on. Should we consider monetary compensation alone[145] or at all, or are there other means of redress? The Office of the United Nations High Commissioner for Human Rights[146] adopted the Basic Principles and Guidelines on the Right to a Remedy and Reparations for Victims of Gross Violations of International Human Rights Law and Serious Violations of International Humanitarian Law (Basic Principles).[147] The document provides several reparative solutions such as access to justice, prompt reparations and information on violations. However, it is immediately striking that the violation to which the reparations are directed is the violation of international human rights law and international humanitarian law.

Already the problem is how to rely on a 'remedy' that was not available at the time the violations took place – that is enslavement. There are ways out of this dilemma. We could utilise the argument put forward by scholars like Wittmann[148] that international law has always existed[149] thus covering the period of the specific violation with the Basic Principles[150] as an affirmation of this. One could also consider the contention of Bracegirdle that, under English law at least, there may be a claim by way of restitution or unjust enrichment[151] which is not barred by the Limitation Act 1980. The Basic Principles provide for both the control of limitation periods[152] in favour of the complainant and the provision of restitution.[153] A more general point is that governments have accepted responsibility for providing reparations for crimes committed before the legislation to make reparations had existed – the most obvious ones are payments to Holocaust survivors and to American Japanese internees. 'In the United States, Canada, New Zealand and Australia',[154] Gifford tells us, 'there have been settlements of various kinds, including a recognition of rights over land and financial payments … [recognising] that the surviving generations of indigenous peoples had the right to a measure of reparations for the crimes committed against their ancestors'.[155]

Having established a chance that claims could be made for reparations the Basic Principles are a useful guide to what reparations would look like in policy terms. The obligation on the part of the state to respect and implement international human rights and humanitarian law;

that states should ensure their domestic law is consistent with international legal obligations; states should respect international human rights law, they should also investigate and prosecute and ensure that limitation periods do not apply to gross violations of human rights. Furthermore, victims should be recognised individually and collectively for the harm they have suffered including physical and mental injury and economic loss. Access to an effective remedy should be available and reparations should include compensation, restitution, rehabilitation, satisfaction and non-repetition.[156] I have argued that positive reparations are anchored in two things: the moral issue of whether reparations are due and, if so, what reparations would look like; and the policy issue. It appears that both questions can be answered in the affirmative. So how does this lead us to positive reparations in practical terms?

Pruitt[157] argues that

> Reparations represents the continued struggle to finish the battles for equality that grew into the Civil Rights and Black Power Movements of the 50s and 60s. Black and white Americans fought those battles together. Black and white people should come together again along with the religious groups and NGOs to produce solutions regarding the legacy of the transatlantic slave trade. All black and white people should initiate the process to eliminate racism and facilitate racial healing, not fight battles about reparations.[158]

Moreover, African-Americans[159]have a long and rich tradition of contributions that has and still does benefit America, this applies to Britain too[160] but this information is not general knowledge, there should be programmes to address this. Understanding the legacy would help with 'improving integration … to enforce laws and policies set forth for blacks to have equal access and receivership of benefits from institutions …'[161]

Social movements and positive reparations

Zerai and Campbell inform us that the Black Radical Congress (BRC)[162] argue that mainstream peace movements have refused to take on the issue of reparations and that of 'genocide against people of African descent'.[163] The BRC were elected in 2001 to commit to a campaign that would include a boost to the struggle for 'peace reparations and justice'.[164] They intended to 'piggy back' on to the tactics used by the Black Feminist Movement (BFM) in order to push forward their cause. Two of those tactics are of particular relevance here. One is 'the importance of remaining organically tied to communities',[165] the other is 'dynamism in social movements'.[166] It could be argued that the work in Jamaica on reparations is organically tied to communities where there has been much consultation and explanation of reparations. Moreover, it could be said that the various vehicles through which reparations has been raised show a drive from sections of differing communities to get reparations for the legacy of the transatlantic slave trade on the table. But the work is done in a peaceful manner not in a way that stirs up anger. This is where positive reparations are important because they encourage people to work together through peaceful means on the issue at hand rather than working in an antagonistic manner.

We have already seen that the various reparations groups do not meet the traditional model of social movements which is one of like-minded people who follow a path and have a leader. It is argued that what we are witnessing is a global movement on reparations. These may be seen as peaceful and sporadic, that have different kinds of leaders and that involve West Indian governments, individuals, NGOs and members of civil society who work organically. An example of an individual pushing the reparations movement can be seen in the address delivered by Professor Sir Hilary Beckles of the CARICOM Commission, House of Commons, Parliament of Great Britain, Committee Room 14 on Thursday 16 July 2014. Here he presented an argument on reparations. There was no report in the general media about this even though Beckles represents CARICOM in the matter of reparations and discussed the global movement for reparations. The importance of this speech should not be ignored because, according to Beckles, it dealt with Britain wanting to shield itself from a past not just of the horrors of slavery, but racial apartheid and the colonial mess left behind for the West Indian governments to clear up.[167] Other examples include the work done by Nathaniel Coleman and the African Reparations Transnational Community of Practice that considers racism in the twenty-first century and that of Professor Verene Shepherd who, along with Professor Hilary Beckles, addressed a conference in Edinburgh entitled: ***Repairing the Past, Imagining the Future: Reparations and Beyond***, in November 2015. Positive reparations calls for change to be made through peaceful means not through aggressive tactics. The key factor is communication and the need for forums to accommodate it and for the resulting conversations to be taken seriously by states.

The Global Movement on Positive Reparations Charter[168]

One thing that groups and individuals working in the area of reparations for the legacy of the slave trade and chattel slavery could do with is a charter. This would form a single instrument around which various organisations and individuals could work without interfering with the particular objectives they are pursuing. Taking the title the Global Movement on Positive Reparations Charter (GMPRC), a possible template for such a charter is laid out below. In putting forward this suggestion, the author is not attempting to provide a westernised model of a social movement, it is rather an attempt to provide a base from which different groups could draw on to a greater or lesser degree.

Introduction

Achieving positive reparations through the recognition that institutional racism is the principal cause of current and continuous racial harm based on the transatlantic slave trade is the aim of the Global Movement on Positive Reparations Charter (GMPRC). This is because a charter would set out how African people[169] were to gain and practise their human rights. A global charter on positive reparations is suggested as one of the most appropriate mechanism through which African people can actively participate. Therefore, the purpose of this charter is to generate this process and to stimulate the achievement of positive reparations.

Definition

A global movement on positive reparations refers to a process whereby, ‘a large base of activists’,[170] together with various elements of civil society and West Indian governments strive towards differing goals that relate to reparations. The role of the GMPRC is to bring to the attention of the state and civil society, the implications for African people of legislation, policies and programmes in any areas and at all levels, that cause racial harm because they are institutionally racist. A charter is a strategic device for making the concerns of African people an integral dimension in the design, implementation, monitoring and evaluation of policies and programmes in all political, economic and social spheres, such that inequality between black and white people is not perpetuated. The ultimate goal is to achieve racial equality and racial justice.

Understanding the role that institutional racism plays in society and the need for positive reparations, is important for human rights because:

- it makes the institutional racism faced by black people and the need for positive reparations central to the policy making process of organisations;[171]
- it ensures participatory governance within organisations;
- it makes full use of human resources and capacities by involving people of African descent;
- it makes institutionally racist issues and the need for positive reparations visible in the mainstream struggle for human rights;
- it takes institutional racism into account within organisations.

The fight to combat institutional racism and implement positive reparations is important for organisations because it ensures an efficient way of using human resources and capacities – and thus promotes the effective running of entities.

The Global Movement on Positive Reparations Charter (GMPRC)

The GMPRC aims to advance the human rights of Africans through the inculcation of the issues raised by institutional racism and the promotion of positive reparations. GMPRC will promote the full participation of Africans as agents and beneficiaries of its work. The importance of racial equality and empowerment is crucial in order to counter institutional racism as a social divider marked by inequality. The racial equality approach will aim to ensure fairness in the way Africans are treated within the organisation and through the policies and projects developed by the GMPRC. To counter historical inequalities, the GMPRC will support the adoption of special measures to tackle racial inequality and increased autonomy.

The GMPR will be spearheaded by an executive committee that will take the lead in committing the GMPR to racial equality by adopting a racial equality mainstreaming approach. This approach focuses on ensuring a racial equality awareness and sensitiveness that will be transportable across the structures and activities of the GMPR. It will also draw attention to the fundamental human rights of Africans within the group. This is to ensure that the racial equality dimension is incorporated into the full range of functions, policies, programmes and projects at all levels and stages of the organisation.

These objectives are challenging. They seek to unearth and eradicate deep-seated barriers to racial equality that will take time to change. The objectives are specific, measurable, achievable, realistic, focused and time-bound. This is to ensure that the processes and outcome objectives of the GMPRC will make certain that the views of Africans their interests and needs shape the GMPRC.

Objectives

The following objectives are considered to be instrumental to a GMPR racial mainstreaming policy:

a To ensure that policy dialogue, views and information flows operate in ways that produce racial equality results.

b To secure racial equality by ensuring that rights or opportunities do not depend on being Black or White.

c To ensure that with every policy, project or programme that differences of race are not reinforced in considering the varying Black-White interests.

d To develop the empowerment of Africans through strategies that will enable people of African descent to access concrete information aiming to increase opportunities for active political participation.

e To advance the equal participation of African people in political decision-making processes, by developing and carrying out programmes that take the diverse potential of young Africans as a starting point for their later active participation and co-determination in politics.

f To promote equal participation of African people as agents of change in the development of the internal and external work of the GMPRC.

g To develop special measures that address policies, procedures, norms, beliefs, practices and attitudes of the state and civil society that maintain racial inequality.

h To develop GMPRC specific racial analysis tools to track and monitor racial inequality.

i To ensure that racial equality policy recommendations are incorporated into all of GMPR activities and outputs.

How to achieve equality through positive reparations?

a Carry out a racial audit of the functions, policies and programmes of the state using a racial mainstreaming kit to find out whether these are racial equality compliant.

b Adopt and apply appropriate research tools that will enable the collection and analysis of qualitative and quantitative data to capture information that will contribute to the achievement of racial equality in the state.

c Carry out institutional racism impact assessments on organs of the state.

d Provide education and training and follow-up action on institutional racism and positive reparations.

e To provide a window of opportunity in a project or programme where resources are invested that promote racial equality through the notion of positive reparations. This should be people centred, make use of skilled professionals, use the expertise of racial discrimination specialists and ensure that a significant number of black people are members.

f To provide the forum for consultation on institutional racism, positive reparations and racial equality issues.

g To provide evidence of systematic work, good practices, methods and initiatives taken from the GMPRC

Goals of the GMPRC

The GMPRC will have a rolling programme of issues that are of direct concern to people of African descent. This rolling programme will look at various issues that concern people of African descent in former slave trading and slave-owning countries. In the case of the UK, the following need immediate attention:

1 STOP THE POLICE FROM USING STOP AND SEARCH TO TARGET PEOPLE OF AFRICAN DESCENT (SUS STOPS)[172]

To have repealed the provision that allows the police to stop and search people without reasonable cause based on their ethnicity. The Sus laws are contained in section 60 of the Criminal Justice and Public Order Act 1994. Section 60 (4) authorises 'any constable in uniform [the] power to stop any pedestrian and search him for anything carried by him for offensive weapons or dangerous instruments and to stop any vehicle and search the vehicle, its driver and any passenger for offensive weapons or dangerous instruments'. Section 4A provides 'A constable may, in the exercise of [the powers conferred by subsection (4) above], stop any person or vehicle and make any search he thinks fit whether or not he has any grounds for suspecting that the person or vehicle is carrying weapons or articles of that kind'. The failure of the person to stop or to stop a vehicle when required to do so, will result in imprisonment or a fine.

2 NO RACIAL PROFILING

To have removed intelligence-led policing that allows the police to target black people because of the colour of their skin. Racial profiling allows the police to target people on the basis of skin colour in order to cut down or prevent crime. The logic behind racial profiling is that it concentrates resources on the 'right' potential suspects, provides a better clear up rate and is therefore more efficient. 'Analysis by the London School of Economics and the Open Society Justice Initiative found that there are 41.6 Section 60 searches for every 1,000 black people, compared with 1.6 for every 1,000 white people – making black people 26.6 times more likely to be stopped and searched ... according to the analysis of Ministry of Justice figures for 2008–2009'.[173] In a Parliamentary Briefing in 2014 it was stated that Black people are stopped and searched around seven times more than white people.[174] According to Ben Bowling, professor of criminal justice at King's College London, 'The police are making greater use of a power that was only ever meant to be used in exceptional circumstances and lacks effective safeguards. This leaves room for increased stereotyping which is likely to alienate those communities which are most affected'.[175] The Home Office states that officers should be careful not to discriminate unless they need to do individual or vehicle stops based on ethnicity, although they say that ethnicity should not be the sole basis for a stop. However there is concern that officers will make such stops anyway.[176]

3 NO RACISM IN SCHOOLS

The GMPR would make sure that all schools have an anti-racist policy and anti-racist active programme in their agenda and in their curriculums. This would be done by working with government and local authorities as well as all schools in a spirit of cooperation.

4 HISTORY AND HERSTORY

The GMPR would work with publishers of school materials to ensure that a fuller account is made of the slave trade, chattel slavery, emancipation, colonisation, racial apartheid and migration. This means working with the Education Secretary/governmental department in charge of curriculums and study to get this onto their agenda first and to convince them that it would be a positive thing to do. The underlying theme would be positive integration and the bringing out of stories of individual men and women who were fighting for emancipation as well as the problems with the periods in question that have made integration difficult to realise.

5 MEDICAL/PSYCHOLOGICAL PROGRAMMES AND EDUCATION

Particularly for the Caribbean there will be medical and educational interventions with respect to the problem with type 2 diabetes[177] and the difficulty with intergenerational post traumatic slave syndrome (PTSS).[178] Both require resources to be put in to deal with diets and to deal with the psychological trauma of PTSS.

Means for achieving the GMPRC

Packages of appropriate instruments required to make a protest:

- Hold a truth, peace and reconciliation commission by inviting representatives from various reparations groups and those sympathetic to the cause. Making sure that the panel was composed of people who are experts in the field as well as ordinary people.
- Use social media such as blogs, Twitter, YouTube and Facebook and Instagram.
- Use musicians to produce a suitable piece of music that would relate to reparations as the legacy of the slave trade.
- Organise a march to 10 Downing Street and Parliament to raise the profile of reparations.
- Use an online petition for reparations, the results of which would be presented to the government.
- Enlist the support of well-respected artists such as Benjamin Zephaniah to create poetry and song for the reparations movement.
- Talk to the media enlisting the support of sympathisers and/or interested parties in print and broadcast media.
- Engage other movements for support, for example, Stopwatch an organisation that campaigns against Section 60 powers.

What does the GMPRC hope to achieve?

The GMPRC hopes to bring about change in the culture and practice of institutions so that institutional racism is exposed and removed by peaceful means. This means that positive reparations would be used to carry out this change.

Conclusion

What we are witnessing is a global movement on reparations that does not operate according to the traditional status quo. In terms of the call for reparations some groups focus on the history of the slave trade and that there should be compensation for that bad history. Others look to the current and argue that there should be reparations for the consequences that stay with us to this day. I argue that the consequences are institutional racism and that is what needs to be tackled. It has also been argued here that the way to tackle the call for reparations for the legacy of the slave trade, institutional racism, is by positive reparations which involves peaceful means where we work in collaboration with one another. The consequences of working in this way would be to the benefit of all. Perhaps as has been suggested in the Global Movement for Positive Reparations charter we need to adopt the tribunal approach and move towards a truth, peace and reconciliation commission.

Notes

1 R.E. Howard-Hassmann, *Reparations to Africa* (Philadelphia: University of Pennsylvania Press, 2008).

2 Ibid., p. 47.

3 S. Staggenborg, *Social Movements* (Oxford: Oxford University Press, 2011).
4 Ibid., p. 5.
5 CARICOM Reparations Commission press statement delivered by Professor Sir Hilary Beckles (Chairman) on behalf of the CARICOM Reparations Commission Press Conference Regional Headquarters, UWI 10 December 2013. Available at: http://caricom.org/jsp/pressreleases/press_releases_2013/pres285_13.jsp (accessed 27 February 2014).
6 Ibid.
7 The Durban Review Conference, Geneva, 20–24 April 2009. For further information see www.un.org/durbanreview2009/pdf/Draft_Report_of_the_Conference.pdf and www.un.org/durbanreview2009/ (accessed 21 May 2015).
8 Durban I was a world conference held on the 31 August to the 7 September 2001 in Durban, South Africa, following which the UN drew up a declaration and programme of action for member states to implement. A number of NGOs attended including the Durban 400 and the representatives of the Pan-African Reparations Movement.
9 'Outcome Document of the Durban Review Conference'. Available at: www.un.org/en/durbanreview2009/pdf/Durban_Review_outcome_document_En.pdf (accessed 29 July 2014).
10 *Durban 400* DVD, directed by A. Santana, 2003, the Drammeh Institute and Al Santana Productions.
11 Ibid.
12 Ibid.
13 Ibid.
14 Meeting at Durban II, Geneva, 23 April 2009.
15 Drammeh Institute. Available at: www.un.org/webcast/durbanreview/archive.asp (accessed 23 May 2014).
16 R. Ramesh, 'More Black People Jailed in England and Wales Proportionally than in US', *The Guardian*, 11 October 2010.
17 Institutional racism has been defined by a number of people one of the most recent in Britain was W. Macpherson, *The Stephen Lawrence Inquiry*(London: Home Office, 1999). In the report institutional racism was defined as: 'The collective failure of an organization to provide an appropriate and professional service to people because of their colour, culture or ethnic origin. It can be seen or detected in processes, attitudes and behaviour which amount to discrimination through unwitting prejudice, ignorance, thoughtlessness and racist stereotyping which disadvantage minority ethnic people' (p. 28, para. 6.34).
18 J. Goodwin and J.M. Jasper, *The Social Movements Reader: Cases and Concepts* (Chichester: Wiley-Blackwell, 2009), p. 12. Also see C.E. Zirakzedeh, *Social Movement in Politics: A Comparative Study* (Basingstoke: Palgrave Macmillan, 2006).
19 The Civil Rights Act of 1964 established prohibited grounds of discrimination of all kinds based on colour, race, religion or national origin.
20 In 1954 the Supreme Court ruled that the 'separate but equal' policy that was custom and practice in the South, and confirmed in the case of *Plessey v Ferguson* (1896) 163 US 537 was in fact discriminatory since Black people were not treated equally. This decision was arrived at in the case of *Brown v Board of Education* (1954) 347 US 483.
21 Zirakzedeh, *Social Movement in Politics*. An example of this is the movement started by Rosa Parks in 1955, a Black woman, who refused to give up her seat to a White person and sit in the 'coloured' section of the bus. Following her arrest Black people boycotted the bus service for over a year. They were led by Martin Luther King, Jr. In 1956 the bus service was desegregated. Available at: www.infoplease.com/spot/civilrightstimeline1.html (accessed 24 May 2015).
22 Zirakzedeh, *Social Movement in Politics*, p. 3.
23 Staggenborg, *Social Movements*, p. 2.
24 Ibid., p. 4.
25 Zirakzedeh, *Social Movement in Politics*, p. 4.
26 C.A. Nathanson, 'The Limitations of Social Movements as Catalysts for Change', in J. Banaszak-Holl, S. Levitsky and M. Zald (eds), *Social Movements and the Transformation of American Health Care* (Oxford Scholarship Online, 2010), see abstract at http://0-www.oxfordscholarship.com.serlib0.essex.ac.uk/view/10.1093/acprof:oso/9780195388299.001.0001/acprof-9780195388299 (accessed 9 May 2015).
27 Ibid.

28 D.D. Porta and M. Diani, *Social Movements: An Introduction* (Oxford: Blackwell, 2006), p. 20.
29 Ibid.
30 R.L. Blumberg, 'The Civil Rights Movement', in J. Goodwin and J.M. Jasper (eds), *The Social Movements Reader: Cases and Concepts* (Chichester: Wiley-Blackwell, 2009).
31 J. Freeman, 'The Women's Movement', in J. Goodwin and J.M. Jasper (eds), *The Social Movements Reader: Cases and Concepts* (Chichester: Wiley-Blackwell, 2009), p. 24.
32 Ibid.
33 Ibid.
34 Ibid., p. 25.
35 Ibid.
36 A. Touraine, 'An Introduction to the Study of Social Movements', in V. Ruggiero and N. Montagna (eds), *Social Movements: A Reader* (London: Routledge, 2008), p. 213.
37 M. Diani, 'The Concept of Social Movement', in V. Ruggiero and N. Montagna (eds) *Social Movements: A Reader* (London, Routledge, 2008).
38 Ibid., p. 271.
39 D.A. Snow and S.A. Soule, *A Primer on Social Movements* (New York: W.W. Norton and Company, 2010).
40 Ibid., p. 5.
41 Ibid., p. 6.
42 Howard-Hassmann, *Reparations to Africa.*
43 D.S. Meyer and N. Whittier, 'Social Movement Spillover', *Social Problems* 41(2) (1994): 277–298, in R. Howard-Hassmann, *Reparations to Africa* (Philadelphia: University of Pennsylvania Press, 2008) p. 47.
44 Available at: www.caricomreparations.org (accessed 24 October 2016).
45 Jamaican Information Service. Available at: www.jis.gov.jm (accessed 24 October 2016).
46 Ibid.
47 '12-Member Reparations Council Named', *Jamaican Observer*, July 2016. Available at: www.jamaicaobserver.com (accessed 24 October 2016).
48 PARCOE. Available at: http://parcoe.com/ (accessed 24 October 2016).
49 PORTCITIES Bristol. Available at: www.discovering bristol.org.uk (accessed 24 October 2016). In this extract Portcities write that between 12 million and 100 million Africans died as a direct result of the slave trade.
50 Ibid.
51 M. Bondi, 'Rise of the Reparations Movement', in M. Martin and M. Yaquinto, *Redress for Historical Injustices in the United States: On Reparations for Slavery, Jim Crow and their Legacies* (Durban and London: Duke University Press, 2007), p. 265.
52 Ibid., p. 265. Although Bondi states that the wording makes it look as though having the slave trade and slavery declared as a crime against humanity, is to be read retrospectively.
53 P. Falk, 'Should U.S. Pay Reparations for Slavery? U.N. Appointed Experts Think So', CBS News, 27 September 2016. Available at: www.cbsnews.com (accessed 25 October 2016).
54 Ibid.
55 A. Gifford, *The Passionate Advocate* (Kingston: Arawak Publications, 2007).
56 H. McD. Beckles, *Britain's Black Debt* (Kingston: University of West Indies Press, 2013).
57 Research Associate on the Philosophy of Race, University College London.
58 F. Brennan and J. Packer (eds), *Colonialism, Slavery, Reparations, Trade: Remedying the Past?* (Abingdon: Routledge, 2012).
59 R.E. Park, *The Crowd and the Public and Other Essays* (Chicago: University of Chicago Press, 1972) p. 22.
60 Zirakzedeh, *Social Movement in Politics*, p. 4.
61 Ibid., p. 4.
62 Ibid., p. 9.
63 Banaszak-Holl, Levitsky and Zald, *Social Movements and the Transformation of American Health Care.*
64 Beckles, *Britain's Black Debt*, chapter 9.
65 Porta and Diani, *Social Movements*, p. 29.
66 Ibid., p. 166.
67 Blumberg, 'The Civil Rights Movement'.

68 *Brown v Board of Education* (1954) 347 US 483.
69 Blumberg, 'The Civil Rights Movement', p. 21.
70 Ibid.
71 Ibid.
72 I. Susser, 'From the Cosmopolitan to the Personal: Women's Mobilization to Combat HIV/AIDS', in J. Nash (ed.), *Social Movements: An Anthropological Reader* (Oxford: Blackwell, 2005), p. 272.
73 Ibid.
74 These issues have been dealt with in the chapter on reparations. Also see J. Curtis, 'Arguments against Reparations for Slavery', *Humanities 360*, 12 March 2009. Available at: www.humanities360.com/index.php/arguments-against-reparations-for-slavery-45353/ (accessed 30 July 2014).
75 'CARICOM Reparations Commission to Boost online Presence', Press release 4 August 2016. Available at: www.caricom.org (accessed 25 October 2016).
76 Ibid.
77 BBC News UK, 6 June 2013. Available at: www.bbc.co.uk/news/uk-22790037 (accessed 30 July 2014).
78 *Ndiku Mutua, Paulo Nzill, Wambugu Nyingi, Jane Muthoni Mara and Susan Ngondi v The Foreign and Commonwealth Office* [2011] Case no. HQ09X02666, High Court, Royal Courts of Justice, London.
79 D. Leader, 'The Mau Mau Litigation – Justice at Last', 3 November 2015. Available at: http://ohrh.law.ox.ac.uk/the-mau-mau-litigation-justice-at-last (accessed 25 October 2016).
80 Ibid.
81 Ibid.
82 Leigh Day Solicitors, UK Law Firm advises the Caribbean Reparations Committee, 26 July 2013. Available at: http://leighday.co.uk (accessed 25 October 2016).
83 Ibid.
84 CRC, 'Ten Point Action Plan'. Available at: www.caricomreparations.org (accessed 25 October 2016).
85 D. Shelton, 'Litigation and Political action to Address Historic Injustices in the United States: Problems and Prospects' in F. Brennan and J. Packer (eds), *Colonialism, Slavery, Reparations and Trade: Remedying the Past?* (Abingdon: Routledge, 2012).
86 CARICOM 'Reparations Commission to Boost Online Presence', press release 4 August 2016. Available at: www.caricom.org (accessed 25 October 2016).
87 CRC, 'The Reparations Movement'. Available at: www.caricomreparations.org (accessed 25 October 2016).
88 A. Whitaker, 'Top Ten Social Movements', InterculturalCom. Available at: http://interculturalcomm.wikispaces.com/Top+10+Social+Movements (accessed 28 May 2015).
89 Ibid.
90 Mohanda Karamchand Ghandi.
91 A. Whitaker, 'Top Ten Social Movements'. Available at: http://interculturalcomm.wikispaces.com/Top+10+Social+Movements (accessed 28 May 2015).
92 Dr Martin Luther King Jr.
93 A. Whitaker, *Top Ten Social Movements*. Available at: http://interculturalcomm.wikispaces.com/Top+10+Social+Movements (accessed 28 May 2015).
94 The Quotations Page. Available at: www.quotationspage.com/quote/27184.html (accessed 28 May 2014).
95 Whitaker, *Top Ten Social Movements*.
96 Porta and Diani, *Social Movements*, p. 165.
97 *Brown v Board of Education* (1954) 347 US 483.
98 Prior to this case in *Plessey v Ferguson* (1896) 163 US 537 the Supreme Court upheld the separate but equal doctrine.
99 The NAACP was created in 1909. Its goal is to use non-violent protest to deal with racism in America, see www.naacp.org/ (accessed 8 June 2014).
100 University College London, 'Legacies of British Slave-ownership'. Available at: www.ucl.ac.uk/lbs (accessed 26 October 2016).
101 By positive reparations I mean those matters that can be looked at and dealt with in a positive light and certainly not pursued on the grounds of guilt or as Howard-Hassmann says 'the major tactic appears to have been shaming', see Howard-Hassmann, *Reparations to Africa*, p. 53.

102 Dr C.W. Worrill, *The Black Commentator*, Issue 318, 2 April 2009.
103 *Durban 400* DVD.
104 Gifford, *The Passionate Advocate*, p. 243.
105 Ibid., p. 243.
106 Ibid., p. 244.
107 'The National Commission on Reparations', Government of Jamaica. Available at: www.jis.gov.jm/special_sections/reparations/background.html (accessed 29 May 2014).
108 Ibid.
109 Human Rights Watch. Available at: www.hrw.org/legacy/campaigns/race/reparations.htm (accessed 29 May 2015).
110 Ibid.
111 Ibid., p. 1.
112 For instance, E. Stanford is a scholar-activist on Pan-African Reparations for global justice. Available at: http://estherstanford.com/about_esther.html (accessed 31 May 2014).
113 R.E. Howard-Hassmann, *Reparations for the Slave Trade: Rhetoric, Law, History and Political Realities* (Waterloo: Wilfrid Laurier University, 2007). Available at: http://humanrights.uconn.edu/documents/papers/Howard-Hassmann_Slavetrade.pdf (accessed 30 May 2014). Also see Lord A. Gifford, 'Formulating the Case for Reparations', in F. Brennan and J. Packer (eds), *Colonialism, Slavery, Reparations and Trade: Remedying the Past?* (Abingdon: Routledge, 2012), pp. 77–96.
114 Gifford, 'Formulating the Case for Reparations', pp. 77–96.
115 Howard-Hassmann, *Reparations to Africa*, p. 33.
116 P. Wheatley, *Poems on Various Subjects, Religious and Moral* (London, 1773).
117 Gifford, 'Formulating the Case for Reparations', p. 84.
118 A. Zunder, 'A New Look on the Economic History of Suriname Including a Methodology to Calculate Reparations for Damage', in M. Schalkwijk and S. Small (eds), *New Perspectives on Slavery and Colonialism in the Caribbean* (The Hague: Amrit/Ninsee, 2012).
119 Gifford, 'Formulating the Case for Reparations'.
120 F. Brennan, 'Slave Trade Reparations, Institutional Racism and the Law', in F. Brennan and J. Packer (eds), *Colonialism, Slavery, Reparations and Trade: Remedying the Past?* (Abingdon: Routledge, 2012).
121 Human Rights Watch. Available at: www.hrw.org/legacy/campaigns/race/reparations.htm (accessed 1 June 2014), p. 1.
122 See paragraph 13 of the *Sources, Causes, Forms and Contemporary Manifestations of Racism, Racial Discrimination, Xenophobia and Related Intolerance in The World Conference Against Racism, Declaration and Programme of Action* (New York: UN, 2002), p. 16.
123 R. Blackburn, *The Making of New World Slavery: From the Baroque to the Modern 1492–1800* (London: Verso, 1998).
124 A. Hochschild, *Bury the Chains: The British Struggle to Abolish Slavery* (London: Pan Books, 2006).
125 S. Salih (ed.), *The History of Mary Prince: A West Indian Slave* (London: Penguin Books, 2000), (1831).
126 UNESCOPRESS, 'Breaking the Silence Surrounding the Slave Trade', Feature no. 7, August 2002. Available at: http://portal.unesco.org/en/ev.php-URL_ID=5653&URL_DO=DO_TOPIC&URL_SECTION=201.html(accessed 4 June 2014).
127 Queen Mother D.B. Lewis, Gyepi III, A. Shakbaba, B. Kwaku Duren, C. Crawford, E. Stanford and S. Moorhead, 'Create the Future: Transformation, Reparations, Repatriation, and Reconciliation Conference', Ghana, 22 July to 3 August 2006. Available at: www.ncobra-intl-affairs.org/Conference.html (accessed 1 June 2014).
128 K. Nimako and S. Small, 'Collective Memory of Slavery in Great Britain and the Netherlands', in M. Schalkwijk and S. Small (eds), *New Perspectives on Slavery and Colonialism in the Caribbean* (The Hague: Amrit/Ninsee, 2012).
129 Also see J. Angelo Corlett, *Heirs of Oppression* (Lanham: Rowman & Littlefield, 2010), p. 161.
130 M. Prince, *The History of Mary Prince: A West Indian Slave*, edited by S. Salih (London: Penguin, 2004 [1831]), p. 7.
131 Ibid.
132 F. Fanon, *Black Skin, White Masks* (London: Pluto Press, 1986 [1952]).

133 Ibid., p. 214.
134 By moral right I take the philosophical position of Gerwith (1981) that there are basic rights that override all other rights. Gerwith argued that a basic right was 'not to be made the victim of a homicidal project', see A. Gerwith, 'Are there any Absolute Rights?', in J. Waldron (ed.), *Theories of Rights* (Oxford: Oxford University Press, 1984), pp. 81–109.
135 According to Williams, although slavery was imposed on people from many colours, eventually it became the pattern to deploy Africans as slaves to work the plantations. See Williams, *Capitalism and Slavery*, p. 29. UNESCO writes that this slavery was a form that fuelled the world economy. Its racial nature is what sets it apart from other forms of slavery. The Black Code, that originated in France, was published as a command by Louis XIV in 1685, and sought to clarify the relations between slave and master. This edict found its way across the Caribbean and Louisiana in the USA. 'The code clearly defines slaves as "moveable property", "people unfit to possess or contract in their own right." Racism was not born with it but legitimised it and 'remains one of its most tragic legacies'. See UNESCO, 'Slavery and Racism'. Available at: www.unesco.org/bpi/eng/unescopress/2001/01-91e.shtml (accessed 11 June 2015).
136 As UNESCO recognises Africans were wrenched from their homes having to leave their possessions behind, see www.unesco.org/bpi/eng/unescopress/2001/01-91e.shtml (accessed 11 June 2015).
137 Fanon, *Black Skin White Masks.*
138 Rawls, *A Theory of Justice*, p. 17.
139 Ibid.
140 Gifford, 'Formulating the Case for Reparations'.
141 Angelo Corlett, *Heirs of Oppression.*
142 Gifford, 'Formulating the Case for Reparations', p. 80.
143 Angelo Corlett, *Heirs of Oppression*, p. 166.
144 At what is called Key Stage 3 of the National Curriculum, this area can be taught or not on a non-statutory basis. Available at: www.gov.uk (accessed 28 May 2016).
145 Bracegirdle informs us that 'in 1999 the African World Reparations and Repatriation Truth Commission me in Accra and issued a declaration seeking the payment by Western states and institutions of $777 thousand billion in reparations'. See Bracegirdle, 'Restitution after Slavery', p. 145.
146 See http://www2.ohchr.org/english/issues/remedy/principles.htm (accessed 12 June 2015).
147 Adopted and proclaimed by General Assembly Resolution 60/147 of the 16 December 2005.
148 N. Wittmann, 'International Legal Responsibility and Reparations for Transatlantic Slavery', in F. Brennan and J. Packer (eds), *Colonialism, Slavery, Reparations and Trade: Remedying the Past?* (Abingdon: Routledge, 2012).
149 Ibid., pp. 5–8.
150 Indeed the Basic Principles constitute 15 years of work by specialists looking at the laws of various states, see OHCHR at http://www2.ohchr.org/english/issues/remedy/principles.htm (accessed 12 June 2014).
151 According to Bracegirdle a successful claim for restitution will come about where the claimant can show there has been unjust enrichment on the part of the defendant and that the latter was unjustly enriched at the former's expense, see Bracegirdle, 'Restitution after Slavery', p. 148.
152 The Basic Principles, paras 6 and 7; see http://www2.ohchr.org/english/issues/remedy/principles.htm (accessed 13 June 2012).
153 Ibid, para. 19.
154 Gifford, 'Formulating the Case for Reparations', p. 82.
155 Ibid.
156 The Basic Principles, para. 19.
157 B. Pruitt, reparations leader and Chairman, Committee for African-American Reparations (CAAR), see www.itsabouttimebpp.com/Announcements/htm/Reparations_Positive_Points.htm (accessed 14 June 2014).
158 Ibid.
159 I would argue that this term should be widened to Black people of African descent.
160 For example 'Ethiopian inventor, Birrou Ayana, London, England, received a patent for a typewriter adapted for use in Ethiopian by the use of special signs on August 9th, 1932', moreover there are thousands of inventors in England who have been granted patents in the field of

technology, see K.C. Holmes, *Black Inventors Crafting over Two Hundred Years of Success* (New York: Global Black Inventor Research Projects, 2008), pp. 32 and 130 respectively.

161 Ibid.

162 The BRC was formed in June 1998 and met again in 2005 to answer the question 'How do we become human again?' See A. Zerai and H. Campbell, 'The Black Radical Congress and Black Feminist Organizing', in *Journal of the Research Group on Socialism and Democracy online.* See http://sdonline.org/38/the-black-radical-congress-and-black-feminist-organizing/ (accessed 14 June 2015).

163 Ibid.

164 Ibid.

165 Ibid.

166 Ibid.

167 Address delivered by Professor Sir Hilary Beckles of the CARICOM Commission, House of Commons, Parliament of Great Britain, Committee Room 14 on Thursday 16 July 2014.

168 The template is adapted from the Gender Mainstreaming policy document that I drew up for the European Human Rights Network, which was adopted by its Executive Committee in 2010.

169 All references to African people mean Africans, Afro-Caribbeans and Afro-Caribbeans in the Diaspora.

170 Howard-Hassmann, *Reparations to Africa*, p. 33.

171 By organisations I mean 'sets of activities in which various physical resources are being used'. There are a number of criteria which relate to the nature and characteristics of an organisation such as size, engagement of members of the group and the degree of social interaction; see J.E. T. Eldridge and A.D. Crombie, *A Sociology of Organisations* (London: George Allen and Unwin, 1974), pp. 27 and p. 33 respectively.

172 According to P. Strickland, black people are stopped seven more times than white people; see House of Commons Library, 'Stop and Search', January 2014 www.researchbriefings.files.parliament.uk (accessed 30 May 2016).

173 M. Townsend, 'Black People are 26 Times More Likely than Whites to Face Stop and Search, *The Guardian*, 17 October 2010; see www.guardian.co.uk/uk/2010/oct/17/stop-and-search-race-figures (accessed 2 July 2014).

174 P. Strickland, 'Stop and Search', Home Affairs section, SN/HA/3878, 23 January 2014. Available at: www.researchbriefings.files.parliament.uk (accessed 26 October 2016).

175 Ibid.

176 Ibid.

177 Type 2 diabetes is prevalent amongst people of African descent. Available at: www.nice.org.uk.

178 J. DeGruy, *Post Traumatic Slave Syndrome* (Joy DeGruy Publications, 2005).

Bibliography

Address delivered by Professor Sir Hilary Beckles of the CARICOM Commission, House of Commons, Parliament of Great Britain, Committee Room 14 on Thursday 16 July 2014. Available at: www.codesria.org/IMG/pdf/sir_hilary_beckles.pdf?3506/708204c9a111bcedd76a9 (accessed 15 December 2016).

Angelo Corlett, J., *Heirs of Oppression* (Lanham: Rowman & Littlefield, 2010).

Beckles, H. McDonald, *Britain's Black Debt* (Kingston: University of West Indies Press, 2013).

Blackburn, R., *The Making of New World Slavery: From the Baroque to the Modern 1492–1800* (London: Verso, 1998).

Blumberg, R.L., 'The Civil Rights Movement' in J. Goodwin and J.M. Jasper (eds), *The Social Movements Reader: Cases and Concepts* (Chichester: Wiley-Blackwell, 2009).

Bracegirdle, K., 'Restitution after Slavery', in F. Brennan and J. Packer (eds), *Colonialism, Slavery, Reparations and Trade: Remedying the Past?* (Abingdon: Routledge, 2012).

Brennan, F., *Race Rights Reparations: Institutional Racism and the Law* (forthcoming).

Diani, M., 'The Concept of Social Movement', in V. Ruggiero and N. Montagna (eds), *Social Movements: A Reader* (London: Routledge, 2008).

Durban 400, DVD directed by A. Santana, 2003, the Drammeh Institute, and Al Santana Productions.

Eldridge, J.E.T. and A.D. Crombie, *A Sociology of Organisations* (London: George Allen and Unwin, 1974).

Fanon, F., *Black Skin White Masks* (London: Pluto Press, 1986 [1952]).

Freeman, J., 'The Women's Movement', in J. Goodwin and J.M. Jasper (eds), *The Social Movements Reader: Cases and Concepts* (Chichester: Wiley-Blackwell, 2009).

Gerwith, A., 'Are there any Absolute Rights?', in J. Waldron (ed.), *Theories of Rights* (Oxford: Oxford University Press, 1984).

Gifford, A., 'Formulating the Case for Reparations' in F. Brennan and J. Packer (eds), *Colonialism, Slavery, Reparations and Trade: Remedying the Past?* (Abingdon: Routledge, 2012).

Gifford, A., *The Passionate Advocate* (Kingston: Arawak Publications, 2007).

Goodwin, J. and J.M. Jasper, *The Social Movements Reader: Cases and Concepts* (Chichester: Wiley-Blackwell, 2009).

Hochschild, A., *Bury the Chains: The British Struggle to Abolish Slavery* (London: Pan Books, 2006).

Holmes, K.C., *Black Inventors Crafting over Two Hundred Years of Success* (New York: Global Black Inventor Research Projects, 2008).

Howard-Hassmann, R.E., *Reparations to Africa* (Philadelphia: University of Pennsylvania Press, 2008).

Macpherson, W., *The Stephen Lawrence Inquiry* (London: Home Office, 1999).

Nimako, K. and S. Small, 'Collective Memory of Slavery in Great Britain and The Netherlands', in M. Schalkwijk and S. Small (eds), *New Perspectives on Slavery and Colonialism in the Caribbean* (The Hague: Amrit/Ninsee, 2012).

Park, R.E., *The Crowd and the Public and Other Essays* (Chicago: University of Chicago Press, 1972).

Porta, D.D. and M. Diani, *Social Movements: An Introduction* (Oxford: Blackwell Publishing, 2006).

Ramesh, R., 'More Black People Jailed in England and Wales Proportionally than in US', *The Guardian*, 11 October 2010.

Rawls, J., *A Theory of Justice* (Oxford: Oxford University Press, 1973).

Ron, J., H. Ramos and K. Rodgers, 'What Shapes the West's Human Rights Focus', in J. Goodwin and J.M. Jasper (eds), *The Social Movements Reader: Cases and Concepts* (Chichester: Wiley-Blackwell, 2009).

Salih, S., *The History of Mary Prince: A West Indian Slave* (London: Penguin Books, 2000 [1831]).

Sheldon, D., 'Litigation and Political Action to Address Historic Injustices in the United States: Problems and Prospects', in F. Brennan and J. Packer (eds), *Colonialism, Slavery, Reparations and Trade: Remedying the Past?* (Abingdon: Routledge, 2012).

Snow, D.A. and S.A. Soule, *A Primer on Social Movements* (New York: W.W. Norton and Company, 2010).

Staggenborg, S., *Social Movements* (Oxford: Oxford University Press, 2011).

Susser, I., 'From the Cosmopolitan to the Personal: Women's Mobilization to Combat HIV/AIDS', in J. Nash (ed), *Social Movements: An Anthropological Reader* (Oxford: Blackwell Publishing, 2005).

Touraine, A., 'An Introduction to the Study of Social Movements', in V. Ruggiero and N. Montagna (eds), *Social Movements: A Reader* (London: Routledge, 2008).

United Nations, *World Conference against Racism, Racial Discrimination, Xenophobia and Related Intolerance* (Durban: UN, 2001).

Wheatley, P., *Poems on Various Subjects, Religious and Moral* (London: 1773).

Wittmann, N., 'International Legal Responsibility and Reparations for Transatlantic Slavery', in F. Brennan and J. Packer (eds), *Colonialism, Slavery, Reparations and Trade: Remedying the Past?* (Abingdon: Routledge, 2012).

Worrill, C.W., *The Black Commentator*, Issue 318, 2 April 2009. Available at: www.blackcommentator.com/318/318_ww_durban_400_printer_friendly_pdf (accessed 15 December 2016).

Zirakzedeh, C.E., *Social Movement in Politics: A Comparative Study* (Basingstoke: Palgrave Macmillan, 2006).

Zunder, A., 'A New Look on the Economic History of Suriname including a Methodology to Calculate Reparations for Damage', in M. Schalkwijk and S. Small (eds), *New Perspectives on Slavery and Colonialism in the Caribbean* (The Hague: Amrit/Ninsee, 2012).

10 Conclusion

The thesis of this book argues that there is a persuasive link between the transatlantic slave trade and the racism (and/or disadvantage) suffered by black people today found in institutional racism. It is further held that as a result of institutional racism reparations are due. In each chapter the relationship between institutional racism and the subject matter under discussion is clear and compelling. The book has tried to link through each chapter the relationship between the subject matter and institutional racism and has found this proved.

Evidence of institutional racism as a continuing problem can be said to have brought itself out onto the streets of Brixton with the 'Brixton Disorders' on the 10–12 April 1981. The factors that led to the disorders focused on the policing of the black community but also the social deprivation in terms of education, housing and unemployment that, Lord Scarman reported, had a disproportionate impact on black people, especially the young. Although Scarman denied that there was such a thing as institutional racism in the policing of the black community and that the problem was insensitive policing The report (*The Scarman Report: Report of an Inquiry by the Right Honourable the Lord Scarman, OBE, presented to Parliament in November 1981*) provided a number of instances where it could be argued that the deeper problems suffered by black people were indeed the result of institutional racism and the disorder on the streets of Brixton was young black people articulating this in the only way they knew how. Furthermore, many witnesses to the inquiry were in agreement that the police racially harassed black people and the police complaints procedure was wanting, and thus there was little confidence in these two public services set up to serve and protect the public interest.

Institutional racism should be a public interest concern. It manifested itself in the disturbances on Broadwater Farm on the 6–7 October 1985 where not only was there disorder from young black people but a police officer was killed. An inquiry into the disturbances was chaired by Lord Gifford QC, to consider the socio-economic conditions in the borough of Haringey (where Broadwater Farm is situated), to look at policing in the area before and after the disturbances, to draw out the racial aspects of policing and to make recommendations. The communities complained about the way stop-and-search policing fell heavily on young black people and argued that it was part of the under-current that led to the disturbances. Furthermore, the reaction to the tragedy where Cynthia Jarrett[1] was involved in an altercation with the police and died, was due to mistrust of the police and could be said to have started the disturbances where black people identified with the sequence of events that led to Jarrett's death in the hands of the police. One disturbing matter that was singled out for complaint was the way the defence appeared to be passive in bail hearings and the fact that the rights of juveniles were not respected such as the right not to have the public and media in the public gallery. The media made a concerted effort to paint black community leaders in a bad light which was not only untrue but led to a reinforcement of institutional racism.[2] It could be argued that the policing of the Broadwater Farm community[3] and the portrayal of the Farm in the media were instances of institutional racism. As one witness said, 'The training for the police is vital. Talking to certain policemen, men who are well meaning in many respects, they don't know what racism is at all. They just have it and they do not realise how much it's affecting other people' (p. 197 of the report).

In 1989 a second report was published where Broadwater Farm was revisited and the report was chaired by Lord Gifford QC. In this report recommendations were made that targeted the treatment of the accused in police custody such as the right to legal representation before being interviewed and the desire for lawyers to inform families in more detail as to 'what is going on during a trial' (p. 140 of the report). That the local council should take a role in employment initiatives on the Broadwater Farm Estate and consult with the local community on community matters and that in terms of education, pressure groups should have a role in the decision-making process.

In 1988 an inquiry was set up by Liverpool City Council published as *Loosen the Shackles: First Report of the Liverpool 8 Inquiry into Race Relations in Liverpool*, to consider the fact that in Liverpool 8[4] black people were concerned about their relations with the police and that, furthermore, the council was concerned about its record of service to the black community. This concern arose out of the uprisings that occurred on the 3 July 1981 (but was not based on that situation) and wider socio-economic issues such as 'employment practices, housing practices and the Council's policies generally, so far as they affect Black people ...' (p. 56). One witness described community relations as 'like shredded paper. We can't put it back together again' (p. 64). The inquiry was 'reminded how ugly the factor of racial prejudice ha[d] contributed to the blighting of people's lives in Liverpool' (p. 65). The recommendations were similar to the ones already portrayed such as the type of policing, better access to housing, education and that the legal system become more aware of the types of charges made by the police against black people.

Then came the Stephen Lawrence Inquiry chaired by Sir William Macpherson of Cluny and presented to Parliament in February 1999. This inquiry arose following the fatal stabbing of a young black man in London by a group of racist killers, some of whom became defendants who were eventually convicted of the crime of murder. The inquiry focused on the issue of policing once more but went into the notion of the 'canteen culture' of the police who work in a way that taints black people, especially black youths. Their encounters with black people were antagonistic and this reinforced a stereotype of them as part of a criminal fraternity. It was with this report that the concept of institutional racism was finally brought out as, 'The collective failure of an organisation to provide an appropriate and professional service to people because of their colour, culture or ethnic origin. It can be detected in processes, attitudes and behaviour which amount to discrimination through unwitting prejudice, ignorance, thoughtlessness and racist stereotyping which disadvantage minority ethnic people' (paragraph 6.34 of the inquiry).

In Chapter 2 it has been argued that there are at least three forms of racism. There are overt forms that are highly visible such as name calling, racially aggravated criminal damage and racially aggravated assaults. Then there are covert forms of racism that are not so visible and take on the forms of indirect discrimination in education, access to health and the use of other services and then there is institutional forms of racism that are extremely hidden and maintained in the culture of institutions by social actors who do not realise they are part of the tapestry of institutional racism. Social actors will not realise their role in institutional racism making until institutional racism and the relationship between it and social actors is exposed.

To get to institutional racism and eradicate it is highly problematic because it is so difficult to detect. The way that institutions work has become the common sense way of doing things. Where did institutional racism come from? It is argued that it is one of the by-products of the transatlantic slave trade. The transatlantic slave trade was a regime of racist exploitation of black people that turned them into chattel slaves so that they could generally be used as beasts of burden. When chattel slavery was abolished in the nineteenth century in British colonies there was no challenge to the hegemony of racism. Instead it remained part of the ideology long after its purpose for being around had become diluted. Whilst overt and covert forms of racism were being tackled in the twentieth century there was no realisation that institutional racism had crept in and become lodged in the social system. It was identified by Macpherson in the late twentieth century but little has been done to curtail it.

In the 1930s a report was published into the 'colour problem' in Liverpool entitled, 'an Investigation into the Colour Problem in Liverpool and other Ports' it revealed 'a number of vile racialist myths covering sexual relations between black and white' people and recommended that the way to tackle white racism in employment was to replace blacks with whites on ships (*Loosen the Shackles*, pp. 29–30). Institutional racism is not that explicit, however, it haunts the very underpinnings of organisations in terms of their cultural practices.

A reparations discussion would provide an ideal space in which institutional racism could be articulated and exposed as a matter that has profound effects on black people in terms of the delivery of public and private services. Reparations would be used in the form of an educative tool where the problem of the hidden nature of institutional racism could be brought out into the open and dealt with in order to eradicate it, a matter that these several reports have alluded to.

In Racismnoway,[5] cyber racism is defined as 'racism which occurs in the cyber world' (Racismnoway, Cyber Racism). In Australia Racismnoway has described cyber racism as 'any use of information and communication technologies to transmit racist attitudes and behaviour including the transfer of offensive content that is intended to cause harm or distress to another person' (Racismnoway.com.au). Cyber Racism and the Future of Free Speech (racismreview.com) reports on two cases: one in Russia and the other in the US. In Moscow a young man formed a group of racists on-line and was sentenced to a one-year suspended sentence. In the US, Pousson was prosecuted for sending a hate-filled email to an African American woman (Cyber Racism and the Future of Free Speech, racismreview.com). Is cyber racism on the Internet just a side effect of free speech? Chapter 3 dealt with cyber race hate and argues that among the social actors responsible for its promulgation are Internet Service Providers (ISPs). In failing to provide a service that is racist free, they show themselves to be institutionally racist and should take responsibility for controlling the use of race hate on the web. It is argued here that race hate is so damaging that it should be seen as one of those rare exceptions to free speech or freedom of expression. Because race hate on the Internet is a violation of human rights.[6] It has consequences in real space in that it is a way of reinforcing racism. Race hate on the Internet takes different forms and is exhibited in different ways all of which could be tackled from a reparations framework. Further research on the issue and the consequences of race hate on the Internet are sorely needed. There is also a need for work to be done to produce legislation that holds the ISP liable for its promulgation.

Global trade is a complex phenomenon and countries in the Caribbean are caught up in this complexity in a way that undermines their bargaining power. In Chapter 4 there was an EU focus and a discussion of the institutional racism meted out to the Caribbean countries in terms of inter-state trade. The argument was also advanced that preferential treatment should have been retained in the international market between the Caribbean and Europe instead of the imposition of Economic Partnership Agreements (EPA). Those who construct and implement the EPAs do not realise that the Caribbean is not sufficiently diversified to be open to international trade. This is the result of its slave trade status based on the plantation system. Guyana is a current example of an economy that relies on a few commodities, such as rice, to trade in the international market. Under the preferential marketing system she could gradually secure the funds to develop a more diversified economy thus making her stronger in the global market. EPAs only serve to open her up to the ravages of competition and make an already weak economy more vulnerable. Behind the decision-making about the use of EPAs is the issue of institutional racism. There is a lack of understanding of the way in which the more dominant economies of the elites in the EU and America have a stranglehold on the market whilst promoting the ideology of liberalisation of the free market.

Here, the case was put for a thorough investigation into the use of EPAs compared with the use of preferences. It is argued that despite the WTOs decision on the use of preferences as illegal under WTO rules, it is necessary to have something like preferences to protect the commercial markets of the Caribbean from markets that are skewed against their independence. This investigation could be conducted on the basis of a moral imperative to seek a reparations framework to deal with the problem of illiberal markets.

We can try to console ourselves that race relations are relatively healthy since there have been no more outbreaks of disorder on the streets of Britain, as was seen in the twentieth century, but institutional racism does not work in that way. It is in-scripted into the cultural mores of institutions and not in the mouths of those who shout racism. Europe seemed to come alive to this in the latter part of the twentieth century with the development of legislation to curtail racism in member states. In Chapter 5 there was a discussion of the Race Directive and its relationship to institutional racism. The Race Directive was implemented into national law (in the UK) with all its interpretive problems and without a notion of institutional racism, one that would have provided a way of focusing on removal of the problem in domestic institutional social relations and sent a powerful message to the polity. A positive recognition that organisations must provide policies to deal with institutional racism, rather the Directive lacked the understanding that it is organisations that fail to provide a professional service to people because of their colour, culture or ethnic origin. Macpherson[7] said this can be seen or detected in processes, attitudes and behaviour which amount to discrimination through unwitting prejudice, ignorance, thoughtlessness and racist stereotyping which disadvantage minority ethnic people. Institutional racism is an evil that has grown into a stranglehold on institutions and has not been recognised and dealt with. The phenomenon is particularly pertinent to those European countries who played a role in the slave trade and whose institutions are institutionally racist. It has been argued here that fresh legislation is needed that specifically deals with institutional racism and focuses on the social actors and social institutions, holding the elite of social actors to account if they do not deal with it.

The death of one person in custody of social actors, by lethal restraint, is one too many. The disproportionate death of black people in custody is of growing concern. Chapter 6 argues that there are hundreds of years of racist ideology that provide an institutionally racist structure within which controversial black custodial deaths occur. The use of restraint techniques for prolonged periods that has led to the death of young black men, in particular, is of great concern. There is also the gendered nature of this area where the custodial deaths tend to affect black men and this is because black men are construed as part of the criminal fraternity even before they are interviewed, charged, prosecuted and convicted. The dearth of prosecutions and convictions against the perpetrators send a signal that the use of these restraint techniques and the lack of a duty of care are part of the norm and not racist in character at all. State actors only serve to reinforce this picture in their day to day social relations with black people. The failure to prosecute those who kill strengthens their hand in the way that black people are treated because state actors become answerable to no one. When you read that between 2002 and 2012 the majority of deaths where black and ethnic minority peoples have come into contact with the police have been deaths in custody this sends a worrying signal to the black community that the service that is supposed to protect them cannot be trusted not to breach their human rights. Rather the services get away with stereotypical views of black people as deserving of this heavy-handed treatment because of what they are perceived to be – big, black and dangerous.

It is argued here that the way to deal with this problem is to make institutional racism part of the training package that goes into training state actors, to make it a statutory duty that the maximum time to hold a person in a restraint position is not more than three minutes and that the cases where there is a black controversial death in custody should be dealt with by our judges (who should also be specially trained on the impact of institutional racism) only without a jury. The latter is necessary because on the few occasions when it has come to prosecuting state actors and controversial deaths in custody, state actors have not been convicted by their peers – the jury. This is because on the rare occasions when a white policeman has been in the dock accused of killing a black dead victim, the jury seem to accept the police version of events. It has been argued by Thomas in *Are Juries Fair?* (Ministry of Justice Research Series 1/10, February 2010) that all-white juries do not racially discriminate against black defendants but that does not address the question of whether they discriminate against a black victim when the police are the accused. To be fair there is far too little evidence to go on with regards juries and the police as defendants when the deceased victim is black because there are few prosecutions. It is in prosecutorial decision-making that the problem lies that is why it is argued that these kinds of cases should be dealt with by judges alone. It is the judge that should make the prosecutorial decision and judges that should replace juries, at least at the evidential stage so as to establish whether there is a case to answer. This might instil more confidence in the black community that their fears of discriminatory practices are taken seriously by the criminal justice system because the decision to prosecute would be conducted in an open manner.

There are several adverts on the Internet that portray the dominant white norm such as 'Shop for L'Oreal white perfect on Google',[8] 'L'Oreal Paris White Perfect',[9] 'L'Oreal White Perfect: Skin Care',[10] 'Givenchy Doctor White 10 Whitening Preparation Lotion/Harrods'.[11] Whitening of the skin is big business in the beauty products market and this whitening of skin as the ideal standard of beauty is pushed by the large multinationals like L'Oreal. There is no equivalent multinational pushing for 'black is beautiful' although it is just over the 50th anniversary of the 'Black is Beautiful' social movement that went viral in the 1960s. That movement aimed to impact on the consciousness of black people and the education of their white peers that the black skin colour was not something to be sneered at but a factor to be embraced. Since the 1980s there has been a backsliding of the black is beautiful campaign giving rise instead to skin whitening and hair straightening. Although there is still a campaign pushing 'My Black is Beautiful' by Proctor and Gamble this is not the norm. Dyer (*White*, London: Routledge, 1997) argues that 'Whites are the one particular group that can take up … the position that claims to speak for and embody the communality of humanity' (p. 223).

Chapter 7 considers the role skin colour plays in the institutional racism of social relations and the gendered nature of these relations since the arena mostly surrounds black women. During the triangular slave trade the differentiation of skin colour between black and white was an easy demarcation line through which to perpetuate the superiority of white people and the inferiority of black people. So much was this the case that skin colour could be used to justify the racist and brutalised treatment of black people as they were construed as chattels. The racism that pervaded permeated into society so that the chattelised black person is inferior and has become a construct that was racially institutionalised. This racially institutionalised inferiority of black skin has continued in modernity in the marketing of imagery in the media and in advertising. White skin becomes the norm through which beauty products, for example, are viewed. The desire to be part of the norm has witnessed some black women 'whitening' their skin with bleaching and lightening products. Some dark-skinned women go to these lengths of bleaching their skin to get away from the stigma dark skin attracts, without the realisation that they are buying into an institutionally racist construction of how a woman's skin should be. So 200 years post the chattel slavery there is still a problem with skin colour. The multinational and national companies perpetuate this division. They are in a particularly strong position to counter this ingrained practice. For example, they could feature black models and black products. This would also make economic sense after all dark-skinned women also wear make-up. This could be part of their corporate social responsibility to balance out the marketing of white-skinned models and products with that of darker-skinned models and beauty products that are aimed at maintaining black skin.

The period 2015–2024 is the International Decade for People of African Descent according to the United Nations, and in this forum it must be remembered that 'people of African descent are among those most affected by racism. Too often, they face denial of basic rights such as access to quality health services and education' (Ban Ki-Moon, United Nations Secretary General, 2015). Moreover, the United Nations General Assembly declared 25 March as the International Day of Remembrance of the Victims of Slavery and the Transatlantic Slave Trade (Resolution 62/122, 17 December 2007). The date 25 March is to honour and remember the history of that slavery and to raise 'awareness about the dangers of racism and prejudice today' (United Nations, International Decade for People of African Descent). These are very important gestures from the United Nations that keep the issue of racism against people of African descent in the public consciousness. However, necessary as these things are, they do not yet get to the crux of the matter which is the question of reparations for the legacy of the transatlantic slave trade, that is, institutional racism.

Chapter 8 addresses this issue. It argues that some reparations arguments are not just about financial compensation. The idea of reparations is a deeper concept than the notion of monetary compensation. From the West Indian call – from CARICOM and Jamaica for reparations they also consider economic, cultural and psychological damage. These matters should be pursued through discussion and negotiation and not primarily through the courts. There should be the development of national strategies to deal with economic, cultural and psychological damage that require deep discussion and carefully planned programmes to deal with the problems of institutional racism that endure in these areas. DeGruy points out that victims continue to suffer from inter or multi-generational trauma brought on by the slave trade and this has affected their self-esteem. Psychologically based programmes need to be put in place to deal with this problem, perhaps a focus on the educational curriculum in schools where more positive and inclusive messages could be transferred from books and teaching to young children. This would help the next generation of black people to grow with a belief that they have a positive place in society as well as help to tackle the institutional racism in the education system.

When dealing with European powers that were involved in the slave trade CARICOM wants to bring the question of reparations to the negotiation table. They have a Ten Point Action Plan that includes a call for apology, repatriation, illiteracy eradication, an African knowledge programme and debt cancellation. However, there is no sense that CARICOM want to talk about institutional racism. It is critical that institutional racism is discussed as part of the issues otherwise the status quo will remain and this window of opportunity to remove the deeply ingrained racism will be lost.

Furthermore, it is my belief that CARICOM should cultivate the backing of NGOs and civil society to ensure the support of those who would primarily benefit from delivery of a reparations programme. This would also strengthen their bargaining power and ensure that negotiations were not a top down exercise.

If reparations for the legacy of the slave trade were to become a matter of litigation it would be very difficult to bring a case. Nevertheless, Leigh Day solicitors have reassured CARICOM that a case for compensation can be sought through the courts of Britain, France and the Netherlands for 'the lingering effect of slavery' (Leigh Day, UK law firm advises Caribbean reparations committee, July 2013).[12] However they will be aware of the problems bringing a case for damages could produce, not least with defining the complainants and the defendants. It is likely that the cause of action would probably be crimes against humanity or restitution. Of course litigation has its own advantages because it might form a way of educating the general public as to the reasons for bringing a case in the first place. If institutional racism were part of the package of complaints the cause of action might pave the way for a public discourse on institutional racism as well as increase pressure on the requirement to make an apology.

Following the Civil Rights Movement in 1960s America, Andrew Young, one of its leaders, became prominent in the political field in the 1970s as US ambassador to the United Nations ('History, Civil Rights Movement', history.com). Young argued that the way forward for race relations was to use the democratic process. Chapter 9 tells us that social movements are a way of moving forward with the debate on institutional racism and reparations. Social movements would be a way of making the argument for reparations more forceful. Yet, it has been argued that although there are developments on the issue of reparations, these do not amount to social movements. There is yet another argument that this constitutes a traditional view of what a social movement is when looking at the argument for reparations for the legacy of the transatlantic slave trade. However, what we are witnessing in the Caribbean is a global movement on reparations.

This global movement on reparations consists of reparations organisations that are creatures of Caribbean governments, together with pan-European and national groupings in the UK and the USA. Groups come together under the broad umbrella of reparations for people of African descent but otherwise tend to co-exist. In terms of the call for reparations some groups focus on a historical view of the cause as a crime against humanity and that reparations should be made for the historical wrong, starting with an apology. Other groups have engaged in a modernity view dialogue arguing that the cause of racism suffered by people of African descent today is based on the slave trade and slavery. Although none of the groups argue that the current problem of institutional racism stems from the slave trade and slavery, nevertheless, the existence of these groups amount to the witnessing of a global movement not typical of social movements depicted in the West and the US.

There are many people that do not believe there is such a thing as institutional racism as well as those who think it has disappeared. This study has sought to prove the reverse – that institutional racism is still with us and has never gone away. It is hoped that the work will spur further research on this topic. I would like to finish off this chapter with a poem from Andrea Cork who had institutional racism in mind when she wrote it.

RACISM
It's In the Way
It's in the way you patronise
The way that you avert your eyes
The way that you cannot disguise
Your looks of horror and surprise
It's the assumptions that you make
On my behalf and for my sake
And in the way you do not hear
The things we tell you loud and clear
It's in the way you touch my hair
The way you think, The way you stare
It's right there in your history
Just like slavery for me
It's in the language that you use
The way that you express your views
The way you always get to choose
The way we lose
It's when you say 'No offence to you'
And then offend me, as you do
It's in your paper policy
Designed by you, for you, not me
It's in the power you abuse
It's on TV, it's in the news
It's in employment, in your school
The way you take me for a fool
It's in the way you change my name
The way that you deny my pain
It's in the way that you collude
To tell me it's my attitude
It's in your false democracy
It's in the chains you cannot see
It's how you talk equality
And then you put it back on me

It's in the way you get annoyed
And say I must be paranoid
It's in the way we have to fight
For basic fundamental human rights
It's in the invasion of my space

It's how you keep me in my place
It's the oppression of my race
IT'S IN MY FACE

(Andrea Cork, in D.G. Green (ed.), *Institutional Racism and the Police: Fact or Fiction* (London: CIVITAS, 2000), reproduced by kind permission of D.G. Green.)

Notes

1 'What Caused the 1985 Tottenham Broadwater Farm Riot?' BBC News, 3 March 2014. Available at: www.bbc.co.uk (accessed 5 April 2016).
2 D. Kuya, 'The Broadwater Farm Disturbances and the Press' (.pdf). Available at: www.berniegrantarchive.org.uk.
3 Available at: http://www.bbc.co.uk/news/uk-politics-35192265.
4 D. Garcia, 'Outside! On the Complexities of Hospitality and Hostility, 2011'. Available at: http://newsfromoutside.co.uk (accessed 5 April 2016).
5 'Cyber Racism Explained, Racism No Way'. Available at: http://www.racismnoway.com.au (accessed 5 April 2016).
6 'Cyber Racism and Human Rights, 2011'. Available at: http://humanrights.gov.au (accessed 5 April 2016). This article states that people have the right to be protected from racism as the right to live without fear. 'The enjoyment of [this] right can be negatively impacted' by the Internet where it 'is used for purposes contrary to respect for human values'.
7 W. Macpherson, *The Stephen Lawrence Inquiry* (London: Home Office, 1999).
8 Available at: www.google.co.uk (accessed 5 April 2016).
9 Available at: www.loreal-paris.com/hk/brandwhite (accessed 5 April 2016).
10 Available at: www.ebay.com/bhp/loreal-white-perfect (accessed 5 April 2016).
11 Available at: http://www.harrods.com/brand/givenchy (accessed 5 April 2016).
12 Available at: www.leighday.co.uk.July-2013 (accessed 5 April 2016).

Index

For Product Safety Concerns and Information please contact our EU representative GPSR@taylorandfrancis.com Taylor & Francis Verlag GmbH, Kaufingerstraße 24, 80331 München, Germany

Batch number: 10726294

Printed by Printforce, the Netherlands